THE HALF-
OPENED DOOR

THE HALF-OPENED DOOR

Discrimination and Admissions at Harvard, Yale, and Princeton, 1900-1970

MARCIA GRAHAM SYNNOTT

CONTRIBUTIONS IN AMERICAN HISTORY, NUMBER 80

GREENWOOD PRESS
Westport, Connecticut • London, England

Library of Congress Cataloging in Publication Data

Synnott, Marcia Graham.
    The half-opened door.

    (Contributions in American History; 80)
    Bibliography: p.
    Includes index.
    1.   Harvard University—Admission—History.
2.   Yale University—Admission—History.   3.   Princeton
University—Admission—History.   I.   Title.
LD2126.S9   378.744'4   78-66714
ISBN 0-313-20617-1

Library of Congress Catalog Card Number: 78-66714
ISBN: 0-313-20617-1
ISSN: 0084-9219

First published in 1979

Greenwood Press, Inc.
51 Riverside Avenue, Westport, Connecticut 06880

Printed in the United States of America

10 9 8 7 6 5 4 3 2 1

To
Howard H. Quint, Mentor and Friend

CONTENTS

TABLES

FOREWORD

Woodrow Wilson, who figures very prominently in this book, declared in a speech to the Princeton alumni of Pittsburgh on April 16, 1910, that because of recent portentous developments, he had devoted every ounce of energy that was within him to the democratization of higher education in the United States. His critics derided him for his alleged demagoguery and accused him of harboring political ambitions and playing to the crowd.

This book well demonstrates that Wilson's perceptions were right, and that his critics were either blind or resented his attack on privilege. What he had seen, at least since 1907, and described graphically in speeches and articles had indeed happened throughout the United States. The new men of wealth had begun to control the boards of trustees of private colleges and universities. More important, the proliferation of fraternities and private clubs had produced a rampaging growth of social snobbery and elitism among the very undergraduates who would be among the leaders of their generation.

Wilson, as Dr. Synnott discloses, knew this fact as well as any college president of his time. He had just been virtually crucified by his opponents in the Princeton community because he had tried to destroy the Princeton eating clubs, the bastions of social privilege and snobbery at the university. And he was near the end of his losing battle to prevent the construction of a sumptuous graduate college—a super deluxe club—presided over by the super elitist, Dean Andrew Fleming West.

This book shows how crucial was Wilson's defeat, not only for Princeton, but also for the country as a whole. The United States had lacked any strong feudalistic and aristocratic traditions, and upward mobility had always depended upon access to educational opportunities. This had been particularly true from 1865 to 1910 on account of the burgeoning of wealth and the radical social changes that had occurred almost overnight.

White Anglo-Saxon Protestants were of course still in the social mainstream in 1910. However, Roman Catholic Irish and German Americans, after more than a century of struggle, were now upwardly mobile, and educational barriers against them were collapsing on all fronts. Blacks, Italians, and other "recent" southern and eastern European immigrants, to say nothing of Orientals and Mexican Americans, for a number of reasons were not yet trying in significant numbers to move into the educational mainstream. The most aspiring group were the sons and daughters of eastern European Jewish immigrants.

Dr. Synnott focuses on how Harvard, Yale, and Princeton reacted to what their leaders thought was a threatening Jewish "invasion" in the 1920s and 1930s. Such concentration by the author was justified, because the Big Three were the pacesetters in educational and social policies; other private institutions usually followed their lead. In addition, Harvard, Yale, and Princeton produced the elite in politics, the professions, banking, and business all out of proportion to their number of graduates.

Dr. Synnott tells a story that will dismay and shock those persons who believe that decency, fair play, and democracy are important values. Harvard led the way when President Abbott Lawrence Lowell did an end run around his protesting faculty and former President Charles William Eliot and established a Jewish quota. (Dr. Synnott contrasts Lowell and Wilson in their social and religious attitudes in a section of this book.) It was the other way around at Yale, where faculty, students, and alumni pressed President James Rowland Angell into adopting a plan for limiting the number of Jewish students. Princeton, under President John Grier Hibben, instituted its Jewish quota quietly and without much publicity or controversy because it had few Jewish applicants. And all during this period it was a rare occasion when a Jew received a tenure appointment, or, for that matter, an appointment of any kind to the faculties of the Big Three. As she points out, it was no accident that these things were happening when antisemitism was on the rise in the United States and finding other manifestations in restrictive immigration laws, the spread of the Ku Klux Klan, and the growth of religious bigotry of all kinds.

But Dr. Synnott shows that there was also a saving remnant in all three universities. Eliot, William Ernest Hocking, and Roscoe C. Pound at Harvard, the Rev. Anson Phelps Stokes at Yale, and the devout H. Alexander Smith at Princeton, to mention only a few of them, never bowed their knees to the Baals of religious and social bigotry.

In her later chapters, Dr. Synnott describes fully and graphically the tremendous changes that occurred at the Big Three (indeed, throughout the entire realm of higher education in the United States) since the Second World War: the impact of the Holocaust and the realization that it was only a monstrous and logical manifestation of anti-Semitism; the consequent collapse of barriers against Jewish students and teachers (the doors were opened first to the latter); the civil rights movement of the 1960s, which aroused concern for blacks, other minorities, and women; and the powerful, perhaps crucial, role that the state and federal governments have played in at least a partial achievement of genuine educational opportunities for all persons regardless of race, religion, and sex. She notes sympathetically the dilemmas that now confront the American society in trying to compensate for centuries of discrimination against blacks, other minorities, and women without impairing the opportunities of other groups who have won the fight against discrimination, most notably Roman Catholics, Jews, and Americans of Italian descent. She has no easy answer, but she does not leave us without hope. What President William G. Bowen said recently about Princeton applies to all private colleges and universities: "We have not yet realized Woodrow Wilson's ideals, but they still shine brightly, and they continue to inspire and challenge us."

This is a remarkable book, one of the most important works in American social history that I have read in many years. Dr. Synnott's research was prodigious. Some readers will say that she has written in too much detail. I do not agree. The story is too important to be treated sketchily. Historical truth lies in facts, not generalizations, and it is the details that give this book its momentum and power. Moreover, Dr. Synnott is no polemicist or sensationalist. She writes fairly and with detachment. She is an historian concerned only about telling the truth. Perhaps that truth will set us free.

It may not be too optimistic to say that it has already set some institutions and persons free. There are many ugly facts in this book. They are drawn from materials in the archives and personal papers in the libraries of Harvard, Yale, and Princeton universities. It is inconceivable that these materials should have been opened to Dr. Synnott or any other scholar twenty-five years ago. Not only were they opened to her, but nothing was held back. This fact is perhaps the most significant indication of the changes that have occurred at Harvard, Yale, and Princeton—and elsewhere—within recent years.

Arthur S. Link,
George Henry Davis '86 Professor of American History and Director of the Wilson Papers, Princeton University.

MONTREAT, NORTH CAROLINA
AUGUST 17, 1978

ACKNOWLEDGMENTS

Professor Howard H. Quint gave generously of his counsel and criticism from this work's inception. The initial research was made possible by a University Fellowship and Teaching Assistantship at the University of Massachusetts. Grants from the University of South Carolina Research and Productive Scholarship Fund and from the Educational Foundation Fund of the Department of History helped to defray the cost of typing and revised manuscript (patiently done by Peggy J. Clark).

Several scholars read parts of my preliminary manuscript and offered constructive criticisms: Professors Arthur S. Link, Frederick A. Rudolph, and George C. Rogers, Jr., and Dr. Barbara M. Solomon. Dean John U. Monro of Miles College shared with me some of his observations as former counsellor for veterans and dean of Harvard College. President Adele Simmons of Hampshire College read the entire manuscript and offered helpful comments from her perspective as the former dean of student affairs at Princeton University. At different stages of the research, Professors George W. Pierson, Rollin G. Osterweis, David Riesman, the late Harry A. Wolfson, Theodore K. Rabb, Lawrence Stone, Harry Barnard, James McLachlan, and Tom E. Terrill, and Messrs. Oscar Cohen and the late M. Halsey Thomas answered my inquiries or letters and added encouragement.

While not forgetting those individuals, often known only by first name, who went repeatedly into the lower depths of the archives for the dusty boxes, I wish to acknowledge especially the help given by the following: Judith A. Schiff and the late Herman Kahn, Manuscripts and Archives, Yale University; Harley P. Holden, curator, Clark A. Elliott, associate curator, and Kimball Elkins, former curator, Harvard University Archives; and Erika S. Chadbourn, curator, Manuscripts and Archives, Harvard Law School Library. At Princeton, I thank the editors of *The Papers of Woodrow Wilson*; Alexander Clark of Rare Books and Special Collections; Dr. Edith Blendon, former acting curator of the university archives; and Constance

Escher, former chief research assistant in Princeton's *Biographical Dictionary* project.

I gratefully acknowledge the permission granted by the following to quote excerpts from both manuscripts and published materials:

The president and fellows of Harvard College; Harvard Law School Library; deans of the Faculty of Arts and Sciences and of Harvard College; Harvard University Archives; Radcliffe College; Samuel H. Fisher Papers, Walter Lippmann Papers, Henry P. Wright Papers, and Yale University Archives, Yale University Library; Princeton University Library; Princeton University Archives; Office of the Committee on Admission and Office of the Secretary, Princeton University.

LeBaron R. Briggs III (for Dean L. B. R. Briggs), Charles W. Eliot II (for President Charles W. Eliot), Dorothea Dde B. Greene (for Jerome D. Greene, secretary and overseer), and Alexander James (for Overseer Henry James, Jr.) for various papers and correspondence and the late Harry A. Wolfson for his "Remarks" in the Harvard University Archives; Richard Hocking (for Professor William Ernest Hocking) for letters in the Harvard University Archives and in the Manuscript Division, Harvard Law School Library; and Dr. Robert B. Allport (for Professor Gordon W. Allport) for a report in the Radcliffe College Archives;

Louis Sachs and Robert Maynard Hutchins for their letters to me;

Princeton University Press for *The Papers of Woodrow Wilson*, volumes 5 © 1968; 6 © 1969; 10 © 1971; 14 © 1972; 15 © 1973; 16 © 1973; 17 © 1974; 18 © 1974; 19 © 1975; and 20 © 1975. Reprinted with permission of Princeton University Press.

Yale University Press for George Wilson Pierson, *Yale: College and University, 1871-1937*, vol. 1: *Yale College: An Educational History, 1871-1921,* © 1952; vol. 2: *Yale: The University College, 1921-1937,* © 1955.

Finally, I want to thank those fellow researchers who shared with me some of their excitement and discoveries, especially Penny Hollander Feldman, Robert D. Shapiro, John R. Thelin, George E. Tomberlin, Jr., and Harold Stuart Wechsler.

INTRODUCTION

By 1900, if not before, academic nativism took root in elite American colleges, among them Harvard, Yale, and Princeton, as new kinds of students, the upwardly mobile sons of Catholic and Jewish immigrants, began to challenge the position of white Anglo-Saxon Protestants (WASPs) on campus. After reviewing the applications for financial aid in 1907, Dean Byron S. Hurlbut of Harvard expressed warm sympathy for

> "the old-fashioned College cases"—sons of families that have been American for generations,—farmers and ministers, and most of all those of families with traditions of refinement and liberal education. Usually this last sort of case is the son of a widow who, used to surroundings of comfort and refinement, finds herself, on the death of her husband, with almost no support. There is another—an increasing class—also interesting,—that is, the foreigners, and especially the Russian Jews. They, however, as a rule accept help with a readiness which cannot but lessen one's interest in them, in comparison with that American spirit which seeks to conceal need.

The newcomers threatened to displace the native-born by their scholastic achievements: They raised academic standards and won a disproportionate share of the scholarships, which had originally been established for the sons of Protestant ministers, New England schoolmasters, and Yankee farmers.[1]

The presence of these immigrant students reopened old questions about the nature and purpose of a university education and raised new ones about qualifications for admission to the academic community. Those having an aristocratic conception of a university would say that it should educate gentlemen for state and national leadership. One of the prerequisites for membership, then, would be proper social standing. The quintessence of this point of view was expressed by Princeton Trustee Bayard Henry when he wrote: "In a University, as well as elsewhere in America, men like to be on their own level, or else to be in a position where they can better themselves." They would not associate with those of lower status. Henry typified the snobbery of many graduates of elite colleges during the first half of the twentieth century. There were exceptions, of course, and among them was Woodrow Wilson. He spoke eloquently about educating the minds of undergraduates through contact with classmates from different geographical areas and social backgrounds. Not until the post-World War II era, however, would private universities adopt the role of educating a democracy, selecting its students for their talents and virtues.[2]

Meanwhile, in the years after World War I, elite colleges found that they had more applicants than space. (Harvard's enrollment rose by over 400 percent from the 1870s to the 1920s.) In order to provide a residential college experience for most undergraduates, classes had to be limited to the number of students who could be fed and housed on campus. Only with the completion of monumental building programs in the 1920s and 1930s would Harvard, Yale, and Princeton approach this goal. But the assumption of paternalistic responsibilities had negative implications for the admission and assimilation of minority students. Universities had to make certain concessions to the social snobbery, if not to the ethnic, racial, and religious prejudices, of their clientele. From the 1920s to the late 1940s, they imposed admissions quotas on Jews and, perhaps, on Catholics as well. (Concurrently, Princeton totally excluded blacks, while Harvard and Yale took only a handful each year.) Under the watchful eye of governing boards and with the guidance of faculties largely committed to traditional mores, these elite institutions fulfilled their primary educational role: they prepared native-born Americans for positions in businesses and professions that were still dominated by alumni or by men of similar outlook. A particular power base exercised leadership at each university. The story behind the decision to restrict Jews gave proof to a saying, then "current at Cambridge, that the 'trustees rule at Princeton, the faculty rules at Yale, and the president at Harvard.'"[3]

In parallel actions, WASP undergraduates limited or excluded altogether the Jews, the Catholics, and the few blacks from their extracurricular organizations and clubs. Membership in these was second in importance only to admission to the right college; they were part of the recruitment and conditioning process that selected the next generation of managers and leaders. Undergraduates of the years between the world wars were conservative, not radical. They did not buck the system, because they were part of it. And in order to make it easier for themselves to climb the ladder to the higher echelons, they saw to it that "outsiders" were barred from the lower rungs.

The pre-World War II campus was particularly anti-Semitic. In his pithy remarks delivered on Harvard Class Day, June 11, 1975, John Kenneth Galbraith commented on his brief experience in the autumn of 1935 as a member of the admissions committee of Winthrop House. He was given a five-columned chart and "told to admit only students of the highest quality" to house residency: "One maximized the number of inmates in the left-hand columns, and most of all the St. GX's [graduates of the most prestigious Episcopal boarding schools: St. George's, St. Mark's, St. Paul's, Groton, and Middlesex], and minimized, at any cost, those on the far right. No. H.S.'s [public high schools]. No X's [Jewish students]." He proved himself "intellectually incapable of mastering the further niceties" by admitting Theodore H. White, who was then an Orthodox Jew and Zionist, the first day and so was dropped from the committee as "incompetent." As he concluded his forty-one-year professorial career at Harvard University, Galbraith quipped that "the greatest change for the better [had been] the conversion of its undergraduates from a slightly ludicrous aristocracy to a somewhat serious meritocracy."[4]

This transformation of the elite colleges was the result of several interacting factors. First, the depression of the 1930s forced the adoption of tougher standards for the recruitment and retention of professors. Faculties became increasingly cosmopolitan with the hiring of European—specifically Jewish—scholars who were refugees from Nazism. Then, in turn, faculty and administrators who had served during World War II were far more willing than their predecessors to select students on the basis of intellectual merit. Admissions policies had to respond to changing national priorities. The scientific and manpower needs of World War II and the postwar era required a larger number of well-educated personnel, especially at the high managerial and professional levels, than the existing pool of college-bound WASPs could provide. At the same time, the scholarly (and grade-conscious) children of immigrants and the veterans on the G.I. bill aided the efforts of the colleges to shift the focus of undergraduate life from the extracurricular to the academic. They eagerly sought the opportunities for career advancement that, in the past, had frequently been closed to their parents.[5]

While retaining the allegiance of its traditional families, Harvard, earlier than Yale and Princeton, began to recruit an economically and socially diversified student body. ("Meritocratic" colleges still welcome qualified alumni sons, for their collegiate loyalty and financial support, and athletes, for the favorable publicity and the other students that they often attracted to the school.) By 1952, Cornell University sociologists estimated Harvard's undergraduate Jewish enrollment at 25 percent, larger than the percentage at ten other universities surveyed, including Dartmouth (15), Cornell (23), and Yale (13). As of 1971, David Riesman thought that Jews were still roughly about a fourth of the Harvard undergraduate body, but that Jewish professors had attained a third of the faculty positions.[6]

A similar rise in Jewish representation occurred at postwar Princeton and Yale, although a decade or so later. By the 1970s, probably about 15 to 20 percent of entering Princeton freshmen were Jewish, and the university was reportedly making an effort to encourage more Jewish applicants. At Yale,

Rabbi Arnold Jacob Wolf, the Jewish chaplain and Hillel director, observed that the percentage "looks like one-third" and that many were "very Jewish Jews" at what was once thought to be "the bastion of quota-protected anti-Semitism." And Catholics, too, totaled about 20 percent, if not more, at each of the three universities. But almost 30 percent of their undergraduates today profess no religious affiliation. In accepting students of diverse or unimportant religious background, these universities have encouraged the spirit of cultural pluralism.7

An analysis of the role of Harvard, Yale, and Princeton as elite WASP institutions—as they most definitely were during the half-century prior to World War II and, to a limited extent, continue to be—should cast light on class structure and values in the United States. It will indicate, moreover, why and how the entrenched position of the WASP upper class was successfully challenged. The educational, and hence economic, mobility of Catholics and Jews will also show other groups—for example, blacks and Spanish-speaking Americans—not only the difficulties that these earlier aspirants had in overcoming class and ethnic barriers, but simply the fact that it can indeed be done.

Aroused by the *Brown* v. *Board of Education* decision, outlawing racially segregated public schools, and by the civil rights movement, blacks demanded access to higher education. In response, the federal government made it a national priority during the 1960s to provide some sort of postsecondary education for all the children of all the people. Private universities, in turn, began seriously to recruit the newer, largely nonwhite minorities. The percentages of blacks at elite institutions doubled or tripled. Then, in the 1970s, such universities as Harvard, Yale, and Princeton realized that American Indians, Asian-Americans, and Hispanic-Americans would add other cultural ingredients to the education of undergraduates. Harvard College now boasts that its "concept of diversity" has broadened from one of geographic residence, extracurricular activities, and career choices—for example, from Californians, farm boys, athletes, and scientists—"to include students from disadvantaged economic, racial and ethnic groups." An applicant's race is now weighed in the admissions decision in much the same way as other nonacademic factors; it may well "tip the balance" in his or her favor.8

Admissions committees justify "goals," even "benign" quotas for racial minorities on the grounds that they have greater obstacles to overcome than had such older white ethnic groups as Germans, Irish Catholics, and Jews. Not only have white people discriminated against racial minorities, but the latter have actually discriminated against themselves by setting limited educational goals or none at all. They had to withstand prejudice, survive the strain of adjusting to urban society, and sustain themselves in a market that offered meager employment opportunities. For people rooted in a rural culture—black or white—the adjustment demanded by urban schools was repressive. Blacks protested in literature and by truancy their feelings of alienation in school systems controlled by whites, who judged them according to middle-class standards of achievement. Yet blacks did graduate from high school; some went on to college. Until recently, however, diplomas were often liabilities, overqualifying blacks for the jobs open to them. Jim Crow had allowed no mobility. Poverty, language, and ethnicity or race also handicapped the educational aspirations of American Indians and Spanish-speaking Americans. But skin color in itself, unless additionally burdened by poverty and cultural deprivation, need not condition students to academic failure. Asian-Americans now attend college in growing numbers, as their parents have moved into the urban middle class. On the other hand, such white ethnic groups as South Italians once resisted compulsory school attendance, because teachers and classmates ridiculed their traditional sources of authority—the family and the home. Of all minority groups, Jews were the most educationally mobile. To Jewish students, whose parents had been denied education in eastern Europe and Russia, teachers were superior beings who pointed the way through the schoolhouse door, their "golden gate" to a better future.[9]

One of the ironies of the history of higher education in the United States is the use of quotas by admissions committees: Restrictive ones were imposed on Jews because they were so successful, whereas benign quotas are currently used to encourage underrepresented minorities to enter colleges and professional schools. Having largely overcome the earlier barriers, Jews and other white ethnic groups are hardly willing to face another kind of exclusion: quotas that may admit blacks, Chicanos, or American Indians ahead of them. The competing claims of both the older and the newer minorities will be the subject of controversy, editorial comments, and court cases for some time to come.

THE HALF-OPENED DOOR

·1·

THE BIG THREE

Why Harvard, Yale, and Princeton?

The collective and individual importance of Harvard (1636), Yale (1701), and Princeton (1746) is the result of a reputation accumulated over two or more centuries. The term *Big Three*, however, originated in the mid-1880s as a newspaper headliner's sobriquet for the country's three best football teams. (Their players monopolized the first All-America team, selected by Coach Walter Camp of Yale in 1889.) Although the three universities were rivals, rather than a triumvirate, they are frequently linked in public estimation: Admission to one of them not only confers social prestige, but also opens doors to the most attractive corporate and professional careers.[1]

From their early years, Harvard, Yale, and Princeton had endeavored to prepare men (and, much more recently, women) for leadership, originally in the Protestant ministry and in the service of the colony and, later, of the nation. And they have ranked, respectively, first, second, and third in producing proportionately more leaders than any other undergraduate college. According to George Wilson Pierson's *Education of American Leaders*, their alumni have been at or near the top in eighty-five occupational and prestige listings, including presidents, Cabinet officers, lawyers, surgeons, industrialists, philanthropists, artists, and scholars. Harvard contributed Theodore and Franklin D. Roosevelt, John F. Kennedy, and Henry Kissinger; Yale trained William H. Taft, Henry L. Stimson, Dean Acheson, and Walt Rostow; and Princeton sent forth Woodrow Wilson, John Foster Dulles, James V. Forrestal, and Adlai Stevenson (and let us not forget the Socialist Norman Thomas). Harvard's poets and intellectuals included Conrad Aiken, Van Wyck Brooks, Malcolm Cowley, E. E. Cummings, John Dos Passos, T. S. Eliot, Walter Lippmann, John Reed, and Wallace Stevens. Yale nurtured Stephen V. Benét, Waldo Frank, Sinclair Lewis, Archibald MacLeish, and Thornton Wilder. From Princeton came F. Scott Fitzgerald and Edmund Wilson.[2]

In addition to its famous alumni, Harvard, Yale, and Princeton educated the solid, if less illustrious, members of America's upper-middle and upper classes, once almost exclusively WASP. With the tremendous business and industrial expansion occurring from the Civil War through the 1920s, affluent Americans sent their children to these elite colleges in the expectation that such training would provide them with the appropriate culture, learning, and social contacts. Academic requirements were modest; students of good character who could pay the tuition were usually admitted.[3]

Until World War II, each of the Big Three was known for the particular kind of man it produced. In his biography of Adlai E. Stevenson (Princeton '22), *A Prophet in His Own Country*, Kenneth S. Davis characterized the typical Princetonian as "'smooth'—that is, socially adroit and graceful," in contrast to the conformity of the Yale man and the individualism of the Harvardian: "It was of his [the Princeton man's] essence that he be neither a strong individualist (to be at all eccentric was to risk being tabbed a 'bird') nor a conformist whose conformity was molded by an openly confessed ambition." On the other hand, the "Yale man" had to "*be* a type: athletic, hearty, extroverted, ambitious, and intensely competitive," one of those chosen by a senior society, preferably by Skull and Bones (in view of later financial connections). But Harvard seemed, Davis continued, "always to have encouraged intellectualism and individualism, the latter sometimes to the point of eccentricity."[4]

Friends as well as critics acknowledged readily that Harvard was a multi-track institution that could accommodate almost any type of student. Like Columbia University and the University of Pennsylvania, Harvard was closely identified with a large city and attracted a high proportion of local students. It was regarded as an "intersectional" university despite the large number it drew from outside New England, because almost 40 percent of its students came from Massachusetts. Moreover, Harvard had fostered graduate and professional training, while still preserving vestiges of the New England college. Within its loose-knit community, historian Henry F. May has noted, "at least five Harvards" coexisted, even before World War I: "a national center of strenuous educational reform, a world center of research, the parochial pleasure-ground of the clubmen (through which passed both Roosevelts), the teaching institution, and, already, the mecca of the disaffected young men who wanted to write."[5]

On the other hand, Princeton and Yale, situated respectively in a borough and a medium-sized city, "had as a result of their age and size developed a national character," said Yale President Arthur Twining Hadley, "and become not so much places of training specialists as places of training American citizens." Princeton was still an intersectional college, because of its high percentage of students from the Middle Atlantic, South Atlantic, and South Central regions. Of the Big Three, Yale had the strongest claim as a national institution—with well-distributed representation and less than 30 percent of its students from its home state. Before World War II, Yale usually outdrew Harvard in the North Central states and the West, though bowing to its major rival in the North Atlantic region.6

Yet no one recognized a Harvard man or a Yale man or a Princeton man more quickly than an alumnus of a rival college. Such an identity, born with each eager freshman's arrival and forged upon the playing fields of Cambridge, New Haven, and Princeton, was cemented after graduation by the good fellowship of graduate clubs and alumni reunions and by generous financial contributions to the alma mater. Not only did this fraternal bond survive two world wars and a depression, but it was strengthened through shared ordeals. Today some alumni of the 1920s and 1930s are disenchanted with the intellectual and social transformation of their colleges, which culminated in the campus revolts of the 1960s. The world of their youth had been simpler. Adlai Stevenson spoke for his college generation when, during a difficult primary campaign in 1956, he recalled fondly his undergraduate days at Princeton: "It was a different time [with] different mores and there are those of us who still shed a salty tear for F. Scott Fitzgerald and the departed glories of the Princeton Country Club."7

"The Life Line of Empire": Student Recruitment

While President James Bryant Conant of Harvard referred to admission policy as an imperial "life line," Vermont-born President James R. Angell of Yale chose a homespun metaphor: "A New England collegiate institution is per se a fairly independent horse, and likely to be affected only by questions of pasturage." And by the mid-1920s, its rivals had to acknowledge that Princeton, once among the "small colleges," had "put herself in the class with Harvard and Yale," which meant "tapping the same sources for students." So jealous were the Big Three in maintaining lines of communication with their respective "feeder" schools and in attracting the best prospects that they cooperated in admission policies only with reluctance. Private day and boarding schools became the principal feeders, since they prepared students almost exclusively in the classical and traditional subjects (Greek, Latin, mathematics, and English) required by the Big Three's own entrance examinations. Consequently, from the early 1900s through the 1940s, about 50 to 60 percent of Harvard and about 70 to 90 percent of Princeton freshmen were private school graduates. Between 40 and 60 percent of Yale freshmen were educated in private preparatory schools, with another 10 to 20 percent adding a year or two at a private school to their public education ("high plus prep").8

Harvard led the Big Three, however, in permitting for admission both alternative subjects (among them, the newer sciences and modern languages) and optional methods of examination. Not only had it been the first of them to drop Greek as a requirement for entrance and graduation (1887), but President Charles W. Eliot had "anticipated 'unrestricted election' in entrance requirements by several years." In January 1898, he told the Board of Overseers that in the future Harvard would insist that "the gate to a university education shall not be closed on the candidate" because he omitted certain subjects, provided his high school course had given him "a sound training of some sort." In order to maintain national leadership in a democracy with "great local diversities," colleges and universities "must be careful not to offer unnecessary obstacles to the admission of young men of adequate though diversified training."9

In May 1904, Harvard preceded Yale and Princeton in voting to join the College Entrance Examination Board. The CEEB held its examinations at various centers and issued certificates of the results, which member colleges would receive in place of their own examinations. Such a system had several advantages; foremost, it insured "a uniform definition of requirements and uniform tests for admission to all participating colleges." Each institution could still decide what it would accept as a passing grade.10

The Yale faculty voted to join the CEEB in 1909, after Dean Henry P. Wright pointed out that better college work was being done by students admitted under the board examination than by those who had taken Yale's own examinations. Princeton followed suit the next year. As of 1916, the Big Three mutually agreed to discontinue June entrance examinations and to "offer one identical paper in each subject" through the CEEB.11

Adoption of the CEEB examinations was only one of the important steps in the modernization of Big Three entrance requirements. While they still insisted on examining applicants in a certain number of subjects—Yale demanded fifteen examinations as of 1911—such state universities as Michigan, Indiana, Wisconsin, and Iowa had begun to admit candidates on certificate from accredited secondary schools during the 1870s. The certificate system invaded the East by 1890, and the future trend was clear when the University of Pennsylvania accepted them in 1907. To attract promising high school students, especially from areas outside the East, Harvard pioneered in 1911 a compromise of the certificate and examination systems called the "New Plan." It required for admission a record of an approved high school course and satisfactory results on four "comprehensive" examinations (English; Latin or, for Bachelor of Science candidates, French or German; mathematics, physics, or chemistry; and a choice of a subject on which the candidate had not already written).12

High school graduates usually sought admission under the New Plan, which emphasized quality of reasoning powers as well as quantity of knowledge and allowed the Committee on Admission to exercise a certain amount of discretion. On the other hand, many preparatory school students preferred the well-known "quantitative" and nondiscretionary "Old Plan" method. While admission was secured by accumulating twenty-six points of subject matter, a candidate could enter "on condition" and make up deficiencies later. As President A. Lawrence Lowell explained to Headmaster Alfred E. Stearns of Phillips Andover Academy, the New Plan would make it harder for the weak student to be admitted from a good preparatory school, but easier for the good student outside the traditional feeder schools. Harvard wanted to extend its educational leadership "by letting in boys from schools in other parts of the country which did not hitherto fit our requirements." The New Plan even caught the imagination of Andrew Carnegie, who praised Harvard as "a Republic of Letters," in which there was "now a clear path for the poor boy from the bottom to the top."13

Although President Hadley of Yale had proposed a system of comprehensive examinations in 1901, his institution did not adopt its so-called Plan B until 1916, four years after Princeton had voted in favor of its own "Alternative Method of Entrance." To facilitate the operation of such new plans, the CEEB began to offer comprehensive examinations in June 1916. A dozen years later, Robert N. Corwin would boast to President Angell about the extension of the New Plan "under Yale's leadership." "To Harvard thus belongs the credit for starting the experiment," he wrote, "and to Yale that of making it workable and generally available."14

As the Big Three expanded their pool of potential applicants to new schools, their representatives became increasingly influential on the College Entrance Examination Board. Robert Nelson Corwin, chairman of the Joint Committee on Admissions for Sheffield Scientific School ("Sheff") and Yale College, represented that university on the CEEB from 1910 to 1934 and was its chairman from 1916 to 1919. As CEEB chairman (1933-36), Radcliffe Heermance, director of admission at Princeton, worked to improve relationships between the colleges and the secondary schools.15

Recruitment policies at Harvard, Yale, and Princeton were shaped largely by the personalities of their first full-time directors. Henry Pennypacker, Robert N. Corwin, and Radcliffe Heermance were old-stock Protestant Americans who championed the virtues of "character," "manliness," and athletic prowess almost as much as the merits of high test scores. In recruiting applicants, they traveled to many schools and alumni clubs. They wooed the audience by their "commanding presence," "resonant voice," and "glad hand act." In selecting incoming freshmen, they relied heavily on the personal interview.16

Both Corwin and Pennypacker were former college athletes and chairmen of their respective university athletic associations or committees. A varsity football player at Yale, Corwin attained the honor of having been elected captain of the championship football team of 1886. (His social success was assured when he was elected to Psi Upsilon fraternity and tapped for Skull and Bones.) After studying for his M.A. and Ph.D. degrees in Berlin and

Heidelberg, Corwin rose through Yale's academic ranks to become head of the German department in the Sheffield Scientific School. For his part, Pennypacker had won the intercollegiate shot put as a Harvard senior. Three years later, in 1891, he began a nineteen-year career at Boston Latin School as a teacher of Latin and Greek, becoming headmaster in 1910. There, given the school's changing student body composition, he became more intimately acquainted with the sons of Catholic and Jewish immigrants than either Corwin or Heermance. From 1920 to 1933, Pennypacker served as chairman of the Committee on Admission at Harvard, the same years that Corwin chaired Yale's University Board of Admissions.[17]

Though a Williams College graduate, Radcliffe Heermance was well suited to direct Princeton's admission office, from its creation in 1922 until 1950. When dealing with young men, he conjured "a vision of a cavalry officer, sabre at point, at full gallop towards a line of green hills." (A major of infantry in the Army Reserve, he commanded a training detachment in Georgia before becoming professor of military science and tactics of the Students' Army Training Corps at Harvard.) As supervisor and later dean of freshmen (1921-42), he gave the "young brats" the rough side of his tongue when their grades fell "far below their predictive group." A genial man of strong moral character who drank no hard liquor, Heermance defended the values of a liberal education to his charges: "You will not solve the problems of middle life, young man, by feats of memory." Like most collegiate paternalists of this era, he prided himself on his ability to judge and mold character.[18]

Financing the Empire: Protestant, Catholic, and Jewish Benefactors

By the 1920s, scholarships and other financial aids were increasingly important in Big Three competition to attract able and deserving students from different parts of the country. The earliest sources of financial support to these and other "private" colleges had been provided by state legislatures. And the earliest form of scholarship aid had been the remission of tuition to sons of clergymen, which was later offered to any qualified student of inadequate pecuniary resources. During the nineteenth century, however, wealthy businessmen or their widows began to give large sums of money to private universities, either as individuals or through foundations. Prominent among such benefactors were Andrew Carnegie, Mrs. Collis P. Huntington, J. P. Morgan, John D. Rockefeller, Mrs. Russell Sage, the Leland Stanfords, the Vanderbilts, and the Whitneys. Each university had its share of wealthy alumni, and sometimes they competed with one another for sons and funds from the same family.[19]

Yale always maintained correctly that Harvard was the wealthier institution, although Harvard graduates, in turn, often claimed that Yale men went into the more lucrative careers. In 1905, discouraged by the response of Yale alumni to the Bicentennial Fund, President Arthur T. Hadley pointed out that Harvard benefited from being more of a local institution, supported generously by wealthy Bostonians. While Yale "had a large hold on the moneyed men of New Haven, and some hold on the Yale moneyed men of New York," once "outside of this you find a distinct unwillingness to give." Bequests were easier to come by, continued Hadley, "but for getting things in life instead of in death one has to work quite carefully." In spite of a smaller budget, he proudly argued that "the amount of instruction per capita given our students is, on paper at least, very much greater than the amount of instruction per capita given Harvard students."20

In addition to such Boston Brahmins as the Lawrences, the Lowells, and Major Henry L. Higginson (who gave funds both for the Harvard Union, an undergraduate social center, and for Soldiers Field for athletics), Harvard had Lamonts, Stillmans, and Wideners. Perhaps its greatest single benefactor of the early twentieth century was Gordon MacKay, an inventor of shoe machinery and a mining tycoon; it was estimated that his 1903 bequest would ultimately bring Harvard well over $23 million for furthering education in the applied sciences. As a result of such gifts, Harvard's endowment increased almost fivefold during Lowell's administration: from $22.7 million in 1909 to $128.5 million in 1933.21

In this same period, Harvard greatly expanded: The School of Business Administration was constructed on the other side of the Charles River, in the university's then characteristic red-brick style, thanks to the $5.0 million gift of George F. Baker, president of the First National Bank of New York. Among the other new buildings were the freshman halls; Lehman and Straus Halls in Harvard Yard; half a dozen laboratories; Widener Library; Fogg Art Museum; Memorial Church; and the Harvard House Plan. When his offer to build residential quadrangles at Yale had not been accepted by his alma mater after almost two years, Edward S. Harkness '97 met with Harvard President Lowell, who accepted the proposal with alacrity. Three months later, in January 1929, Harvard received a written promise of $11.4 million to launch the Harvard House Plan. Fortunately for Yale, Harkness agreed a year later, after considerable negotiations, to donate $15.7 million to build eight units of Yale's College Plan.22

Yale's great building program, in the Gothic revival style, was financed largely by Harkness, heir of wise investments in Standard Oil Company, and by John W. Sterling '64, New York corporation lawyer. Sterling's bequest of $15.0 million capital in 1918 was "the greatest gift an American university had ever received." And $22.8 million of the almost $39.0 million ultimately appropriated for Yale University by the trustees of Sterling's estate went into buildings. Beginning with the Harkness Memorial Tower and Quadrangle (1920), the gift of Mrs. Stephen V. Harkness, Yale's building program culminated in the 1930s with Sterling Memorial Library, Sterling Law Buildings, the Hall of Graduate Studies, and ten residential colleges (Sterling Quadrangle was the ninth, and the bequest of Frederick W. Vanderbilt provided for the tenth). In addition, the family of Payne Whitney '98 gave Yale a magnificent gymnasium. And during President Angell's administration (1921-37) Yale's endowment more than quadrupled: from $25.7 million to $107.6 million. 23

Scions of big business and banking were also to be found among Princeton's moneyed men: Junius S. Morgan '88; Childs Frick, B.S. '05 (from Henry Clay Frick's bequest, publicized in 1919 as being worth $15.0 million, Princeton had realized only $5.9 million by 1932); Firestones (a new university library); McCormicks; and Rockefellers. Among the numerous buildings—mostly in Gothic revival architecture—constructed at Princeton during the boom decade of the 1920s were seven dormitories, Baker Rink, McCarter Theater, a new school of science, and a new chapel. In 1911-12, Princeton's endowment had been a relatively modest $5.2 million; twenty years later, it totaled $24.7 million. 24

Most of the big donors were Protestants, because Harvard and Yale had been founded by the Congregationalists and Princeton largely by the Presbyterians. But as Catholic and Jewish students began to attend these colleges in the late nineteenth century, some of them also became loyal alumni contributors. Harvard had the most Catholic and Jewish alumni and, hence, donors, because it was the first of the Big Three to cut ties with its sectarian past. For example, in 1925, the widow of Charles Joseph Bonaparte '71, who had been Harvard's first Catholic overseer (1891-1903), endowed a scholarship in her husband's memory to be awarded to the outstanding junior concentrating in government. (Bonaparte, the grandson of Napoleon's brother Jerome, had been a successful Baltimore lawyer before becoming Theodore Roosevelt's secretary of the Navy and then his attorney general.) In 1902, James Byrne '77, the first Catholic fellow of the Harvard Corporation (1920-26), had founded the Class of 1877 Scholarship and fifteen years later endowed the Byrne Professorship of Administrative Law. 25

Another Irishman, William Stanislaus Murphy '85, left his entire estate of more than $53,000 to be used as a scholarship fund "for the collegiate education of any young man or men named Murphy who in the judgment of the faculty should prove deserving of this kind of encouragement." The son of a Boston harness maker, Murphy had lived at home during his four years at Harvard. He then worked for almost thirty years as a clerk in the surveyor's office of the Boston customhouse until his death in 1916. According to an editorial in the *Harvard Alumni Bulletin*, the bequest "was a fine, impersonal, yet tribal wish . . . worthy of all honor." Murphy's gift was only one of many —including Harvard's first scholarship, endowed in 1643 by Lady Ann Mowlson of London—that gave preference to kinsmen or to applicants from a particular place or area. "Although this gift may possibly give the Murphys at Harvard a slight advantage over the less fortunate Cabots and Lowells," quipped the *Boston Herald*, it did "not prevent the faculty from teaching the truth to the Murphys, Cabots, and Lowells." 26

One of Harvard's more generous alumni was George Smith '53, who left his alma mater about a quarter of a million dollars. After it accumulated to $450,000, it was to be spent for the construction of three residence halls for freshmen. His real father had been an Irish porter named Connelly, an employee of Smith & Partridge, St. Louis merchants. Orphaned at a young age, George had been informally adopted by the senior partner and his wife, James and Persis Smith, a childless, middle-aged couple. Sent to Harvard, young Smith offended his eastern classmates by wearing long, curly hair in the style of Buffalo Bill. He also wrote a letter impetuously challenging Dr. James Walker, president of Harvard (1853-60), to a duel. Much later, after a bitter, though successful, contest over his benefactors' estate, Smith became an eccentric recluse who immortalized the family by naming the three halls after himself, James Smith, and Persis Smith. 27

To be sure, "the clan of Smith" was "well worth going after," but had the halls been named "Connelly," shrewdly commented an alumnus to President Lowell, it might have increased Harvard's "prestige with the Irish, who seem to be the coming over-lords of Massachusetts." The Smith Halls, along with Standish (the gift of Mrs. Russell Sage) and Gore (built by alumni subscriptions), were opened in 1914 as the freshmen halls. With the addition of McKinlock Hall in 1926 (given by parents in memory of their son, George Alexander McKinlock, Jr., '16, killed in World War I), the four quadrangles provided on-campus housing for most freshmen. 28

Jewish alumni also began to give generously to Harvard, although its first major Jewish benefactor, Jacob H. Schiff, head of Kuhn, Loeb & Company, had not attended college. In 1889, he had founded the Semitic Museum at Harvard, and he gave about $275,000 to its construction and its activities (which included purchase of specimens, exploration in Palestine, and publications) before his death in 1920. 29

Most of Harvard's wealthy Jewish alumni were from interrelated German Jewish families who had become well established in banking and commerce. In addition to Lehmans (Arthur '94) and Strauses (Jesse Isidor '93, Percy S. '97, and Herbert N. '03), who donated money for the construction of halls in Harvard Yard, there were Goldmans, Sachses, Loebs (of Kuhn, Loeb & Company; in-laws of Jacob Schiff), Littauers, Warburgs (who intermarried with the Schiffs and the Loebs), and Wertheims. The Sachses and the Warburgs contributed substantial sums to the Fogg Art Museum as well as loaning works of art for exhibition. Paul Sachs '00, who had become a Unitarian, was an associate professor of fine arts (1922) and a director of the museum. 30

Morris Loeb '83 left $500,000 to Harvard for the advancement of chemistry and physics (1914), while his brother, James Loeb '88, bequeathed $500,000 to the Department of Classics (1934), established the Loeb Classical Library Foundation (1933), and endowed the Charles Eliot Norton Fellowship in Greek Studies (1901). Lucius N. Littauer '78 chose to strengthen the study of Jewish literature and philosophy at Harvard by establishing the Nathan Littauer Professorship in honor of his father (1925), by making other large bequests, and by giving thousands of volumes of Hebrew books to the library. In 1935, this glove manufacturer and former Republican congressman from New York donated $2 million for the endowment of the Lucius N. Littauer Foundation for Public Administration; two years later he added $250,000 for a new building to house the foundation.[31]

Harvard and Yale were pleased, of course, to accept the gifts of men known as the "Jewish Grand Dukes." But some of their administrators and faculty resented the immigrant Jewish and Catholic students, who competed successfully for financial aid with sons of the salaried native-born middle class, the backbone of Yankee Protestant culture. These "people of education and refinement" also needed scholarships to compensate for a loss of purchasing power. Since the professoriate came from the same social background, it was anxious to protect its own kind from such academic—and hence economic—competition, by carefully allocating scholarships and by specifically restricting the percentage awarded to Jewish students.[32]

Nevertheless, ambitious immigrants from the public feeder schools (Boston Latin and Boston English Schools for Harvard and Hillhouse High School for Yale) won not only scholarships, but also prizes with cash awards. Indeed, a number of scholarships were established at Harvard for the metropolitan area's high school graduates: Daniel A. Buckley, Cambridge, Price Greenleaf, Harvard Club of Boston, and Harvard Club of Somerville. Alumni founded other Harvard Club scholarships for high school graduates from a particular city, state, or region. As of the late 1920s, the average scholarship ranged from $300 to $500, the highest being $975. Smaller amounts of financial assistance—from $50 to $300—were available through the beneficiary, loan, and aid funds. The total amount of financial aid was then about $210,000, but the cost of tuition, medical fees, and room and board (together with estimates for clothes, transportation, books, laundry, and miscellaneous) had risen to a minimum of $1,100—a 240-percent increase within twenty years—according to Seymour E. Harris's *Economics of Harvard*.[33]

Harvard's rivals also provided scholarship aid for needy students. Yale was, Professor Pierson has written, "a place where a poor boy could go and make his way, financially as well as socially and athletically." Not only did the university maintain its tuition at $155 a year from 1888 to 1914 (and then increased it just $5), but its Bureau of Appointments helped students to find part-time jobs. "To strengthen . . . connection with the schools of Connecticut," the Yale Corporation voted in 1911 that freshman tuition scholarships be offered to the state's public high school graduates, fifteen to Connecticut as a whole and two additional ones to New Haven. The number of scholarships was increased substantially in the 1920s, when about $1.0 million from the Sterling bequest was used to endow freshman tuition scholarships and scholarships for graduates of New Haven and Connecticut public schools. Believing in geographical balance, Yale established in 1928 special university regional scholarships for the South Atlantic, Southwest, and Far West (adding the Middle West in 1934). By 1936-37, about thirty students a year from six noneastern regions were selected to come to Yale by criteria similar to those of the Rhodes Scholarship.[34]

In spite of these gains, Yale was facing serious competition from Princeton as well as Harvard. As of 1912, Princeton had 88 university and general scholarships. But in 1919, the university launched an endowment campaign, one purpose of which was to fund regional and memorial scholarships. By 1921, it had almost 300: 40 university for students of Group I and Group II standing; 61 general; 22 regional; 51 war memorial; and 120 memorial prize scholarships. The latter, which paid $200 per annum, were apportioned thirty to each entering freshman class in such a way that fifteen different regional districts received at least one apiece.[35]

Even with similar maximums set on scholarship aid, Harvard's greater resources allowed it to capture "more than its share of the really bright students," Professor Pierson has noted with regret. Through its attractive national scholarships (with stipends of $1,000), Harvard began in 1934 to recruit a student body "as national as Yale's" and gained in prestige, while "Yale lost an opportunity for intellectual leadership." Competition among the Big Three was a boon to many enterprising high school graduates, especially to those from the West.[36]

The Changing Campus: World War I and the Beginning of Restrictive Admissions

World War I changed colleges in at least three ways: Most importantly, by dramatically increasing enrollments through returning veterans, it opened the way for the development of more selective standards of admission. Second, the success of the United States Army in classifying 1,726,966 officers and men by standardized tests—known as Alpha and Beta, for both the literate and the illiterate—was "irresistibly suggestive" to colleges and universities faced with screening a rapidly growing number of applicants. Third, by becoming apologists for the United States' conduct in the war, members of the professoriate "were bound to compromise their critical judgment," Carol S. Gruber has written. Not only did faculties accept and participate in military training programs on campus (SATC), but they also yielded on issues of academic freedom and failed to denounce the rising public hysteria. Having once "compromised the ideal of their calling" during a war for "civilization," they would not find it so difficult to acquiesce when again the ends seemed to justify the means.[37]

The war aroused the passions of religious intolerance and ethnic or racial prejudice, which reached their fullest pitch during the "tribal twenties." Across the country, native-born groups fearing aliens and radicals rallied under the banner of 100-percent Americanism. And in the hysteria of the red scare, two Italian anarchists and draft dodgers, Nicola Sacco and Bartolomeo Vanzetti, were convicted of murder and robbery largely because they appeared to be the most likely suspects. Their guilt was subsequently upheld by an advisory committee appointed by Governor Alvin T. Fuller of Massachusetts. Three members of the WASP establishment reviewed the case: President A. Lawrence Lowell of Harvard University, chairman of the committee; President Samuel W. Stratton of the Massachusetts Institute of Technology; and Judge Robert Grant. These men lent their prestige to a controversial verdict and execution in which ethnic and political prejudices may have been decisive. Lowell's role was significant, given both his concurrent advocacy of immigration restriction and the proposed quota on Jews at Harvard. Although he had vigorously defended professorial rights to freedom of speech during and after World War I, his toleration of differences was limited. Like many contemporary academic spokesmen, Lowell's judgment was shaped by certain class and racist assumptions.[38]

The Big Three's decision to limit enrollments and to impose quotas on Jews should be seen in the light of parallel national trends that resulted in the Immigration Quota Laws of 1921 and 1924. Just as a nation had an obligation to select its future constituency with care, their argument ran, so also did universities, because they educated the leaders of tomorrow. Since eastern and southern Europeans were somehow less "desirable" than those of northern European origin—not only as citizens, but also as collegians—their numbers had to be restricted to tolerable proportions.

In limiting the size of their freshman classes (at Harvard to 1,000, at Yale to 850, and at Princeton to 600), the Big Three favored their middle- and upper-class WASP clientele. Alumni preference operated to reduce the admission of immigrant and minority students. But by the 1920s, Catholics fared better than Jews in admissions and on campus: They were Christians and, partly for that reason, seemed less threatening. While both college officials and undergraduates held favorable stereotypes of Irish (and Welsh) students, their conceptions of Jews were negative. For example, Dean Byron S. Hurlbut recalled "a cheerful Irishman" who worked as a policeman during the summer. He would "someday be heard from in politics," the dean predicted and hoped that his "Harvard education [would] help him to stand for what is right." Another Harvard student, a Welshman with an occasional "miner's cough," was "jolly, full of fun, cheerful in the darkest days," in spite of having to work his way through college. On the other hand, Dean Frederick S. Jones of Yale blamed the declining interest in scholarship among Gentiles on the academic success of the Jewish student, who was seen as "the greasy grind." Undergraduates would no longer compete for "first honors," because they did "not care to be a minority in a group of men of higher scholarship record, most of whom are Jews."[39]

Another reason for their different receptions was the fact that proportionately more Jews than Catholics sought admission to Harvard, Yale, and Columbia. Jews did not found denominational colleges, but preferred to attend existing private and public institutions. Commented President James R. Angell of Yale, neither the Jewish students themselves, "nor their families would be likely to look upon a Jewish university as satisfactorily meeting their requirements, unless it were notably more liberally endowed, staffed and equipped than other existing institutions." In contrast, Catholics often believed that religious training was an integral part of education itself; and they built an educational system extending from parish schools through universities. Consequently, although Catholic immigrants had arrived earlier than the bulk of Jewish immigration, they did not enter the mainstream of secular higher education until at least a generation later.[40]

According to a survey by the Bureau of Jewish Social Research published in the *American Jewish Year Book*, 20 of the 106 institutions studied had 10 percent or more Jewish enrollment by 1918-19 (see Table 1.1). While Jewish students constituted 9.7 percent overall, or 14,837 of a total enrollment of 153,084, the heaviest concentrations were almost invariably in eastern urban institutions. City College of New York had the highest Jewish academic enrollment—78.7 percent—followed by New York University (47.5), Hunter College (38.7), Saint Lawrence University (31.7), and Polytechnic Institute, Brooklyn (29.4). The more expensive private universities had lower percentages: Columbia University (21.2), University of Pennsylvania (14.5), and Harvard (10.0).[41]

At first, the "foreign element," as it was called, was too small to cause alarm. But by their May 1918 meeting at Princeton University, several members of the Association of New England Deans voiced their fears:

> *Dean Wren* [Frank G., Tufts College]
> I find that more and more the foreign element is creeping in and now, because of the enlistments, the American boys are getting less and less. We now have more new students than old at the end of the year and about twenty per cent of them are Cubans. How can we get the boys of American parentage to come to college?
> *Dean Sills* [Kenneth Charles Morton, then Acting President, subsequently President of Bowdoin College]
> We do not like to have boys of Jewish parentage.
> *Dean Randall* [Otis E., Brown University]
> They tried to establish a Jewish fraternity at Brown.

Table 1.1
PERCENTAGE OF JEWISH STUDENTS AT THIRTY COLLEGES AND UNIVERSITIES, 1918-19

College	Enrollment Jewish	Total	Percentage
College of Dental & Oral Surgery, New York	477	589	80.9
College of the City of New York	1,544	1,961	78.7
Long Island Hospital Medical College	189	343	55.0
New York University	2,532	5,536	47.5
Hunter College	502	1,295	38.7
St. Lawrence University	169	532	31.7
Polytechnic Institute of Brooklyn	97	329	29.4
Fordham University	290	1,247	23.2
Columbia University	1,475	6,943	21.2
Tufts College	310	1,635	18.9
University of Chicago	761	4,106	18.5
Johns Hopkins University	322	1,983	16.2
Armour Institute of Technology	95	605	15.7
Western Reserve University	269	1,838	14.6
University of Pennsylvania	596	4,072	14.5
Temple University	266	1,854	14.3
Adelphi College	42	309	13.5
University of Pittsburgh	443	3,627	12.2
Trinity College, Hartford	29	237	12.2
Harvard University	385	3,843	10.0
Boston University	169	1,714	9.9
Baldwin-Wallace College, Berea, Ohio	55	565	9.8
Cornell University	317	3,505	9.1
Brown University	34	1,140	2.9
Dartmouth College	33	1,173	2.8
Princeton University	30	1,142	2.6
United States Military Academy at West Point	22	994	2.2
Amherst College	8	421	1.9
Bowdoin College	14	774	1.9
Williams College	7	481	1.4

Source: Adapted from: Table I Number and Proportion of Jewish Students Enrolled in 106 Colleges, Universities and Professional Schools in the U.S. for Scholastic Year 1918-1919, pp. 387-89, "Professional Tendencies Among Jewish Students in Colleges, Universities, and Professional Schools" (Memoir of the Bureau of Jewish Social Research), *American Jewish Year Book, 5681,* Vol. 22 (September 13, 1920, to October 2, 1921), pp. 381-93.

Q. Does Brown feel the effects of Jewish students?

A. Yes.

Dean Jones [Frederick S., Yale University]

I think we shall have to change our views in regard to the Jewish element. We should do something to improve them. They are getting there
rapidly. If we do not educate them, they will overrun us. We have got to
change our policies and get them into shape. A few years ago every single scholarship of any value was won by a Jew. I took it up with the Committee and said that we could not allow that to go on. We must put a ban
on the Jews. We decided not to give them any scholarships but to extend
aid to them in the way of tuition.

Dean Burton [Alfred Edgar, Massachusetts Institute of Technology]

We always ask of our Jewish students whether or not they will be obliged to leave college if they do not receive assistance. In every case they
say they will, but we have found by experience that such is not the case.

There was no evidence that the deans made any collective resolutions at this
time. But before the 1920 meeting of the Association of Administrative Officers in New England, held at Middletown, Connecticut, Dean Randall of
Brown proposed for discussion the "limitation in the enrollment of Jews and
Negroes." And at subsequent meetings during the 1920s, limitation of enrollment and of size of the freshman class was frequently discussed. [42]

The first universities to adopt some form of restriction, specifically a quota
on Jewish students, were those in New York City, particularly Columbia University and New York University. Columbia cut its undergraduate Jewish enrollment in order to regain its former status as an elite institution for native
American sons of downtown business and professional men, its clientele
prior to moving to Morningside Heights. Even before World War I, Frederick
P. Keppel, dean of the college, was asked: "Isn't Columbia overrun with
European Jews, who are most unpleasant persons socially?" [43]

In his well-documented book entitled *The Qualified Student: A History of
Selective College Admission in America*, Harold S. Wechsler has explained
both Columbia's attraction for immigrants, especially eastern European
Jews, and then the reasons that the undergraduate college and the College of
Physicians and Surgeons imposed quotas on them. Initially, President Nicholas Murray Butler made access to Columbia easier by improving relations
with the New York City public secondary schools and by modernizing admission requirements through the establishment of the College Entrance Examination Board. Columbia's combined course, moreover, allowed students to
begin professional training as undergraduates, thereby saving both expense
and time. [44]

But because the city high schools were not "properly" performing "the selective function" of steering "undesirables" away from Columbia, Admissions Director Adam LeRoy Jones and the college faculty began to develop

criteria that included social characteristics as well as academic record. For example, new application blanks asked for the candidate's birthplace, religious affiliation, and father's name, place of birth, and occupation. Students were also to submit photographs and to present themselves for a personal interview, if possible. [45]

While the new admissions process was "affirmative"—having the objective of bringing better students to Columbia, rather than merely limiting the number of Jews—the next step was to screen applicants by giving them the Tests for Mental Alertness, devised by E. L. Thorndike of Teachers College. During World War I, Columbia had used such tests to determine the "general mental ability" of candidates for the Students' Army Training Corps. In 1919, it began to allow candidates with satisfactory school records to take Thorndike's "intelligence examination" in place of the entrance examinations. Fitness for college work would then be decided by record of preparation, "character and promise," health, and intelligence. [46]

Herbert E. Hawkes, Keppel's successor as dean of Columbia College, subsequently argued that required intelligence or psychological tests would provide a "rational" means of selection. A Yale alumnus who had been considered a possible successor to President Arthur T. Hadley, Hawkes had close contacts with men at his alma mater. In 1922, Admissions Director Corwin reported to Yale's Committee on Limitation of Numbers the results of Columbia's new admissions policy. According to Corwin, Hawkes explained that "most Jews, especially those of the more objectionable type, have not had the home experiences which enable them to pass these tests as successfully as the average native American boy." As a result, "the proportion of Jews in Columbia has been reduced from about forty percent to about twenty." But the belief prevailed "among some not connected with Columbia," added Corwin, "that these tests, by enabling the Board of Admissions to review again the records of all candidates, may in some cases be arbitrarily made to serve the end desired." [47]

Yet in spite of this device, said Wechsler, "at all times through the mid-1920s at least 40% of the freshman class was from immigrant families"; the number of Catholic students, Italian Americans in particular, increased as the number of Jews declined. But Catholics, too, were subject to some kind of limitation during the late 1920s or early 1930s. The freshman class of 572 that matriculated in the fall of 1934 was 58 percent Protestant, 25 percent Catholic, and 17 percent Jewish. These figures suggest the operation of some sort of percentage limitation on the admission of Catholic and Jewish students to Columbia. [48]

Columbia's College of Physicians and Surgeons also slashed its Jewish enrollment, which was almost 50 percent in 1919, to 18-20 percent in 1924. Since training cost much more than tuition fees, every Jewish applicant admitted to medical school was seen as another expensively subsidized competitor of the native-born American. And every Jewish doctor allegedly took a position away from a native American doctor. Not until the late 1920s were there any efforts to limit enrollment and to adopt selective admissions for the law school. Even then, Jewish students continued to be strongly represented in the school and on the law review board. [49]

New York University, sensitive to developments at Columbia, evidently began its sifting process in 1919-20, using "a group of coordinated principles" to measure "moral values." By 1922-23, all four undergraduate classes at the University Heights campus were on "a selected basis." According to the secretary of the NYU branch of the Intercollegiate Menorah Society, the percentage of Jewish students declined from over 40 to 25; but he also argued that the smaller number profited more from their education. [50]

Discussion or adoption of a Jewish quota at one private eastern university sparked similar consideration or debate at other institutions. Even colleges like Amherst, Dartmouth, Princeton, and Williams became more selective, although they had "no pressing Jewish problem." Certain factors aided them by limiting the number of potential Jewish applicants. First, their small-town locations discouraged both local Jewish residents and outside Jewish applicants. Other deterrents were the required chapel attendance and the exclusiveness of clubs and fraternities. In 1918-19, Jewish enrollment at Dartmouth was 2.8 percent; at Princeton, 2.6; at Amherst, 1.9; and at Williams, 1.5. [51]

Given such a pervasive climate of opinion and their own Jewish enrollments, it was inevitable that sooner or later Harvard, Yale, and Princeton would reexamine admissions policies. The proportion of Jewish freshmen who had been regularly admitted to Harvard, had risen from 7.0 to 21.5 percent (150) between 1900 and 1922. While the increase in Jewish students at Yale was smaller, it caused as much official concern. In 1901-02, there were 18 Jews in the three upper classes, or 2.0 percent of the enrollment. Twenty years later, 13.4 percent (71) of the Yale College class of 1925 was Jewish. In 1900, six Jewish undergraduates enrolled at Princeton; in 1922, there were 25, or just under 4.0 percent, of the class of 1926. By 1911-12, at the very least, judging from the 250 members of the campus St. Paul's Catholic Club, several hundred Catholic students attended Harvard. Yale College had fewer: 30 Catholics were among the 357 members of the class of 1912. And fewer than 20 Catholics matriculated each year at Princeton until 1908, when 25 enrolled. Although officials at the Big Three may have kept an occasional count of Catholic students, their numbers did continue to increase slightly, even after quotas were imposed on Jewish applicants. [52]

With considerable resistance at Harvard (in spite of the will of a majority of the faculty), less at Yale, and virtually none at Princeton, all three universities began to limit Jewish students by various and not particularly subtle means. They ranged from photographs attached to admission forms, specific questions regarding the applicant's race and religion, personal interviews, and restriction of scholarship aid. Beginning with the class of 1928, Yale aimed at stabilizing its proportion of Jewish students at around 10-12 percent. During the same year, 1924, Princeton almost halved its number of successful Jewish candidates in order to admit no more, and usually less, than the percentage of Jews in the national population—about 3 percent. Two years later, with the class of 1930, Harvard began to reduce its Jewish enrollment from about 25-27 percent to about 10-16 percent.[53]

Drawing the Caste Line: From Admissions to Extracurricular Activities

Collegiate anti-Semitism and anti-Catholicism arose in part from and were sustained by the Big Three's dependency on private preparatory schools for a large proportion of their undergraduates. Less than half of these students, however, were really part of the so-called prep school crowd of the socially elite. But they exercised an influence on campus life far out of proportion to either their numbers or their academic attainments. The other private school graduates were really in Yale's "high plus prep" category—the sons of middle-class business, professional, and even farming families, who attended a local or neighboring private school of modest social reputation for a few years before going off to college. If they made their mark in extracurricular activities, they, too, might be admitted to an exclusive social club or fraternity. Few public high school graduates had any presumption of social success in college. Although "proper Bostonians" like Charles W. Eliot had once attended the public Boston Latin School, by the 1890s "a lad of Mayflower and Porcellian ancestry who entered from a high school was as much 'out of it' as a ghetto Jew," wrote Samuel Eliot Morison, historian of Harvard.[54]

Noting that the New York elite had already departed from Columbia to be with more pleasing companions at such smaller colleges as the "Little Three" of Amherst, Wesleyan, and Williams, the Big Three took care to shield their upper-class patrons from undesirable contacts or jostling from social inferiors. Not only were they "paying customers," but members of this social class could be counted on to contribute generously both time and money to alumni activities and fund-raising campaigns (indeed, many of them came to the Big Three because of their alumni lineage). Frequently dubbed the prep school crowd, they usually shunned honor grades and threw themselves wholeheartedly into more "gentlemanly" pursuits: editorships, managerships, and athletic competitions. (Yale students even voted the "Y" to be of more esteem than Phi Beta Kappa.) As candidates for Harvard's "final" clubs, Yale's junior fraternities and senior societies, and Princeton's eating clubs for upper classmen, they created college life.[55]

It was partly to prevent the desertion of the upper class from Harvard that President Lowell urged the adoption of a percentage system for any group of men who did not mingle indistinguishably with the general stream,—let us say Orientals, colored men, and perhaps . . . French Canadians, if they did not speak English and kept themselves apart; or we might limit them by making the fact that men do not so mingle one of the causes for rejection above a certain percentage. This would apply to almost all, but not all, Jews; possibly, but not probably, to other people.

Lowell's concern for the social relations among students was in marked contrast to the attitude of his predecessor, Charles W. Eliot. The fact that some students did not intermingle or receive invitations to join social organizations was not, in Eliot's view, reason to limit their access to the university.[56]

Like President Woodrow Wilson of Princeton, however, Lowell felt that a congenial academic atmosphere would help students to mature. To this end, Lowell and Wilson independently developed residential housing plans for their respective colleges, drawing in part on Oxford and Cambridge universities as models. Whereas Wilson envisioned his Quadrangle Plan primarily as a means of elevating intellectual standards by displacing the upperclassmen's eating clubs as the focus of undergraduate life, Lowell stressed the social intermingling that his House Plan would encourage. Wilson's failure at Princeton strengthened the Harvard president's own convictions about potential undergraduate and alumni resistance to enforced residential mixing. Consequently, administrators and masters supervising the allocation of students among Harvard's freshman halls and houses and among Yale's colleges made only limited efforts prior to World War II to counteract snobbery and cliques based on economic status, ethnic or racial background, and school groups.

During this period, moreover, clubs and fraternities competed successfully for the loyalty and time of undergraduates with social aspirations—and credentials. At Princeton, for example, the upper-class eating clubs offered bids to the most promising sophomores during the annual spring selection, known as "bicker week." The five oldest and most prestigious clubs were Ivy (1879), Cottage (1886), Colonial (1891), Cap and Gown (1892), and Tiger Inn (1892). According to one observer, they tended to attract, respectively, the following types of students: snobs, literary men like Fitzgerald, social register members, noble Christians, and football players. In the period 1920-23, the percentage of private school graduates was 100 in Ivy, 86 in Cap and Gown, 81 in Cottage, 76 in Colonial, and 72 in Tiger Inn. If one considers all five clubs, almost 84 percent came from private schools, about 11 percent from other colleges, and only 5 percent from high schools. Some preparatory schools provided better club connections than others. Just one man each from Groton and Polytechnic Prep entered a top club in that four-year period, while Lawrenceville sent 31 men to four of the five (excluding Ivy), and Hill sent 22 of its 24 graduates to Ivy, Cottage, and Cap and Gown. Gilman almost evenly divided its 17 graduates between Ivy and Cap and Gown, while Phillips Exeter sent 8 of 11 to Tiger Inn. Membership seemed almost predetermined.[57]

Concurrently, Princeton had the reputation of giving Jewish students a hard time. Two leading novels of the 1920s recorded this treatment. In *This Side of Paradise* by F. Scott Fitzgerald, Amory Blaine and his friends amused themselves by filling "the Jewish youth's bed with lemon pie," a fairly mild form of hazing. But to protect himself from possibly more serious abuses, Robert Cohn in Ernest Hemingway's book *The Sun Also Rises* became the college middleweight boxing champion. Cohn, whose character was apparently drawn from one of Meyer Guggenheim's grandsons, was the scion of both wealthy and old New York Jewish families. At military school he had been a good football player, and "no one had ever made him feel he was a Jew, and hence any different from anybody else, until he went to Princeton."[58]

Such social discrimination was especially hard to endure at Princeton, since too few Jewish students were there prior to World War II to establish more than informal groups. Some of them may have joined the Liberal Club and the Society for the Study of Socialism. (These more daring campus organizations were moribund, if not defunct, by the end of the 1920s.) A few well-to-do Jewish students who were willing to become "pet Jews" probably had a good time. Many more may have experienced the reception given to Robert Cohn. Then they either learned to fight or transferred to another college.[59]

Columbia, Harvard, and Pennsylvania were generally more hospitable. Accordingly, Mrs. Phillip J. Goodhart, one of the leading lights of New York German Jewish society, "believed . . . that boys should concentrate on Harvard or Columbia, not Princeton." One of her sons went to Yale, but "Princeton had graduated too many people she did not visit."[60]

On the other hand, some Harvard men felt that "the liberality" of Princeton's club system was "superior" to theirs, because a higher proportion of Princeton upperclassmen was elected and all clubs were ostensibly of equal rank. At Princeton, moreover, clubhouses were opened to nonmembers as well as to those belonging to other clubs. As late as 1947, Cleveland Amory, author of *The Proper Bostonians*, maintained that "as currently constituted Harvard's club system is probably the most exclusive of that in any college in America." First, in order to be in the social swim at all, a man had to be among the 150 selected out of a class of about 1,000 for membership in Hasty Pudding—Institute of 1770. One's position in this organization, which produced a musical comedy in the spring, was further defined by the presence of the letters DKE. If he was a "Dickey," a man was among the first forty-five sophomores chosen for membership and "hence very definitely a social somebody." But the ultimate goal was to be elected to one of Harvard's ten final clubs (about 11 or 12 percent of the sophomore, junior, and senior classes).[61]

The path to these social pinnacles was strewn with hurdles: residence in one of Mount Auburn Street's "Gold Coast" halls, invitations to Boston Society events, and avoidance of certain taboos. Among the most damaging, if violated, were "overcareful dress, undue athletic exertion, serious literary endeavor, rah-rah spirit, long hair, grades above C, and Radcliffe girls." Proper behavior was nurtured, of course, by the right preparatory school background. The best were the Episcopal boarding schools—the "St. Grottlesex" group—followed by schools like Milton Academy, Noble & Greenough, Pomfret, and several country day schools. The preparatory school cliques were so powerful, wrote Corliss Lamont '24, son of Thomas W. Lamont, chairman of the board of J. P. Morgan and Company, that eighty-two of the eighty-five selected from the class of 1923 for final club membership were private school graduates. 62

These top ten clubs were ranked in three groups by prestige. The two best were Porcellian (to which belonged such prominent Bostonians as the Cabots, Lowells, and Saltonstalls, as well as some suitable New Yorkers like Theodore Roosevelt) and A.D. In the second group were Fly (Franklin D. Roosevelt), Spee, Delphic or Gas, and Owl; and a third cluster comprised Fox, D.U. (James B. Conant), Phoenix, and Iroquois. Surprisingly, not all "proper Bostonians" made one of these final clubs. A. Lawrence Lowell '77 became an honorary member of Fly in 1904. And Charles W. Eliot '53 turned down an invitation from Porcellian, judging it "given to dissipation"; however, he joined the Institute of 1770, then concerned with debating and literary activities, and Alpha Delta Phi, intended for those with scientific interests. 63

An undistinguished background was not an insurmountable bar, if an individual was truly exceptional. Even an Irish Catholic might be admitted to an exclusive campus organization, especially if he were a good athlete and personable. For example, Joseph Patrick Kennedy '12, a graduate of Boston Latin and member of St. Paul's Catholic Club, belonged to Hasty Pudding—Institute of 1770, DKE, and Delta Upsilon. His son, John Fitzgerald Kennedy '40, was chosen by fourth-ranked Spee. The elder Kennedy had played on the freshman and university baseball teams, while his son John, a graduate of Choate, was on the junior varsity football team and the swimming squad and played golf, hockey, and softball. 64

On the other hand, old-stock Americans rarely extended invitations to blacks, Italians, and Jews. Not only were Jews almost entirely absent from social club rosters, but they were often excluded from athletic teams of the major sports, debating societies, editorial boards, and musical clubs. Acknowledging these social realities, Bernard Berenson '87—born in the Jewish Pale of Settlement in Lithuania and educated at Boston Latin School and Boston University before coming to Harvard—"preferred the conversation of James, of Toy, of Climer, of Wendell, to that of my fellow students." These professors were "better worth while" and "more accessible." "Nothing," he maintained, was "so clicky and exclusive as the schoolboy or the schoolboy-minded Anglo-Saxon of all ages." As one member of the Harvard class of 1924 commented, there was "no use talking of a 'spirit of common brotherhood' between the graduates of St. Mark's and the Menorah Society."65

In order to gain some leverage in campus affairs, Jews formed parallel cultural and social organizations. The first was the Menorah Society, begun at Harvard in 1906, whose purposes were religious and cultural as well as social. Within six years Harvard had three Jewish fraternities, one of which was the Tau chapter (1912) of the national Zeta Beta Tau. Founded in 1898 "to interest college men in the Zionist movement," ZBT had broadened its appeal from Zionism to Judaism and had evolved into a Greek letter society by 1910. Although the charter members of Tau encountered strong opposition from those who argued that "Harvard isn't a fraternity college," the chapter had thirty-five members by 1916, some of whom were on the football, baseball, and soccer teams as well as on the *Lampoon* and in drama organizations. In 1921, it purchased a second house for its growing membership and shortly thereafter abolished physical punishment during the initiation of pledges. And in 1918, Zeta Beta Tau, Sigma Alpha Mu (1909), and Argo Club (1911) had been joined at Harvard by three other Jewish fraternities: Kappa Nu, Tau Delta Phi, and Tau Epsilon Phi. Only through such organizations could Jewish students really find any social life outside the classroom.66

Similar developments occurred at Yale, although until the early 1910s it had been reasonably liberal in regard to social distinctions. Yale College had senior societies and junior fraternities (the latter fed its members), while Sheffield Scientific School had societies and fraternities (which housed members). Graduates of Phillips Andover and Hotchkiss and of such Episcopal boarding schools as Groton and St. Paul's were in a strong position to be tapped for these social honors.67

Exceptions were sometimes made for young men of distinguished Jewish lineage, for example, John Mortimer Schiff '25, grandson of investment banker Jacob Schiff of Kuhn, Loeb & Company. Schiff had considered joining the Alpha Lambda chapter of Zeta Beta Tau, established at Yale in 1921, but his father, Mortimer L. Schiff ex-'96, a member of Beta Theta Pi at Amherst, persuaded him to join the Yale chapter of his own fraternity. (Around the same time, another Jewish student, whose father had been a former head of Beta Theta Pi, was denied membership.) Certainly, young Schiff had the proper credentials for admission to a Gentile fraternity at Yale: a graduate of the Taft School; a member of the class crew squad, including the championship class crew of May 1924; the assistant business manager of the *Yale Record*; and the manager of the varsity swimming team. At some point in life, he became an Episcopalian; he also married Edith Baker, granddaughter of banker George F. Baker, and carried on his own family's business of Kuhn, Loeb & Company.68

Although not the first Jewish fraternity founded at Yale, ZBT was the most exclusive. It gave preference to German and Spanish Jews from private schools and to those whose fathers had graduated from Yale or from another elite college. Hence, a boy whose father had belonged to a ZBT chapter at a less prestigious institution, for instance, Syracuse, might be denied admission to the Yale chapter. To gain status in the eyes of Gentiles, some chapters of Jewish fraternities imitated the snobbishly exclusive practices of Gentile fraternities that had led to the establishment of separate Jewish social organizations in the first place. [69]

Jews of eastern European origin usually joined the Sigma Alpha Mu chapter, begun in 1917, or Tau Epsilon Phi, founded the next year. Pi Lambda Phi (started in 1917, but not officially recognized until 1923) and Phi Alpha also offered social comfort. Often existing unofficially for several years, Jewish fraternities were designated as university fraternities, which meant that they drew members from both the college and Sheffield. Two social worlds had developed at Yale, as at Harvard, by the 1920s. [70]

Obvious parallels existed between the collegiate social segregation of most Catholic and virtually all black and Jewish students and the prejudices of the Ku Klux Klan. Most undergraduates would have protested that they neither condoned the Klan nor participated in similar activities. After all, hazing Jewish students and pugilistic confrontations with the townspeople (heavily Catholic in Cambridge and New Haven) were done in a "spirit of fun." A certain amount of boisterous boyish behavior and pranks received parental winks, if not sly approval. Indeed, it was preferable to driving fast cars, chasing faster girls, and drinking questionable booze. "I am no great Puritan," wrote one Yale alumnus to Dean Frederick S. Jones, "but the mixing up of Champagne and chorus girls and society halls indicated a degeneration from the time when young men drank whiskey and licked the towns-people— which on the whole indicated a more wholesome atmosphere." [71]

In keeping with the undergraduate temper of the 1920s, student response to the Klan ranged from a protest riot to a journalistic hoax. Not only did student editorials at Princeton denounce the Klan as "un-American," but more than eight hundred students rioted in 1924 against the appearance in the borough of a number of hooded kleagles, who had to be rescued by police. On the other hand, the *Harvard Crimson* had facetiously announced on October 22, 1923: "Ku Klux Klan At Harvard Awaits Moment To Strike." Believing this undergraduate Halloween trick to be true, James Weldon Johnson, secretary of the National Association for the Advancement of Colored People, sent a telegram to President Lowell and the Board of Overseers urging expulsion from the university of those who brought the Klan to Harvard. "It would be better to close the university," Johnson said, "than to permit it to become a vehicle for disseminating the poison of race and religious hatred upon which the infamous Klan depends in recruiting its membership." Though unfounded, these allegations of a Klan at Harvard were an ominous symptom of the times. [72]

· 2 ·

PORTRAITS AND PHILOSOPHIES
OF TWO HARVARD PRESIDENTS:
CHARLES W. ELIOT AND
A. LAWRENCE LOWELL

> I have known well four generations of Lowells, beginning with John Amory Lowell, who was for forty years a member of the Corporation. To no member of the whole family of these four generations should I apply the word "disingenuous." In every generation they have shown themselves resolute, eager to win in any controversy upon which they entered, credulous in regard to alleged facts which go their way, and incredulous with regard to alleged facts which do not go their way, often sudden in making decisions, and then ingenious, though abrupt, in justifying those decisions.
>
> Charles W. Eliot to Jerome D. Greene, June 7, 1922[1]

President Abbott Lawrence Lowell led the movement for restrictive admissions at Harvard College, supported by a substantial minority of the faculty and a majority of the alumni. The so-called Jewish problem would have emerged at Harvard, whoever was president, but Lowell's role was crucial in determining the direction that the controversy took. Deeply opposed to his successor's advocacy of a Jewish quota, President Emeritus Charles William Eliot felt it incumbent on the corporation and the Board of Overseers to "keep incessant watch against his defects of judgment and good feeling." Lowell had not been Eliot's choice as successor when he stepped down in 1909, after forty years as president of Harvard University. He would have preferred Jerome Davis Greene '96, his former secretary, who became the first secretary to the corporation and, later, an overseer. Eliot's presence in Cambridge until his death in 1926 proved an embarrassment to Lowell. The president emeritus became the unofficial rallying point for all the dissident elements within the Harvard family. Even though both men came from similar backgrounds, their temperaments, educational objectives, and social philosophies were in sharp contrast. A comparison between them may suggest why Boston Brahmins not quite a generation apart in age came to hold such different interpretations of Harvard's educational role and responded in opposite ways to the problems posed by ethnic diversity within both the college and the United States as a whole.[2]

Family Background and Personality

Eliot and Lowell were descended from old Yankee stock. By the late eighteenth and early nineteenth centuries, the Lowells and Lawrences, on the one hand, and the Eliots and Lymans, on the other, had become established merchant princes. Financial success was allied with social eminence and also with a record of substantial contributions to culture, education, military service, philanthropy, and politics. A. Lawrence Lowell's great-great-grandfather, Judge John Lowell, for example, had served in the Massachusetts legislature and Congress during the late eighteenth century; his maternal grandfather, Abbott Lawrence, had been an influential New England Whig in Congress and minister to the Court of St. James's. Charles W. Eliot's father, Samuel A. Eliot, and his uncle, Theodore Lyman, had been mayors of Boston during the 1830s. The former also served in the state legislature and Congress. When eventually the time came that men of inherited wealth and social prominence could no longer control elective offices, the Lowell and Eliot families redoubled their endeavors in the realms of culture and philanthropy. The Lowells founded and directed the Lowell Institute, which brought many distinguished scholars to Boston. Lawrence Lowell's father, Augustus Lowell, was a prominent member of the corporation and executive committee of the Massachusetts Institute of Technology. Samuel A. Eliot, president of the Boston Academy of Music, was also a pioneer of prison reform.[3]

Harvard College was the most important recipient of the benefactions of the Lowells and probably of the Eliots. Lawrence Lowell especially had what amounted to a proprietary interest in Harvard. His was the sixth generation of Lowells to attend the college; three of his relatives had previously served on the Harvard Corporation; and among the family's generous benefactions to Harvard was $100,000 for the founding of Lawrence Scientific School. On their side, the Eliots presented a similar story. Grandfather Samuel Eliot anonymously gave $20,000 to establish a Greek professorship in the college, while father Samuel A. Eliot, treasurer and a fellow of the corporation, helped raise money for the Harvard Observatory. Clearly, family tradition strongly reinforced in both Lowell and Eliot a love for Harvard and a vision of its leadership in American higher education.[4]

Hard times came to the Eliots, however, when the family lost its fortune during the Panic of 1857. After a business association bankrupted not only his father but his mother as well, Eliot had to assume financial supervision of the family's affairs and provide housing for his parents and three unmarried sisters. His situation was eased somewhat with his promotion to assistant professor of mathematics and chemistry at Harvard. At a comparatively young age, Eliot learned to cope with adversity and to shoulder responsibility. (He also overcame the embarrassment caused by a birthmark on the right side of his face.) His early testing prepared him for later administrative and educational battles during his forty-year presidency of Harvard University. [5]

Family religious training also molded Eliot's personality. Not only was his uncle, Andrews Norton, a prominent Unitarian and the professor of sacred literature at Harvard, but his father, Samuel A. Eliot, had even written a book for the religious guidance of his children. Not surprisingly, Eliot declared: "I am a Unitarian by birthright and environment, and have never accepted any of the common creeds, dogmas, and catechisms, or believed in the God they describe." While he respected other creeds and applauded any cooperation and federation among different churches that would lead eventually toward "a universal church," he distrusted religious ritual and superstition. During a two-year sojourn in Europe (1863-65), when an alien culture confronted his Yankee and Unitarian way of life, he wrote that cathedrals were "bad things," because they inspired "superstitious awe in ignorant minds." Catholicism, he believed, limited freedom of thought, the touchstone of Unitarianism. "Institutional Christianity," Protestant as well as Roman Catholic, could "still be very un-Christlike," he observed. [6]

In contrast to Eliot's militant Unitarianism, Lawrence Lowell's religious beliefs were less precisely defined. Although second cousin William Lawrence was an Episcopal bishop, Lowell himself seemed to have been a nondenominational Protestant. He worshipped at several different churches and read the Bible regularly. For some time he was treasurer of King's Chapel in Boston, the Unitarian church attended by the Eliots. According to his biographer, Henry Aaron Yeomans, a contemporary professor of government and dean of Harvard College, Lowell "respected any sincere creed, but he did not admire a creed to which he could not subscribe nor could he admire another's subscribing to it." Lowell was no fanatic, but there were limits to his religious toleration. [7]

To the family influences and religious outlook of both men may be added the accidents of history and traits of temperament. Born in 1834, Eliot came to majority during the height of the New England renaissance. Yankee orators, reformers, and writers of this era were generally optimistic about mankind's capacity for progress. Such optimism was not a denial that problems existed; the very multitude of reformers and their causes—abolition, education, prison conditions, temperance, and women's rights—were proof of social evils. By believing that almost any problem could be solved by "democracy, utilitarianism, and the scientific method," Eliot united the natural optimism of his personality with the confidence of an age. [8]

Born in 1856, Lawrence Lowell grew up in a period of intense national strife and painful reunion—Civil War and Reconstruction. Three of his relatives, nephews of James Russell Lowell, were killed in action fighting for the Union. Yet, noted Eliot, Lowell "never seemed to take any interest in Robert Gould Shaw or any of his like" nor, as president of Harvard, in Memorial Hall, which honored Harvard men who had fought and died during the Civil War. Contrariwise, Lowell believed in reconciliation with the South and criticized northern philanthropists for what he considered their mistaken reconstruction policy in regard to the Negro.9

The mature Lowell witnessed the rapid industrial growth of the United States, with its attendant economic and social conflicts. Among other things, massive immigration from eastern and southern Europe began to change the complexion of the American character—to erode it, many were convinced. No longer was immigration preponderantly from northern Europe, the wellspring of white Anglo-Saxon Protestants; it had become increasingly Catholic and Jewish. The new America and the new Americans raised questions of national purpose and destiny. Lowell was uneasy with the changes that he saw and feared the future they portended. Finally, the years of his presidency of Harvard, like those of his youth, paralleled times of national crisis: World War I and its aftermath. History itself had challenged the cultural values that he shared with other old-stock Americans. The preservation and endurance of these values, Lowell believed, depended on the ability of the United States to retain its original and essential homogeneity.

Charles W. Eliot succinctly portrayed his successor as aloof, strong willed, and self-righteous. Eliot himself was detached, decisive, and outspoken. Neither man as president courted the affection of students. But Eliot's strength was tempered by a capacity to listen. His toleration of professorial digressions was little short of remarkable: "The Faculty," he wrote, "is a ruminating animal, chewing a cud a long time, slowly bringing it into a digestible condition; then comes the process of assimilation which is gradual and invisible, so that by-standers do not perceive the growth and expansion of the animal." In contrast, when Lowell once decided on a course of action, he rarely brooked further faculty discussion or hesitation. He could not understand why that which he himself saw so clearly was not self-evident to everyone else.10

Educational Philosophy

In his love for Harvard, Lowell had no peer; but his conception of the college was that of a homogeneous society of elites. Eliot also wanted Harvard to train elites, but under his administration its student composition began to diversify significantly, in comparison with its two closest rivals, Yale and Princeton. In fact, by the nineteenth century Harvard was largely liberated from the inhibiting spirit of Puritanism, as were Eliot and, to a lesser extent, Lowell. As president, Eliot consistently advocated toleration of all creeds. Lowell, too, felt "that after childhood the motives for attending any religious service had better be religious, not disciplinary." He also defended the policy of professors' presenting "the facts of evolution as they do any other facts in science," since conflicts between the theory of evolution and the account of creation in Genesis would not undermine essential religious beliefs.[11]

After Harvard abolished compulsory chapel in 1886—with faculty approval—a board of five preachers from different Protestant denominations shared the services in the college chapel with the professor of Christian morals. (Until 1903-04, the university rented seats in neighboring churches for both Catholics and Protestants, a practice that had originated during the days of active Unitarianism on campus.) In keeping with this spirit, Harvard refused gifts with denominational strings attached, as for example, a bell tower offered with the condition of required religious instruction. Eliot did welcome a proposed endowment of a college chapel by George Wigglesworth, because it would establish the principle of educating ministers and "conducting religious services in a manner free from denominational control or bias—in the only manner, in short, in which a modern university can either teach theology or maintain religious services."[12]

Harvard's evolution toward nonsectarianism was noted with disapproval elsewhere. After listening to its representatives at a meeting of the New England colleges, Dean Frederick S. Jones of Yale concluded that Harvard had "practically abandoned all thought of exerting either moral influence or restraint among her students." Yet Yale's insistence on chapel aroused considerable resentment among its own undergraduates. Protestants, particularly Episcopalians, as well as Catholics objected to the required ten-minute service in the campus Battell Chapel before or after going to their own church in New Haven. Finally, and somewhat reluctantly, Yale abolished compulsory daily and Sunday chapel, beginning with the 1926-27 academic year. (The Yale Sheffield Scientific School had never required attendance at either morning prayers or Sunday services.) Princeton had made morning weekday chapel voluntary in 1915 and silenced, at least partially, undergraduate grumblings with the dedication in 1927 of an impressive Gothic-style university chapel. But by 1935, Princeton grudgingly waived all chapel attendance for juniors and seniors, though requiring freshmen and sophomores for almost another thirty years to attend a certain number of services.[13]

Harvard's comparative openness encouraged non-Protestants to seek admission. By the early twentieth century, Catholics and Jews had their own religious organizations: the St. Paul's Catholic Club (1893) grew to 250 members by 1911-12, only 50 less than the Episcopalian St. Paul's Society, while the smaller Menorah Society (1906) sponsored a prize established by Jacob H. Schiff for the best undergraduate essay on "the work and achievements of the

Jewish people." To be sure, Harvard continued to preserve a broadly Protestant religious orientation. It was during Lowell's administration, for example, that a ruling was established barring non-Christian private services in Memorial Church, which had been erected in memory of Harvard men who had died in World War I. This policy remained unchanged until 1958.14

In spite of such exceptions and the virtually exclusive Protestant dominance on the governing boards, Harvard was freer than its rivals to attract a more cosmopolitan faculty, to experiment in admissions policy, and to reform the curriculum. Both Eliot and Lowell contributed to Harvard's academic reputation, but they viewed the nature and purposes of higher education from different perspectives. For Eliot, the graduate and professional schools were the center of the university. In building them up, some critics charged, Eliot had neglected the college. For Lowell, the college was the heart of the institution. He therefore dedicated himself to revamping the undergraduate curriculum and to bringing students together in residential units.

Eliot's Harvard was preeminently an academic institution, little concerned with social relations. Because he considered undergraduates as potential graduate students, he introduced in the college a broad elective system. Its major purpose was to educate individuals according to their particular areas of interest. Students were admitted on an equal basis to lecture halls, to laboratories, and to such large associations as the Harvard Union. Eliot did not occupy himself with problems of residential dispersion among freshmen or the existence of living quarters for the wealthy, known as the Gold Coast. It was enough, he wrote, that the university recognized "among its officers and students neither class, caste, race, sect nor political party."15

On the other hand, Lowell advocated a structured and largely prescribed undergraduate curriculum as a means to reinvigorate intellectually "the descendents of old, well-to-do American families." As a professor at Harvard, he served on various committees to improve academic standards and social welfare. He had been a leading member of the committee of 1902-03 that inquired into ways to improve the quality of work done for the Bachelor of Arts degree. (Preferring to teach only undergraduates, he actually declined to offer an advanced course in government at Harvard.) Answers to questionnaires sent to the faculty and students showed the committee that little work was done on the average and that the amount varied considerably from course to course. The committee made several important recommendations: that all courses require approximately equivalent amounts of preparation, that each subject be related to the purpose of a liberal education, and that able students be urged to undertake honors work. Lowell was also a leading member of the committee on the award of degrees with distinction, whose report was adopted in 1904. And four years later, he chaired a "Committee appointed to Consider how Tests for Rank in College may be made a more Generally Recognized Measure of Intellectual Power." Submitted to the faculty just two weeks after Eliot resigned the presidency, the committee's report modified the elective system by requiring both "concentration and distribution" in undergraduate studies. An honors college, which Lowell first proposed in 1907, would be the capstone of the curriculum. [16]

As long as Eliot was president, he had to bide his time, all the while extending his influence. Disturbed by the social polarizations among students, Lowell drafted the report of a committee to advise the corporation on methods of assigning college rooms. He feared "that with the loss of that democratic feeling which ought to lie at the basis of university life," Harvard would lose its "moral hold upon a large part of the students" unless it provided residential housing. The rich congregated on Mount Auburn Street's Gold Coast, the poor in off-campus private rooms, and the Jews in Walter Hastings Hall, nicknamed "Little Jerusalem." [17]

As soon as Lowell became president, he set out to achieve most of his major academic and social ideals. His inaugural address epitomized his educational philosophy by focusing entirely on the college. He insisted that Harvard College should "produce an intellectual and social cohesion, at least among large groups of students, and points of contact among them all." Virtually every measure that he instituted during his presidency was aimed at creating an educational totality for the young men coming to Harvard. Accordingly, he wrote, "no man ought to be given a degree, certifying a liberal education, who has not in college read some good literature, and learned something of history, of the conceptions of modern science and of methods of abstract thought." [18]

Lowell's campaign to restore "liberal culture" at Harvard was supported by a number of professors—notably, by Le Baron Russell Briggs, professor of English and dean of the Faculty of Arts and Sciences. Lowell and Briggs had become disenchanted, wrote historian Laurence R. Veysey, with "Eliot's tireless insistence upon rational individualism, unmitigated diversity, and curricular do-as-you-please." "Intellectual cohesion" would be fostered by requiring undergraduates to take two-fifths of their courses in one field, as well as studying several broad disciplines. The natural consequence of systematic studies was the creation of general examinations to test scope and depth of knowledge. First begun for the class of 1917 in the Division of History and Political Science, general examinations were adopted by most departments outside of mathematics and natural sciences for the class of 1922. Then, influenced by Woodrow Wilson's preceptorial system at Princeton, Lowell established Harvard's tutorial system to unify a student's course work as well as to prepare him for the general examination. Finally, a three-week reading period was provided at the end of each semester to encourage self-education and to relieve the burden on tutors and instructors. Lowell's innovations and reforms, which have continued with some changes until the present day, were criticized by his predecessor. Jerome D. Greene, a friend of

Eliot, maintained that even though these reforms actually tried to make the best use of the elective principle, "President Lowell tended to identify the needs of the minority of undergraduates who came from socially privileged families and schools with the needs of Harvard College as a whole." They required more intellectual prodding than bright public high school graduates, who were serious and mature enough to select courses on the basis of concentration and distribution. [19]

Promotion of "social cohesion" was equally important to Lowell. As early as 1887, he envisioned a residential college system for Harvard. The first step was the opening of freshman halls in 1914. By intermingling most freshmen in these halls, Lowell hoped to prevent the formation of cliques based on schools and geographical distribution. But Eliot strongly opposed the segregation of classes by dormitories on the grounds that students of similar interests, though of different ages, should be allowed to live together. Compulsory residency in the freshman halls, he felt, was "much the worst happening at Harvard since 1909." [20]

In contrast to Eliot's critical attitude toward his successor's educational goals was Woodrow Wilson's warm praise. On the occasion of his visit to Harvard to deliver the Phi Beta Kappa oration in 1909, Princeton's president found Harvard's entire atmosphere changed: President Lowell was "of an absolutely different type from Mr. Eliot, cordial, natural, friendly, open to all ideas, and very democratic indeed." He had "brought Harvard back already into connection with the rest of the academic world." The affinity between Wilson and Lowell dated from their days as young professors. They were strong Anglophiles and enjoyed each other's company socially. Both believed that college should educate undergraduates in "liberal culture." Like Lowell, Wilson opposed Eliot's elective system and indifference toward the quality of undergraduate social life. Because Lowell wanted to reduce the prestige of the Gold Coast, make residence "compulsory" in the freshman halls, and unite the three upper classes in residential units, Wilson considered him "very democratic indeed." And Lowell thoroughly sympathized with the aims of Wilson's Quadrangle Plan, which had "taken some long strides" toward improving collegiate organization. [21]

In December 1914, Lowell wrote that "it would be far better to have the whole college housed in halls of this kind, with the classes intermingled," but he was sensitive to the "grave difficulty, which Wilson encountered at Princeton." In proposing to extend a hall system to the three upper classes, Lowell was careful not to appear too far in advance of alumni and undergraduate opinion. For some years, many people had been thinking about the value of smaller residential units. In 1926, for example, the Harvard Student Council recommended that the student body be divided into such units; and two years later, its report on the clubs suggested that some of their bad effects could be remedied by a house system. Although Edward S. Harkness, generous benefactor of both the Harvard houses and Yale colleges, told historian Henry W. Bragdon that "he had not been inspired by Wilson's efforts at Princeton," the Quad Plan controversy ultimately "helped to create a favorable climate of opinion making it easier for President Lowell to introduce the House Plan in 1929." Dunster and Lowell were opened in 1930-31; five more houses followed. 22

Lowell's hopes of overcoming segregation along school and geographical lines were, for the most part, realized by the freshman halls and the House Plan. But his solution to the problem of racial and ethnic segregation, recognized in 1902, was to exclude Negroes from the freshman halls and to impose a quota on the admission of Jewish students to the college and to the houses. Those who allegedly did not or could not assimilate threatened the success of his policy of social cohesion, which depended on a fairly homogeneous student body. Professor Yeomans wrote of Lowell that "the poor, hard-working student, native-born or immigrant, Gentile or Jew, white or black, never had a warmer friend, although many excellent persons criticized at times his way of showing friendship." But the weight of evidence indicates that Lowell interpreted the meaning of friendship differently than did Harvard's immigrant, Jewish, and black students. 23

Social Philosophy: Free or Restricted Immigration?

A close connection existed between the educational and social philosophies of Eliot and Lowell. Their opinions on a wide range of subjects—among others, immigration restriction and minority groups—were frequently expressed in their voluminous presidential correspondence. Today, Eliot's image is that of an educator generally more liberal than his times. He frequently rejected antidemocratic and racist attitudes in his correspondence and maintained that considerable ethnic diversity was compatible with democratic government and the advancement of civilization. Lowell, however, was more restrained; at times the very lack of comment in his letters created a certain ambiguity about his personal feelings. But his correspondence revealed that he disagreed strongly with Eliot's philosophy in regard to the questions of immigration restriction and student diversity within Harvard University.

Free immigration, which had pumped new blood into the nation's population for almost three centuries, came under attack in the late nineteenth century. Foremost among the critics of America's open door were members of the Immigration Restriction League, founded in Boston in the spring of 1894. The key promoters were Harvard-educated Bostonians: Prescott F. Hall '89, Robert De Courcy Ward '89, Joseph Lee '83, Charles Warren '89, and Richards M. Bradley '82. They soon attracted to the league many prominent college presidents and professors: William De Witt Hyde of Bowdoin, David

Starr Jordan of Stanford University, and John R. Commons and Edward A. Ross of the University of Wisconsin. The league had a small core of dedicated votaries in the Harvard family. In addition to Ward, a professor of climatology (1900-31), and Lee, a lecturer on education and an overseer, there were about a dozen other Harvardians who supported the league in one way or another. Four overseers and two fellows contributed to its success: John Fiske, Henry Cabot Lodge, Charles Warren, Owen Wister, Henry Lee Higginson, and John Farwell Moors. In addition the league claimed the support of such well-known professors of political economy as Thomas Nixon Carver and William Z. Ripley and that of Nathaniel Southgate Shaler, dean of the Lawrence Scientific School (1891-1906). Lawrence Lowell assumed the national vice-presidency of the league three years after becoming president of Harvard University. Significantly, eight of these members of the Harvard establishment were active and influential during the 1920s, when the university debated the issue of restrictive admissions to the college. 24

Lowell opposed the continued large-scale immigration of "alien races," firmly convinced that American political and social institutions could not survive in a heterogeneous society. In 1918, he declined to join Sidney L. Gulick's League for Constructive Immigration: "Having started life prejudiced concerning the restriction against Chinese immigration, I long ago came to the conclusion that no democracy could be successful unless it was tolerably homogeneous." Lowell was absolutely certain that some Europeans could not be easily assimilated into American life; the same was true, of course, of the Chinese and the Negro. His study of government reinforced this attitude. In some cases, such as Switzerland, a degree of racial diversity was compatible with democracy, he noted. Although that tiny country had three "races" and two religious creeds, its population shared certain common aims and ideals. But countries like Austria-Hungary and Ireland, which lacked the homogeneity to create an accepted and effective communal psychology, faced increasing ethnic and nationality tensions. The United States had no choice but to ponder the problems posed by ethnic diversity: Without some national homogeneity and political consensus a country might break apart in civil war. If the masses of immigrants, wrote Lowell, could be completely assimilated within a few generations and become "an indistinguishable part of the population, well and good;" otherwise they endangered democratic institutions. Refusing to acknowledge positive contributions of the new immigrants to the melting pot, Lowell focused on their differences in customs, language, and values—all of which constituted a threat to native-born Americans until neutralized by the assimilative process. 25

Two letters from Lowell to Rhode Island Senator Le Baron B. Colt, chairman of the Senate Committee on Immigration, clearly revealed the Harvard president's bias. The first letter was written on March 31, 1922, at the suggestion of Robert De Courcy Ward, who had published during the previous summer an article in support of a permanent percentage limitation on immigration. Lowell, too, urged that the Senate concur in a House resolution extending the Three Per Cent Immigration Law for at least a year. "In old times," Lowell wrote, "[European immigrants] were energetic and adventurous people who sought to improve themselves." But in recent years they had more often been people who, unsuccessful in their native country, were brought over by shipping companies to provide cheap labor for big corporations. Assuming that the newer immigrants from eastern and southern Europe were less worthy of admission than earlier ones from the British Isles and northern Europe, he vested in the first comers the right to shut the door. Accordingly, he wrote to Senator Colt two years later: "The essential thing about any nation is its population, and it seems to me that every nation is entitled to decide what additions from outside to its population it will receive." In fact, it owed such selection to posterity. At the instigation of Richards M. Bradley, Lowell endorsed the Reed Bill as "very sensible," because it took "into account the older stocks in distributing the number of immigrants" and set a 300,000 total limit. The Johnson-Reed Act, which became law in 1924, was based on quotas of 2 percent of each foreign-born nationality resident in the United States as of 1890.[26]

Whereas Lowell was predisposed to accept the assumptions on race then prevalent among many of his fellow New England Brahmins, Eliot's optimism withstood almost all the alarms of the Immigration Restriction League. Although he expressed concern over the growing political power of alien groups in Boston and New York City, such unease never became a gnawing resentment. Contrariwise, he made dozens of generous statements, some published and widely circulated on behalf of the National Liberal Immigration League, affirming a vibrant faith in the capacity of the United States to assimilate immigrants without obliterating their individuality.[27]

Even more important, Eliot's outlook broadened as the opposition to unrestricted immigration increased. One of the principles of the platform that he drafted for the mugwump, or independent, Republicans in 1884 endorsed immigration "without distinction of race, nationality or religion." Another early view was revealed in his reply, in November 1892, to an inquiry from the *Home Journal*. He argued that all immigrants should be admitted except "criminals, paupers, and diseased persons," because the United States was not overpopulated and could use "every healthy and honest laborer" and his family. Immigration restriction by the present inhabitants, moreover, was "a peculiarly ungenerous and ungrateful proposal," since they themselves were descended from a similar class of mechanics and farmers. Eliot slyly pointed out that even those who claimed English ancestry were actually descended from "a mixed people made up of Danes, Norwegians, Dutch, Germans, Normans, and Saxons—a veritable ethnological conglomerate very much like that which is now forming on a larger scale in the United States." At this time, he drew the line on the assimilation of colored races. Negroes, Chinese, and Japanese presented the "real difficulty," while all the Europeans seemed "capable of complete assimilation under the influence of free schools, free churches, equal laws, and democratic social mobility." But it should be noted that, as was characteristic of his day, Eliot often applied the term *race* uncritically to Italians, Jews, and other European ethnic groups.28

By 1906, however, Eliot could not "admit the doctrine that the United States should be reserved for the white race"; the country could use all able-bodied laborers, Orientals as well as Europeans. Provisions should be made, he said, for different races to live separately within the United States, "beside each other in the same territory, at peace and under just industrial conditions, but without admixture." Eliot then added: "That is what we must do for the Africans, and what we ought to do for the Indians; and . . . we might do it also for a few Chinese, Japanese, and Filipinos." The same year, Eliot forcefully expressed to Richards M. Bradley his disagreement with the policies of the Immigration Restriction League, which "struck" him "as vicious,—economically, politically, and sentimentally." Although he "should feel safer" in agreeing with such men as Bradley, John Farwell Moors, and Joseph Lee, it was "a real case of different faiths and expectations."29

Having written in 1900 that neither the native American stock nor the foreign-born should make special efforts to prevent intermingling, Eliot subsequently came to believe that amalgamation or miscegenation was "not only extraordinarily slow, but of doubtful issue as to the strength and viability of the offspring." The preservation of ethnic differences among the population might even be a blessing. What he wrote during the 1920s in regard to the Italians could apply to all immigrant groups: It was "not desirable that they more than the Irish or the Jews should lose their racial characteristics here." The Italians gave "the unfortunate descendants of the Puritans, who would not have any music to speak of in their own churches," the gift of "the love of music."30

Just as Eliot modified his earlier beliefs about the assimilation of European immigrants, so he also became more optimistic about the presence of the supposedly nonassimilable races in the United States. Because very little amalgamation had or would occur—there was no American melting pot—the country could benefit from an almost infinite diversity "of many races, many religions, and many varieties of human nature, forming one liberty-loving, stable democracy." When Madison Grant, author of *The Passing of the Great Race in America* (1916), misconstrued the meaning of his denial of the melting pot thesis and welcomed him to the ranks of the restrictionists, Eliot promptly enlightened him.31

Student Diversity Within Harvard University

The beliefs of Eliot and Lowell on immigration restriction almost paralleled their attitudes toward student diversity, because Harvard University,

like the country, confronted problems of cultural assimilation. Eliot maintained that just as the country could profit from unassimilated peoples and
races living side by side in harmony, so Harvard could benefit by educating
students of diverse backgrounds, talents, and interests. During his administration, Harvard not only opened its doors to students from all races and
many ethnic groups, but it also became a truly cosmopolitan university by
encouraging professorial exchanges with European universities and American colleges and by educating the larger community through its extension
courses and summer school. On the contrary, just as Lawrence Lowell
thought that American democracy required a largely homogeneous population in order to survive, so he also believed that Harvard could best fulfill its
academic mission by educating an assimilated student body. Unquestionably, he lent his prestige as president of Harvard to furthering the work of the
Immigration Restriction League. In return, he received both implicit and explicit support from certain league members for his proposal to place Harvard
College admissions on an equally selective basis. As Richards M. Bradley
suggested, during the 1920s Lowell tried to make the student body "reasonably representative of the country's racial and social makeup, but at the same
time distinctively representative of the best of what has made Harvard distinctive." As a scholar seeking to enhance Harvard's intellectual prestige,
Lowell favored admitting foreign students and professors as nonquota immigrants. But since foreign students composed a mere 1 or 2 percent of the undergraduate body during the 1920s, they hardly threatened the college. 32

Neither president, however, saw Harvard as a microcosm of the United
States; it was the academe for the nation's elites, not a cross section of its population. The degree to which Harvard's student body had diversified during
the late nineteenth and early twentieth centuries was indicated by the report
of the Immigration Commission entitled *Children of Immigrants in Schools:
Higher Educational Institutions* and based on data collected in the autumn of
1908 (see Table 2.1). Of the 2,196 Harvard academic students reporting,
1,783 were native-born of native fathers; all were white except for five Negroes. The total number of native-born of foreign fathers was 281, of which
106, or 37.7 percent, were either Jewish or Irish. Of the 132 foreign-born students, Jews numbered 39, or 29.5 percent. Counting both native-born of foreign fathers and foreign-born, Jews numbered 95 students, whereas the other
ethnic groups trailed far behind: Irish, 54; Germans, 53; English, 49; and
Canadians (other than French), 49. By the third generation, Germans, Irish,
and Jews may well have classified themselves as native-born of native
fathers, while most English and English-speaking Canadians had probably
amalgamated with native white Anglo-Saxon Protestant stock. 33

The presence of Irish Catholics, Jews, Negroes, Chinese and Japanese, and
other foreign students in the Yard was a sign of Yankee willingness to share
Harvard's educational advantages with outsiders. Eliot helped to open the

Table 2.1

NATIVITY OF ACADEMIC STUDENTS AT HARVARD UNIVERSITY, 1908-09

Nativity and race of student	Under 18 years of age	18 to 20 years of age	21 to 24 years of age	25 years of age or over	Total
Native-born of native father:					
White	123	1,062	547	46	1,778
Negro		1	3	1	5
Total	123	1,063	550	47	1,783
Native-born of foreign father, by race of father:					
Canadian, French		4	2	2	8
Canadian, Other	1	19	13	1	34
Cuban		1			1
Danish		1	1		2
English	4	19	16	1	40
French		5	5		10
German	6	30	8	1	45
Greek		1	1		2
Hawaiian	1	1			2
Hebrew, German	3	5	2		10
Hebrew, Polish		1			1
Hebrew, Roumanian		1			1
Hebrew, Russian	9	25	4		38
Hebrew, Other	1	4	1		6
Irish	2	31	15	2	50
Italian		1	2		3
Japanese		1			1
Magyar		1			1
Norwegian		1	1		2
Ruthenian			1		1
Scotch	1	9	2	2	14
Spanish-American			2		2
Swedish		4	1		5
Welsh			2		2
Total	28	161[a]	80[a]	12[a]	281
Total native-born	151	1,224	630	59	2,064
Foreign-born:					
Bulgarian				1	1
Canadian (other than French)		5	6	4	15
Chinese		1	7	11	19
Cuban			1	1	2
Danish		1			1
English		4	4	1	9
Filipino			1		1
French		1			1
German		2	4	2	8
Greek			1		1
Hawaiian			2		2
Hebrew, German			1		1
Hebrew, Polish	1	2			3
Hebrew, Roumanian		1			1
Hebrew, Russian	3	18	9	3	33
Hebrew, Other		1			1

Table 2.1 (Continued)

Nativity and race of student	Under 18 years of age	18 to 20 years of age	21 to 24 years of age	25 years of age or over	Total
Hindu		1	1		2
Irish			1	3	4
Italian (not specified)			2	3	5
Japanese		1	3		4
Negro			1		1
Porto Rican		1	2		3
Portuguese			1		1
Russian		1			1
Scotch		2	3		5
Spanish				1	1
Spanish-American			1		1
Swedish			2	1	3
Welsh	2				2
Total foreign-born	6	42	53	31	132
Grand total	157	1,266	683	90	2,196

Source: U.S. Congress, Senate, Reports of the Immigration Commission, *Children of Immigrants in Schools,* 61st Cong., 3d sess., 1910-1911, S. Doc. 749, vol. 5, *Students in Higher Educational Institutions,* Table 1, "Number of students within each specified age group, by institution and by general nativity and race of student," Academic, Male, Harvard University, Cambridge, Mass., p. 725.

aThese totals, here published exactly from the original source, are incorrect. They should read, in order, 165, 79, and 9.

gates by emphasizing education for qualified individuals. Although believing that Harvard should continue to educate some outsiders, Lowell felt that the trends begun under Eliot could not go unchecked without baneful consequences for the college.

Irish Catholics

Beginning in the 1870s, Irish Catholics were the first of the minority groups to enter Harvard University in substantial numbers. But relations between Catholics and Protestants remained highly sensitive, if not hostile. Some Catholics were quick to take offense at Protestants' slights, unintentional or otherwise, while certain Protestants exacerbated the problem by allegations of papal plots. During the 1880s, for example, Harvard students expressed in speeches and themes a strong distaste for Irish peasants and a distrust of Irish politicians. [34]

Understandably, the Irish in Cambridge were suspicious of Yankee professions of friendship, especially when tinged with noblesse oblige. In 1903, an address by a Harvard senior in Boston's Park Street Church on the Harvard Christian Association's work in East Cambridge, as reported in the *Boston Herald,* angered the clergy of the Sacred Heart Church. They distributed at all masses ten thousand free copies of a pamphlet entitled *Is East Cambridge a 'Whitechapel' Town?* The pamphlet denounced the student's address, "Student Religious Work," because it described East Cambridge as "the most neglected district within a radius of ten miles of Boston." "Thank God," wrote Father John O'Brien, "our boys and girls, our men and women, are decent, Christian people, who like their Saviour, know how to bear calumny and if need be, to turn the other cheek." The Catholic clergy saw Harvard students, "outside of college bounds, whether on a lark in the city or playing reformer," as "a nuisance and a menace to peace and order." Town and gown, Irish Catholic and Harvard Yankee, were poles apart. 35

Yet overt anti-Irish prejudice in Massachusetts had begun to bow to political expediency, when Henry Cabot Lodge launched his long career in the United States Senate in 1893. Politically, however, Charles W. Eliot had his differences with Irish politicians, and he regretted loss of political power by the Yankees. In a letter to Mayor James M. Curley, he recalled that his father, as mayor of Boston (1837-39), had read the riot act to stop a throng of Americans from attacking the city's Irish inhabitants. Like him, Eliot condemned violence by Americans against minority groups and use of similar tactics by Irish Americans. Eliot complained to James Bryce in 1922 that the Irish in America defended violence by labor unions and "promoted corruption and inefficiency in our municipal governments, including New York, Boston, Cambridge, and most of the larger Eastern cities." Because of widespread corruption among local Democrats, in 1923 Eliot supported Godfrey L. Cabot, an Independent Home Rule candidate for mayor of Cambridge, while voting the Democratic ticket in national elections. 36

In his general capacity as educator, Eliot occasionally disagreed with the Catholic hierarchy over parochial schools. On the one hand, he criticized separate schools for Catholic children, because he felt that youths of different backgrounds should intermingle. On the other, he believed that the Catholic hierarchy ought to maintain parochial schools in a democratic country, because they would have to compete with public schools for the financial support of Catholic families. In Massachusetts, he observed, the majority of Catholic families preferred "the free schools for their children." But Eliot favored popular election of the Boston School Committee, since it was then appointed by the mayor of Boston, who was most likely to be a Roman Catholic and in all probability a man under the hierarchy's control. At the same time, he was willing to ally with some Catholic leaders in a common cause. According to Hugh Hawkins in *Between Harvard and America: The Educational Leadership of Charles W. Eliot*, the Harvard president had argued in the 1870s that all property used for educational and religious institutions should be tax-exempt. He was motivated both by the need to protect Harvard from taxation and by his sincere belief in religious toleration. 37

The academic qualifications of Jesuit college graduates constituted the one major educational controversy between Eliot and Roman Catholics and the only issue that directly involved him in his capacity as president of Harvard University. Although some Catholics attended Harvard College, others preferred to enter the university's professional schools after graduating from Catholic colleges, notably those under Jesuit control. After all, Harvard was still a Protestant, not a nondenominational, college. Jesuit colleges provided moral instruction for Catholic undergraduates, while Harvard University offered opportunities for professional training. A conflict developed, however, between Harvard and several Jesuit colleges following the publication of Eliot's June 20, 1893, letter in the Boston *Pilot*, the diocesan paper. Highly incensed by the Harvard president's argument that course work in Catholic colleges was not the academic equivalent of that in other undergraduate institutions, the president of Georgetown College, the Reverend J. Havens Richards, S.J., urged public retraction. On further consideration, Eliot agreed that Georgetown, Boston College, and Holy Cross might be included in the Harvard Law School list (published from 1893 to 1904), which exempted graduates of its colleges from entrance examinations. 38

But the issue was not settled; five years later Fordham argued for similar privilege. As a result, the academic merits of all Catholic colleges were reexamined. When a faculty committee on admission to Harvard College held that Boston College graduates were not qualified for even junior class status at Harvard, the law faculty removed from its list all Catholic colleges except Georgetown. This decision stirred up a nasty public controversy. The more understanding among both Catholic clergy and laymen seemed to appreciate that religious prejudice, as such, had no part in the law faculty's action. 39

At the very time that this controversy was occurring, the Reverend Timothy Brosnahan, S.J., of Woodstock College in Maryland took strong issue with Eliot's article, "Recent Changes in Secondary Education," appearing in the October 1899 *Atlantic Monthly*. The article had focused on arguments for extending the elective system to secondary schools. But Eliot also referred briefly, by way of contrast, to the prescribed curriculum of Jesuit and Moslem schools, which had "remained almost unchanged for four hundred years, disregarding some trifling concessions made to natural science." In a reply in the *Sacred Heart Review* entitled "President Eliot and Jesuit Colleges: A Defence," Father Brosnahan used Georgetown University to show that only 53 percent of the course time was now devoted to Latin and Greek rather than 100 percent, as in the seventeenth-century Catholic university. The remaining 47 percent was "conceded" to English, mathematics, modern languages, and natural science. In counterattack, Father Brosnahan pointed out that under the elective system a student could graduate from Harvard College without taking any natural science. Although the Reverend John O'Brien, editor of the *Sacred Heart Review*, invited Eliot to publish in detail his objections to Jesuit instruction, the Harvard president declined. "It was not for a

Protestant," he said, "to make a public statement concerning the inferiority of the Jesuit colleges in both programme and method."[40]

Many informed Catholics were, indeed, well aware of the academic inferiority of Jesuit colleges, and few, if anyone, believed that Eliot had "determined to crush out Catholic education." Eliot was later pleased to learn that representatives of the Jesuit colleges had conferred about broadening their programs and introducing laboratory work. Such changes would help to deal with the difficulties that their graduates were having in the medical and the law schools. Over the years, hundreds of Catholics (they numbered about three hundred in 1894) were welcomed as students at Harvard and treated eminently fairly.[41]

Even though Eliot's differences with Catholicism and Irish Catholics were frequently sharp—blending a militant Unitarian's hostility to religious hierarchy, a Brahmin's dislike of corrupt politicians, and a democrat's belief in religious and cultural pluralism—he did not oppose election of Catholics to the governing boards of the university. His relations with Overseer Charles J. Bonaparte were cordial. And when the first Irish Catholic was elected a fellow of the corporation in 1920 (James Byrne), Eliot expressed his approval to Jerome Greene: "The advent of a *rational* Catholic to the Corporation may have various good consequences [because] it thoroughly illustrates the genuine liberality of the characteristic Harvard spirit" [italics added].[42]

By the 1920s, Lawrence Lowell, too, commented favorably on the progress of Irish Catholics in the United States. He believed that they, unlike newer immigrant groups, were capable of almost complete cultural assimilation. But in the *Forum* of 1887—before the effect of eastern and southern European immigration had generally begun to be felt—Lowell had written of the increasing difficulty in naturalizing Irish and other immigrant groups. These foreigners, he insisted, had to become "so merged in the American people that they cannot be distinguished as a class, by opinion or sentiment on any subject, from the mass of the population of which they form a part." At this time, the Irish were the most recalcitrant of all immigrant groups in preserving their distinctive characteristics. Accounting for their social defiance were racial feeling, clannishness, Roman Catholicism, and poverty. Politics especially drew the Irish together, with Lowell noting their new "boldness." Agitated by discussions of the Home Rule Bill in the British Parliament, the Irish had even tried to prevent Boston's Faneuil Hall from being used to celebrate Queen Victoria's Jubilee. Anti-Irish, or "Know-nothing feeling," which came in response, only aggravated the problem. "What we need," wrote Lowell, "is not to dominate the Irish but to absorb them." Moreover, he claimed that "we want them to become rich, and send their sons to our colleges, to share our prosperity and our sentiments."[43]

Some thirty years later, Irish Catholics were meeting Lowell's criteria for true Americans. In a revealing letter to Overseer John Pierpont Morgan '89,

Lowell defended James Byrne's election to the seven-member corporation. Morgan had preferred to restrict membership on that body to "Protestant Christians." He pointedly assured Morgan that "of a Jew there is no suggestion at the present time." The corporation's choice of Byrne, a New York lawyer, was an acknowledgment of the importance of maintaining good relations with Catholics, who composed a large percentage of the country's population and almost half that of Massachusetts. Lowell recalled that during his youth there was opposition to electing anyone except a Unitarian to the corporation, but he was glad that this principle was no longer followed. Then he asked: "Would it not be a grave misfortune for our country if our institutions of higher learning were divided in such a way that part were only attended by Protestants and the rest only by Roman Catholics?" Harvard could not "take the ground that a Roman Catholic [was], in the nature of things, unfit to be a member of the Corporation," without aiding the efforts of certain of their hierarchy to keep Catholics from attending the university. In defending Byrne and Harvard's obligation toward a populous and influential minority, Lowell linked the university's greatness to its welcoming of "all classes of people."[44]

Jews

Although biographer Henry Yeomans maintained that "thirty-five years after Lowell's article appeared in the *Forum* he might have been willing to substitute 'Jew' for 'Irish,' 'Palestine' for 'Ireland,' and let the writing stand," this parallel could not be sustained. Irish Catholics had always a greater potentiality than Jews for the assimilation that Lowell demanded: They were Christians and ethnically and culturally similar to other Britons, the stock from which Yankees descended. Consequently, toward Jews his welcome was considerably more restrained.[45]

Prior to the 1890s and early 1900s most Jewish students at Harvard were of German background and practiced Reform Judaism. Their parents and grandparents usually had emigrated to the United States during the middle decades of the nineteenth century. Now their ranks were swelled by Jews from eastern Europe, particularly by those from Russia, at a time when many Americans were beginning to question the benefit of the New Immigration. If we count both sons of immigrants and the foreign-born (refer back to Table 2.1), Russian Jews numbered 71 of the 95 Jewish academic students in 1908. Unlike the German Jews, the Russian Jews observed the very traditional Orthodox faith.[46]

Conflicts developed between German Jewish students and these newcomers. Early in November 1901, Rabbi Charles Fleischer of Temple Adath Israel of Boston talked with President Eliot about the corporation's providing religious instruction for Jewish students. Eliot replied that if Jewish students organized and asked "of the Corporation a convenient room for the conduct of religious services," he had "no doubt" that it would be provided. However, Professor Francis Greenwood Peabody, Eliot's brother-in-law, and Professor George Herbert Palmer "thought that the Synagogue Jews could not be brought to associate in a religious service with the Temple Jews." Like most Gentiles, Eliot was not particularly sensitive to the deep cultural and religious differences separating the Reform and Orthodox Jews. But he followed the advice of Professors Peabody and Palmer to let the Jewish students themselves choose their own religious organization.[47]

German Jewish students had mixed quite well in their social relationships— John Weiss, A.B. '37, a Jewish barber's son from Worcester, was a member of the Institute of 1770, a Phi Beta Kappa, and the secretary and poet of the Hasty Pudding. Other German Jewish students received similar social recognition, at least until the last quarter of the nineteenth century, when the process of excluding Jews from clubs and similar organizations had begun. Russian Jews, who were far more culturally exclusive and generally poorer than the German Jews, rarely, if ever, received a cordial welcome.[48]

When Eliot noted in 1901 that Jews were "better off at Harvard than at any other American college" and "therefore, likely to resort to it," he also recognized that a concentration of Jewish students in particular halls, as then was forming in Hastings, might pose a problem. Probably parental attitudes were largely responsible for social anti-Semitism on campus, with students reflecting the value judgments of their elders. Occasionally, however, a few students acted independently of parental wishes, as the following incident illustrated. In the autumn of 1915, President Lowell received complaints from an aunt and father because the latter's son was "assigned a Jew as a chum." Since the assignment could not be "a congenial one," the boy would lose his friends. Lowell reported to the father that "great care" was taken in the selection of roommates. The "Jewish" roommate was an alumni son and Roman Catholic in religion, while his father was considered "an agreeable person socially." The protesting parent was also informed that his son was given the choice of another "chum," but stated his satisfaction with the existing arrangement. Apparently, the son felt that he would have less time to study if he changed roommates. This seems to be the only extant complaint of its kind.[49]

But President Lowell was not tolerant of religious differences among Harvard students when they conflicted with the university calendar. He took a hard line against requests from Rabbi Harry Levi of Temple Israel, Boston, that Harvard reschedule for Jewish students its September 1915 entrance examinations. He suggested instead that Jewish students who had scruples against writing examinations on the Day of Atonement dictate their answers. The rabbi replied that proper religious observance required all-day attendance at the synagogue. While admitting that Lowell should have been informed earlier of the dates of the Jewish holidays, he pointed out that both

Boston and Tufts universities had allowed Jewish students to be examined on other days. But Lowell countered that the setting of entrance examinations presented special problems; Harvard afforded only two opportunities to pass them, in June and September. Third opportunities were not granted, even for students who were ill. This general rule, he argued, was applied to all students equally (including Catholics and Episcopalians, should one of the examinations be scheduled on Good Friday). Yet his opposition to greater flexibility was based on the suspicion that "the real object of the protest is not any hardship on individuals, but a desire for recognition of the Jewish religion by Harvard University."[50]

The following year, Lowell received a letter protesting the scheduling of the first day of course enrollment on the Jewish New Year. In reply, he questioned whether there was "anything in the nature of a sacrilege or a violation of religious duty for a man to enroll himself in a course on that day?" In subsequent years, Harvard may have made some effort to avoid these conflicts, but complaints over scheduling continued into the 1950s.[51]

A similar attitude was apparent in Lowell's protest (as one of more than fifty prominent Boston lawyers) to the president of the Senate against Louis D. Brandeis's confirmation as a justice to the United States Supreme Court. Lowell insisted that his opposition was based on Brandeis's "untrustworthy" character and his "unscrupulous" legal practice, not on his economic and social views. Indeed, Brandeis's dissenting opinions "should very properly be represented in the Supreme Court." In defense of dissent, Lowell claimed such a right for himself in voicing his opposition. Yet Brandeis's Jewishness was unquestionably his primary concern.[52]

By contrast, Charles W. Eliot numbered several Jews among his friends. One was banker Jacob Schiff, a summer neighbor at Mount Desert Island, Maine. Eliot was also on cordial terms with other Jewish benefactors of Harvard, James Loeb and Jesse Isidor Straus. He treated them as he would any cultivated gentleman. Personally free of the prejudices of many of his Brahmin class, Eliot once had to quash a rumor that anti-Semitism had kept a prominent Jew from being nominated for the Harvard Board of Overseers.[53]

Though he also denounced Henry Ford's anti-Semitic articles in the *Dearborn Independent*, Eliot did occasionally criticize Jews and their practices. He opposed, for example, a bill introduced in the New York legislature to allow the operation of Jewish businesses on Sunday, and he even suggested that the Jews shift their Sabbath twenty-four hours. Eliot was concerned, moreover, that the Jews used "their new freedom in the British Empire and the United States with an intelligence and an industry which give them control" of newspapers, motion pictures, sports, banks, and department stores. And while he believed that they lacked the Anglo-Saxon gift "of slowly improving political and social conditions under party government and by long discussion followed by compromise," he nevertheless considered American Jews to be "trustworthy in regard to the theory of political liberty."[54]

On the whole, he thought Jews to be "the most resistent and prepotent race in the world." Consequently, it would be best, he said, that Christians and Jews not intermarry, since the latter might well dominate. (He was not greatly influenced by the eugenicists, however, because most of them tended to urge immigration restriction.) Eliot observed a "Jewish strain" in several old New England families, his own among them. He saw it not only in his uncle Andrews Norton, but also "in the physiognomies of some of his children, and very strongly in some of his grandchildren." Such an identification by facial characteristics was more a surmise than a fact. Yet at least one famous New Englander, James Russell Lowell, said Eliot "was sure he had Hebrew blood in his veins through the Russells; and he decidedly liked to testify to that fact."[55]

In their attitudes toward these two non-Protestant groups, Irish Catholics and Jews, Lowell was somewhat more favorable to the former, while Eliot was definitely more friendly to the latter. Another major Catholic group in Massachusetts, the Italians, who numbered over 60,000 in greater Boston around 1920, were hardly even represented at Harvard. In 1908-09, the total of Italian-Americans and Italians at the college was 8 out of almost 2,200 students; there also were 5 others, 1 each in engineering, medicine, and postgraduate work and 2 in law. Far more Italians attended Syracuse University, where they founded a fraternity, Alpha Phi Delta, in 1914; another chapter was established at Columbia University the following year. But the number of Italians at Harvard remained small. There were only 6 Italians in the Harvard Class of 1926 of a roster of over 750. Four were born in Massachusetts, 1 in Rhode Island, and 1 in Italy.[56]

Negroes

Despite their small numbers at Harvard, Negroes became the subjects of two major controversies during the first half of the twentieth century: the membership of blacks on Harvard athletic teams and the residency of blacks in the freshman halls. Blacks had begun to enter the university before Eliot's administration, but most came after about 1890. Of the approximately 160 blacks who matriculated in Harvard College between then and 1940, about half received their degrees and a number had distinguished academic and athletic careers. In his survey of black students at Harvard during this fifty-year span, Paul D. Davis '40, a former member of varsity track squad, counted an All-American football center, two varsity baseball players, and two track stars, holding Harvard records in the broad jump and hammer throw. In addition, blacks wrote for undergraduate publications, debated, belonged to political clubs, and were class day speakers and officers as well as class orators. They also won scholarships and departmental honors; eight were elected to Phi Beta Kappa. Unquestionably, the records of Harvard's black graduates were equal to or better than those of most white students.[57]

While the first Negro to enter any Harvard department was Martin R. Delany, who attended the medical school in 1850-51 (and served as a major in the United States volunteers in Louisiana during the Civil War), the first Negro graduate from Harvard College was Philadelphian Richard Theodore Greener, who had prepared at Phillips Andover Academy and Oberlin College. After graduation in 1870, Greener, winner of first Bowdoin Prize during his senior year, taught philosophy and logic at the University of South Carolina (1873-77). There he received his law degree before becoming dean of the Howard Law School (1877-80). He later served as chief examiner of New York City and County Civil Service and was appointed by President William McKinley as United States consul first in Bombay and then in Vladivostok.[58]

While Greener's career was remarkable, the most famous black to graduate from the college during this early period was W. E. Burghardt Du Bois '90. In *Dusk of Dawn* (1940), Du Bois described his life at Harvard. Accepting the fact of social segregation from his white classmates, he devoted his energy to study and reading. Moreover, he enjoyed the friendship of William James and Albert Bushnell Hart. Du Bois placed second in the Boylston Oratorical Contest behind another Negro, Clement G. Morgan, who broke a long-standing caste and racial barrier when a revolt among classmates resulted in his election as the first black class orator. Du Bois, however, delivered one of the commencement speeches. After receiving his Ph.D. in history from Harvard, he began a long career as author and editor. As a spokesman for blacks, Du Bois was a militant idealist, in contrast to Booker T. Washington, who urged his people to accommodate themselves to whites. Washington was the first Negro to receive a Harvard honorary degree, an M.A. in 1896.[59]

It was not for their intellectual attainments that blacks most readily won recognition from their white classmates; it was rather, commented President Eliot in 1907, "on account of their remarkable athletic merit." Among these talented black athletes was football All-American William Henry Lewis, Harvard Law '95, who was credited with inventing the "roving center." But they met considerable discrimination from other teams in intercollegiate contests. Black baseball players, for instance, were frequently targets for the spikes of opposing base runners. And when a Virginia team insisted in 1903 that Harvard bench "star third baseman," William Clarence Matthews '05, the university decided against playing baseball with that institution. Eight years later, some protest also arose over sending shot-putter Theodore Cable '13 to the Oxford-Cambridge track meet, but it was "immediately checked by graduate pressure." Not until many years later, however, did the corporation make an official statement against racial discrimination in intercollegiate athletics. This decision was reached only after Harvard had bowed to pressure from the lily-white United States Naval Academy at Annapolis. On April 5, 1941, Harvard benched Lucien V. Alexis, Jr., '42, from a lacrosse game with Navy. Harvard lost, 12-0. During its southern trip, Alexis had previously played against the universities of Pennsylvania and Maryland. At Annapolis, Superintendent Rear Admiral Russell Willson offered the Harvard team three choices: First, Navy would bench a player to compensate for the benching of Alexis; second, Navy would forfeit the game; or third, the Harvard administration would be phoned for a decision. The third course was followed. Harvard Athletic Director William J. Bingham then reversed his earlier decision to play Alexis. After spring vacation, Harvard students petitioned the athletic director to explain his stand and to give assurances that it would not be repeated. Subsequently, the corporation "suggested that the Athletic Committee 'should make it plain to other institutions with whom we are competing that it is Harvard's principle that there should be no racial discrimination among our students.'"[60]

On the issue of housing black students in the freshman halls, Harvard also reversed its position, but only after a long and painful public controversy. Prior to the opening of the freshman halls in 1914, the faculty had voted that all first-year students be required to reside in them, "except those who are permitted by the Assistant Dean of Harvard College to live elsewhere." Black students were thus *persuaded* to seek other accommodations. By accident, two black freshmen were assigned to the halls during World War I. To prevent a similar recurrence, William Knox, Jr., was told, after appearing for the June 1921 examinations, to return his registration card for a room in Standish Hall because all rooms had been assigned.[61]

In December 1922, Roscoe Conkling Bruce, a black Phi Beta Kappa and magna cum laude graduate of the class of 1902, applied for a room in the halls on behalf of his son, who planned to enter the class of 1930. Not only had Bruce held several scholarships at Harvard, but he had also won both the Pasteur Medal and the Coolidge Debating Prize and delivered the class oration. Since Bruce, Jr., the grandson of a former United States Senator, Blanche K. Bruce of Mississippi, would not graduate from Phillips Exeter Academy until 1926, his father may well have intended to make this application a test case. Both Bruce and his son had become accustomed to associating with middle- and upper-middle-class whites through their preparatory school training. And although they claimed their Negro identity with pride, both were light skinned.[62]

After President Lowell personally turned down Bruce's application for his son, they exchanged letters, which were published in January 1923 in the Boston *Transcript* and the New York *World*. Bruce expressed his shock and said that he had believed culture, not race, was "the basis of sound nationality." He put his argument succinctly:

> Few words in the English language, I submit, are susceptible of more poignant abuse than the two you have seen fit to employ. The first is 'race'; the second, 'necessity'. As the one is often nothing more than a term of so-

cial convenience, so the other is quite as often a means to buttress prejudice. But, *Veritas* is less elusive.

Lowell's reply revealed his firm belief in the "reasonableness" of exclusion:
"We owe to the colored man the same opportunities for education that we do
to the white man; but we do not owe to him to force him and the white man
into social relations that are not, or may not be, mutually congenial." This, of
course, was simply a variation of the "separate but equal" doctrine. While
Harvard gave blacks "freely opportunities for room and board wherever it is
voluntary," Lowell argued that the social benefits of compulsory residence
for white freshmen—"99 ½% of the students"—should not be jeopardized
"because the remaining one half of one percent could not properly be in-
·cluded."[63]

His application of "compulsory residence" was admittedly "arbitrary"; he
justified exclusion of blacks on the grounds that "no one has a right to live in
any one of the Freshman Dormitories." But since there were not enough
rooms in the halls to accommodate all freshmen, a number of whites, mostly
local boys, were allowed to live off campus. White southerners who objected
to integrated halls could have been given the same permission to live elsewhere. Few of them, however, refused to associate with blacks in the dormitories and dining halls open to all upperclassmen.[64]

Lowell seemed to have believed that integration of the halls "would cause a
revulsion and reprisals in a good many places" against Negroes. After all, the
previous twenty years had witnessed a high watermark in Jim Crow laws and
lynchings in the South. Commenting in a March 1923 letter on the poor treatment of Negroes in the United States, he blamed the "philanthropic people in
the North" who were "wholly unwilling to face the negro problem as a problem, but have insisted that the color line ought to be wholly disregarded."
Such a mistaken notion led to "the blunders of reconstruction, followed by
the treatment of the negro by the Southerner as he pleased, without rational
influence by Northern thought." In his chapter entitled "Race" in *Conflicts of
Principle*, Lowell also pointed to the hypocrisy of the North, which rejected
in principle legal discrimination, while denying Negroes practically all opportunities to better themselves. On the other hand, the South, which imposed social segregation by statute, at the same time offered more opportunities for Negro employment.[65]

Reconstruction, then, failed because it ignored the fact of racial differences
between whites and blacks. To buttress his argument, Lowell drew upon the
writings of historian James Ford Rhodes. Lowell's decision in regard to
Roscoe Conkling Bruce's son already had brought down upon his head a
storm of protest from a number of Harvard alumni. In January 1923, he
wrote to Rhodes that he felt like "Saint Sebastian, stuck full of arrows which
people are firing at me." The historian reassured Lowell that his interpreta-

tion of Reconstruction was supported by volumes 6 and 7 of his *History of the United States from the Compromise of 1850*. In fact, Rhodes was far more disparaging than Lowell of the Negro, who could "never be elevated to a social level with the whites; he is a million years behind in civilization."[66]

Another ally was Booker T. Washington, whom Lowell considered "the wisest guide the colored man ever had in this country," because he did not urge social equality. The views of alumnus W. E. B. Du Bois, he implied, were less reliable. Lowell referred to the following extract from *Up From Slavery*: "The wisest among my race understand that the agitation of questions of social equality is the extremest folly," and that only through "severe and constant struggle," not "artificial forcing," could "progress in the enjoyment of all privileges" be made. Washington, said Lowell, "felt that the important thing was to train the men of his race in character and efficiency, believing that when this was accomplished the question of their rights would present less difficulty."[67]

But for all of Lowell's ratiocinations, the crucial question remained whether Harvard's policy helped or hindered Negro progress. His argument that Harvard would lose influence in the South, just as the North had after Reconstruction, if it tried to enforce social equality among its students, was largely vitiated by the fact that so few blacks had attended the college. And Professor Albert Bushnell Hart, a trustee of Howard University, doubted "whether any southern student in the last forty years has stayed away from Harvard because he knew there were some negro students here." Though believing in Negro inferiority and opposing racial mixing, Hart did not think northerners should "take responsibility for the prejudices of the Southern people." Since "Chinese, Japanese, Filipinos, Indians and rather dark Latin Americans are received without comment," he argued that the exclusion of black freshmen from the halls was "an unnecessary discrimination," which filled him with "pain and apprehension."[68]

From his experience, Hart found Harvard students to be relatively tolerant in their treatment of black classmates, even to the point of rooming next door to "a respectable colored student." And when All-American William Henry Lewis was refused service by a Harvard Square barber, students had boycotted his shop. On the other hand, some southerners, an alumnus recalled, described one of the entrances of Hollis Hall as a "nest of negroes." But southerners had to accept blacks in competition for extracurricular activities. One of them even welcomed the challenge of a Negro candidate for a university debating team, "because the only way he could get on the team ahead of the negro was to show his superior quality."[69]

Hart was not the only prominent Harvardian to question President Lowell in regard to his treatment of blacks. Charles W. Eliot had never sanctioned an official policy of racial discrimination, although in personal attitudes he and Lowell were not very far apart. In the era after the *Plessy* v. *Ferguson* decision

(1896), the two Harvard presidents, like most white Americans, endorsed the "separate but equal" doctrine and accepted Booker T. Washington as the spokesman for American Negroes. No less than Lowell, Eliot was concerned by the attitude of black leaders who had migrated from the South to the North in the early 1920s. They seemed "to abandon the methods of Hampton and Tuskegee in favor of more combative or violent methods."[70]

In two letters written in 1909 to W. Monroe Trotter, '95 and M.A. '96, editor of the *Guardian*, Eliot summarized his views on social segregation. While libraries and parks should not exclude Negroes, he suggested that if their numbers grew, "it might be more convenient to provide in libraries separate tables or desks for colored people." At this time, segregation certainly was not "necessary" in the Boston and Cambridge public schools. But if "in any Northern state the proportion of negroes should become large," said Eliot, "I should approve of separate schools for negro children." Nor did he have any "theoretical objection to the separate car laws of the South," if both races had "equally good accommodations." Laws against racial intermarriage, of course, received his warm approval. Though considering most Negroes several generations behind whites in civilization, Eliot believed, nevertheless, that they "should have access to all trades and professions" and be able to vote if they, like the whites, met educational qualifications and paid the poll tax.[71]

During the course of an extensive correspondence with Frederick George Bromberg '58, a Liberal Republican and a lawyer from Mobile, Alabama, Eliot maintained that political equality for blacks did not confer social equality, which was a matter of "similar tastes and habits." As a New England aristocrat, Eliot chose his intimate associates on the basis of their culture, education, and common interests. "It would never occur to me," he wrote, "not to invite to my house an educated Chinaman or Japanese because their skin is yellow or brownish, or to avoid asking a negro to my table if he were an intelligent, refined and interesting person." On the same basis, he took an interest in the career of Roscoe Conkling Bruce and viewed with approval President Theodore Roosevelt's much criticized invitation to Booker T. Washington to dine at the White House.[72]

Eliot and Lowell both thought racial tension would be decreased if Negroes and whites lived as separate entities under equal protection of the laws. They probably mirrored the racial views of the eastern academic establishment, whose concern for the education of the Negro was limited to those few talented blacks brought to their attention by educators and ministers. On the other hand, since American Indians already lived separately from whites, Eliot and Lowell actively opposed the infringement of their rights and wrote Massachusetts Congressman Frederick W. Dallinger on behalf of several tribes. Few, if any, American Indians would attend the modern university (part of the original 1636 college, named for benefactor John Harvard in

1638, had been known as the Indian College) until official efforts undertaken to recruit blacks in the early 1960s were expanded a decade later to include other nonwhite groups and Spanish-surnamed Americans. [73]

Foreign Student Enrollment

In regard to the admission of students from foreign countries, the Lowell administration continued, but did not expand substantially the policies and practices of its predecessor. President Eliot had made Harvard a more cosmopolitan university in four ways: by encouraging qualified foreigners to study at Harvard; by providing university extension courses for the community, especially for schoolteachers; by educating Cuban and Puerto Rican schoolteachers at Harvard Summer School; and by promoting exchange professorships with certain European universities and western United States colleges. Harvard became one of the leaders among the American universities that opened their doors to foreign students and professors. [74]

From the turn of the century until World War I, the enrollment of foreign students at American universities steadily, and in some cases dramatically, increased. In 1908-09, for example, Harvard ranked fourth among American universities in terms of the total number of foreign students enrolled. The University of Pennsylvania was the leader with 225, followed by Columbia with 166, Cornell with 157, and Harvard with 147. Far behind them came Yale (86), California (76), Massachusetts Institute of Technology (72), Northwestern (71), Michigan (69), and Illinois (62). Princeton had only 13 foreign students. Foreign student enrollment was largely determined by the advantages offered at the different graduate and professional schools—for example, Pennsylvania's dental school—since this training was the kind most eagerly sought. [75]

At Harvard, the college enrolled about 40 percent of the foreign students and the Graduate Schools of Arts and Sciences about 30 percent (see Table 2.2). They ranged from the most familiar—Canadians—to the most exotic—Chinese, Japanese, and Siamese. The admission of Chinese and Japanese to Harvard did not arouse fear of a yellow peril, because the percentage of American-born Orientals living in the eastern United States was very small and because almost all of these students were foreign nationals. Instead the education of Orientals appealed to American altruism and belief in the "white man's burden." Some Chinese, however, especially those among the nobility, decided to send their sons to European, rather than American, universities because of the Chinese Exclusion Acts. [76]

Chinese students had attended Harvard in the late nineteenth century; its first professor of Chinese, Ko K'un-hua (1879-82), had been brought to the university by Boston businessmen in the China trade. Although the number of Chinese students declined around the turn of the twentieth century, well

Table 2.2
FOREIGN STUDENTS REGISTERED IN HARVARD
UNIVERSITY, 1900-01 AND 1904-11

Foreign Countries	1900-01	1904-05	1905-06	1906-07	1907-08	1908-09	1909-10	1910-11
Argentine Republic			1	3	5	2	1	1
Armenia							3	2
Asia Minor					1			
Australia		5	1		3	1		
Austria-Hungary				1			1	1
Bermuda					1			
Brazil		1				1	1	
British West Indies	1	3	2	3	1	2	2	1
Bulgaria	1	1		1	2	2	2	2
Canada	45	34	38	43	47	35	35	51
China		1	2	20	25	25	22	23
Colombia				1	1	1	1	1
Costa Rica				2	2			
Cuba	2	3	2	1	4	5	4	
Denmark								1
Dutch Guiana							1	1
East Africa								1
Egypt					1	2		1
France	5	5	6	4	3	6	9	5
Germany	4	3	4	3	4	12	9	7
Great Britain & Ireland	3	9	8	14	9	13	5	8
Holland		1	1			1		1
Iceland			1					
India	1	1	1	3	3	6	5	9
Italy	1	1	3	3	3	3	2	3
Japan	8	13	13	10	8	7	14	8
Korea				1	1	1		
Mexico	2	3	6	5	4	2	2	3
Morocco	1	1	1					
New Zealand		3	4	3	1	2	1	1
Norway	1		1					
Panama					1		3	3
Peru						1	2	1
Portugal				1				
Roumania					1	1		
Russia	1			1	3	5	6	4
Siam					1	1	3	1
South Africa		1	1	4	3	2	2	
Spain	2	1					1	
Sweden					2			1
Switzerland	1			2		1	1	1
Syria			1	1	1			
Turkish Empire	1	4	5	3	1	2	3	5
Total foreign countries	80	94	102	133	142	142	140	147
Dependencies								
Hawaii	10	6	8	9	6	8	10	9
Puerto Rico	0	1	3	3	3	4	5	4
Philippines	0	2	0	1	1	1	1	2
Total dependencies	10	9	11	13	10	13	16	15
Total foreign countries and dependencies	90	103	113	146	152	155	156	162
Total university enrollment	4,314	4,192	4,009	4,149	4,065	3,918	4,213	4,123

Sources: Harvard College Scrap Book Registration, Geographical Distribution, Harvard University Archives; and *Harvard University Catalogues, 1900-1911*. Different sources gave slightly different figures.

over a hundred were enrolled during the period from 1906 to 1911. This increase was due to a combination of factors: edicts of the Chinese government recommending that sons of the nobility receive their education abroad; the progress made by Western missionary schools and colleges in preparing Chinese students; and the remission of the Boxer Indemnity funds by the United States for the purpose of educating Chinese students. 77

Harvard hoped that China would follow Japan's example in sending its best upper-class students, men who would do for China what four Japanese graduates of Harvard University had done for their country, "namely, absorb, modify, adapt, and improve western ideas for eastern use." Count Jutaro Komura, Harvard Law '77; Viscount Kentaro Kaneko, L.S. '78; Shinichiro Kurino, A.B. '81, minister to Russia and later ambassador to France; and Baron Tanetaro Megata, L.S. '74, former financial administrator of Korea, were among the architects of modern Japan. For the education of China's future elite, Harvard offered to Sir Chentung Liang Cheng, his imperial Chinese majesty's minister plenipotentiary, to provide both special admission terms and an adviser as well as free tuition and financial aid. In addition, a fund of $10,000 was raised through subscription by Major Henry L. Higginson to contribute toward their tuition and expenses. At the time, this sum was the largest raised on behalf of any group of foreign students. 78

In July 1906, Dr. Charles D. Tenney brought over some forty Chinese students to Harvard Summer School before distributing them to other colleges throughout the country. Dr. Tenney, a Harvard graduate, was eminently qualified for the position of director of Chinese government students by his career as a missionary and educator in China. After studying English, German, and French in preparation for the Harvard entrance examinations, fifteen of the group enrolled in September. 79

Not surprisingly, among the main impediments to the admission of Chinese and Japanese students were the language requirements. While Orientals had to speak and write English quite well in order to complete the baccalaureate, it was an added burden to require them to know Greek and Latin as well as the classics of their own literature. In 1908, Jerome D. Greene was asked by the Committee on Admission to propose revisions subsequently accepted by the faculty, in the rules governing the admission of Oriental students. After consulting with Dr. Tenney, Greene recommended, first, that the Chinese and Japanese classics be given equal recognition and rated as ancient languages. Second, he proposed that Oriental students be exempted from offering French or German for admission, although they would have to take one of these modern languages for their degree. The Japan-born Greene, whose father, the Reverend D. Crosby Greene, and mother were the first missionaries sent to Japan by the American Board of Commissioners for Foreign Missions, was both friend and advocate of Oriental students at Harvard. 80

By contrast, A. Lawrence Lowell never shared the enthusiastic interest of Charles W. Eliot and Jerome D. Greene in Oriental students. In fact, he had long believed in restricting Oriental immigration to the United States. Although Lowell once mentioned the importance of maintaining goodwill among the Chinese students, some of whom might become China's "future leaders," no additional funds were subscribed during his administration for their education at Harvard. In 1918 it was decided to use the $107 that remained of the $10,000 fund as small loans to Chinese students in the college.[81]

When Lowell assumed the presidency of Harvard University, he inherited an institution committed to cosmopolitanism and scholarship. Professors from great European institutions of learning came to lecture at Harvard, and its graduate school had international representation and reputation. On the one hand, Lowell wanted to keep these doors open by continuing the professorial exchanges and by supporting scholarly inquiry. But on the other, he felt he had to guard Harvard College from the ethnic challenge. The results of Professor Albert Bushnell Hart's survey of the family backgrounds of forty-two students in Government 13b showed that the challenge had become serious. In February 1922, Hart assigned a classroom paper entitled "Personal Race and Descent," which was to cover four major points: "Territorial Relations and Immigration"; "Family Tree"; "Status and Services of the Family"; and education of family members and reasons for coming to Harvard. Hart expressed to Lowell his surprise at the findings. "Only a fifth" were descended from English colonial ancestry, while a fourth were from Scotch and Scotch-Irish. "Fifty-two percent" were thus "outside the element from which the college has been chiefly recruited for three hundred years." Hart classified the forty-two students into seven groups: nine English colonial stock; eleven Scotch and Scotch-Irish; four Irish; five Continental (Danish, Norwegian, Swedish, Polish Catholic, and Swiss); eight Jewish (four from Germany, Austria, or Hungary; two from Russia; and two intermarried with Protestants); three Africans; and two Asiatics (Chinese). One of the Chinese had the longest lineage—to A.D. 700.[82]

Although educational advantages, prestige, and proximity were the three main reasons that students attended Harvard, there were some interesting variations in the answers given by the different groups. Three young men of English colonial stock replied, respectively: "Harvard is in my blood, so to speak"; "Always wanted to come here as it appealed to me more than any other college, even when it was just the colors that I thought of"; and "I followed the tide of my friends in quest of further education." One of the Negro students was attracted by Harvard's "heralded democracy and efficient curriculum," while another, who served in France during World War I, came because he "saw the need of higher education for the Negro race," which prejudice made "impossible" for him to obtain in the South. The latter felt that "going to a mixed school and coming in contact with different races would help [him] to try to solve the problem of" his own people.[83]

But President Lowell feared that so many ethnic and racial contacts would undermine the position of old-stock Americans in the college. The diversity that might be tolerable in the university threatened college traditions. Whereas Eliot had tried to bring the university into the college, Lowell wanted to protect the college from the cosmopolitanism of the university. That was why he advocated both a quota for Jewish students and a limitation on the freshman class to 1,000 during the 1920s.

· 3 ·

HARVARD: DEBATE ON RESTRICTION, 1922

> The President stated that there could be no doubt that the primary object in appointing a special Committee was to consider the question of the Jews and that if any member of the Faculty doubted this, let him now speak or forever after hold his peace.
>
> President A. Lawrence Lowell
> to the Faculty of Arts and
> Sciences, June 2, 1922.[1]

The question of increasing numbers of Jewish students at Harvard—and hence their "desirability"—was hotly debated in faculty meetings, private gatherings, personal correspondence, and the public press in 1922-23. The internal controversy was precipitated, in part, by several decades of festering anti-Semitic feeling in the nation. In leading Harvard's "caste establishment," President A. Lawrence Lowell was motivated by expediency probably as much as by personal conviction. According to President Emeritus Charles W. Eliot, Lowell's proposal to limit Jewish admissions developed in response to pressures from graduates in New York City, Louisiana, and Texas in January 1922. While on a western trip later in the spring, Lowell himself heard that one reason that alumni clubs had trouble recruiting students was due to Harvard's "reputation of having so many Jews." He also learned that "the same talk" was "heard in the great preparatory schools." An alumnus of the Harvard Club of Southern California asked whether Harvard was considering any plans "which would leave our University free of this plague" that was "enveloping Yale" and had "completely submerged Columbia." Since the Endowment Committee had launched a campaign to raise $15 million in 1919-20, Lowell expediently decided to pacify influential Harvardians.[2]

Although personally denying anti-Semitic feeling, Lowell agreed substantially with alumni criticisms that there were too many Jews at Harvard. A social problem had developed on campus, but the president's methods were arbitrary. He was convinced that the only way to reduce anti-Semitism within the Harvard community, as within the nation, was to limit the number of Jews allowed to associate with Gentiles. In hindsight, some may see merit in part of Lowell's argument: It may be necessary to impose controlled ethnic and racial mixing in schools (and residential neighborhoods and jobs) in order to overcome persistent social polarizations, whether voluntary or involuntary. Few today would dispute the need to transform ghettos into vital neighborhoods and to resist the demands of those who would divide the United States into separate nations. But Lowell put the entire burden of proof on the Jewish students, whose records were usually above the class average, instead of sharing it with their Gentile classmates. Had he been so disposed, he could have used his moral influence to counter the petty snobbery of campus cliques and alumni gatherings. In fact, his very emphasis on the social values of undergraduate education contributed to some of that snobbery. Coincidentally, academic standards became less rigorous during the last years of his administration. Had Lowell begun to raise admission requirements to the scholastic heights necessitated by the competitive applicant pool of the era after World War II, he would, of course, have lost alumni support. Yet in all likelihood, those alumni sons who made the academic grade would have been more willing to judge classmates on the basis of individual talents and virtues rather than on family social status.

First Inquiries

Over a two-year period, Lowell came to the conclusion that Harvard had a "Jewish problem." On receipt of a letter from an alumnus in February 1920, he had inquired into the number of Jewish undergraduates. Noting the problem of determining their exact number because of name changes, the dean's office surmised that it was "about what it always has been here and that during the war the percentage of Jews was larger than it had been before." Apparently, this initial inquiry did not go further; but in January 1922 the dean's office observed that "Mr. Lowell feels pretty strongly that of the scholarships controlled by us the percentage allotted to Jews in their first year in Harvard College should not exceed the percentage of Jews in the Freshman Class." The Committee on Scholarships and Other Aids for Undergraduates pointed out that the present announced terms for awards made it difficult to reject academically qualified applicants. After consulting with Lowell, however, the committee voted to adopt new terms, to be published in the university catalogue. While awards would continue to be made "primarily on the basis of high scholarship," holders also had to be "men of approved character and promise."[3]

These discussions within the administration came to the attention of Julian W. Mack, LL.B. '87, judge of the United States Circuit Court, New York, and the first Jewish member of the Board of Overseers. In March and April 1922, Judge Mack, past president of the first American Jewish Congress (1918-19) and former head of the Zionist Organization of America, conferred with President Lowell, who explained that Harvard had a "duty" to admit as many sons of immigrants as it could "effectively educate: including in education the imparting, not only of book knowledge, but of the ideas and traditions of our people." Immigrant sons of Russian Jews, Armenian Christians, and Russian Slavs in particular, implied Lowell, so resisted Harvard's benign tutorial influences that their numbers should be limited to about 15 percent of each class. Since Jewish students already numbered about 20 percent of the freshman class, Lowell urged that the college exercise its discretionary authority more strictly in regard to provisionary freshmen and transfer students, among whom was found a high percentage of Jews. The president estimated that "if we excluded all but the clearly desirable Jews who came from other colleges or who had not fully passed the examinations under the new plan, the percentage would have been reduced to 15%." Such discretion would not, however, be used to question the desirability of students who achieved satisfactory grades on the regular extrance examinations.[4]

When Judge Mack asked the dean's office for statistics on the scholarship stand of Jewish students, Lowell shifted his argument: "The question that troubles us is the discipline for offenses of a moral nature, dishonesty, etc.; where the difference of background, of foreign standards, etc., counts heavily." "By what test," Mack retorted, "do you determine which Jews or which immigrant Jews or which individuals, of the immigrant classes, are 'clearly desirable'?" He found Lowell's method "as much of a subterfuge as Columbia's psychological test,—a test that you had said had cut the percentage of Jews from 40 to 16, and as you and I believed, aimed primarily, if not solely, at this result." In reply, Lowell contended that while the same objection applied to other immigrants who lacked "American traditions," it was "natural to speak of the Jews in this way, because they are the only immigrants in this condition who come to us in large numbers." Hence the terms *Jew* and *immigrant* ostensibly were interchangeable in his mind.[5]

He apparently believed that the amount of student—or, in reality, Jewish student—wrongdoing was in the nature of an iceberg: the largest part remained undetected. In pursuit, Lowell dispatched the following memorandum to the dean's office:

> You have basely gone back on me. Somebody told me that of the fourteen men dismissed last year for cheating and lying about it, thirteen were Jews. Now you make out that there were twelve of them, of whom only five were Jews. Please produce at once six more![6]

But Judge Mack was not to be appeased with material and statistics prepared by the dean's office and approved in advance by President Lowell. And by April 1922 several other overseers also became concerned, among them Jerome D. Greene, who represented in large measure Eliot's point of view on matters involving Harvard's traditional admission policy. Speaking for the Overseers' Committee on Harvard College, Greene presented his analysis to Lowell: "The real kernel" was not "the relative delinquency" of Jews, but "the actual disinclination, whether justified or not, on the part of non-Jewish students to be thrown in contact with so large a proportion of Jewish undergraduates." To alleviate this "Jewish problem," he suggested that the corporation authorize a faculty study of the entrance examination system as well as other methods of admission. The object would be to devise a method of selection limiting the student body "to the most promising individuals without reference to any question of race or religion." While such a method would exclude many Jews "of objectionable personality and manners," it should not bar Jews as such, especially not "the sort who are of unquestionable character and all-round promise." Moreover, Greene and the committee counseled delay and further study of the admissions problem.[7]

President Lowell wanted an immediate change of policy. In fact, by April 14, the day before Greene wrote his letter, the president had sent two propositions to the Committee on Admission. They were aimed specifically at Jewish applicants.

(a) That Hebrews applying for admission to Harvard College and the Harvard Engineering School by transfer from other colleges and technical schools be rejected except such applicants be possessed of extraordinary intellectual capacity together with character above criticism.

(b) That in determining questions of admission under the New Plan all doubtful or line cases shall be investigated with the nicest care, and that such of this number as belong to the Hebrew race shall be rejected except in unusual and special cases.

In presenting these propositions, Lowell was acting in stealth as well as in haste. If the Committee on Admission had accepted them, he would have succeeded in bypassing both the overseers and the faculty in establishing special, subjective admissions tests of intellect and character.[8]

But Chairman Henry Pennypacker told President Lowell that its members unanimously "felt that the Committee should not practice discrimination without the knowledge and assent of the Faculty," of which it was "merely the administrative servant." Although expressing "some concern" over the increase in Jewish students, the committee's vote revealed a clear-cut recognition that the two proposals involved discrimination. At the heart of the growing controversy over Jewish admissions at Harvard was the genesis of a conflict over authority between a strong-willed President Lowell and a hesitant, yet generally enlightened, faculty.[9]

About a week after his reply to Lowell, Pennypacker addressed the meeting of the Faculty of Arts and Sciences on May 9, 1922. This was to be the first of four such faculty meetings on the Jewish question, couched in terms of delegating to the Committee on Admission "a larger measure of discretion in the selection of candidates for admission to the College." Since the discussion on May 9 was of a general nature and did not lead to a vote, it was unlikely that the faculty as a whole was then aware of the issues. Moreover, only 88 members out of a possible total of 193 professors and administrative officers were present.[10]

The next faculty meeting, on May 16, was attended by 98 members. Attention focused on the proposal introduced at the previous meeting. During the ensuing discussion, several faculty members introduced significant resolutions. The first, by Arthur Norman Holcombe, chairman of the Department of Government, stated that the faculty had "heretofore approved the policy of including in the educational process at Harvard College due care for the moral development and social discipline of the students," an object that was to be achieved by residence in the university dormitories. He resolved that no transfers or line cases be admitted unless they had "the moral character and social capacity to profit by and duly contribute to the serviceability" of a Harvard education.[11]

Albert Bushnell Hart and William Ernest Hocking, however, proposed to delay immediate action. Hocking, professor of philosophy, made the motion that would ultimately be carried at a later meeting: "That a special committee be appointed by the President to consider principles and methods for more effectively sifting candidates for admission in respect to character." Its purpose would be to study objectively Harvard's character requirements with the intention of restoring them as criteria, rather than allowing them to be the "subjective caprice" of a particular committee. This meeting was adjourned without a vote being taken.[12]

Impatient with the slowness of faculty deliberations, Lowell was busy building his case. He collected from the different schools within Harvard University statistics on the percentage of Jews in each class, the percentage of Jews subject to disciplinary action, and the percentage of Jews falling in each group on the rank list and earning degrees with distinction. Such figures were hardly conclusive because of the difficulty in determining accurately who was and was not Jewish. At the law school, for example, two members of the staff relied on their personal recollections over a twenty-two-year period. The medical school said that the only means it had to determine whether a student was Jewish was his name and, after the institution of a new requirement in the spring of 1922, his photograph, which, of course, proved nothing. In spite of these limitations, Lowell believed that the statistics would ultimately persuade most of the faculty of the need for a Jewish quota.[13]

During May 1922, Lowell also presented his views in writing to some members of the faculty. One of his most interesting exchanges was with William Ernest Hocking, who pointedly asked about the specific object of limitation: Was it Jews per se or just "undesirable" ones? This distinction, Hocking wrote, would make "a further and rather explosive difference as to whether a given course is 'candid' or not." Initially he saw the problem as one of "individual character," not of race, which could be ameliorated by "the combined efforts of our Jewish alumni and of additional tests on our own part." (Williams College had tacitly agreed to let older Jewish alumni screen its Jewish applicants.) Another possible method was use of the still imperfect psychological tests. With the elimination of "undesirable Jews" at Harvard, the issue of their proportion "would automatically disappear," because their "presence . . . casts a spot-light on all . . . compatriots and makes them conspicuous." The faculty debates, however, revealed to Hocking the broader dimensions of the problem: What ultimately should be "the constituency of the nation"? For some time, that question had been raised in terms of immigration; it was "now being echoed in the schools of the nation; and the 'Jewish question' is a part of it."[14]

Whereas Hocking called for a broad inquiry into admissions policy, the Harvard president would direct attention exclusively toward Jewish applicants. Lowell contended that it was not simply the "individually undesirable" Jews, but "the fact that they form a distinct body, and cling, or are driven, together, apart from the great mass of the undergraduates." To buttress his argument, he presented an implied analogy between Jews at Harvard College and Jews driving away Gentiles from a summer hotel, from a private school run by one of his friends in New York City, and from Columbia College. He did not want Harvard to suffer the same fate, but it "would be wholly wrong" for a college to refuse to admit any Jews, like many summer hotels.[15]

For his own part, Lowell preferred "to state frankly" and publicly the reasons for the proposed quota. Despite "some protest," he believed that "reasonable people" would recognize it as "the wise and generous thing." Yet "tests of character in the ordinary sense of the word [would] afford no remedy," he concluded, because not enough Jews could be excluded by objective tests of any kind. Therefore, "any vote passed with the intent of limiting the number of Jews should not be supposed by anyone to be passed as a measurement of character really applicable to Jew and Gentile alike."[16]

Lowell explained his justification for such a double standard in a similar letter to Rufus S. Tucker, an economics instructor. The accepted theories— "that all men are born free and equal, etc.—are not absolutely true, but true within certain limits," Lowell argued. Having rejected this tenet of the liberal creed, he could easily take the next step and deny that Jews should be treated as individuals. In an earlier, homogeneous society, one "could consider only the qualities of the individual." But "we are now faced by an actual group segregation, in which the important factor is not the quality of the individual but of the group." Lowell believed that he was approaching the problem as a scholar and man of science examining "group psychology."[17]

Faculty Meetings of May 23 and June 2, 1922

The May 23 faculty meeting, which followed three days of debate, revealed a confusion in the minds of many faculty, 109 of whom were present. Sometime during the early part of the meeting, Admission Director Pennypacker presented a chart showing the increase of Jewish enrollment since 1900. The fact that the percentage of Jewish students had tripled—from 7 to 21 percent—made many faculty members, in the words of Professor Hocking, "quite panicky." Additional statistics, based largely on data collected for 1920-22, were presented to show that Jews were a special group within the student body: In relation to the total number, Jews constituted 11.2 percent of those under discipline, but 40 percent of those dismissed for improper conduct. On the other hand, almost half of those in Group I of the rank list were Jewish. At this point, Lowell's brother-in-law and "intimate friend," James Hardy Ropes, professor of divinity, made a three-part motion, which would become the subject of intense debate at this and at a subsequent, special faculty meeting. He proposed that in considering the admission of transfer students and marginal candidates, the Committee on Admission should be, first, "convinced that their presence as members of the College will positively contribute to the general advantage of the College [and, second,] instructed to take into account the resulting proportionate size of racial and national groups in the membership of Harvard College." The final part of his resolution stated, "In the opinion of this Faculty it is not desirable that the number of students in any group which is not easily assimilated into the common life of the College should exceed fifteen per cent of the whole College." Not only did Ropes urge that the Committee on Admission consider the size of racial groups in admitting transfer students and marginal candidates, but he also wanted the faculty to agree to a general 15-percent limitation on minority groups. The phrase "not easily assimilated" was a thinly veiled reference to Jews.[18]

Before the motion was passed, however, several others were made. At this time, David Gordon Lyon, professor of Hebrew and curator of the Semitic Museum, moved that a faculty committee be appointed to confer with "representative Jews, and others, among whom shall be graduates of the College, with the object of finding some solution acceptable to all interests concerned, and consistent with the liberal, democratic spirit of the University."[19]

Finally, Edmund E. Day of the economics department asked that Ropes's controversial motion be so divided that sections one and two could be considered separately, on the ground that the first was a one-year emergency measure intending no racial discrimination. Following the president's affirmative ruling, Ropes moved that the first section of his motion, with certain amendments, be adopted:

> That from the following groups of candidates for admission to Harvard College
> (a) Candidates for admission by transfer from other colleges and technical schools;
> (b) Candidates for admission by examination who have not adequately satisfied all the requirements;
> the Committee on Admission be instructed to admit, for the academic year 1922-23, only applicants concerning whom the Committee is not merely satisfied (as at present) as to their mental attainments and moral character, but, in addition, is convinced that their presence as members of the College will positively contribute to the general advantage of the College.

It was carried without a recording of the affirmative and negative votes. Most faculty members probably reasoned, as Day himself apparently did, that an emergency existed and that a fair application of the above stated principle would exclude Gentiles as well as Jews, although more of the latter on personal grounds. William Ernest Hocking abstained, because he did not think that an emergency existed. His letters to law professor Felix Frankfurter and to Jerome D. Greene in May and June illuminated the motives behind these faculty votes. [20]

On the second paragraph the debate was heated, Hocking recounted. To insure its adoption, Lowell made his coup. He implied that it would be insincere or dishonest to reject the second part after approving the first. But Day argued that the original motion had been divided because the first two parts did not infer the same result. Henry Wyman Holmes, dean of the graduate School of Education, "rather furious" at Lowell's allegation, "demanded to know why the President, if he valued frankness so much, was not more frank." To test "the 'honesty' propaganda," Holmes moved to substitute a specific statement on keeping "the Jewish group . . . at its present relative position." He received only token support. [21]

When the faculty voted on the second part of Ropes's motion, it read, as amended:

> That, pending further action by this Faculty, the Committee be instructed, in making its decision in these cases, to take into account the resulting proportionate size of racial and national groups in the membership of Harvard College.

Under the influence of "the President's moral bludgeon," it was carried by 56 to 44, with two not voting. One of those was Jewish (Leo Wiener, professor of

Slavic languages and literatures). Hocking, of course, voted against the motion. But the fact that many moderate and even liberal men, including one of Jewish background (Paul Joseph Sachs), voted in its favor, while one or two who preferred a more explicit measure voted against it, showed it to be a measure about which many had grave doubts. 22

The faculty next voted, 50 to 37, to replace Professor Lyon's motion about the appointment of a committee with the briefer May 16 motion of Professor Hocking, as amended by Professor Hart. It provided "that a special committee be appointed by the President to consider principles and methods for more effectively sifting candidates for admission." This motion was adopted, Hocking subsequently explained to Felix Frankfurter, "with the unwritten understanding that it absorbed the purport of Lyon's motion, namely that racial constituency of Harvard should come within the scope of the enquiry and that leading Jews should be asked to help in the discussion." Shortly thereafter, the meeting adjourned. 23

Within five days, the faculty seemingly awoke to the implications of what it had done and circulated two similar petitions addressed to President Lowell, requesting that he call a special faculty meeting to reconsider the votes. The petitions recognized that the recent action "relating to controlling the percentage of Jews in Harvard College is a radical departure from the spirit and practice of the College [and is] so precipitate that fair notice" could not be extended to candidates for the fall of 1922. The signers, moreover, believed "that racial considerations should not influence the Committee on Admission before a careful and deliberate study of the whole question of the Jews shall have been made by the Faculty." Of the thirty-one petitioners, nineteen had voted against the second part of Ropes's motion, four had voted for it, and the remainder had apparently been absent from the meeting. Few of Harvard's big names in the humanities signed the petitions; the exceptions were Charles H. McIlwain (history and government), Byron S. Hurlbut (English; formerly dean of the college), Edward C. Moore (theology), and David G. Lyon. Many faculty may have been unwilling to sign a petition for a variety of reasons unconnected with their personal feelings about Jews. 24

One major Harvard figure, Dean Le Baron Russell Briggs, raised serious questions about the votes in a letter to the president, with whom he was on friendly terms. Uncertain about the true purport of the motions, Briggs had voted against the first, but for the second, "to avoid camouflage" of the issue. The faculty's dilemma was painful: The contemplated change seemed "contrary to the best Harvard traditions; yet, paradoxically, without a change of policy the best Harvard traditions may be destroyed." "Dissatisfaction [arose] from a feeling that we are taking one of the most important steps ever taken in the history of the college . . . without knowing thoroughly the ground we step on." The vote had been too close—only a dozen more in the affirmative than in the negative—to justify a new departure in admission policy. As Briggs subsequently wrote Judge Mack, he and several other faculty members wanted the president to confer first with a number of prominent Jews. Harvard's "responsibility to the Jews who have given us money," Briggs acknowledged, was "pretty serious." Because of the dangers of mishandling the problem as well as the need to find a plan behind which the faculty should unite, Briggs counseled delay and the calling of another meeting.25

Meanwhile Harry Wolfson, assistant professor of Jewish literature and philosophy, was meeting with Harvard friends to prepare a strong statement against those who favored a quota on Jewish students. Professor Wolfson and Dr. Henry M. Sheffer, who was also Jewish, had voted against the second part of Ropes's motion. Although Wolfson never formally presented his paper to the faculty, because that body rescinded its controversial votes on June 2, 1922, it was an effective counterattack. The Lithuanian-born Wolfson well knew what quotas meant to Jews in Russia; he did not want to see them imposed at Harvard. "You assume," he addressed proponents of restriction,

> that Jewish students coming to the University bring with them ideals and loyalties different from those of other students, that they are still to go through the so-called process of assimilation and be made over into good Americans, that assimilation is not complete until no two Jews are ever seen to walk together in the College Yard, and that the assimilation of Jews beyond a certain percentage is impossible. I say that all this should be made a subject of thorough study and investigation.

Referring to statistics on Jewish students to forecast their future behavior, Professor Wolfson asserted that there were "many among us who believe neither in old-fashioned fatalism nor in new-fashioned statistical pre-ordination." And personal interviews with local committees of Harvard graduates were also unreliable. "It may be readily admitted," he said, "that outward appearance is a proper test for selecting book agents, bond salesmen, social secretaries and guests for a week-end party," but scarcely "a proper test for the selection of future scholars, thinkers, scientists, and men of letters."26

Professor Wolfson's statement was pointed, but temperate. He gave Lowell credit for saying that he would "take the best scholars" among the Jewish applicants, "irrespective of their social backgrounds," admitting not just "the sons of the rich Jews," but "the best Jews, even of the poorest families." Lowell treated him well and approved of his promotions. In 1924-25, with money for his chair provided by Jews outside the university, Wolfson became the Nathan Littauer Professor of Jewish Literature and Philosophy.27

As might be expected, President Lowell was hardly pleased by these developments. In his view, the faculty had voted to limit the number of Jewish students when it passed the first motion by such a margin that no one even called for a show of hands. At the very least, he wanted to keep intact this vote, although he showed some signs of yielding temporarily in regard to the second.[28]

Lowell received another candid letter from Professor Hocking, who chose this means to express his views rather than signing the petition. As a result of his conversations with Professors Felix Frankfurter, Paul Sachs, and Harry Wolfson and with Dr. Henry Sheffer, Hocking mentioned to Lowell a plan for limiting the admission of Jews through Jewish agencies and pointed to "a remote analogy" with the Japanese government's limitation on emigrants. While Hocking now believed that "a Jewish problem" existed at Harvard, he did not think that it was "primarily racial, nor national, nor religious," but suspected it was "historical." Like many other Harvardians, he wanted to preserve the character of the college. He had "no desire to see the undergraduate body become a Cosmopolitan Club," although taking "pride in the cosmopolitan character of our Graduate School." Yet he essentially agreed with Ralph Barton Perry, a colleague in the philosophy department on leave in Italy, who expressed his concern about developments at Harvard: "The best things about Harvard [were] a thick skin, a healthy appetite, looseness or absence of social organization, tolerance,—in short, individualism in dear W. J.'s [William James's] sense." The "temporary emergency" did not merit the radical measure enacted by the second vote on May 23.[29]

Lowell agreed with Hocking that Harvard should cooperate with prominent Jews and said that several had been consulted before the faculty became involved in the discussions. The Jewish students themselves were the problem, he insisted. "More than half the difficulty would be overcome," Lowell would later write to Professor George F. Moore (religion), if they should "on admission be overcome with an oblivion of the fact that they were Jews, even though all the Gentiles were perfectly aware that they were Jews." Otherwise, their number would have to be limited to reduce anti-Semitism. While Lowell did not object to an investigation, he argued that the Committee on Admission should apply the first vote "in such a way that there should be no substantial change in the composition of the student body in the coming year." But the president had not counted on either the strength of the faculty revolt or the opposition of a great majority of the Board of Overseers.[30]

Lowell agreed to call a special meeting of the faculty—111 of whom attended—for Friday evening, June 2, 1922. The article in the docket was the "Further consideration of the votes passed on Professor Ropes's motions at the meeting of May 23, 1922." Professor Day, who had voted against the second motion and who subsequently signed the petition, moved that these votes—both sections of Ropes's motion—be rescinded. But Lawrence J. Henderson (biological chemistry) introduced a substitute motion for the same two votes: "That the Committee on Admission be instructed, pending the report of the special committee, to keep the proportion of Jews in Harvard College what it is at present." Such a measure would, in fact, fulfill Lowell's objectives. The issue at stake was clear: Would the faculty accept any measure specifically limiting the admission of Jews?[31]

Meanwhile three professors—Briggs, William McDougall (psychology), and Paul J. Sachs—explained why they had voted affirmatively on the second motion of May 23. In a letter that he read to the faculty, Sachs explained that he voted against the first motion, but for the second, in order to make clear the purpose behind the first. Had the motions been presented as a whole, rather than being divided into three separate parts, Sachs would have cast one negative vote. The faculty applauded Sachs's statement, and Lowell asked him shortly thereafter to serve on the investigating committee.[32]

After hearing the three professors, the faculty rejected Henderson's substitute motion in what was probably the first reliable index of its sentiment: 64 negative to 41 affirmative votes. Although a majority was decidedly against any specific limitation on Jews until after investigation—a defeat for President Lowell—a number of big Harvard names, past, present, and future, supported restriction prior to the report. But the day was carried by the liberals and moderates when, by a show of hands, 69 to 25, the faculty rescinded the first two votes of May 23, leaving only the third vote extant—regarding the appointment of a special committee "to consider principles and methods for more effectively sifting candidates for admission." Hocking believed that this committee should examine the national constituency "with racial and vocational questions in mind among others, to discover what college education has to do for it in the immediate future, and how, *in view of these facts, we propose to define and select ("sift")* the constituents of our own small community, Harvard College."[33]

Professor Charles J. Bullock (economics) then argued that if publicity were given to the activities of this committee, the president should state that its purpose was indeed "to consider the matter of the increasing number of Jews applying for admission to the College." Lowell, according to Professor Day, "turned this down flatly with the suggestion that the Faculty need not instruct him concerning the way to give publicity to the Faculty's action." To make certain that no one misinterpreted his blunt words, the next morning Lowell dictated to George W. Cram, secretary of the Faculty of Arts and Sciences, a statement to be incorporated into the minutes of the June 2 meeting: "The primary object in appointing a special Committee was to consider the question of the Jews." And if any faculty member still did not understand this, Lowell said: "Let him now speak or forever after hold his peace."[34]

Privately, Lowell told George Lyman Kittredge that he was at least partially satisfied with the results of the meeting, because the faculty now understood that it was confronted with "a Jew problem." Believing that the faculty would accept a restriction on Jews, if the committee reported it to be necessary, Lowell "did not see any object in being a 'die hard.'" And in his own mind, he had "no doubt that they will so report, because I think I know the situation well enough to be persuaded that there is no other solution."[35]

Appointment of the Committee on Methods of Sifting Candidates for Admission

Because of the far-reaching and sensitive nature of the special committee's task, the thirty-member Board of Overseers voted, on June 5, to expand both its representation and scope from the Faculty of Arts and Sciences to include the other university faculties. The committee would focus on admission requirements to the college, since the graduate and professional schools had their own specialized prerequisites. But the university would also be affected by whatever general admission principles it endorsed for the college.[36]

Seven of the thirteen men appointed to the committee were from the Faculty of Arts and Sciences, two were from medicine, while business administration, education, engineering, and law were each represented by one. Under the chairmanship of Charles H. Grandgent '83 (romance languages), the committee also included: Henry Pennypacker '88 (chairman of the Committee on Admission); Chester N. Greenough '98 (English; dean of Harvard College); Roger I. Lee '02 (hygiene); Theodore Lyman '97 (physics; director of Jefferson Physical Laboratory); Paul J. Sachs '00 (assistant director of the Fogg Art Museum, he was promoted to associate professor of fine arts in 1922); Harry A. Wolfson '12 (Jewish literature and philosophy); Lawrence J. Henderson '98 (biological chemistry); Milton J. Rosenau, honorary '14 (medicine); Wallace B. Donham '98 (dean of the Graduate School of Business Administration); Henry W. Holmes '03 (dean of the Graduate School of Education); Harry E. Clifford (engineering); and Samuel Williston '82 (law). Most of these men had already voiced their opinions in the preceding faculty meetings, and they would all share the work of preparing the committee's report.[37]

Lowell's appointments were interesting because of both whom they included and whom they did not include. For example, there were three Jews: Rosenau, Sachs, and Wolfson, but the militant Felix Frankfurter of the law school was conspicuously absent. As counterbalance, Lowell chose at least two representatives of his own position, Donham and Henderson (although the latter was too much the independent thinker and scientist to be just a presidential mouthpiece), and probably more—that is, Lee and Pennypacker. Also on the committee were men like Greenough, who had voted nay on both motions. For the most part, it represented both the different faculties and points of views within the university.[38]

Underneath the surface calm, dissatisfaction was widespread within the Harvard family; the June 5 overseers' meeting had been far from tranquil. In fact, according to both Jerome D. Greene and Judge Mack, the overseers had approved a broad interpretation of the committee's scope: an evaluation of Harvard's present and future educational obligations to the American people. Since the direction that any committee took was determined largely by its personnel, it was essential, Mack wrote to the president, that the committee reflect the thinking of the overseers. 39

Although some members of the committee were satisfactory—Samuel Williston, for example—the judge wanted the inclusion of such men as Felix Frankfurter and Dean Roscoe Pound of the law school or Dean David Linn Edsall of the medical school. Of all the Jewish faculty members, Mack told Lowell, Frankfurter would be the best possible choice. Not only did he have the legal training, but he was a Vienna-born German Jew who was well acquainted with eastern European Jews. he would be able to evaluate fairly the problem created in part by these Jewish applicants, whose numbers were increasing in the college, but whose fitness for a Harvard education was being called into question. Frankfurter was thus qualified to serve on the committee, and, most importantly, "he would go there as a Jew."40

On the other hand, appointee Paul J. Sachs was "far removed from the element" that was of particular concern to the inquiry. A member of the committee to raise $10 million in 1924, Sachs was connected with the German-Jewish elite in the United States. And while Harry Wolfson understood "all classes of Jewish students," he was "such a scholar pure and simple" that when he sought Mack's counsel, the judge advised him to decline the appointment. Although Mack was expressing his own opinions, he was also a Harvard spokesman for a number of prominent Jews: lawyer Louis Marshall, president of the American Jewish Committee; Supreme Court Justice Louis D. Brandeis; Judge Irving Lehman of New York; Julius Rosenwald of Sears, Roebuck; lawyer Joseph M. Proskauer of New York; Boston merchant Louis E. Kirstein; Cleveland clothing manufacturer Richard A. Feiss, '01 and LL.B. '03; author and college professor Horace M. Kallen; and writer and editor Walter Lippmann. Brandeis and Kallen, in particular, praised Mack's strong opposition to the imposition of a quota system. Moreover, Mack was authorized by a friend in the event that the corporation lacked sufficient funds to pay at least one-fourth of the cost of the investigation, provided that its total expense was not over $10,000. 41

Lowell was cool to the judge's proposal. He did not anticipate that the expenses of the investigation would be high. Dean Pound was unavailable since he was in Europe; and, as for Professor Frankfurter, Lowell did not believe him suitable for service on the committee. Frankfurter, like Brandeis in 1916, was not trustworthy:

> All the members of the Committee ought, if possible, to be persons in whom all Harvard men feel confidence, and you know that there are

> many people—including many on the Governing Boards of the Univer-
> sity—who have not that feeling towards Professor Frankfurter. Their
> sentiment may be unjust, but it is real; and the very fact that it exists
> would have an unfortunate effect. Many people with a high opinion of
> Professor Frankfurter's ability do not trust the solidity of his judgment.

True enough, Frankfurter had some critics on the governing boards, but
Mack did not surrender easily. Contacting Lowell again by letters and telegram, he pointed out the Dean Pound was returning from Europe in June and
reiterated his confidence in Frankfurter, which was shared by William Ernest
Hocking. [42]

Frankfurter himself was surprised to hear that Lowell regarded his views as
"violent and extreme," inasmuch as they had "never discussed this subject."
To this Lowell replied that he wanted an "open-minded" committee, but
Mack's insistent endorsement of the law professor made Frankfurter an advocate of the judge's views. Frankfurter countered that while Lowell might appoint to the committee Jews who passively held Mack's views, the president
was opposed to an active advocate. Lowell, he believed, was counting that
his three Jewish appointees would be no more than token representatives:
Sachs did not share Mack's views, Wolfson was "a naive bookish man," and
Rosenau would be abroad at the time that the committee defined its methods
and scope. [43]

On at least two occasions, Frankfurter accompanied Judge Mack and a
Jewish medical student on their visits to the president emeritus of Harvard.
As Eliot reported to Jerome Greene, Mack felt that Lowell was "disingenuous" in both word and deed and that those who voted for restrictive measures
on Jewish students at the recent faculty meetings were either " 'mentally con-
fused,' or in a foolish panic, or . . . 'disingenuous.' " For his part, Frankfurter
believed that Lowell was "not only disingenuous, but tricky, in discussion
and executive action." The young man "was so depressed about his own experiences as a Jew in the Harvard Medical School" that he said nothing, his
silence expressing "sadness and hopelessness." Discrimination against Jews
was also evident among alumni. About two weeks later, Mack wrote Eliot
that the Admissions Committee of the Harvard Club of Boston had asked
him to withdraw Harry Wolfson's name for nonresident membership, after
postponing the application twice and asking for letters from contemporaries. [44]

While Eliot had no intention of making public statements about the situation at Harvard, it was "a grave disappointment and astonishment" to him
that "so considerable a proportion of the Faculty of Arts and Sciences lost
their heads, even temporarily, on these fundamental questions in Harvard
policy." As for President Lowell, Eliot questioned whether he was in fact
"disingenuous"; sadly he described his successor as a man who was "reso-

lute," even tactless, in his pursuit of what he believed to be the truth, yet "ingenious, though abrupt, in justifying those decisions." Because Eliot was temperamentally so different from Lowell, he became the rallying point for all those opposing the latter's campaign to change Harvard's admission policy. Though staying in the background, Eliot, even at eighty-eight years of age, could not remain silent during the coming months. 45

Alumni, Undergraduate, and Public Reaction

In spite of efforts by Eliot, Mack, and others to keep the controversy from the public domain, the mere hint that Harvard was considering a new departure in admission policy was sufficient to arouse the Boston press, which generally catered to its readers' prejudices by labeling the university as undemocratic. And Lowell himself announced at commencement the appointment of the Committee on Methods of Sifting Candidates for Admission. Once the alumni got wind of the situation, they began to write letters to Eliot and Lowell. As might be expected, those who wrote the former president condemned the new developments, while many of those writing Lowell favored some limitation on Jews. The volume of correspondence was further swelled by the growing alumni awareness, in June 1922, that Harvard excluded Negro students from the freshman halls. The time lapse between May and June 1922, when these controversies became public, and March and April 1923, when Harvard reported its decisions in regard to the Jewish and Negro questions, contributed to both public rumors and private suspicions.

Student and alumni reactions as well as the newspaper reports of the controversy cast light on the depth of ethnic and racial prejudice in America of the 1920s. Jews might come to Harvard, but that did not mean they were accepted as equals by their WASP classmates. Since Lowell's actions had been motivated in some measure by alumni criticism of increasing Jewish enrollment, he was confident that this vocal opposition represented the majority opinion. Eliot, for his part, hoped that the contrary was true. Although he declined to write an article explaining Harvard's admission policy for the *Harvard Graduates' Magazine*, Eliot spoke briefly to a meeting of the Associated Harvard Clubs in Sanders Theatre on June 16, 1922. When President Clarence C. Little of the University of Maine, former secretary to the Harvard Corporation, demanded that Harvard disavow any intended discrimination in admissions, Eliot strode forward, usurping the stage from President Lowell, to head off "a row in the meeting over the Jewish question." Unfavorable publicity must be avoided, Eliot believed, while Lowell and the investigating committee were being persuaded that "a decided majority of the Alumni and of the students [were] strongly opposed to any such departure from the traditional policy of Harvard College." The best vehicle of alumni opinion would be editorials and letters in the *Harvard Graduates' Magazine* or the *Harvard*

Alumni Bulletin. Strong statements against racial quotas would be fairly and widely publicized by the newspapers. While the alumni made its influence felt in this way, Eliot, Frankfurter, and Judge Mack would quietly confer with the members of the investigating committee. [46]

But the debate could not be kept within the Harvard family. The first anonymous leak to the press came on May 31 in the *Boston Post*, whose headline blared: "Jewish Ban Is Opposed at Harvard," followed by "Leaders of Student Body Organized to Fight Propaganda Started Outside Ranks of University—Believe in Equal Opportunity" and by "Some Think Agitation Is Scheme Fostered by Henry Ford." Without this scoop by an energetic reporter, William A. Coblenz, the whole matter might have been settled quietly within the university. But soon other Boston and the New York papers took up the hue and cry. [47]

To explain Jewish student reaction and correct any misrepresentations, however, Harry Starr '21, president of the Harvard Menorah Society, the major Jewish organization on campus, wrote an article entitled "The Affair at Harvard, What the Students Did," for the *Menorah Journal.* As good Harvard men, Jews were indignant over sensationalist newspaper accounts, such as the *Boston American* report of June 3, 1922, that Jewish students had named Professor Roger B. Merriman (history) and Professor Richard C. Cabot (clinical medicine and social ethics) as being President Lowell's appointed "anti-Jew drive leaders." And Jewish undergraduates were dismayed by the June 5 *Harvard Crimson*, which included an unofficial letter from one of its subeditors, Charlton MacVeagh '24, who blamed the *Boston American*'s outburst against discrimination at Harvard entirely on false statements allegedly supplied by Jewish students. MacVeagh branded them as cowards, examples of the "objectionable qualities" shown by Jews--"slandering an innocent person behind his back and then running away." [48]

This invective evoked from a number of Jewish students—among them Harry Starr—strong denials of any complicity with leaks to the press. He pointed out the rather obvious fact that the stories were usually pasted together from several sources and embellished by vivid reportorial imaginations. While some reporters were genuinely concerned with helping Jews, others were merely interested in making good copy by attacking Harvard. On the whole, Starr felt that MacVeagh spoke for only a minority of the Gentile students. [49]

In actuality, student concern over anti-Semitism on campus had predated the faculty debates of May and early June. David Stoffer, chairman of the Jewish War Relief Drive, was told by a prominent Gentile undergraduate that there was "a growing prejudice against the Jew in the University." Stoffer talked with Starr, and together with three representatives of Jewish social organizations—Zeta Beta Tau and Sigma Alpha Mu fraternities and the Argo Club—they conferred with their faculty advisers, Professor Wolfson and Dr.

Sheffer. The Jewish students then attended an informal conference held April 12 at the *Harvard Crimson* building. There they met with campus leaders: R. R. Higgins, football player and student council member; J. Corliss Lamont, a *Harvard Crimson* editor, "whose father [was] renowned among America's financiers for his economic liberalism, and who himself represented the best type of fresh American boyhood, combined with much Yankee 'horse sense'"; and B. Del Nash, secretary to the editorial board of the *Harvard Lampoon*. Also present was a faculty member and prominent Bostonian, "who, in that manner peculiar to New England, reveres the democratic ideal while not relaxing his faith in the destiny of his own kind." Yet the Jewish students confronted misconceptions and stereotypes. For instance, a Jew was considered as a Jew when trying out for the athletic teams and other extra-curricular activities. Allegedly, they were treated fairly. Indeed, Jews captained three sports. And though they were excluded from social clubs, so were many Christians. 50

After the meeting ended, the Jewish committee talked with Dean Greenough, who supported their fact-finding endeavors, but told them of his difficulties in counteracting undergraduate anti-Semitism. It was not a question of particular Jews, wrote Starr:

> we learned that it was *numbers* that mattered; bad or good, *too many* Jews were not liked. Rich or poor, brilliant or dull, polished or crude— *too many Jews*, the fear of a new Jerusalem at Harvard, the 'City College' fear.

Because of such feelings, the second conference, on May 8, came to an impasse. 51

On hearing of the faculty discussions in regard to limitation, the committee again went to Dean Greenough and insisted that "the vast majority of self-respecting Jews stood on their absolute right to be at Harvard." They considered themselves first and foremost "Americans." On the advice of Professor Wolfson, the five Jewish students wrote a strongly stated letter to the dean just before the May 16 faculty meeting, rejecting either general limitation or categorization of some Jews as "undesirable." While unable to estimate the letter's effect on the faculty as a whole, they did meet with several members and were especially appreciative of Professor Lyon (he had voted against the two racially discriminatory motions of May 23 and June 2), whose "logical forceful arguments" persuaded others against limitation. And they expected that the recently appointed Committee on Methods of Sifting Candidates for Admission would pursue its investigations impartially. 52

The other side of the undergraduate story was revealed by student answers to Dr. Richard C. Cabot's social ethics examination.

> Discuss as fairly as you can this question: For the good of *all* persons con-
> cerned, is a college ever ethically justified in limiting to a certain percent-
> age the number of any particular race who are admitted to the freshman
> class each year?

Of the eighty-three upperclassmen responding, thirty-four opposed restriction, seven of whom were Jewish; forty-one justified "a policy of race-
limitation under certain circumstances"; and eight were undecided, including one Jew. Although agreeing that Harvard was a private institution with a
public role, the restrictionists were convinced that it should maintain a racial
balance. Since Harvard had been founded by Anglo-Saxons, they shuddered
at the possibility that it would graduate so many Jewish alumni that control
of the university would pass into their hands. The purpose of a college education, moreover, was to train future leaders: Jews were generally deficient, the
restrictionists believed, in those traits of character and personality that were
part of leadership. While many Jews were able scholars, others were mere
grinds, who "memorize their books!"[53]

Some distinguished between the exceptional Jewish students, who were
truly cosmopolitan like the Chinese, and the less gifted, but "arrogantly objectionable" Jews. Others, however, would extend the principle behind Oriental exclusion not only to Jews, but also to Irish, "or what amounts to the
same thing, the Catholics." One student wished that Jews would follow the
example of Catholics, who "long ago saw the folly of forcing themselves on
the American college, and built institutions of their own," or Negroes, who
also attended their own colleges. While antirestrictionists agreed that undesirable individuals should be excluded, they objected when universities told
"a Cohen, whose average on the college board examinations was a 90, that he
cannot enter because there are too many Jews already, while a grade of 68 will
pass a Murphy, or one of 62 a Morgan."[54]

The implication that Harvard was an institution for rich men's sons, but
not for poor immigrant boys, was also part of a long-standing town-and-
gown conflict. Consequently, Harvard and Lowell had to endure criticisms
from the press, politicians, and labor leaders. The Boston *Telegram* entitled
its June 6 editorial "Down Hill from Harvard to Lowell." The day before, the
Telegram headline read "Harvard to Limit Number of Its Irish." According to
an unnamed "Harvard man," the Irish were "the real problem at Harvard,"
because they shouldered aside the preparatory school boys to be elected team
captain. The university had had an "Irish problem" for some time, but during
his administration Charles W. Eliot had defended them for "deep in his heart
he thought the Irish added a lot to college life." One disgruntled prep school
graduate complained of "the air of a public school" at Harvard and of the difficulty in knowing "just who he can pick up with."[55]

This threat to the Irish as well as to other immigrant groups provided ammunition for Boston's Mayor James Michael Curley, speaking at the annual banquet of the Bunker Hill Council, Knights of Columbus:

> These people seek to bar men because of an accident of birth. . . .
>
> God gave them their parents and their race, as he has given me mine. All of us under the Constitution are guaranteed equality, without regard to race, creed or color. When Harvard loses sight of that fundamental we, who are not yet discriminated against, should assist those who are [in] obtaining their equal rights as guaranteed them as American citizens.
>
> If the Jew is barred today, the Italian will be to-morrow, then the Spaniard and Pole, and at some future date the Irish.

As a man of immigrant Irish parents, Curley spoke on behalf of all immigrant groups who might be excluded from a Harvard education by the WASP elite.[56]

In June, two state representatives introduced motions calling for an investigation of Harvard. George Pearl Webster of Boxford proposed that during the General Court's recess a joint special committee of the Senate and House inquire into "the alleged or proposed discrimination against persons of the Jewish race existing or recommended in respect to the matriculation of students in Harvard University." In order that applicants of "all races and nationalities may have equal rights and opportunities for admission," the committee should make recommendations and any necessary changes in the law and the state constitution. Acting at the request of the *Telegram*, Stephen C. Sullivan of Ward 1, East Boston, presented an order to consider "the necessity or desirability of permitting Harvard, should its plans to become a private and restricted institution be consummated, to enjoy exemption from taxation upon its realty and holdings." Although Harvard was within its legal rights to change admission policies, President Lowell certainly did not want a confrontation with a hostile legislature, especially since the university's tax-exempt status had always meant a higher tax rate for Cambridge property owners. On June 3, Lowell had personally explained to House Speaker B. Loring Young the faculty vote on the appointment of the Committee on Methods of Sifting Candidates for Admission. Harvard was not without allies on Beacon Hill: More than 150 Harvard graduates sat in the state legislature, including Speaker Young. No formal investigation followed. If this adverse publicity were not enough, Lowell received a resolution from Samuel Gompers, president of the American Federation of Labor, opposing Harvard's alleged religious discrimination in admissions.[57]

Jews, of course, spoke eloquently against restrictive admissions as in the well-publicized correspondence in June between Alfred A. Benesch '00, a Cleveland attorney, and President Lowell. Benesch, head of the local branch of B'nai B'rith's Anti-Defamation League, argued that scholarship and character should be the only tests for admission and pointed out that many Jews, himself included, had contributed generously to Harvard. Lowell replied with his standard arguments about the growth of anti-Semitic feeling in the country and maintained that there was "perhaps no body of men in the United States, mostly Gentiles, with so little anti-Semitic feeling as the instructing staff of Harvard University." But he insisted that the only alternative to the creation of ethnically separate universities was the controlled mixing of Gentiles and Jews within each university. Benesch countered, however, that the strong feeling of Jewishness was "the result rather than the cause" of Anti-Semitism. A university, he said, should try to lessen this antipathy by means other than exclusion. He urged Lowell to call a conference of Jewish graduates, other concerned graduates and undergraduates, and members of the corporation. [58]

As chairman of the first subcommittee, which was to confer with representative Jews, Paul J. Sachs counseled "patience and extreme self-restraint, and, above all, no further outbursts in the public press" in his conversations with Julius Rosenwald, Louis Marshall, and Judges Lehman and Mack. Sach's urged that the committee of thirteen "high-minded men" be given "a chance, with a full realization that they earnestly desire to cooperate, in the real sense of the word, with the leading Jews of the country." [59]

While avoiding public controversy, a number of Jewish alumni voiced their concern to President Emeritus Eliot. Jesse Isidor Straus, one of the "Jewish Grand Dukes" and a leading retailer with three generations of Harvard connections (his father had served on one of the visiting committees), had heard that "the catastrophe" was caused by the increase in the number of Jewish commuters from East Boston. As he confided to Eliot, "there might have been found some less obnoxious method of discriminating against *them*." Straus had thought that anti-Semitism was waning in the United States until the recent outbursts of Henry Ford and the Ku Klux Klan and "the anti-Semitic storm" at Harvard. Neither he nor his son, who graduated in 1921, experienced prejudice during their undergraduate years; his younger son would enter Harvard the following autumn. But "his pride in Harvard was shocked" by these developments; and he shared "the conviction with many with whom I have discussed the matter, that in your day, no such thing could have transpired." [60]

Straus did not feel that Jews should take "any formal steps as Jews." He was very cool to Zionism and saw Jews only as members of "a religious sect." He hoped, however, that suspicion and rumor could be dispelled by "stating what the Protestants (for it appears to be largely they who are fomenting any anti-Semitic feeling) would have Americans of Jewish religion do." Since assimilation involved more than the Jews—other immigrant groups as well as such foreign students as Chinese, Japanese, Indian, and "Near Eastern-European"—the faculty investigating committee should endeavor to handle the problem without discriminating against any particular religious group. Then the faculty would have to decide how many of these could be educated "without affecting the traditional American atmosphere of the college."[61]

Another prominent Jew who agreed that the more recent immigrants, not just Jews, should be limited in the interests of assimilation was Dr. Felix Adler, founder and philosopher of the Ethical Culture movement. Speaking to the Boston Ethical Culture Society on the "Persistence of Prejudice," the Columbia University professor said that race prejudice was fostered by differences in religion and standards and by economic competition. The major conflict within the colleges was "between Anglo-Saxon standards and traditions and those of recent immigrants." Consequently, immigrants residing in the United States less than ten years should not be allowed to concentrate in only a few colleges. Adler thus believed that the best of other races "should be grafted" upon Anglo-Saxon traditions, rather than creating a truly pluralistic culture within American universities.[62]

Fear of the consequences of discrimination united Jewish opinion. Well-educated upper-class Jews might acquiesce, perhaps unwillingly and guiltily, in a restriction on the less couth applicants of immigrant stock, be they Catholic, Protestant, or Jewish. And perhaps these Jews sensed that some concession was necessary, given the increasing anti-Semitism of the past quarter century. But the thought that Harvard might discriminate against all Jews must have hurt, since that university, among all others, had been a special symbol. It had stood for liberalism, cosmopolitanism, and opportunity.

There was as much, if not more, diversity of opinion over restrictive admissions among non-Jews. One graduate, with alumni connections dating back to colonial times, wrote President Lowell that all immigrants "must be amalgamated into good Americans." Harvard, where he had first met Jews—"some of the finest men"—should "encourage" them to attend. On the other hand, a Brooklyn attorney expressed full support for Lowell's views; he had had some unpleasant encounters with Jews or they with him: "We Americans, (and my great grandfather was a Revolutionary soldier) are not prejudiced against the Jew on account of his race or religion, but that the prejudice is against his practices in business and in social life." Apparently, one Jewish businessman had bragged to him that "within five years they would own the City of New York," which was already "in entire control of a combination of Jews and foreigners that we cannot possibly dislodge." The same frustration and resentment was voiced by another New Yorker who feared that his children, "taught to be good rather than clever," could not "compete with the new element." Recalling the comment of Will Rogers on election night—"the Republicans in Texas have about the same amount of prestige as the Gentiles have in New York City"—he decided to "go West" with his family. President Lowell tried to reassure the disgruntled father by telling him that "the Americans" could "compete with the Hebrews. . . . and win when they choose to do so; but a great part of our American boys from well-to-do families are brought up to believe that in their early years they should not work hard, but play rather than labor." In pointing out that some of the native-born were lazy in comparison with many of immigrant stock, Lowell unwittingly echoed one of President Emeritus Eliot's arguments for continued immigration. 63

While the debate at Harvard did not capture abroad anywhere near the level of attention commanded by the Sacco and Vanzetti case, the few foreign comments were significant. A graduate of both the college and the law school who was connected with Nan Kai College in Tientsin, China, sent Lowell a clipping from the August 15, 1922, *North China Star*, the local American newspaper. Drawing on the Chung Mei Foreign Service and the New York *World*, the article described in detail the functions of the investigating committee. "Articles like this will deter our Chinese students from coming to Harvard," he wrote Lowell, "and also make them feel that democracy is a failure in America." Harvard stood for educational opportunity and Yankee hospitality to many Chinese, but a restriction on Jews might well be extended to other groups, especially to Orientals. 64

By the early autumn of 1922, Lowell was beginning to solidify alumni opposition to his discriminatory policies. In September, the columnist contributing "From a Graduate's Window" to the *Harvard Graduates' Magazine* argued that the addition of racial and religious requirements as tests for admission would have "mischievous results." Since scholarship alone was an inadequate method of weeding out the "undesirables," the application of tests of "character, personality, and general mental ability" would be justifiable. But if Jews met these tests as well as the academic one, they should be admitted, no matter what the percentage. While the writer did not think that any racial group would have proportionally a larger number in the college than it had in the country as a whole, if such a group did prove itself worthy, "so abundantly as to acquire of right a dominating representation in Harvard University, that right must be accorded to it." 65

The Negro Question

During the same month, Lowell received a petition signed by 143 alumni opposing the exclusion of black students from the freshman halls. News of it had already been leaked to the New York newspapers in June. This "Memorial" to the corporation, with an accompanying letter, was sponsored by a committee of seven: William Channing Gannett '60; Moorfield Storey '66, president of the NAACP; Charles C. Burlingham '79; Alfred Jaretzki '81; John Reynolds '07; Edward Eyre Hunt '10; and Robert C. Benchley '12. The sponsors urged the administration to desist from its "Jim Crow policy" and return to "the Alma Mater of Channing, of John Quincy Adams, of Sumner, of Robert Gould Shaw of the 54th Massachusetts Infantry . . . the tradition of Harvard liberalism, tolerance, and justice." Since the freshman halls were spacious enough to accommodate black students without antagonizing southerners, the latter should be required to conform to Harvard's customs in regard to Negroes—attending the same lecture halls, eating in the same dining room, albeit at separate tables, and sleeping in the same dormitory, although in different rooms. 66

In addition to the committee, there were 136 other signers, whose classes ranged from 1850 to 1920. Among them were Francis G. Peabody '69, James Loeb '88, Herbert Croly '90, Oswald Garrison Villard '93, Heywood Broun '08, Samuel Eliot Morison '08, C. C. Little '10, and Walter Lippmann '10. Some of the signers had also opposed discrimination against Jews: Broun, Lippmann, Little, and Loeb. While the committee had not intended to link the Jewish and Negro questions (they apologized for the leak to the press), the connection was inescapably there. 67

Lowell tried to present the discriminatory policy instituted by the corporation in 1914 as *"un fait accompli,"* in the words of Professor Albert Bushnell Hart. But the alumni were not appeased by Lowell's offer to meet with the committee nor with his discussion of the matter at the annual dinner of the New York City Harvard Club. The Negro question actually generated more response and perhaps a more sympathetic one than the Jewish question. There was, of course, the difference in numbers. 68

As Professor Hart wrote to Lowell: "You have heard me in the Faculty express the conviction that something ought to be done in the case of the Jews, because they were becoming so numerous and are so strongly and aggressively united." But the same argument did not apply to the few Negro students at Harvard, who were "not likely to be numerous, simply because the number of colored boys whose parents can find the money to send their sons to Harvard is limited." A handful of blacks in each class could hardly be considered a threat; but Jews constituted over 20 percent of the class of 1925. Also the type of discrimination applied to the blacks differed from that proposed against the Jews. Once admitted, blacks were a small enough group to be segregated or ignored. Another reason for stronger alumni opposition to discrimination against black students lay in the fact that there was no organized, official group within the university speaking on their behalf. In contrast, the university had already responded, in part, to the protests of those opposing a restriction on Jews by creating the investigating committee. Whereas most alumni were willing to leave the decision regarding the Jewish question to the committee, many felt that they must speak out against exclusion of the blacks from the freshman halls. Some signed the petition; others wrote letters to President Lowell, the *Harvard Alumni Bulletin*, or one of several magazines and newspapers. As Lowell ruefully acknowledged: "The flare-up of such men as Villard and Storey did frighten the alumni. . . . there was a great outcry on the part—among others—of alumni, and the press was hot with denunciations of me from one end of the country to the other." 69

The proponents as well as opponents of discrimination came from all sections of the country, North as well as South. For example, a Connecticut alumnus '01, who returned to Cambridge for the Harvard-Yale game expressed shock at the number of "Kikes" in the Yard. His hostility mounted as he saw "two Jews and a negro, fraternizing." He was particularly aggrieved that Jews could not be barred by raising academic qualifications,

> whereas by the same process of raising the standard "white" boys ARE eliminated. And is this to go on? Why the Psychology Test if not to bar those not wanted? Are the Overseers so lacking in genius that they can't devise a way to bring Harvard back to the position it always held as a "white man's" college? Does the possible flare-up of such men as Villard and Storey frighten them? Why not come out into the open and take the "gaff" of criticism for a year or so and save our University for our sons, grandsons and for our posterity?

The writer believed that his New England parentage and attendance at Harvard gave him a proprietary interest in the university; now he threatened to send his son elsewhere. Letters of this sort, however, were few in number. 70

As was to be expected in these years, most southerners opposed any form of social equality between the races. From Beaufort, North Carolina, the Reverend George W. Lay, D.C.L., who had been educated at St. Paul's School in New Hampshire and at Yale '82, argued that northern colleges must respect the race feelings of southern whites if they wanted to attract students from that region. A white southerner who acted as the social equal of a Negro would lose his influence in the South; consequently the social barrier was never to be crossed. A former Mississippian '98 began his letter by quoting a clause from his will, which bequeathed to Harvard an amount up to $50,000 to become "a Scholarship Fund for the education of native born boys from the States that seceded from the Union." If Negroes roomed with white men in the freshman halls, intermarriage between white women and blacks would follow, he believed, because "social equality—marriageability, if you will—is implied in sharing 'bed and board' with another." Eating at a separate table in a public restaurant was "allowable, but to—well, 'sleep with a nigger'—is a horse of another color." Though more restrained in his language, a Chicago alumnus sent a similar message: Any social contact that implied equality between the races was or should be forbidden, and Negroes who sought such equality had overstepped their place. 71

Yet there were also thoughtful comments from many born in the South. Georgia-born George Foster Peabody, honorary A.M. '03, argued against exclusion on political, religious, and scientific grounds. The democratic principle was at stake, he declared, if blacks were excluded solely on the basis of race. Furthermore, both Christianity and "the most advanced scientific theory of the origin of man would seem to agree as to their being one original derivation of the human species." Another southerner, James C. Manry '14, also dissented from the exclusion policy. He had taught at Ewing Christian College in Allahabad, India, and had done a year's relief work for the Polish universities, during which he had endeavored to abolish racial discrimination. Having had his own eyes opened by his undergraduate experience at Harvard, where he made friends with a Negro, this alumnus felt it would be best if it were "understood that Harvard proposes to force negroes and white men to live in the same building and eat at the same table."[72]

One northern opponent of exclusion who did not sign the petition was Hamilton Fish, Jr., '10, former Crimson football captain and Republican congressman from New York. The grandson of President Ulysses S. Grant's secretary of state, he had also served in France during World War I as captain of colored infantry (15th New York Volunteers, which became 369th Regiment Infantry). In his letter, which was given to the newspapers, he attacked the Jim Crow dormitory policy: "Harvard is not a private school, but a great National University with its gates wide open to all who can comply with the entrance requirements, based on scholarship, not on race, color, or creed." There were, of course, several other critical letters, both published and unpublished. According to Edward S. Drown '84 of the Episcopal Theological School, the issue was clear: Harvard must affirm "the principle of equal rights" for all students and reject "a narrow and partisan concept of social status."[73]

Dr. Louis T. Wright, a graduate of Harvard Medical School in 1915 and the first black to be appointed to the staff of a New York City hospital (Harlem Hospital), added his protest. He remembered that in conversation with black students, Lowell had "always stressed the point that they were so few in number that should discrimination occur their rights could not be considered." Often Lowell laid himself open to misinterpretation by the blunt and tactless way in which he expressed himself. He probably said that black students should expect to encounter discrimination at Harvard, a true, yet unconsoling observation about life in the North as well as in the South.[74]

But his policy of excluding blacks from the freshman halls could not be explained simply as a misunderstanding. Lowell acted primarily because his point of view was expedient—southern whites were more valuable to Harvard than blacks—and, secondarily, because he probably thought he was "protecting" black freshmen. "The Civil War is on again," wrote an aroused alumnus, George L. Paine '96, a student pastor. He then proceeded to "fire ten shots on the side of those fighting for justice and brotherhood." Two of his shots were aimed at the small number of students, black and white, who were the subjects of this controversy: Of the forty-two blacks in the university, seventeen were in the college and twenty-five more in the graduate schools, but only one was a freshman; there were only sixty-seven students from ten southern states. Of the black students in the college, ten resided in campus dormitories: seven in Weld, two in Perkins, "and one, if you please, in Claverly on the 'Gold Coast.'" Twenty-two others were in private houses, and ten lived outside Cambridge. There was no record that any white students moved out of the integrated dormitories.[75]

George Paine thought that "an extraordinary proportion" of Negroes had made their mark intellectually and athletically in terms of their numbers. At the June 1922 commencement a white senior from Atlanta, Georgia, delivered the Latin and class orations, while a black resident graduate in the divinity school who later became president of Howard University, Mordecai W. Johnson, addressed the audience on "The Present Condition of the Negroes in the United States."[76]

A majority of the alumni agreed that Lowell's policy of excluding blacks from the freshman halls was wrong, judging from editorials in both the *Harvard Graduates' Magazine* and the *Harvard Alumni Bulletin* and the volume of letters to the editor of the *Bulletin*. "From a Graduate's Window" regretted the stand taken by President Lowell and praised the willingness of white athletes to participate with a black athlete: "to work with him, play with him, strip with him, go to the showers with him." Invoking the memory of Robert Gould Shaw, the *Bulletin* argued that "for Harvard to deny to colored men a privilege" accorded to white students appeared "inevitably as reversal of policy if not as positive disloyalty to a principle for which the University has hitherto taken an open and unshaken stand." From mid-January to mid-March 1923, almost sixty alumni wrote letters to its editor. Of this number, approximately two-thirds rejected the policy of racial exclusion, while somewhat under a third supported Lowell's stand; the remainder were either suspending judgment until all the facts were known or favored some form of discrimination—toward Jews, but not toward black freshmen. It was against this background of swelling alumni protest that the corporation would have to reconsider its decision in regard to the freshman halls. And this decision would be influenced, at least in part, by the work of the Committee on Methods of Sifting Candidates for Admission. Harvard's traditional liberalism was on trial. The country, as well as alumni, faculty, and students, awaited the verdicts.[77]

·4·

HARVARD: METHODS OF SIFTING CANDIDATES FOR ADMISSION, 1920S TO 1950S

> With regard to the Jew as a Harvard student, the following facts may be culled from the statistics. He is, on the average, a better scholar than the Gentile. In morals, he seems to be more prone to dishonesty and sexual offenses, but much less addicted to intemperance. About a third of the Hebrews are non-residents. In social club life, there has come to be almost complete separation of Jew and Gentile. In athletics, on the other hand, there is commingling, with the Jews in fair and increasing representation. Further meeting-ground—aside from lectures and other exercises—is offered by debates, music and dramatics.
>
> Letter accompanying the report to
> President A. Lawrence Lowell,
> April 7, 1923[1]

The "Report of the Committee on Methods of Sifting Candidates for Admission" affirmed that Jewish students contributed to the academic life of Harvard College and participated in extracurricular activities to the extent that their Gentile classmates permitted them to do so. Where individual merit was the test of acceptance, as, for example, in athletics, debating, music, and dramatics, Jews made successful entry. But the same was not true of social life, where many Gentile students, like their elders, chose and generally valued their companions on the basis of family background and future social connections. That Jewish students did participate in college activities, despite their large percentage among commuters, disproved one of President Lowell's major arguments—that they did not assimilate into the life of the college.

This finding raised several interesting questions: What did Lowell mean by assimilation? Did he truly think that Jews would not assimilate or did he fear that they would displace the native-born Protestants by assimilating too much? At his most extreme, Lowell virtually demanded as the price of admission to Harvard that Jewish students "be overcome with an oblivion of the fact that they were Jews." In opposition, Harry Wolfson argued that those Gentiles who denied Jews the right to be themselves—to be seen walking together in the College Yard—were as much a cause of anti-Semitism as Jewish students allegedly were. If one views the problem of assimilation from another perspective, however, an educational institution must consider whether its service to the large majority of students would be impaired by granting freedom of opportunity to a controversial, possibly troublesome, minority. Such a balancing of interests would be necessary in situations in which groups of people were mutually antagonistic. Even outright restriction might be justifiable in regard to such politically disruptive groups as Nazis and neofascists. But Harvard's Committee on Methods rejected any quota on Jewish students, because their presence on campus contributed to, and did not detract from, the educational experience of all students in the university. When Lowell finally realized the committee's report would go against him, he expediently accepted the decision. Shortly thereafter, he began to argue that Harvard could educate effectively only a fixed number of undergraduates and that consequently the size of the freshman class should be limited to 1,000 students.[2]

Investigation by the Committee on Methods

The Committee on Methods had commenced its work in the summer of 1922. At its own organizational meetings on June 21, the thirteen members were assigned to four subcommittees, each with specific functions. The first subcommittee, under the chairmanship of Paul J. Sachs, included Professors Henderson, Rosenau, and Wolfson and was to correspond or meet with Jewish alumni and prominent Jewish citizens. The second, directed by Deans Greenough (chairman), Donham, and Holmes, was to gather statistics about Jewish students within the university. The third, with Pennypacker (chairman), Clifford, and Grandgent, was to contact other colleges and universities to learn if they confronted a similar Jewish problem and, if so, how it was being handled; it also was to sound out various headmasters on the advisability of admitting top secondary school students without entrance examinations. Meanwhile, the fourth subcommittee, chaired by Lyman and assisted by Lee and Williston, was to sample undergraduate opinion during the coming fall semester.[3]

Chairman Charles H. Grandgent defined the committee's major problem as one of "determining whether or not the recourse of Jewish students to the University should be limited." Dean Wallace B. Donham, for his part, divided Jews into "two radically divergent groups," those wanting "complete assimilation" and those insisting on their separate identity within the community and the university. He felt that a large group of the latter within Harvard would lead to "very serious racial antagonism." Convinced that "maximum service to the nation" was of most importance, Donham thought that the committee would have to broaden its investigation to "the whole problem of racial groupings in the University and the entire question of sifting candidates for admission." Contrary to Judge Mack's initial expectation, Harry Wolfson argued forcefully that "a distinction should be drawn between a real problem involving fundamental conflict of interests between racial groups and a problem . . . arising solely from the existence of race antagonism." Neither he nor Paul J. Sachs favored "the development of a distinctive Jewish group" within Harvard, although Wolfson wanted to promote "among Jewish students a more accurate and more intelligent understanding of things Jewish." He also urged that the first subcommittee authorize a survey of the social background of both Jewish students and the communities from which they came, because "rich and prominent Jews" were not representative of "the feelings and ambitions of the mass of the Jewish population." After all, the voting power of these Jews, by far more numerous, might elect unfriendly candidates to the legislature or to the governorship who could pass legislation hostile to the university.[4]

None of the three Jewish members would accept the adoption of any form of quota system as a solution. The committee in general opposed adoption of a percentage limitation on Jews, but some members would reluctantly consent to one "as a last resort." In keeping with the vote of the majority of the faculty, which had turned down Lowell's proposal for a quota in early June, the committee's task would be to decide whether there was a Jewish problem and, if there was, to determine what means, short of a quota, should be used to handle it.[5]

At their second organizational meeting, on the evening of June 21, the committee agreed to inquire extensively into the numbers and achievements of Jewish students at Harvard. The work of culling the relevant data from student records would be supervised by a statistician. It then adjourned until October 2, when it held its first meeting of the academic year. From that date to the final meeting of March 29, 1923, the committee met seventeen times, almost on a weekly basis during the last three months.[6]

While not imposing his personal views on the Committee on Methods, President Emeritus Charles W. Eliot visited Chairman Grandgent in July 1922 and subsequently wrote him several letters arguing against either a restriction on the admission of Jewish students or any limitation of enrollment. According to certain statistics that Eliot sent Grandgent in August, Harvard's capacity to educate students had grown with, if not exceeded, the increased enrollment over the past two decades. In November, Eliot related to Grandgent several complaints and reactions that he had received concerning the work of the committee and its subcommittees.[7]

From one or more of his inside sources—Dr. Milton J. Rosenau, Professor

Felix Frankfurter, and Overseers Jerome D. Greene and Julian W. Mack—
Eliot had heard that the committee's report was being delayed by personal
incompetency and faulty research methods used in the gathering of statistics. But most interestingly, he learned that undergraduates expressed a wide
difference of opinion on "the right means of excluding undesirable Jews."
Probably "the better sort of college undergraduate," Eliot wrote Grandgent,
objected to the assignment of rooms "through a student committee . . . instructed to segregate Jews, and to some extent Irishmen, in certain dormitories." They preferred assignments to be made by lot.[8]

In February, Eliot was pleased to hear of the committee's unanimous opposition to racial discrimination against candidates for admission. On the one
hand, he did not object to questions on the Harvard application form about
the "genealogy, history, and background" of the candidate and his parents.
On the other, he was suspicious of proposals for "an oral, unrecorded, personal interview"; the "closing of the back road" to transfers from neighboring colleges; "easier terms" of admission for candidates living outside New
England and the Middle Atlantic states; and use of psychological tests. If re-
jections increased under any new admission test, he insisted on the publication of their "distribution . . . geographically and genealogically" in the next
departmental reports to the president.[9]

Eliot also opposed "admission on certificate," believing its adoption would
undermine Harvard's long effort to persuade secondary schools to raise their
standards. (Most American colleges admitted without examination students
with acceptable certificates from approved secondary schools.) In response,
Professor Grandgent maintained that the committee was not considering the
usual "certificate method," but one that would offer admission to seniors
standing in the "highest seventh" or top 15 percent of their class. Ultimately,
Eliot lost out because the plan received substantial support from both the
committee on methods (with the exceptions of Dr. Rosenau and Henry Pennypacker) and the schoolmasters.[10]

As important proposals came up in the committee, Dr. Rosenau turned to
Eliot for advice, especially with respect to changes in admissions policy.
Rosenau's principal adviser, however, was Felix Frankfurter, because Judge
Mack had urged him to confer "right along" with the law professor. "In case
of doubt in your mind," said Mack, "accept his judgment," which was "invariably excellent." Frankfurter thus served—unofficially, of course—as the
fourteenth member and fourth Jew on the committee. With the counsel of
Frankfurter and several others [Louis E. Kirstein (whom Eliot described as
"the leading Jew in Boston"), Alfred Cohn, and David A. Ellis], Rosenau
drafted a "memorandum of proposals," which was presented to the committee on February 2, 1923. It reaffirmed the "traditional ideals of Harvard," the
university's "adherence to the policy of the open door," and "equal opportunity and academic freedom." Admission requirements, said Rosenau, should
rest on the "two basic principles" of "scholarship [and] character."[11]

He subsequently moved that the committee present a short report that simply stated its unanimous decision against racial and religious discrimination. Although the committee believed that a more comprehensive report was needed and decisively turned down his motion, Rosenau acquiesced in its final vote. The committee could then "present a united front" to the faculty and governing boards. He thought the report "would satisfy fair-minded persons," yet confided to Eliot his belief that Lowell and the Committee on Admission to Harvard College would "exclude Jews all the same." Eliot did not think that could happen; "Chester Greenough would prevent it, if tried."12

Of the thirteen members of the committee, Professors Lawrence J. Henderson and Roger I. Lee and Dean Donham came closest to favoring an outright restriction on the admission of Jewish candidates. Consequently, Jews, both on the committee and within the larger Harvard family, sought to impress their point of view upon these three. For example, in August 1922, Judge Mack and Professor Sachs had a three-hour meeting with Professor Henderson, who, noting the substantial increase in Jewish students over the past twenty years, commented on the "very objectionable and morally inferior" conduct and manners of many of "the new Russian or Polish Jewish element." Their character defects, which required policing in the chemistry department, were caused, he thought, by the parental ghetto environment. Although two Russian Jews were admittedly his best students, Henderson maintained that many others were the poorest of his ninety. In explaining their qualitative difference, he argued that since a higher proportion of Jews attended college than Gentiles, "it was but natural that the Jewish cream should be, on the whole, weaker as it was more diluted than the non-Jewish, unless it were true, —and he did not believe it,—that the Jews as a race were intellectually superior to other races."13

To counter such arguments, Felix Frankfurter enlisted the support of Walter Lippmann, a most influential alumnus. Lippmann met with Henderson on October 25, 1922, and tried to discuss the issues. He "lost his temper," however, when Henderson initially favored higher intellectual standards but then suggested a loophole for future "business and social leaders" who could not pass the hardest examinations. Lippmann acknowledged that the increasing concentration of Jewish students at Harvard, especially from immigrant families, had created "a conflict of manners and appearances." The solution, he believed, was not to exclude and segregate Jews, but to encourage them to develop new social habits through contact with a "more catholic environment." Before acting, the committee on methods should master the facts and assess the probable results of various kinds of tests. Raising the passing grade on entrance examinations "would be a form of selection wholly without offence to the Jewish people." But "every administrative device" adopted would become "as a result of Harvard's dominant intellectual position a pattern for the country."14

Although Henderson did not change his mind, other Harvard men were

well aware that any questionable innovations in the college admission policies would soon attract the spotlight of national attention. They, too, applied
pressure on Lowell and his administration. In January 1923, Jerome D.
Greene declared that if Lowell did not voluntarily convene a special meeting
of the overseers, he would seek to do so, acting as chairman of the executive
committee of the board. But the president avoided a confrontation by sailing
for Europe. His purpose was to invite two English tutors from either Oxford
or Cambridge to Harvard for a semester to explain their new tutorial system.
At the same time, two Harvard tutors went to England to observe the system
firsthand. Before Lowell left, however, the corporation met on January 22 to
reconsider the Negro question. It had supported the policy of exclusion during two previous discussions; now its members began to shift their ground,
judging from Lowell's own changed attitude. Greene reported to Eliot that
when Lowell became "reasonably convinced" that he could not "have his
way," he was "apt to discover a graceful method of retreat." This was "as far
as his open-mindedness [went]." Eliot doubted that Lowell had found "a
graceful method of retreat"; his "withdrawals" had always "been extremely
abrupt." After returning from England in mid-March, Lowell not only had
remained "silent," Eliot observed, but he had "become so nervous and agitated that he [was] compelled to leave his work and go away for rest and
quiet."15

Until the overseers received the report, Greene did not feel that he should
involve himself with the committee's activities, even though each overseer
had been officially invited to visit or write a statement. Judge Mack also re-
frained from communicating with the committee, because some of its members "would resent what they could plausibly call a 'butting in' by an Overseer and that, too, by a Jew." Moreover, he thought that Eliot's letters to
Chairman Grandgent already had presented the issues effectively. In late
March, Eliot could write the judge that the opinion of the overseers was so
unmistakable that he would not need to return for the board's spring meetings. And early in April, Felix Frankfurter was similarly optimistic. He expressed appreciation for Eliot's leadership and except for "one point"—probably the highest seventh proposal—called the report of the committee of
inquiry "a gratifying result."16

Denial of Racial Discrimination in Housing and Admissions, 1923

Within a period of just fifteen days, between March 26 and April 9, 1923,
both Lowell's policy of excluding blacks from the freshman halls and his proposed limitation on Jewish students received major setbacks, though not permanent defeats. On March 26, for example, the corporation voted

> that up to the capacity of the Freshman Halls all members of the Fresh-
> man Class shall reside and board in the Freshman Halls, except those who
> are permitted by the Assistant Dean of Harvard College to live else-

where. In the application of this rule men of the white and colored races shall not be compelled to live and eat together, nor shall any man be excluded by reason of his color.

An "explanatory statement" accompanied the publication of this vote to the effect that "social intimacies or friendships" among students would be matters of personal discretion. [17]

An interoffice memo among the college deans, following a conversation with Lowell, explicitly stated the president's "general policy" of "doing not a bit more or less for them [Negroes] than for other students." Lowell expected few black applicants. Each of them would receive a special letter indicating room prices. But if a black student could neither "afford our cheapest single room in Standish" nor "get any negro to room with him," he could not reside in Standish, nor for that matter in "any of the Freshman Halls." Historian Nell Painter has claimed that black students were not permitted to reside in the freshman halls until the class of 1957. She based this statement on personal interviews with two black alumni. No doubt a quasi-Jim Crow situation persisted at Harvard because only an occasional black student could afford one of the few inexpensive single rooms; furthermore, there were not many available black roommates. In May 1939, Dean A. C. Hanford stated that black students were assigned to all college residences: freshman halls, the houses, and other college dormitories. Of the *five* black students then enrolled in the college only one was living in the freshman halls; he had been admitted to Adams House for his sophomore year. Thus the absence of black freshmen from the halls in any one or several years was more likely the result of small enrollment and the fact that most black students were commuters than of official policy. [18]

Even though the governing boards had voted against exclusion in principle, they permitted the administration a certain amount of discretionary authority in carrying out that decision. Some flexibility was also present in the guidelines set down by the Committee on Methods of Sifting Candidates for Admission. On April 7, 1923, the committee sent President Lowell its report, along with a "volume of statistics." In an accompanying letter, the committee summarized its activities. Professor Sachs, for example, had devoted much of his time to conferring with over eighty "representative Hebrews"; others gave him unsolicited advice. "Virtually all" opposed a quota system of any kind. And nearly a hundred non-Jewish alumni "protested with earnestness, either emotionally or argumentatively, against the principle of racial discrimination." A few suggested "indirect restriction," but hardly anyone favored "frank limitation." [19]

Among the noteworthy communications that the committee received was a letter from Judge Learned Hand, a graduate of both the college and the law school. The judge recognized that the ethnic composition of the college had changed since his graduation, thirty years before, but insisted that

> if the Jew does not mix well with the Christian, it is no answer to segregate him. Most of those qualities which the Christian dislikes in him are, I believe, the direct result of that very policy in the past. Both Christian Jew are here; they must in some way learn to live on tolerable terms, and disabilities have never proved tolerable.

The proposal to limit Jewish students was even "worse," because those admitted were "effectively marked as racially undesirable." To Lowell's frequently advanced argument that Jews should be apportioned among several colleges and universities to prevent their concentration in a few, Hand countered that such involuntary dispersion would still make them "social inferiors." Until someone should develop an "honest" character test, the only valid method of selection was scholarship. "A college may gather together men of a common tradition, or it may put its faith in learning," as he did.[20]

On the whole, headmasters expressed support—"from mild approbation to enthusiastic advocacy"—for admission without examination of the top seventh of the graduates from good high schools. While the highest seventh plan was designed to attract more "country boys" from the South and the West, the stricter requirements proposed by the committee could be counted on to cut off transfers from Boston and New York colleges and to weed out candidates with weaker secondary preparation in, for example, English composition. This meant, of course, students from the public high schools, which sent Harvard "about three-quarters" of its Jews, but "only about one-third of [its] Gentiles." The committee estimated the number of Jews who would have been eliminated from among the successful candidates in 1921, had their new measures been in operation: "55 very bad scholars" would have been exchanged for "15 presumably good ones."[21]

The Board of Overseers gave their overwhelming approval to the report on April 9, and the newspapers were so informed the same day. On Lowell's advice, a substantial six-page report, dated April 11, was printed and circulated. But both the interpretation of the proposed changes, as explained in the committee's letter to Lowell, and the statistical tables were kept strictly confidential.[22]

Response from the press was indeed gratifying. Boston, New York, and East Coast papers generally carried both editorials and a column or two summarizing the major provisions of the report as well as the corporation's vote on admitting blacks to the freshman halls. During the month that followed, glowing headlines appeared in newspapers from all parts of the country: "Harvard Opens Portals Wide" (*Times*, Buffalo); "Harvard Will Bar None for Race or Sect" (*Oklahoman*, Oklahoma City); "Harvard's American Decision" (*Virginian Pilot*, Norfolk); "Hats Off to Harvard" (*Union Record*, Seattle); "Harvard Rings True" (*News*, New York); "Harvard Repents" (*News*, San Jose); "Harvard Will Open Doors Wide, Racial Discrimination Taboo" (*Rocky Mt. News*, Denver); and "Old-Fashioned Americanism"

(*Register*, Sandusky, Ohio; *News*, Bangor, Maine; and, in California, *Chronicle* of Calexico, *Press Democrat* of Santa Rosa, and *Independent* of Stockton). Critical comments were few in number; one exception was the Socialist Milwaukee *Leader* of April 11: "Harvard Board Evades Issue of Admitting Jews." But then it reported only the overseers' votes and not the text of the report. [23]

An interesting commentary appeared in the *Jewish Tribune and the Hebrew Standard*. Rabbi Louis I. Newman's article, "The Harvard Report: An Analysis," was thoughtful and sympathetic, calling the report a "document of true liberalism, vindicating pristine Harvard traditions of freedom of educational opportunity for all." Harvard's desire to be a "national university," he observed, did not threaten prospective Jewish applicants as did the "geographical" tests of Columbia, Dartmouth, and New York University. Columbia, for example, had sought "to balance the 50 per cent. metropolitan with the 50 per cent. non-metropolitan registration." Dartmouth, limiting its enrollment to 2,000 students, used Columbia's "Personal Rating System," by which an alumnus and the preparatory school principal appraised applicants. And New York University was "said to give preference to students who can live on or near the campus, as opposed to applicants, largely from the East Side," who commuted. On the other hand, the Harvard report explicitly repudiated "even so rational a method as a personal conference or an intelligence test" and was against "an arbitrary limitation" on enrollment. While its new provisions would bring in more applicants from the South and West, they would not necessarily reduce the number of "metropolitan" students. But Dr. Newman hoped that Harvard would drop questions of race, religion, and name change from its admission form. [24]

Profile of the Jewish Student at Harvard: "Statistical Report"

The unpublished volume of statistical tables, compiled under the direction of the Subcommittee Appointed to Collect Statistics (Deans Greenough, Donham, and Holmes), revealed the degree to which racist concepts had permeated academic circles by the 1920s and provided a fascinating collective portrait of Jewish students at Harvard during the first twenty years of the century. The only prior study of ethnic groups at Harvard had been conducted under the auspices of the United States Immigration Commission in 1908. It differed from the later Harvard study because it collected information on all students in school, with particular emphasis on those of the various immigrant stocks. The Harvard statisticians—Edward R. Gay, an assistant dean of the college, and Dr. A. J. Hettinger, Jr., of the Graduate School of Business Administration—focused almost exclusively on Jewish students. And instead of drawing only on cards completed by students at registration, they delved into a wide variety of sources: admission forms, parentage cards filled out at registration; records in the bursar's office; and senior class albums. Their report, submitted on December 21, 1922, traced the enrollment of Jewish students principally in the college and, to a limited extent, in the graduate and professional schools. 25

Virtually no aspect of the Jewish student's college career went unexamined. Assisted by the Bureau of Business Research, the statisticians computed the percentages of Jews and non-Jews among each of the following: high school and preparatory school graduates; transfer students; line cases; recipients of degrees, both with and without distinction; ranking scholars and unsatisfactory students; disciplinary cases; participants in athletics and other extracurricular activities; members of social clubs and the Harvard Union; commuters; recipients of financial assistance; and undergraduates in various fields of concentration. Vocational choices of Jewish graduates, along with the number of them entering Harvard's graduate and professional schools, were also tabulated. The methods employed probably gave "results as trustworthy as any can be," the committee on methods believed, "when the object of research [was] as undefined and undefinable as the Jew."26

First, Hettinger and Gay had to determine which students were Jewish and which were not in those years since 1900 that were chosen for study. After an independent examination of the records by each statistician, about eight thousand names were culled by their "composite judgment." But Judge Mack complained about their methodology when applied to the law school. The statisticians "later rejected forty-five per cent" of the initially selected law school records as being those of Gentiles. Questioning both the accuracy of the original data and the conclusions deduced from it, especially in regard to disciplinary cases, Professor Wolfson asked to examine the original cards for those Jewish students under discipline. After checking the class album, he believed that the statisticians had placed in the class of 1914 more Jewish students than were actually enrolled. The other committee members proposed that Wolfson consult with the statisticians concerning their methods of classification. 27

Although they did not avoid certain assumptions—Jews were definitely classified as a racial type—the statisticians did steer clear of certain pitfalls. There would be no measurements of skulls and other parts of the body during the prescribed physical examinations and training of freshmen. Their work primarily involved filling out a "racial classification" form on all students assumed to be Jewish. They relied on a combination of factors for a positive identification:

  1. Name
  2. Birthplace
  3. Father's Name
  4. Father's Vocation
  5. Mother's Name

6. Bondsmen's Names
7. Admitted to Harvard from
   a. Preparatory School
   b. College or University
8. Home Address

According to the statisticians, names were incomplete evidence because

> there were a sufficient number of changes in name or instances of a name that might have been, for instance, either German or Jewish. . . . Changes in the father's name were less frequent. The mother's maiden name, very seldom altered, was of material help. Such items as birthplace, father's occupation and home address, when considered in light of the evidence as a whole possessed a value beyond that which could be ascribed to them as isolated facts.

And if the bondsmen had Jewish names, it was likely that the student was also Jewish. But contrary to expectation, photographs in the freshman red book and the senior album "afforded practically no additional information." Lastly, the biographical data in the senior album provided a final check.[28]

The "Jews" so selected were divided into three groups and labeled J1 ("conclusively" Jewish), J2 (indicatively), and J3 (possibly, but not probably). Of the total number of college students admitted between 1918 and 1923, 17.0 percent on average were placed in the J1 category and only 2.5 percent each in J2 and J3. Since the first two categories together gave "the most probable estimate" of Harvard's Jewish students, the statisticians based their analysis only on J1 and J2. While mistakes in classification might occur, "the number of men wrongly classed as 'J1' or 'J2'" would be "counterbalanced" by those assigned to J3 or undiscovered. In the case of Harvard College, which had the largest enrollment of any school within the university, statistical errors would alter the percentages much less than in the dental school, which had the smallest enrollment. (Changing the classification of only one dental student would alter by 4 percent the proportion of Jews.)[29]

Tabulations for the World War I years, said the statisticians, should be treated with particular care, since enrollment during that time was unstable. And although the results for Harvard College were generally reliable, they recognized that tabulations for disciplinary cases, which were based on a small number of students, had to be analyzed cautiously. On the whole, their report had three virtues: painstaking research, uniform procedures, and acknowledgment of possible inaccuracies in both classification and results.[30]

As Table 4.1 indicated, the enrollment of Jewish students at Harvard College had dramatically increased from 7.0 percent in 1900 to 21.5 percent in 1922. By that later date, there were also substantial percentages of Jews in the law school (14.4), medical school (16.1), and dental school (12.5).

Much of the increase in the proportion of Jewish freshmen, regularly ad-

Table 4.1

NUMBER AND PERCENTAGE OF JEWISH STUDENTS TO TOTAL
NUMBER OF STUDENTS ADMITTED TO VARIOUS SCHOOLS
WITHIN HARVARD UNIVERSITY IN SPECIFIED
YEARS, 1900-22

Year Admitted	College Regulars			College Transfers		
	Total Number	*Number of Jews*	*Percentage of Jews*	*Total Number*	*Number of Jews*	*Percentage of Jews*
1900	511	36	7.0			
1903	490	35	7.1			
1906	559	42	7.5			
1909	551	54	9.8	109	17	15.6
1912	611	77	12.6	84	12	14.3
1913	581	85	14.6	114	14	12.3
1914	664	100	15.1	119	26	21.9
1915	649	91	14.0	139	28	20.2
1916	647	96	14.8	123	33	26.8
1917	536	70	13.1	78	13	16.7
1918	499	99	19.8	319	91	28.5
1919	504	90	17.9	274	68	24.8
1920	578	103	17.8	284	81	28.5
1921	716	141	19.7	217	69	31.8
1922[a]	698	150	21.5	134	36	26.9

	College Special Students			Engineering School		
1900						
1903						
1906						
1909						
1912						
1913						
1914						
1915	37	2	5.4			
1916						
1917						
1918	29	4	13.8			
1919	66	4	6.1	122	17	13.9
1920	68	11	16.2	154	20	13.0
1921	58	10	17.2	126	11	8.7
1922[a]	20	3	15.0	107	5	4.7

	Graduate School of Arts and Sciences			Law School		
1900	180	3	1.7	242	22	9.1
1903	134	6	4.4	293	19	6.5

Table 4.1 (Continued)

	Graduate School of Arts and Sciences			Law School		
1906	213	9	4.2	243	25	10.3
1909	281	20	7.1	314	23	7.3
1912	260	13	5;0	372	26	7.0
1913	259	15	5.8	323	25	7.7
1914	310	15	4.8	356	35	9.8
1915	343	18	5.2	377	29	7.7
1916	301	23	7.6	398	51	12.8
1917	169	14	8.3	127	21	16.5
1918	225	34	15.1	224	33	14.7
1919	319	26	8.2	485	51	10.5
1920	261	17	6.5	451	61	13.5
1921	345	33	9.6	431	65	15.1
1922[a]	311	27	8.7	452	65	14.4

	Medical School			Dental School		
1900	198	8	4.0	43	3	7.0
1903	78	2	2.6	50	1	2.0
1906	91	8	8.8	21	4	19.0
19091	60	7	11.7	47	9	19.1
1912	70	4	5.7	69	14	20.3
1913	84	8	9.5	80	15	18.8
1914	98	8	8.2	68	19	27.9
1915	105	16	15.2	90	29	32.2
1916	109	15	13.8	94	12	12.8
1917	94	10	10.6	42	12	28.6
1918	108	29	26.9	37	12	32.4
1919	120	22	18.3	84	23	27.4
1920	126	12	9.5	79	16	20.3
1921	130	12	9.2	25	6	24.0
1922[a]	124	20	16.1	48	6	12.5

Graduate School of Business Administration

	Total Number	*Number of Jews*	*Percentage of Jews*
1900			
1903			
1906			
1909	42		
1912	76	5	6.6
1913	67	2	3.0
1914	111	6	5.4
1915	117	5	4.3
1916	142	8	5.6
1917	42	6	14.3

Table 4.1 (Continued)

Graduate School of Business Administration

	Total Number	Number of Jews	Percentage of Jews
1918	111	18	16.2
1919	305	17	5.6
1920	300	20	6.7
1921	265	16	6.0
1922[a]	260	24	9.2

Source: Compiled from "Statistical Report of the Statisticians to the Subcommittee Appointed to Collect Statistics: Dean Chester N. Greenough, Chairman, Dean Wallace B. Donham, Dean Henry W. Holmes" (Hereafter cited as "Statistical Report"), Abbott Lawrence Lowell Papers, Harvard University Archives, 1922-1925, #387 Admission to Harvard College, Tables 1-10 on "Study of Admissions," pp. 7-16.
[a]Note to Table 1 reads, "1922 percentages, except in case of Harvard College, based on preliminary survey made early in October."

mitted, was due to their growing numbers in the Boston area high schools. For example, Boston Latin School sent a contingent of Jewish students to Harvard College: 19 in 1918, 18 in 1919, 23 in 1920, and 27 in 1921. The largest number of Jewish transfer students also came from the Boston area—from Tufts College and Boston University. About one-third of the Jewish students commuted—twice as many, proportionately, as among the Gentiles. Of the 210 Jewish students (transfers as well as regulars) admitted to the college in 1921, 83, or 39.5 percent, were commuters. In contrast, while the percentage of Jewish students coming from the South had tripled between 1901 and 1922, their numbers from that region had increased, according to a rough estimate, from 2 to only 6![31]

Among those admitted between 1912 and 1918, about three-fourths of the Jewish and Gentile regular students completed the college course and received degrees. Moreover only 15.5 percent of 958 Jewish students regularly admitted between 1912 and 1921 were ever reported for unsatisfactory records, while 37.2 percent of the 5,027 Gentile regular students were so cited. And proportionately more than twice as many Jewish regular students received degrees with distinction. With only about 15 percent of the regular students, Jews earned 28 percent of the degrees with distinction (see Table 4.2). Jewish transfer students, about one-fourth of the total number admitted from other colleges, earned over one-third of the degrees with distinction. Approximately 30 percent of the Group I and Group II scholars (Table 4.3) and almost 15 percent (35) of the students elected to Phi Beta Kappa from 1914 to 1920 were Jewish.[32]

Table 4.2
PROPORTION OF JEWS TO TOTAL NUMBER OF STUDENTS
RECEIVING DEGREE WITH DISTINCTION
(Data for Students Admitted 1912-18)

Kind of Distinction	Number of Students Receiving Degree with Distinction		Percentage of Jews to Total Receiving Degree with Distinction
	Total	*Jews*	
All kinds			
Regulars	738	207	28.1[a]
Transfers	89	30	33.7
Summa cum laude			
Regulars	53	12	22.7
Transfers	2	0	0.0
Magna cum laude			
Regulars	152	40	26.3
Transfers	17	5	29.4
Cum laude in special subject			
Regulars	211	64	30.3
Transfers	35	13	37.1
Cum laude in general studies			
Regulars	322	91	28.3
Transfers	35	12	34.3

Source: "Statistical Report," Table 3 on "Scholarship," p. 32.
[a]Note to Table 3 reads, "Proportion of Jews to total obtaining degree:
Regulars 14.6
Transfers 25.7"

With respect to disciplinary cases, the committee's April 7, 1923, letter disregarded the cautionary advice of the statisticians and generalized that Jewish students seemed "more prone to dishonesty and sexual offenses, but much less addicted to intemperance." Yet only 4.7 percent of all Jewish students and 3.0 percent of all non-Jewish students were under discipline of any kind

Table 4.3
PROPORTION OF JEWS AMONG FIRST AND SECOND GROUP
SCHOLARS, 1915-16 TO 1922-23

Year	First and Second Group Scholars		Percentage of Jews to Total First and Second Group Scholars
	Total	*Jews*	
1915-16	228	71	31.1
1916-17	227	63	27.7
1917-18	204	66	32.3
1918-19	135	45	33.3
1919-20	171	52	30.4
1920-21	135	32	23.7
1921-22	160	49	30.6
1922-23	136	42	30.9

Source: "Statistical Report," Table 4 on "Scholarship," p. 33.

during the years 1912-22 (see Table 4.4). Except for "offenses involving dishonesty," only about 1 percent of either Jews or Gentiles were guilty of misconduct—drunkenness, improper conduct, or other offenses. For dishonesty, 131 Gentiles, or 2.0 percent of their total number, were disciplined and

Table 4.4
PROPORTION OF JEWS TO TOTAL NUMBER OF STUDENTS UNDER
DISCIPLINE, 1912-13 TO 1921-22, INCLUSIVE

Offense	Number of Students under Discipline		Percentage of Jews to Total under Discipline	Percentage of Students under Discipline to Total in Group	
	All Students	*Jews*		*Jewish Students*	*All Other Students*
All offenses	256	66	25.8	4.7	3.0
Offenses involving dishonesty	183	52	28.4	3.7	2.0
Drunkenness	32	2	6.3	0.1	0.5
Improper conduct	26	7	26.9	0.5	0.3
All other offenses	15	5	33.3	0.4	0.2

Source: "Statistical Report," Table 3 on "Disciplinary Cases," p. 43.

52, or 3.7 percent, of the Jews. These almost insignificant figures did not indicate that Jews were proportionately more dishonest than Gentiles, since only 2 non-Jews and 3 Jews were expelled for dishonesty; and only 1 Jewish student was expelled for "improper conduct" (see Table 4.5).[33]

Tables on athletic participation, based on a larger number of students, were more reliable. By 1918, for example, over 30 percent of Jewish regular students and some 13 percent of Jewish transfer students participated in athletics. According to the 1922 senior album, 48.5 percent of the Gentile and 25.0 percent of the Jewish students went out for athletics. In the same class, about three times as many Gentile as Jewish students participated in nonathletic extracurricular activities. During the years 1900-18, Jews were most active in music and debating, then in campus newspapers and magazines, class offices, dramatics, and social service (see Table 4.6). Table 4.7, concentrating on the class of 1922, showed Jewish students to be well represented in debating and music, but entirely unrepresented in dramatics. Although impossible to measure, Gentile social attitudes probably accounted for the limited participation in or exclusion of Jewish students from extracurricular activities.[34]

Jewish students relied on each other for social companionship. In the class of 1922, forty of the forty-six Jews belonging to social clubs were members of Jewish fraternities. At that time, Harvard had six Jewish fraternities: Sigma Alpha Mu (1909), Argo Club (1911), Zeta Beta Tau (1912), and Kappa Nu, Tau Delta Phi, and Tau Epsilon Phi, all founded in 1918. The fact that chapters of three Jewish fraternities began at Harvard in one year suggests that as the percentage of Jewish students increased in the college, the proportion taken into the Gentile fraternities did not rise correspondingly. The Speaker's Club, which had accepted as many as five Jews from the class of 1918, had none from the class of 1922, although the Institute of 1770 and Hasty Pudding each had two Jews from the same class. Of Harvard's ten final clubs, only four—Owl, Delta Upsilon, Phoenix, and Iroquois—took any Jewish members from the classes admitted between 1912 and 1918. Owl, ranked sixth in Harvard's hierarchy of clubs, admitted three Jews from the class of 1920. Delta Upsilon, Phoenix, and Iroquois, which ranked eighth, ninth, and tenth, respectively, together accepted eight others from the classes of 1917 to 1920 and 1922. All were regular students; none had transferred to Harvard from another college. Of the Jewish students listed in the 1922 senior album, 27.4 percent belonged to social clubs, but only 3.6 percent were affiliated with Gentile clubs. In contrast, almost 59 percent (314) of the non-Jews so listed were club members.[35]

In terms of undergraduate fields of concentration, Jewish and Gentile students tended to share similar interests. Economics was the clear favorite for almost a quarter of the Jewish students admitted in 1921, followed by English, chemistry, and history and literature (each chosen by between 10 and 16

Table 4.5

JEWISH AND GENTILE STUDENTS UNDER DISCIPLINE, BY FORM OF DISCIPLINE,
1912-13 TO 1921-22, INCLUSIVE

Discipline	All Offenses		Offenses Involving Dishonesty		Drunkenness		Improper Conduct		All Other Offenses	
	Gentiles	Jews	Gentiles	Jews	Gentiles	Jews	Gentiles	Jews	Gentiles	Jews
All discipline	190	66	131	52	30	2	19	7	10	5
Expelled[a]	2	4	2	3	0	0	0	1	0	0
Dismissed	19	13	13	12	4	0	2	0	0	1
Put on Probation	93	32	74	29	11	0	1	1	7	2
Probation closed	18	4	16	3	1	1	1	0	0	0
Required to withdraw	35	7	16	2	5	0	14	4	0	1
Admonished	15	3	7	3	4	0	1	0	3	0
Suspended	3	0	0	0	3	0	0	0	0	0
Degree withheld	5	2	3	0	2	1	0	0	0	1
Deprived of Scholarship	0	1	0	0	0	0	0	1	0	0

Source: Compiled from "Statistical Report," Tables 4 and 5 on "Disciplinary Cases," pp. 44-45.
aOn the basis of this data, the statisticians noted that a higher percentage of Jewish students under discipline (25.7) than Gentile students under discipline (11.0) were "expelled or dismissed," p. 38.

Table 4.6
PERCENTAGE OF JEWS PARTICIPATING IN INDICATED NONATHLETIC ACTIVITIES, REGULARS AND TRANSFERS

Year Admitted	Total Number of Jewish Students Admitted	Papers		Dramatics		Musical		Debating		Class Office		Social Service: Phillips Brooks House	
		No.	% of Total	No.	% of Total	No.	% of Total	No.	% of Total	No.	% of Total	No.	% of Total
1900	36	0	0.0	0	0.0	1	2.8	7	19.4	1	2.8	0	0.0
1903	35	0	0.0	0	0.0	3	8.6	0	0.0	0	0.0	0	0.0
1906	42	3	7.1	0	0.0	3	7.1	2	4.8	1	2.4	0	0.0
1909	71	3	4.2	1	1.4	4	5.6	5	7.0	4	5.6	1	1.4
1912	89	1	1.1	5	5.5	9	10.1	9	10.1	2	2.2	2	2.2
1913	99	3	3.0	3	3.0	10	10.1	9	9.1	4	4.0	0	0.0
1914	126	6	4.8	5	3.0	15	11.9	6	4.8	3	2.4	2	1.6
1915	119	7	5.9	2	1.7	5	3.2	5	3.2	5	3.2	2	1.7
1916	129	10	7.8	2	1.6	14	10.9	12	9.3	4	3.1	0	0.0
1917	83	3	3.6	0	0.0	5	6.1	8	9.6	0	0.0	0	0.0
1918	190	3	1.6	0	0.0	10	5.3	5	2.6	2	1.1	1	0.5

Source: "Statistical Report," Table 3 on "Non-Athletic Activities," p. 60.

Table 4.7
PROPORTION OF JEWS TO TOTAL NUMBER OF STUDENTS
PARTICIPATING IN INDICATED NONATHLETIC
ACTIVITIES, SENIOR ALBUM OF 1922

Nonathletic Activities	Number of Students Participating in Nonathletic Activities		Percentage of Jews to Total Participating in Nonathletic Activities
	All Students	*Jews*	
Papers	74	3	4.1
Dramatics	12	0	0.0
Musical	52	10	19.2
Debating	13	5	38.5
Class office	42	2	4.8
Social Service: Phillips Brooks House	11	1	9.1

Source: "Statistical Report," Table 5 on "Non-Athletic Activities," p. 57.
Note: Senior album did not include 22 of the 190 Jewish and 92 of the 628 Gentile students admitted in 1918

percent of the Jewish sophomores). Over one-fourth of the Gentiles chose English, with much smaller percentages selecting economics, history and literature, and romance languages. Significantly, these majors related only indirectly to career choices.[36]

After graduating from the college, a considerable portion of Jewish students entered one of the Harvard graduate and professional schools: 50 out of 190 in 1922. In order of preference, they chose Harvard Law School, Medical School, Graduate School of Arts and Sciences, Business School, and School of Engineering. Of the Jewish graduates (from selected classes admitted between 1900 and 1918) whose vocational choices were known, 30 percent entered mercantile businesses; 15 percent, law; and 11 percent, manufacturing. According to statistics compiled from the secretary's reports for the classes of 1896, 1901, 1906, 1911, 1916, and 1921, Harvard graduates increasingly had entered business occupations. Whereas 35 percent of the class of 1896 had gone into business, over 55 percent of the class of 1916 had opted for commercial and industrial occupations. Such a trend occurred partly at the expense of medicine, but principally of law and education, both of which dropped during that twenty-year period. About 11 and 8 percent, respectively, of the class of 1916 became lawyers and educators. (And the number entering the ministry continued its two-hundred-year decline "until it . . . nearly reached the vanishing point.") Comparison of these two sets of statistics indicated that a majority of Harvard graduates became businessmen, but that almost three times as many Jewish alumni were engaged in mercantile pursuits as in manufacturing. [37]

Faculty Adoption of the Committee on Methods' Report

Despite reservations about the validity of some of the tables, reservations that the statisticans themselves acknowledged, their report assembled an impressive amount of data. The weight of evidence showed that Jewish students were constructive citizens of the Harvard community, not an alien body. But few people outside the committee on methods and some of the members of the governing boards ever saw these statistics. Yet the intention of the printed report was clearly stated: reject racial and religious discrimination in admission, eliminate weaker students, and attract more applicants from the South and West. [38]

On April 10, Grandgent presented the document to the Faculty of Arts and Sciences for their consideration. Although slightly irritated because it had been released to the press before they saw it, the faculty adopted the report (which had already received the corporation's approval) without lengthy discussion at a special meeting on April 24. No opposition was raised to the first eight of the proposed nine changes in admission policy. The most important were the first five:

(a) That in the administration of rules for admission Harvard College maintain its traditional policy of freedom from discrimination on grounds of race or religion.

(b) That, as a general policy, transfer of students from other Colleges be confined to such candidates as have lacked opportunity to prepare themselves for admission by the usual methods.

(c) That insistence be stricter on full compliance with the published requirements for admission.

(d) That no candidate be admitted whose examination in English composition is not passable. This rule is not to apply to candidates for whom English is a foreign tongue.

(e) That the number of satisfactory grades under the Old Plan be raised from five to six, announcement being made that a greater increase is likely in the near future. [39]

On the ninth and final recommendation, Clifford H. Moore (Latin) asked that the votes be recorded. By 73 ayes to 20 nays, out of 100 present, the faculty adopted "as an experiment" the highest seventh plan, the most "radical" of the proposals:

> Pupils who have satisfactorily completed an approved school course such as is outlined in the description of the New Plan, and whose scholastic rank places them in the highest seventh of the boys of their graduating class, may, if recommended by their school, be admitted to College without examination.
>
> This method of admission is intended to facilitate access to College by capable boys from schools which do not ordinarily prepare their pupils for college examination.

The faculty now voted unanimously to approve the entire report. Then, on May 8, Henry Pennypacker submitted for the Committee on Admission its statement on administering the new regulations. Put to the test of experience, would these measures work to the satisfaction of all concerned? [40]

Limits on Enrollment in Harvard College: The Beginning of Restriction on Jewish Students, 1926

Hardly had the faculty and governing boards adopted the report when President Lowell introduced another scheme of limitation. He was dissatisfied with the results of the committee on methods, yet aware that his approach had stiffened opposition to a Jewish quota. In May 1923, Lowell wrote President Alexander Meiklejohn of Amherst College about Harvard's recent decision on "the race question." Said Lowell: "We have dealt with it in both cases by compromise, which was the only possible thing at the time, though it can hardly be said to be fully satisfactory to anyone." But in December 1925, Lowell assured those alumni who were concerned over the increase of Jewish students at Harvard that they "need not doubt that the matter is thoroughly understood by the authorities here." Alumni letters had convinced the president that he "was not wholly wrong three years ago in trying to limit the proportion of Jews." However, in a postscript, he admitted: "My plan was crude, and its method was very probably unwise." [41]

On the other hand, a proposal to limit enrollment of students to a number that Harvard could effectively educate seemed far more reasonable. In December 1923, the Faculty of Arts and Sciences approved the report of a special committee on the advisability of limiting the size of the freshman class to 1,000 students. The following month, the Faculty of the Engineering School voted to include first-year engineering students within the 1,000 total, but to exclude freshmen who were applying for readmission after having been dropped for academic reasons. After it was submitted to the Board of

Overseers, they, in turn, relayed it to Henry James, Jr., chairman of their Committee to Visit Harvard College. 42

With Jerome D. Greene having completed his term as overseer, Henry James, author, lawyer, and son of philosopher William James, emerged as one of the few critics of Lowell's policy. In addition to his service on various overseers' committees, James was to contribute greatly to the history of Harvard by his Pulitzer Prize-winning two volumes, *Charles W. Eliot, President of Harvard University, 1869-1909* (1930). 43

After this committee's report endorsed limitation as a "temporary" measure, the president of the Board of Overseers appointed a Special Committee on the Limitation of the Size of the Freshman Class, under the chairmanship of Henry James. It included representatives of the corporation (President Lowell and James Byrne) as well as overseers and faculty members. In a year, it was to report "on numbers in relation to equipment, personnel, standards, and the scope and function of the College."44

Meanwhile, Lowell was instructing the dean's office to keep a count of the Jewish students, particularly those admitted under the highest seventh plan. In June 1923, for example, Jews had constituted 32.1 percent of the 134 applicants admitted without examination and came largely from New England and the Middle Atlantic states. Later, after checking through the parentage cards of 880 new freshmen in the autumn of 1925, the dean's office classified 243 students as Jewish—J1 and J2. Within the past three years, their percentage had risen from 21.5 to 27.6. This figure did not include 38 students classified as J3. Almost 42 percent (115) of the 276 successful highest seventh (now called "honor plan") candidates were Jewish. And Jewish students constituted 25 percent of those receiving "freshman aid," roughly their proportion within the class. These statistics must have convinced President Lowell that the Committee on Admission would have to exercise greater discretionary authority. He moved more cautiously, however, than he had in 1922. 45

For one thing, President Emeritus Eliot, although ninety, was still vigorously objecting to any change in Harvard's "open door" policy for all qualified candidates. Some Jews, Eliot related to Jerome D. Greene, had gone "directly to President Lowell to inquire insistently if the present limitation movement" was aimed at them. Lowell had "assured them" that it was not! Eliot also expressed his views to Overseer Langdon P. Marvin, law partner of Franklin D. Roosevelt and past president of the Associated Harvard Clubs. He was disturbed that Marvin apparently showed no concern about the possible use of a character test to reduce the percentage of Jews in the college. At the same time, Eliot kept in touch with Dr. Rosenau, Professor Frankfurter, and Judge Mack. 46

Except for a few ripples, harmony seemingly prevailed in the Harvard community as Lowell worked assiduously to achieve the objective he had failed to accomplish three years before. In November 1925, he persuaded

Henry James, chairman of the special committee, that a limitation of the size of the freshman class was necessary to enable the Committee on Admission to select the "best" candidates. "To prevent a dangerous increase in the proportion of Jews," Lowell advocated

> a selection by a personal estimate of character on the part of the Admission authorities, based upon the probable value to the candidate, to the College and to the community of his admission. . . . If there is no limit, it is impossible to reject a candidate who passes the admission examinations without proof of defective character, which practically cannot be obtained.

Lowell insisted, of course, that he was proposing not racial discrimination, "but a discrimination among individuals." Believing that Jews then constituted "a very large proportion of the less desirable" candidates, he gave the overseers three choices: either they must take responsibility for the increasing numbers of Jews, or they must say how the situation should be handled, "or they must leave the administrative officers of the University free to deal with it."47

Henry James yielded in part and with great reluctance to Lowell's point of view. "*Everything* in my education and bringing up makes me shrink from a proposal to begin a racial discrimination at Harvard—there's no use my pretending that that isn't the case," he wrote the president. On the other hand, James could support "discrimination among individuals" and thought that "such a discrimination would inevitably eliminate most" of the troublesome "Jewish element." While he, himself, did not fear "any competition" from Jews, he felt their intellectual "precocity" gave them "a head start." By late 1925, however, he told Lowell that the overseers proposed a motion at their autumn meeting that "named the Jews and was on its face a racial discrimination." Many of those who shared Lowell's "concern about the increasing numbers are advocating what they call a candid regulation excluding all but so many or such a proportion of 'Jews.' "48

Thus after many discussions and meetings over almost a two-year period, the Special Committee on the Limitation of the Size of the Freshman Class issued its thirty-two-page printed report. Replete with eighteen pages of tables and graphs, the report pointed out that Harvard's enrollment had dramatically risen since 1870-71. In that year, the college had had 608 students and the university, 1,316; by 1924-25, the figures were 3,041 for the college (a 400.16-percent increase) and 7,075 for the university (a 437.61-percent increase). Harvard's total enrollment was larger than any of the other private eastern colleges and universities, except for Columbia and Pennsylvania. Moreover, nine of these institutions—Amherst, Bowdoin, Brown, Columbia, Cornell, Dartmouth, Princeton, Williams, and Yale—had adopted or were considering some limitation on undergraduates, even if only on an informal basis. 49

Yet up to 1925, freshman enrollment had not even attained its 1,000 "quota." When it became necessary to be more selective, the committee believed it would be "neither feasible nor desirable to raise the standards of the College so high that none but brilliant scholars can enter and remain in regular standing." At present, "in spite of certain complaints which have recently been heard," the academic demands were not "too high for serious and ambitious students of average intelligence." Nor would the committee object if Harvard "become somewhat harder . . . to enter" than other colleges. 50

On January 11, 1926, Henry James submitted the report of his committee to the Board of Overseers, which accepted it, with amendments. Although phrased in reasonable terms, the Board of Overseers had implicitly agreed to subjective admission standards, which very easily could be used to exclude Jews:

> 1. That, during the next three years, 1926-27 to 1928-29, the limit of 1,000 Freshmen shall include dropped Freshmen as well as those newly admitted to the College and Engineering School, but not thereafter, save with the approval of the Governing Boards.
> 2. That the application of the rule concerning candidates from the first seventh of their schools be discretionary both as to schools and candidates with the Committee on Admission.
> 3. That the rules for the admission of candidates be amended to lay greater emphasis on selection based on character and fitness and the promise of the greatest usefulness in the future as a result of a Harvard education. 51

On January 19, 1926, the faculty voted to accept the first proposal as it stood, to amend the second and third, and to add one of their own. The latter provided for the admission of candidates whose examinations and school records were judged by the Committee on Admission to be equal to those of Harvard undergraduates in the highest four groups of the rank list and those with "unquestionably good" examination averages. The best students would be admitted, whether or not they were Jewish. Since two of the overseers' recommendations would grant considerable discretionary authority to the Committee on Admission, the faculty voted in favor of two changes. The major one made application of the first seventh rule "discretionary" only "as to schools," not to candidates within the same school. But the Committee on Admission could withdraw its offer of admission without examination from a particular school or from all schools within certain localities. To obtain information on "character and fitness and the promise of the greatest usefulness in the future as a result of a Harvard education," Chairman Henry Pennypacker would interview many applicants, as individuals and in groups,

during his visits to private preparatory and public high schools. "For purposes of identification and for later use by the Dean's office," a passport-sized
photograph was subsequently "required as an essential part of the application for admission."[52]

At the same January 19 faculty meeting, President Lowell announced that
Professor Robert De Courcy Ward and Dr. Kenneth B. Murdock had been
appointed to the Committee on Admission, replacing Professors Charles H.
Grandgent and George S. Forbes, who had resigned. Since Professor Ward
had been one of the leaders of the Immigration Restriction League, it was
more than likely that he brought similar assumptions about immigrant
groups to his work on the Committee on Admission.[53]

Statistics showed that the Committee on Admission began to use its discretionary authority to exclude candidates from New England and the Middle
Atlantic states whose academic records were good enough for admission. Although the ethnic origin of these rejected applicants was not given, one may
guess that a high percentage was Jewish. Well into the 1930s, the application
for admission to Harvard College included questions on ethnic identity and
religious affiliation, while the secondary school principal or master was
asked to check the applicant's religious preference on the "Personal Record
and Certificate of Honorable Dismissal." And Clarence W. Mendell, who
visited Harvard in December 1926, during his first year as dean of Yale College, learned from Chairman Pennypacker that Harvard was

> now going to limit the Freshman Class to 1,000 including dropped and
> rated which means about 850 new men. After this year they are going to
> discontinue—for the East at least—the "first seventh" arrangement
> which is bringing in as high as 40% Jews. They are also going to reduce
> their 25% Hebrew total to 15% or less by simply rejecting without de-
> tailed explanation. They are giving no details to any candidate any
> longer. They are getting small representation from the West and none
> from the South and have no plan for improving the situation. . . .[54]

By the mid-1920s, Harvard had yielded to a selective system of admissions,
which, with no apologies, aimed at reducing the percentage of Jews in the college. This system certainly continued throughout Lowell's presidency, because he believed that it should operate without time limit until the "problem" was corrected. And it persisted into the administration of James Bryant
Conant, since he, too, favored a limitation of students within the college.
Symbolic of Lowell's victory at Harvard was the death of Charles W. Eliot on
August 22, 1926.

The Harvard Houses: Apportionment of Students by Type of Secondary
School and by Race

In his annual *President's Report* of 1936-37, James Bryant Conant reviewed the accomplishments of the Harvard House Plan during its first seven years of operation. The first two houses—Dunster and Lowell—had opened in September 1930, followed the next year by Adams, Eliot, Kirkland, Leverett, and John Winthrop. (When their halls became the cores of the last three houses, the freshmen—"Yardlings"—were relocated in the Harvard Yard dormitories.) Four houses were named to honor individual Harvard presidents; Henry Dunster, first president of the college; John Leverett and the Reverend John Thornton Kirkland, presidents, respectively, in the early eighteenth and early nineteenth centuries; and Charles William Eliot. Adams House (named for John Adams, second president of the United States) and Lowell House acknowledged the contributions of many generations of those two families to both the nation and the university, while John Winthrop House honored Massachusetts Bay Colony's first governor and his lineal descendant, a distinguished Harvard astronomer and mathematician. [55]

It was "no accident," wrote Conant about A. Lawrence Lowell, "that the House Plan was introduced by a President of Harvard who opened his inaugural address with these words, 'Among his other wise sayings, Aristotle remarked that man is by nature a social animal.'" Even more than the physical facilities—libraries, common rooms, squash courts, and dining rooms—the houses provided a most desirable intellectual and social climate for student and student-faculty exchanges. When daily life was arranged "in such a way that the future doctor, the future lawyer, the future banker, the embryo scientist, and the youthful poet all lunch and dine together day after day," said Conant, "the most powerful of the forces making for a liberal education are set at work." The houses also offered opportunities for art exhibitions, quartets, bands, orchestras, and plays. Nor should the benefits of intramural athletics be overlooked, Conant noted. Virtually all students could participate on the house squads and teams, not just the superior athletes. Beyond question, the House Plan added a vital dimension to the Harvard educational experience. Each of the seven residential houses domiciled between 230 and 300 men; this meant that slightly more than a third of the members of the three upper classes were per force excluded from them. Consequently, admission to the houses became secondary in importance only to admission to the college itself. [56]

The policy of limiting the size of the freshman class had been extended by a faculty vote of October 16, 1928. But instead of referring the measure back to the governing boards after that academic year, the Lowell administration simply assumed that limitation should be continued by implication. Freshman enrollment in Harvard College had reached 1,063 in 1925-26, but then had dropped into the 900s. To counteract such a decline, 1,117 freshmen were admitted in 1932-33. Thereafter, total freshman enrollment averaged well above 1,000 (with engineering school freshmen phased out after 1935). [57]

Even with a flexible quota on enrollment, the Committee on Admission rejected hundreds of qualified as well as unqualified applicants during the 1930s. An undeterminable number of the rejected applicants were Jewish. According to the "Supplementary Memorandum Explaining Method of Arriving at Estimate of Size of Class of 1946," among those "eliminated by the Admission office," were two categories: "a. *Because of quota for a certain type* [italics added]. b. Because of insufficient academic promise." Of the total number of 886 nonscholarship applicants eligible for admission in May 1942, it was estimated that 70 would attend another university, leaving 816, of whom "*about 100 will be lost on account of the 'quota'*" [italics added]. Another 76 students would probably be cut, leaving 640 who would be admitted, though "a good many . . . would not even have been approved for admission in previous years." Of the 1,162 scholarship applicants, it was assumed that 525 would receive aid or decide to come on their own resources. [58]

The exact annual percentage limitation on Jewish students admitted to the college is not known, but it may be deduced that the quota fluctuated between 10 and 16 percent of each freshman class in the late 1920s and 1930s. (There is no firm information to indicate that the graduate and professional schools imposed similar quotas.) In 1938-39, for example, about 165, or 16 percent, of the 1,028 freshmen admitted were Jewish (of whom about 117 lived on campus and 48 commuted). World War II, however, caused a decided increase in Jewish enrollment. At least 19 percent of the freshmen entering the class of 1946 were Jewish. [59]

Jewish students also encountered a quota, roughly equal to their proportion within the class as a whole, when applying for admission to the houses as sophomores. By the spring of 1933, Lowell and the masters had agreed that the House Plan was in "serious danger" if students were allowed choice of residence. They detected a growing "social consciousness of an unfortunate and disagreeable kind among the undergraduates." Already the houses were becoming classified, with the likely result that "some of our most 'fashionable' and 'successful' students will refuse to enter the Houses at all unless they gain admission to one of the two or three 'socially eminent' ones." [60]

The masters made a considerable, though only partially successful, effort to entice the prep school crowd and then to keep it in residency. Specifically, these were the students of the eight or nine schools that saw half or more of their graduates chosen by the Hasty Pudding Club, a prerequisite to admission to one of Harvard's ten final clubs (attained by only 11 or 12 percent of the three upper classes). At the core of the "selected private schools" were the five Episcopal boarding schools—the St. Grottlesex group—followed by Brooks, Milton, Noble and Greenough, and Pomfret. Belmont Hill, Gunnery, Hill, Kent, and Santa Barbara (for the California elite) were subsequently placed on this list; Deerfield and Hotchkiss were added by the 1940s. [61]

At their best, the prep school crowd were like the Holmeses and the Roosevelts. At their worst, they formed cliques whose members either declined to apply for house residence or, having been denied their first choice, refused to accept their second—and the common board and discipline of the houses. In 1933, according to Seymour Harris, who was then an assistant professor of economics and later senior tutor of Dunster, nineteen students who were graduates of seven select private schools left house residency to live in a "rabbit-warren" on Plympton Street. None had made the dean's list at midyear, while eight had below passing grades. 62

Indeed, during the 1930s, final club members would desert the houses. Whereas 70 percent of the 266 clubmen had lived in the houses in 1932-33, the percentage fell off during the next four years until only about 50 percent resided there. And in 1939-40, only six of the twenty-eight members of Porcellian and fourteen of the thirty-eight in Fly lived in a house. Lowell, Kirkland, and Dunster had the poorest record—which may indicate other virtues—while Winthrop, Eliot, and Leverett had the best in attracting clubmen. Eliot House enjoyed for many years a reputation for "social éclat." Commented one freshman of Eliot in 1953: "Behind that 'cold exterior,' there is a cold interior."63

To prevent the houses from becoming nicknamed Gold Coasts or Little Jerusalems, President Lowell appointed in March 1933 a central committee, consisting of himself, Dean A. Chester Hanford, and Dean of Freshmen Delmar Leighton, to work with the masters and to confer with the freshman class officers. First, they estimated the number of probable freshman applicants among the class of 1936 (all freshmen then residing in college dormitories were included, as well as those who had been dropped from their class, but would seek readmission). Students who lived in off-campus housing or who commuted—almost 30 percent of the class—were excluded from four classifications, designed to apportion those applying to the houses:

> A. *Race*; B. *Scholarship rank*; C. *Private schools*, with some subclassifications to distinguish the very few fashionable private schools from the schools like Andover and Exeter, and to distinguish these schools from the large group of other private schools; D. *Public Schools*. . . . a definite percentage could then be fixed for each House for each classification, on the basis of the proportion of that classification in the total number of applicants or the College as a whole.

This principle of apportionment, known as "the cross-section," reflected a sensitivity to and an acute realization of the reputation that certain school groups then had in Harvard College and tried to achieve a balance among them. At the same time, it perpetuated these very divisions by giving greater weight in the selection process to social standing than to intellectual achievement. 64

In addition to the category of "selected private schools," the administration and the masters made three other school groupings: "Andover-Exeter," "other private schools," and "public schools." Andover and Exeter were put in a separate class, because together they sent on an average about one hundred men a year to Harvard. Academically, their graduates did somewhat better than the St. Grottlesexers, though lacking the latter's social prestige. For example, in the classes of 1939, 1940, and 1941, 127 (43.3 percent) of the St. Grottlesexers made a final club, but only 8 of 112 Andover graduates and 6 of 228 Exeter men did so. The importance of coming from the "right" school, to established cliques at Harvard, was further underscored by the fact that of the 293 clubmen in these three classes, only 23 had graduated from one of the "other private schools" and just one from a public high school.[65]

One other social group was identified, not by school, but by "race" (see Table 4.8). Jewish students among the probable freshmen applicants and returning upperclassmen were marked by a J, X, or * (meaning the "starred" group) for purposes of identification.[66]

To decide which applicants would be rejected, scholastic rank would be taken into account, and the Jews on the whole were better students than Gentiles. Almost 32 percent of Jewish freshmen made dean's list, while less than 8 percent had unsatisfactory records (see Table 4.9). But for the entire freshman class only about 19 percent achieved dean's list standing, while over 16 percent were less than satisfactory. The contrast between the Jewish group and the "selected private schools" was striking: More than 20 percent of the latter were unsatisfactory, while just over 11 percent were on dean's list. As a student's social prestige rose, his academic standing often declined.[67]

To be sure, other factors were considered in assigning students to the houses—for example, fields of concentration and room prices. Since each house had a head tutor, several resident tutors, and a number of nonresident tutors, students would generally choose or be assigned where they might receive instruction in their fields of concentration. To promote an intellectual cross section, many different fields should be represented in each house. Room prices varied, however, from $100 to $500 per student during the mid-1930s, with the average being $262. As was to be expected, there was a keen demand for lower-priced triples and quadruples. Geographical distribution was also given some weight. Tables compiled in 1933 on the numbers and percentages from each major region showed that almost three-fourths of students in the houses came from New England (over 40 percent) and the Middle Atlantic regions.[68]

Even if one makes allowances for tutorial quotas and economic factors, the evidence indicated that some students were denied admission to the houses because of "racial" prejudice. House representatives could rate the desirability of freshmen applicants on the basis of the required personal interview. Professor Seymour Harris has noted, moreover, that "there were under-

Table 4.8

RESIDENT FRESHMEN APPLYING FOR HOUSES, BY TYPE OF SCHOOL AND BY RACE, 1933-42

Year[a]	Selected Private Schools		Andover and Exeter		Other Private Schools		Public Schools		Total Freshmen	Proportion of Jewish Freshmen to Total	
	No.	%	No.	%	No.	%	No.	%	No.	No.	%
1933	149	19.0	85	11.0	322	42.0	216	28.0	772	93	12.4
1934	125	17.0	121	16.0	288	39.0	204	28.0	738	73	9.9
1935	165	20.4	129	15.9	263	32.5	253	31.2	810	88	10.9
1936	185	22.8	122	15.0	239	29.5	265	32.7	811	120	14.8
1937	188	23.8	104	13.1	240	30.3	260	32.8	792	111	14.0
1938	178	22.4	90	11.4	261	32.9	264	33.3	793	122	15.4
1939	179	22.1	68	8.4	255	31.4	309	38.1	811	117	14.4
1940	164	20.3	103	12.7	260	32.2	281	34.8	808	129	16.0
1941	140	17.6	97	12.2	274	34.4	286	35.8	797	112	14.1
1942	166	19.4	85	10.1	255	29.6	352	40.9	858	138	16.1
Total[b]	1,639	20.48	1,004	12.58	2,657	33.38	2,690	33.56	7,990	1,103	13.8

Source: Compiled from: Table 1, most frequently entitled "Distribution of Probable Freshman Applicants for Houses According to Rank List, Race, Type of School Represented," in Dean of Harvard College Correspondence File, 1933-57 (and some earlier), box on Houses (Parietal Rules—Tutorial), Houses (Adams—Winthrop), folders on Statistics, 1932-42; from box on House Plan—Houses (to 1938), folders on Houses, 1933-38; and from box on Houses 1939-52, folder on Houses 1938-40.

[a]To determine the year of graduation, add three years. The totals tabulated are the classes of 1936 through 1946.

[b]The final totals are based on the revised figures for 1935.

Table 4.9

RANK LIST DISTRIBUTION OF PROBABLE FRESHMAN APPLICANTS FOR HOUSES,
BY TYPE OF SCHOOL AND RACE, 1933–42

Rank at Midyear[b]	Selected Private Schools		Andover and Exeter		Other Private Schools		Public Schools		Freshman Total		Proportion of Jewish Freshmen to Total	
	No.	%	No.	%	No.	%	No.	%	No.	%	No.	%
I[a]	7		2		18		31		58		16	
II[a]	31	11.0	28	13.9	101	16.3	210	29.1	370	19.3	101	31.9
III[a]	143		110		315		543		1,111		235	
IV	292	17.8	196	19.5	540	20.3	710	26.4	1,738	21.7	296	26.8
V	621	37.9	368	36.7	861	32.4	741	27.6	2,591	32.4	309	28.0
VI	216	13.2	117	11.7	288	10.9	189	7.0	810	10.2	66	6.0
Unsatis-factory	329	20.1	183	18.2	534	20.1	266	9.9	1,312	16.4	80	7.3
Total	1,639	100.0	1,004	100.0	2,657	100.0	2,690	100.0	7,990	100.0	1,103	100.0

Source: Compiled from Table 1, most frequently entitled "Distribution of Probable Freshman Applicants for Houses According to Rank List, Race, Type of School Represented."
[a] Groups I–III constitute dean's list. Group I: at least 3.5 As, 0.5 B; Group II: at least 1.5 As, 2.5 Bs; Group III: at least 3.5 Bs, 0.5 C; Group IV: 2 Bs, 2 Cs; Group V: average Cs; Group VI: average Ds; and Unsatisfactory: failing several subjects.

standings about the equitable distribution of Jewish students among the houses and even some enthusiasm for quotas." Indeed, the percentage of Jewish freshmen as resident students (as opposed to those who commuted) dropped sharply in 1934 to 9.9 percent and rose by only 1 percent the following year (see Table 4.8). Following a 4-percent rise in 1936, the percentage of resident Jews fluctuated thereafter between 14 and 16; the percentage admitted to the houses averaged only slightly higher. [69]

A memorandum on "Suggested Procedure for Assignment to Houses" advised the masters to take "care [that] the total of Jews accepted does not exceed what 'the traffic will bear,' " but that "superior Jews" not be "vetoed" so late that they would not be able to apply to another house. One master complained, however, that while almost fifty Jews made his house their first choice, he would accept only a dozen of them. He therefore asked the central committee to "relieve" him of "a few [of his] most expensive Jews" in order to "improve the complexion of the House." Another felt that "it would be unwise to have any House at any time run over ten per cent of its total membership on 'black spots.' " He hoped for a more positive method of identification, "since our sad experience has been that names mean very little." One way of identifying Jewish applicants was to look up their ancestry or make pointed inquiries. Each house kept a separate list of Jewish students admitted. [70]

Some alumni fathers complained that their sons failed to secure a room in any house, although they had better academic records than some of those accepted and although rooms were still available at the price they offered to pay. On at least one occasion a parental letter evidently opened the door to a house for an alumni son in spite of the reluctance of the masters to "increase their racial quota." But in many more cases, the rejected students had to seek other accommodations. In December 1936, Dean Hanford reported to President Conant that there were "now 195 names on the House waiting list," of which "112 belong to a particular group of whom the Masters will not take more than a certain percentage." [71]

The Masters at Harvard—and at Yale

Each master cultivated a certain social atmosphere in his house. As observed by Professor David Riesman '31, who had roomed in Dunster House during his senior year, "the House masterships with notable exceptions were in the early years filled by Ivy-League-type men in English or history or classics." The first two masters were Julian Lowell Coolidge, a kinsman of the Harvard president, and Chester N. Greenough, former dean of Harvard College. Coolidge, master of Lowell House, was a mathematician and amateur astronomer, while Greenough, master of Dunster House, taught English. When the five other houses were opened in 1931, the following professors were appointed as masters: Roger B. Merriman (history), Eliot House; Ronald M. Ferry (biochemical sciences), Winthrop House; Kenneth B. Murdock (American literature), Leverett House; Edward A. Whitney (history and literature), Kirkland House; and James P. Baxter (American diplomatic history), Adams House. All were graduates of Harvard College, except Baxter, who had attended Williams College; he returned to his alma mater to be its president from 1937 to 1961.[72]

Julian Lowell Coolidge, summa cum laude in mathematics '95, personified institutional loyalty and Boston Brahmin values. After Harvard, he studied at Oxford and then for the Ph. D. at the University of Bonn. On his return, the former track star became a well-recognized cyclist around Harvard. In addition to Mrs. Coolidge's frequent teas, the Monday night "high table" (it had an eighteen-inch lift) became a Lowell House institution: Coolidge, the tutors, prominent guests, and selected students dined in dinner coats on a platform at one end of the hall.[73]

The impact of his mastership was well noted in 1940, the year he retired, in Thomas Stephenson's feature article, "Lowell House in the Coolidge Manner," appearing in the *Boston Herald*. The master took "minute interest in selecting" the applicants and insisted on "good scholarship." Usually, a higher percentage of Lowell House members were found in the first four groups of the rank list than was the case in any of the other houses. "Star athletes and final clubmen," reported Stephenson, were "noticeably absent." (Lowell House had only 7 of the 293 final club members in the classes of 1939, 1940, and 1941.) Coolidge preferred "a well rounded type of undergraduate."[74]

While all of the first seven Harvard masters had studied at Harvard, the first ten Yale masters had received, in addition to Yale degrees, academic training at Cambridge and Oxford, Harvard, Johns Hopkins, Columbia, and Denver universities. They were, wrote Yale historian George Wilson Pierson, "anything but inbred." In developing its College Plan, however, Yale both drew upon and modified the models provided by Harvard and the English universities of Cambridge and Oxford. For example, the Yale units, the first seven of which opened in September 1933, were limited to 150 to 250 students, at least 50 less than Harvard's largest house (Eliot). And when the problem of assigning rooms had to be considered, Yale was well aware that the Harvard Plan "had unexpectedly accentuated the differences between" the residential students and "the outcast commuters." At Yale, only about 10 percent of the students lived at home; these men, it was hoped, would become nonresident associates of the colleges (but until the commuters got associate membership in the 1940s, their only campus facility was Byers Hall). Benefactor Edward S. Harkness did provide bursary funds for work scholarships so that some fifty students in each college could earn part of their board. To unify campus life further, Sheffield Scientific School students were brought together with Yale College men in the same residential units.[75]

But after a detailed tabulation of data on the classes of 1934-36 by A. B. Crawford and the Department of Personnel Study, the Yale masters rejected rigorous cross-sectioning. Students were allowed to choose their college—and 70 percent of the accepted applicants got their first choice—in accordance with personal preferences, family ties, and friends. But it was also agreed "to have an even distribution of the self-help and religious groups, and . . . to set up a tribunal to adjudicate rival claims." After each master indicated a limited number of first choices, the lists were sent to the Committee on Allocation for final distribution. Some would be left out of the residential units by lack of space. Wiser than Harvard in this respect, Yale decided that seniors and juniors would first receive accommodations, while sophomores on the dean's list could compete for the 175 places remaining out of the 1,250 then available.[76]

Aside from these differences. Yale followed Harvard in generally accepting the recommendations of the masters. Yale also had its charts of "Data Relating to Allocation of Students to the Colleges." In April 1934, of the 1,433 residents and new applicants, 485 were fraternity men, both Yale College and Sheffield; 275 were bursary students (but together with other self-help students, the percentage in this category was expected to double); and 123 were Jews (9 percent), identified by a penciled X. Each of the residential colleges would thus take "a proportionate quota of self-supporting students as well as of Jewish students," dean's list scholars, and fraternity men.[77]

The Students Outside the Houses

By its handling of room assignments and nonresident students, Yale seemed largely to avoid aggravating on its campus the two social problems that festered at Harvard during the 1930s: the long-delayed efforts to raise the status of commuters, who were generally relegated to the margins of campus life, and the limited administrative concern for the several hundred upperclassmen, Gentiles as well as Jews, who were rejected each year for admission to the houses.

In 1933-34, 804 students, 23.3 percent of the total Harvard College enrollment of 3,450, lived at home either in Cambridge or in one of the twenty-one other neighboring communities. While their percentage declined to 16.5 by 1942-43 and to just under 11 percent by 1955-56, they remained a significant group. Recognizing their need for a fuller collegiate experience, the Phillips Brooks House Association, a social service organization open to all Harvard students, presented in 1935 a "Report on the Commuting Student Situation in Harvard College." It urged that the university provide a building for commuters, which would be managed by an undergraduate organization and maintained by a $10 annual membership fee. In response to this report as well as to concern expressed by alumni and overseers, the Harvard Corporation voted that a Committee on the Harvard College Non-resident Student Center assume responsibilities for the first floor of Dudley Hall, which would be opened in September. The members of this committee, under the chairmanship of Allston Burr '89, had volunteered their services.[78]

In at least two ways, Dudley Hall fulfilled an important role. Established to bring the economically "less fortunate" students into greater contact with Harvard undergraduate life, it functioned almost as an eighth house. Dudley competed in nine team sports, despite the fact that juniors and seniors left the center as vacancies opened up in the seven residential houses. And those who worked with the commuters found the experience to be an education in "overcoming race prejudice." Although the number of Jewish commuters cannot be exactly determined, a check of the names of the 217 commuting freshmen in the class of 1942 indicated that 48, or about 22 percent, were probably Jewish. During Dudley Hall's second year of operation (1936-37) about two-thirds of the 268 members were Jews, many of them graduates of the Boston Latin School, and Jews were strongly represented on the center's house committee. After graduation, Dudley's former members went "well on their way to positions of promise in virtually all phases of American life."[79]

By 1941, the administration was also considering ways to expand Harvard's service to greater Boston. Of the ten thousand young men graduating annually from the area's 101 public high schools, about one-quarter went on to college. Less than one-tenth—and the number was decreasing—came to Harvard. To attract more of the very best students from these high schools, it was proposed to provide three National Scholarships for Massachusetts applicants and ten Greater Boston Non-resident Scholarships.[80]

During the late 1930s, the administration had, as well, to respond to mounting student pressure on behalf of the unsuccessful applicants for the houses. Some of the masters were "somewhat disturbed by the number of good *'s who are being left out of the Houses." (Of the 184 members of the classes of 1939, 1940, and 1941 still on the house waiting list in October 1938, 84 were "starred.") Earlier in May, a committee of twelve freshmen, among them the class president and the chairman of the Freshman Union committee, had met with Dean Hanford and Walter Clark, master of Kirkland House. Although eleven of the group had been admitted to a house, the committee was formed to express the "smouldering" feeling of "the large number of men who cannot get into the Houses." The dean explained that the housing situation would improve after the graduation of the larger classes of 1938 and 1939, since the incoming freshman class of 1942 would be strictly limited to 1,000. But the freshmen were not convinced: The committee asked that the university consider either expanding housing facilities or creating associate memberships, with privileges of using dining halls, library, and common rooms and of participating in house sports. They strongly recommended that the university guarantee all juniors admission to a house.[81]

In a subsequent "Memorandum to Freshman Committee of the Houses,"

Dean Hanford rejected its proposals. Not only would the creation of associate memberships lead to overcrowding and a reduction in the number of
sophomores admitted, but this new category would heighten the distinction
between those inside and those outside the houses. In October the masters declined to follow Yale in "guaranteeing" admission to a house to every junior
and senior. [82]

In his annual report of January 1939, however, Dean Hanford became the
first ranking administrator to advocate the construction of a new house as a
solution, if funds were available. About the same time, the Student Council
decided to study and make major reports on "The Problems Offered by Men
who are not Admitted to any House" and on "Methods of Selection to the
Houses." (In 1926, its "Report of the Committee on Education" had recommended that the college be divided into smaller residential units—two years
before E. S. Harkness's gift.) In its report on the problems, the council proposed that each house take ten or twelve nonresident memberships; that juniors and seniors be given sufficient preference to enable them to reside in a
house at least one year; and that provision be made for informal athletics for
upperclassmen living in college dormitories. The masters agreed to all three.
With reluctance, they voted to admit to each house ten to twelve associate
members from the waiting list, as an experiment in 1939-40. [83]

Concerning methods of selection, the Student Council modified its initial
recommendation on dean's list students, because it realized "the impossibili-
ty" of definitely guaranteeing them admission, given such factors as room
prices. Publicly, the council declared its unanimous support for "the present
system of having a cross-section of students in each House based on their
school and general social background" as well as a cross section by academic
concentration. Privately, the council sanctioned the principle that each house
admit the same percentage of Jews. The publicized proposals were sharply
criticized by the *Harvard Crimson* in its April 13, 1939, editorial, "Deep
South." The council, it argued, should direct attention to improving "the
methods by which Masters ascertain the qualifications and antecedents of
applicants." [84]

Many freshmen were still impatient and bitter. Eleven Yardlings with
house acceptances wrote a protest letter to the central committee and then circulated a "Freshman Class Petition on the House Problem." It secured 210 sig-
natures (more Gentiles than Jews). The freshmen's most important request
was that dean's list students be promised admission to one of the houses, as
well as all freshmen in Group IV who actively participated in three major extracurricular activities. Judging as "inadequate" the interviews with house
representatives, the freshmen urged that "merit" play a greater role in the
selection process. (As of the spring of 1939, 80 men with unsatisfactory
academic records resided in the houses.) Although the Student Council defended the existing policy of selection—voting against any category of

assured admission—it had helped undergraduates win significant concessions from the administration and the masters, notably the nonresident memberships. [85]

World War II opened the houses to most upperclassmen. In February 1942,
the faculty and governing boards approved the recommendation of the masters and the Administrative Board that, beginning with the class of 1945 and
continuing throughout World War II, "all undergraduates, except those who
live at home or have special permission to live elsewhere, shall reside in College halls." The policy of compulsory campus residency, which had been applied to freshmen in 1914, would now be extended to upperclassmen, thus
fulfilling President Lowell's vision of Harvard College as an intellectual and
social community. Since more than half the wartime undergraduates would
be accelerating their academic studies, house residence would give them the
collegiate experience, while benefiting Harvard financially. If any vacancies
remained, freshmen would be allowed to enter the houses. [86]

Complete statistics were not kept during World War II, but an analysis of
the composition of Adams, Dunster, and Lowell on March 30, 1944, showed
that 178—31.7 percent—of their 562 undergraduates were Jewish. With the
war's end, the masters resumed cross-sectioning. Of the 2,731 residents in the
houses in 1946-47, 464, or 17.0 percent, were Jewish, the same percentage
that it had been in May 1941. At the same time, the percentage of public high
school graduates had increased to well over 40 percent, largely at the expense
of those from "other private schools." [87]

But the social priorities of Harvard during the 1930s would not survive
long into the postwar period. The older administrators as well as several of
the original masters had retired. Many of the younger men, who joined or
returned to the Harvard faculty or administration after military service, did
not share the social attitudes of their predecessors. Sometime between the fall
of 1946 and the fall of 1950 (the exact date may well be found when the papers
of President James Bryant Conant are opened to examination), the administration recognized that its school and social classification scheme was beginning to lose its relevance.

While the final clubs still counted socially among the classes of 1949, 1950,
and 1951, the St. Grottlesexers had yielded some of their preeminence to Exeter, Andover, and the "other private schools" (more than 20 percent of their
graduates were now members). Even the "high schools" were modestly represented by twenty-seven men. Porcellian and Fly, still dominated by the graduates of Groton, Milton, St. Mark's and St. Paul's, each admitted only one
man from Exeter and none from Andover or the "public schools." [88]

In the early 1950s, an alumnus of Jewish lineage who served on Committee
to Visit Harvard College was concerned that the college's social system often
discouraged applications from able men outside of the eastern prep school
crowd. "A Levi Jackson or a [Dick] Kazmaier would have been lost at Har-

vard College," he argued, "whereas at Yale and Princeton they received every honor." Jackson, a black member of the Yale class of 1950, was elected captain of the 1949 football team and tapped for Skull and Bones, while Kazmaier, the son of a Libby-Owens glass worker, became in 1951 the third Ivy League football player to win the Heisman Trophy. The alumnus felt that the social systems at Princeton, Yale, and Dartmouth gave "a boy a circle of close friends" that Harvard clubs, with their "astounding medieval features," could not offer. Yale fraternities and honor societies not only elected more high school graduates than did those at Harvard, but its fraternities also invited nonmembers to lunches and dances. Even while continuing to bar nonmembers as guests, Harvard clubs were becoming less attractive to the prep school crowd because of required board payments to the houses. [89]

In May 1950, moreover, the masters agreed that every applicant for a house be given a permanent assignment, as either a resident or a nonresident. Heretofore, a student or clique could refuse to accept an assignment considered uncongenial in the hope of later receiving a more preferable one. As President Lowell had probably anticipated, the houses eventually eroded much of the prestige of the clubs. But the houses have not as yet become the "laboratory for determining a more ideal freshman class," which Christopher S. Jencks and David Riesman proposed, by experimenting with "the 'mix' of various types of students." House recruitment has slowly moved away from administrative allocation and masters' preferences toward student choice and computer assignment. For example, the "Analysis of House Applications" in April 1951 and 1952 *omitted* the "starred" group (Jewish students) from its tabulations. Rank list and type of school—S, OP, AE, and HS—seem to have been the only factors included. These two charts may well have signaled the beginning of the end of an era in Harvard undergraduate social policy and perhaps in admissions as well. [90]

To be sure, cross-sectioning, with its quotas of school groups modified by students and masters' first-choice preferences, continued to be applied in the postwar period. Finally, in 1973, the masters yielded their preferences, although Harvard probably retains certain distribution-type criteria. Some official intervention may be necessary, from time to time, to prevent the formation of voluntary enclaves, especially among black students. And sex ratios became factors in assignments when Radcliffe and Harvard students were admitted to each other's houses. At present, resident students list their choices of houses from one to twelve (including three in the Radcliffe Quadrangle), together with names of roommates. This information is fed into a computer that randomly selects from those applying to each house the number necessary to fill vacancies. In 1974, 67 percent received their first choice; over 80 percent, one of their top five choices; and over 90 percent, one of their first nine. [91]

Harvard experienced one of the major educational crises of the twentieth century when its traditional admission preferences and residential allocation policy confronted new social groups. Whether its administrators—President Lowell, most conspicuously—were realistic or short-sighted in their treatment of Jewish (and black) applicants and students depended on whether alternative solutions existed. Harvard's largely, but not exclusively, meritocratic post-World War II admission policies suggested that there were options. But the Lowell administration seemed neither to perceive the existence of alternatives nor to recognize that its own method of long-term Jewish quotas would perpetuate the very divisions that the president claimed he desired to heal. In responding to the crisis at Harvard, Lowell proved himself, like his contemporaries at Columbia, Princeton, and Yale, to be bound by the prejudices of his social class and times.

·5·

YALE: REACTION AND STABILIZATION, 1900S TO 1940S

> I am urging him because he is Dean of the Yale Medical School, and as Dean should naturally be invited to become a member of the Club, unless there is stronger objection to him than that which is based on the fear that the Hebrew element in the Club may become too large.
>
> President Arthur Twining Hadley to Professor
> Frederick B. Luquiens, November 25, 1920

> The Corporation's Committee on Educational Policy has asked me to report at an early date on the number and status of students of Jewish origin now in the Undergraduate Schools and to discuss with them the advisability or necessity of concerting measures for limiting the number of those of this race or religion to be admitted to college.
>
> The restrictive measures enforced or to be enforced at other colleges which draw from the same sources as we make the serious consideration of this question imperative.
>
> Robert N. Corwin, chairman of the Board of Admissions, to Frederick S. Jones, dean of Yale College, May 3, 1922[1]

In 1920, President Arthur Twining Hadley wrote a strong letter endorsing the admission of Milton Charles Winternitz, dean of the Yale Medical School, to the Graduate Club in New Haven. It was of prime importance to the president that the dean of the medical school have access to those places that served as a forum for Yale affairs. While Hadley did not think that the Graduate Club should elect a man just because he was connected to Yale, he deplored the club's "policy of race discrimination," one that it had "not always practiced." In the present situation such a policy would "exceptionally effect the Yale Medical School" and cause public discussion. Hadley's very advocacy of Winternitz proved the prevalence of anti-Semitism—of that intangible, but deadly gentlemanly sort—on Yale's Old Campus.[2]

Less than two years later, Yale began its own examination of Jewish students within the undergraduate schools. "Old Blues" in the administration and on the faculty were reacting to news carried by the academic grapevine as well as to official announcements at other universities, especially Harvard. Any admissions decision that Harvard made was bound to affect Yale because the two universities drew upon a similar pool of applicants. A memorandum of May 12, 1922 by Admissions Board Chairman Corwin pointed out that Columbia had "reduced the number of its Jewish students by half," that Harvard was "taking measures leading to the same result, and that several other eastern colleges [were] limiting numbers partly with this same end in view." Given this situation, it seemed "necessary that we should take some action if we are not to add to our present quota those . . . refused admission" elsewhere. At the same time, Yale, if not necessarily its new president, James R. Angell, was having doubts about the overall quality of its Jewish students. To this point, Corwin asked Dean Jones two leading questions: Was it "desirable, for reasons purely scholastic in the larger sense, to limit the number of Jewish students admitted to Yale?" Was "the present proportion of Jewish students . . . too great when the interests of the whole undergraduate body [were] taken into consideration?" And if these questions were answered affirmatively, as they were to be, Corwin added a third: "What measures" should be adopted to accomplish such a limitation?[3]

President Arthur Twining Hadley and the "Yale Spirit"

Though of "unimpressive face and figure," President Arthur Twining Hadley '76 was a man of sound principles and strong convictions. Born in 1856, the same year as A. Lawrence Lowell of Harvard and Woodrow Wilson of Princeton, Hadley was a descendant of an old New England farming family, which in recent generations had entered the educational and legal professions. His grandfather had gone to Dartmouth, but Hadley and his father, James, were Yale College graduates. Both were to become professors at the college, the father in Greek and the son in political economy. Arthur Hadley achieved unqualified academic and social success at Yale. He was class valedictorian and held prestigious scholarships throughout his years of undergraduate and postgraduate study. He also was a member of the junior fraternity, Delta Kappa Epsilon, and of the senior society, Skull and Bones. An additional measure of the esteem in which he was held was his election in senior year as alumni class secretary.[4]

In many ways, Hadley was the ideal Yale man, exemplifying the virtues of the Christian gentleman, the scholar, and the public servant. His religious faith, while strong, was not fanatical, and in this respect, he was well suited to become Yale's first lay president. Preferring membership in a nonsectarian Protestant organization to affiliation with an established denomination, Hadley belonged to the Church of Christ in Yale College. He believed that Yale's president should participate in religious services that drew together many denominations. In addition to his professorial duties, Hadley was commissioner of labor statistics of the State of Connecticut from 1885 to 1887. His correspondence as president showed an active concern for issues of the day, although his replies were usually brief, due to the pressure of his regular work. In his commitment to "God, Country, and Yale," Hadley merited the praise lavished on him by Charles Seymour, a later Yale president: "With all his brilliance, with all his fame, we thought of him always simply as the truest Yale man of all."[5]

Hadley administered Yale as a "moderator [or] mediator rather than master," and according to Yale's historian, George W. Pierson, his presidency was best described as "the Consulship of Hadley." His reluctance to dictate policy allowed conflicts to develop within the faculty, and these, in turn, sometimes forced him to reverse his previous decisions. He accepted, moreover, the custom that allowed the permanent officers of Yale College far more independence in running their own affairs than was permitted the faculty at Harvard and Princeton. In 1908, for example, the Yale faculty exercised its prerogative of choosing a successor to Henry P. Wright, who was retiring as dean of the college. [6]

Hadley's administration, nevertheless, encouraged Yale's lay alumni to assume a larger role "in the clerically-dominated hierarchy." In keeping with this new spirit, the Corporation of Yale University voted in April 1906

> that the President be authorized to certify to the Trustees of the Carnegie Fund that no denominational test is imposed in the choice of trustees, officers, or teachers, or in the admission of students, nor are distinctly denominational tenets or doctrines taught to the students of Yale University.

By a self-perpetuating authority to choose their successors for two centuries, only ordained ministers had served as trustees of the Yale Corporation. By the 1920s, however, laymen constituted six of the ten successor trustees.[7]

At the end of World War I, the alumni were in a position to demand and then to push through a major reorganization of Yale University. Their reform movement had several objectives: improve the quality of undergraduate teaching and curriculum; bring Yale College and Sheffield Scientific School into closer relationship; modify entrance requirements so as to increase western representation; build up the graduate and professional schools; augment the university's endowment; and raise faculty salaries. Hadley initially hesitated and then opposed these changes on the grounds of excessive cost. But ultimately he accepted "reorganization," which had effected the following changes: Sheff's course of study was extended from three to four years; the college began to award the Ph.B. (formerly given in Sheff's select course) for those who entered without Latin; and the freshman year, Yale College, and Sheff admissions were to be combined under a newly created Board of Admissions. Freshmen admitted under this new procedure would participate in a common freshman year, before electing to study at Yale College or Sheff for the remaining three years. Finally, the faculty would be organized into university departments, under university divisions, which in turn would be represented on a university council headed by a provost. While Hadley's last years as president were marred by disagreements with the alumni and corporation, it was nevertheless during his administration that Yale evolved from an uncoordinated association of schools into a balanced university. Yale had combined, with some success, the ideals and organization of the English and German universities. By his two principal achievements—the Memorial Quadrangle and the university press—the president had fostered the unity of spirit and intellect.[8]

As Yale developed into a university capable of sustaining comparison with European models, it also began to attract a more cosmopolitan faculty and a more socially diversified student body. Though the overwhelming majority of professors in the university were white Anglo-Saxon Protestant, a few Catholics and Jews began to appear on the faculty roster around 1900. The latter groups were usually connected with Sheffield Scientific School or with one of the professional schools. Jews who received tenure before 1930 numbered well under a dozen—and none were tenured in Yale College before 1940. Among the earliest Jewish faculty members were two instructors of Russian, one for just a few years around 1900 and the other, Max Solomon Mandell, from 1907 to 1924. Dean Frederick S. Jones opposed offering Mandell a permanent position largely because his "accent and idiom" were "peculiar to the Russian Hebrew." (Ironically, as the Western world watched with fascination the Bolshevik experiment in Russia, the Yale faculty voted to discontinue instruction in Russian at the end of the 1923-24 academic year.)[9]

Among the other Jews teaching at Yale were a musician and four professors of medicine or science, notably, Dr. Milton C. Winternitz, honorary M.A. '17, professor of pathology and bacteriology, who served as dean of the School of Medicine from 1920 to 1935, and Lafayette B. Mendel '91, professor of physiological chemistry from 1903 to 1921 (department chairman in 1920), who was appointed to a Sterling Professorship in 1921. During the 1930s and 1940s, several other Jews achieved prominence at Yale, as attested by the Sterling Professorships they held, but the road was difficult.[10]

Even a faculty appointment did not insure social acceptance. The elite social club for Yale men and faculty in New Haven was the Graduate Club Association. Though founded by Yale graduates, non-Yale men who were appointed to faculty positions could also be proposed and accepted for membership, as was the case of Hadley's successor, University of Michigan-educated James R. Angell. The number of members was limited to 500-600 residents and to 1,200 nonresidents. A Committee on Admissions passed on recommendations for membership. Under their "secret and confidential" proceedings, "two negative ballots shall be sufficient to exclude; one negative ballot shall be sufficient to defer consideration of a candidate's name for one regular meeting." A minimum of four affirmative ballots (half) were required for election. [11]

Three decisions regarding admission or its denial to Jews provided salient illustrations of the effect of the Jewish question on the Yale community. President Hadley argued against the exclusion of Dean Winternitz on professional and social grounds. Above all, the dean needed the club as a place in which to hold conferences, "partly because most of the men will be Graduate Club members, and partly because the Graduate Club is regarded by the public, and rightly so regarded, as the natural place for the discussion of Yale affairs by intelligent graduates." As an Old Blue, Hadley understood that a gentleman's club was a key decision-making institution on the campus no less than in the downtown business district and in suburbia. His arguments carried weight with the club's Committee on Admissions: Dean Winternitz was elected a resident member in 1920. [12]

But Hadley's powers of persuasion did not succeed in the case of another Jew, who was "a graduate of Yale, an active leader in educational and charitable work, and thoroughly likable man." "The commercial characteristics which are often so disagreeable," said Hadley, "have not been marked either in him or in his father," both prominent New Haven businessmen. Nevertheless, certain stereotypes influenced his personal attitudes toward Jews: the socially uncouth, commercially aggressive Jew as opposed to the well-educated, culturally assimilated Jewish community leader. Jews were racially different from Gentiles, Hadley believed, but this difference ought not stand as barrier to their advancement and social acceptance. His professions of friendship for the *right kind* of Jews were sincere. [13]

Hadley realized that many on the Yale faculty did not share his views and furthermore disliked working on a committee with a Jewish professor. Hence, someone other than Professor Lafayette B. Mendel would be a better choice for "a committee on Library site," because "while everybody likes him, the fact of his race has kept him in some measure apart from the life of the place." Though a Yale man and a member of the Graduate Club, Mendel was not an Old Blue, a member of the inner group. In the 1920s, he did represent Sheffield Scientific School on the all-important Board of Admissions. His participation might have been a matter of administrative expediency. In comparison with other professors of Jewish origin, Mendel and Winternitz had achieved comparatively elite positions in the Yale community. [14]

During the 1920s and 1930s, this community closed its ranks socially. A frequently told, though never fully documented, story illustrated this trend. A world renowned professor of Jewish origin, Edward Sapir, had been appointed Sterling Professor of Anthropology and Linguistics in 1931. He was refused membership in the Graduate Club. [15]

Minorities at Yale: Jews, Catholics, Negroes, and Foreign Students

Prior to the early 1920s, relatively little faculty criticism or hostility was expressed toward Jewish students. Although one incident was reported in late 1915 of a professor's "discourteous treatment" of two Jewish students, Yale was relatively accessible during these years. A Jewish alumnus, Louis Sachs, counted 20 Jewish students of a total enrollment of 361 in his Yale College class of 1914. Moreover, he was one of six brothers who graduated from Yale: one each in the classes of 1913, 1914, 1915, and 1922 and twins in 1927. Significantly, all of them lived at home as undergraduates. Two of the brothers received virtually full tuition scholarships; three were elected to Phi Beta Kappa; and three subsequently attended the Yale Law School. "The above roster of admissions from one family," he continued, "would seem to indicate that up to that time at least there was no real imposition of a quota system." He believed that quotas began in later years "when the number of Jewish boys passing the entrance exams became 'too large' for the college authorities." Yale also permitted the organization of Jewish social and cultural groups. The Menorah Society, which had branched out from Harvard to other colleges, received official recognition and was given a meeting room in a university building. [16]

While Jewish students were generally tolerated, there was occasional "evidence of some prejudicial conduct on the part of an official, but none on the part of a teaching professor or instructor," Sachs recalled. When he entered Yale in the fall of 1910, students were permitted eight class cuts a semester. Since the Jewish High Holidays occurred within the opening weeks of college, Sachs used all his cuts and feared that he might hurt his academic standing. After explaining his position, the dean of Yale College replied: "Young man this is neither a Jewish nor a Mohammedan institute. This is a Christian college and you will have to abide by its rules." On his way out, the youth passed through the room of the assistant dean, a man of broader sympathies, who told him: "Don't pay any attention" to Dean Jones; "if you get into difficulty come in and see me and I will take care of you." Since Sachs stayed in good health, he did not need the assistant dean's intercession, but the two were warm friends thereafter. [17]

By way of comparison, Catholic-Protestant relations at Yale seemed on the surface at least to have been harmonious. The degree to which Catholics had assimilated into the university as well as into American society was measured by the fact that they did not suffer from the restrictive policies aimed at more recently arrived immigrants, particularly the Jews. There was no evidence that Yale had any quota for Catholic students. Although Protestants, especially Episcopalians, dominated undergraduate life, many Catholics were varsity men. Catholic students were elected to Yale fraternities and even to senior societies. Nearly all Catholic fraternity members were from well-to-do families and had been educated at preparatory schools. Of the four Catholics among the fourteen Football Y men of 1912, two had graduated from Andover, one from Hotchkiss, and one from Williston Academy, after attending Hotchkiss. All were elected to one of the Yale fraternities or Sheffield societies: two in Delta Kappa Epsilon, one in Alpha Delta Phi, and the fourth in Sheffield's Berzelius. In addition, the two DKE's were tapped by Elihu (one of them achieved further distinctions by serving on Senior Council and class day committee); the ADP man was circulation manager of the *Yale Record*; and the Berzelian was a member of Sheff's Aurelian Honorary Society. In terms of social club membership, then, Catholics were comparatively well represented (see Table 5.1).[18]

This tabulation was suggestive, not conclusive. First, there was a considerable decline in Catholic membership in the senior societies from the class of 1912 to the class of 1927. Second, Psi Upsilon had no Catholic members in either year. And third, in both years one fraternity—DKE in 1912 and Alpha Sigma Phi in 1927—had a larger Catholic representation than any of the others. Further information probably lies in the private fraternity records. Whatever it may reveal, Catholics enjoyed a greater degree of social success at Yale than any other minority group.

Occasionally there occurred incidents that offended Catholic sensibilities. Yale undergraduate literary efforts sometimes revealed a strong Protestant bias, as in a poem published in 1901 in the *Yale Courant*. "Wooster Square" briefly chronicled in verse the settlement of South Italian immigrants in what had once been a fashionable New Haven residential area. The second stanza described:

> The old white church in Wooster Square
> Where godly people met and prayed—
> Dear Souls! They worship Mary there,
> Italian mother, man and maid
> In gaudy Southern scarfs arrayed;
> The horrid candles smoulder where
> The godly people met and prayed.
> Alas! The fall of Wooster Square!

By 1900, 7,780 Italians lived in New Haven, about one-third of them born in the United States. During the next thirty years, the Italian population in the city rose from 7.2 to over 25.0 percent. Only a small percentage of their children graduated from high school; consequently, few attended college,

Table 5.1
SOCIAL CLUB MEMBERSHIP OF CATHOLIC STUDENTS IN YALE COLLEGE, 1912, AND IN YALE COLLEGE AND SHEFFIELD SCIENTIFIC SCHOOL, 1927

Yale College			Sheffield Scientific School[a]	
Senior Society	*1912*	*1927*	*Societies*	*1927*
Skull and Bones (1832)	2	0	Berzelius ("Colony," 1848)	1
Scroll and Key (1842)	2	0		
Wolf's Head (1883)	2	1	Book and Snake ("Cloister," 1863)	4
Elihu Club (1903)	2	2	Theta Xi ("Franklin Hall," 1865)	0
Junior Fraternity[b]			Delta Psi ("St. Anthony," 1869)	0
Alpha Delta Phi (1836)	3	2		
Psi Upsilon (1838)	0	0	Phi Gamma Delta (1875) ("Vernon Hall," 1908)[d]	0
Delta Kappa Epsilon (1844)	9	1		
Zeta Psi (1888)	4	2	Chi Phi ("York Hall," 1878)	1
Beta Theta Pi (1906)	0	2	Delta Phi ("St. Elmo," 1888)	3
Alpha Sigma Phi (1924)	..	5		
Chi Psi (1924)	..	2	Phi Sigma Kappa ("Sachem Hall," 1893)	1
University Fraternities[c]				
Book and Bond (1899)	0	1		
Alpha Chi Rho (1905)	0	1		
Acacia (1909)	0	0		

Source: Compiled from "Yale College 1912 Statistical Blanks," filled out by seniors for *History of the Class of 1912, Yale College,* vol. 1, Yale University Archives; and from Yale and Sheff seniors listed as members of the Catholic Club in *Yale Banner and Pot-Pourri* 19

(1927): 202. See also "Foundation of Societies," *Yale Banner and Pot-Pourri* 22 (1930): 171. Total number of Catholics in Yale College class of 1912: 30, of whom 13 had neither senior society nor fraternity membership. Total number of Catholics in Yale College and Sheffield Scientific School class of 1927 was not precisely known. Figures were based on the 61 senior members of the Catholic Club in 1927, of whom 36 were in the college and 25 in Sheff. One nonmember was included on the basis of additional information. A varsity football player, Rupert Bloomfield McGunigle, Sheffield '27, entered a Roman Catholic monastic order in 1930. Of these 62, 26 belonged to social clubs.

[a]Prior to 1920, Sheffield offered a three-year undergraduate course, which made comparisons between Sheff and Yale College classes difficult. Sheff students who entered in 1908 graduated in 1911.

[b]Dates given indicate year in which each was recognized as a junior fraternity. At one time, ADP and BTP had been academic fraternities and ASP a sophomore society and then a university fraternity.

[c]University fraternities drew members from both the college and Sheff. Alpha Chi Rho, which began as a university fraternity in 1905, became a college (1924) and then a junior (1928) fraternity.

[d]Phi Gamma Delta functioned as both a Sheffield fraternity and a university fraternity before becoming the Sheffield Society known as Vernon Hall in 1908.

and very few went to Yale. In the Yale College class of 1927, for example, there were only four students of Italian descent; three of their fathers had been born in Italy. Eight Italian Americans were in the Sheffield class of 1927, and ten years later, Italian-born Paul Pasquariello graduated with the highest four-year average, a 98, attained in Yale College. [19]

Like Harvard, Yale was hospitable to the few Negro applicants who sought admission each year. There is no way of ascertaining how many applied, in excess of those admitted, but there seems to have been no objection against admitting a handful. Socially their status was considerably lower than their white fellow students, reflecting the condition of blacks in the outside community. Until about 1923, Negro waiters served in the Commons and Negro hallmen cleaned dormitory rooms. After they were replaced by student waiters and white maids, Negroes continued to perform many of the menial jobs in the university—their service, rendered with "Uncle Tom" cordiality, was one of Yale's traditions. [20]

Yale encouraged truly exceptional blacks to attend by awarding them scholarships. Some were transfer students from such southern Negro colleges as Talladega and Tuskegee, while a few came from New England private schools. Several were local youths, like Edward Alexander Bouchet, who in 1874 became the first Negro to graduate from Yale College. The first black member of Phi Beta Kappa, Bouchet earned a Ph.D. in chemistry and physics in 1876 and then became a teacher at the Institute for Colored Youth in Philadelphia. [21]

The career of William Pickens '04 was also of particular interest because of his friendly relationship with Dean Henry Parks Wright. Pickens, born in Anderson County, South Carolina, graduated from the College Department of Talladega College. He was recommended for admission to the junior class at Yale by the Reverend A. F. Beard, a corresponding secretary of the American Missionary Association of New York. Beard believed that "the promise of his future is the more hopeful as he is an earnest and consistent Christian man." Any interest that Dean Wright took in the young man would be "a good investment for his race." In spite of the necessity of working his way through two years at Yale by washing pots and windows at the YMCA, Pickens was elected to Phi Beta Kappa and won the Ten Eyck Oratorical Contest prize. After graduation, he returned to Talladega as a teacher of Latin, German, English, and Esperanto. He next taught at Wiley University and later became dean of Morgan College. In addition, Pickens published several books, among them *The New Negro* (1916), a series of essays, and *Bursting Bonds* (1923). By then, he was also a field secretary for the NAACP. [22]

Although Pickens had found his Yale years to be a great opportunity, most aspiring black students favored other eastern, private colleges. In 1909, Alfred E. Stearns, principal of Phillips Andover Academy, asked Wright's successor, Dean Frederick S. Jones, whether a Negro student would be as welcome at Yale as at Dartmouth or Harvard. The only Negro student at Andover at that time had been urged to seek a good education by a former Yale man, but he had come "to feel that he would have a better chance at Harvard." Stearns recommended him as

> a good clean fellow, much better than the average 'darkey' and a boy who has in the main stood very well in his work here, indeed on several occasions he has been on our honor lists, although lately he has found the work harder, as almost all boys of his race do.

Whatever Jones replied, the black student decided to enter the class of 1914 at Harvard, where he won a major letter in track. And twenty-five years after graduation, he recalled that his "school days at Phillips-Andover and college experiences at Harvard were the happiest years of my life." [23]

Yale continued to admit a few Negroes most years, but as of 1931 there was only *one* Negro in the three undergraduates schools. The general economic situation may have been largely responsible. In answer to a request by W. E. Burghardt Du Bois, editor of the *Crisis*, for a statement on "The Negro and Yale University," President Angell suggested that he write directly to the one black undergraduate, Edward Morrow '31, of Huron, South Dakota. Morrow had written a considerable part of the recently published *Life of Paul Robeson* and planned to become the concert artist's secretary after graduation. Before replying to Du Bois, Angell had consulted with Admissions Director Robert N. Corwin, who said that as far as he knew "there has never been any negro question here, nor has the necessity been felt for adopting a policy for determining our acceptance of negroes or our treatment of them."

Angell asserted, too, that he was unaware of any discrimination against Negroes at Yale, nor had he heard any complaints in that regard. He thought that "colored boys, when they come here, are accepted on their merits and so dealt with just as are other students." Many years later this observation would be verified when Levi Jackson, the black football captain, commented on his selection by Skull and Bones: "If my name had been reversed, I never would have made it." But Jackson turned down Bones, joining Berzelius instead to be with friends. 24

During Arthur Twining Hadley's years as president, Yale attracted foreign students to its classrooms. Of these, Yale felt a special concern for the Chinese, dating from the days of Yung Wing, who graduated from the college in 1854. Yale's first Chinese graduate was largely responsible for encouraging the imperial government to send an educational mission of 120 students to the United States in the 1870s. But, following a change of policy in 1881, the imperial government recalled the students. Not until almost twenty-five years later, between 1905 and 1911, did another sizable group of Chinese students seek entrance to American universities. This time foreign study was made possible by the United States government's remission of the Boxer Indemnity, which the imperial government subsequently used to send students abroad. Like Harvard, Columbia, and several other American colleges and universities, Yale did its part in educating the Chinese. 25

The Yale faculty was cautious, however, about watering down admissions requirements and allowing substitutions for Greek and Latin. If it gave in too much to the Chinese, the door would be open to similar requests from the Japanese and even from the Russians. While desiring "to aid China by assisting to train up Chinamen to serve their country well," the faculty stated:

> Yale College can do more for China, in the future as in the past, by giving her best to a few Chinamen of high character and ability, than by giving something less good to a large number of inferior men, unable to receive her best. It would be poor service to China to relax our standard.

Indeed, the college faculty considered permission to substitute Chinese classics for Greek as a temporary exception; no substitutions would be accepted for Latin. More realistically, Harvard did not require Latin of Chinese students who had prepared in foreign schools. Yet, paradoxically, Yale continued to enjoy a high reputation in China in spite of its rigid admission requirements. 26

Several scholarships were established to help defray the expenses of Chinese students at Yale. The two Chinese viceroys, envoys to the United States, nominated candidates for two permanently endowed scholarships. Yale offered ten other $150 tuition scholarships from 1906 to 1910. These were to be filled on the recommendations of the Chinese legation in Washington, D.C.; its commissioner, Sir Chentung Liang Cheng, was honored by Yale in 1906 with the Doctor of Laws degree. [27]

Yale men were sympathetically concerned with China. Some had even visited the country, among them James R. Angell, who had spent a year and a half there as a youth, while accompanying his father on a trip around the world. Many of them took pride in the fact that their university had been "the first," according to the Reverend Anson Phelps Stokes '96, "to undertake through its graduates the creation of an educational mission in the Far East." Ya-li in China graduated its first class in 1912. Wrote F. Wells Williams '79, assistant professor of modern Oriental history, like Yale in New Haven, the college in Changsha stood "for Christianity and an example of a Christian— but not sectarian—institution." And in 1911-12, plans were being made to build both a new college campus and, nearby, a new Changsha Yale Hospital. Thus, claimed Stokes, the foreign medical, educational, and missionary work of other American universities—Harvard, Princeton, and the universities of Michigan and Pennsylvania—had "been largely influenced by the Yale enterprise." [28]

To be sure, the University of Pennsylvania, Columbia, Cornell, and Harvard drew far more foreign students than Yale. Of those who came to New Haven, more enrolled in the Yale graduate and professional schools than in the college. Because of Yale's limited scholarships, with none restricted to particular nationality groups, foreign students usually had to compete on the same basis for aid as Americans. As in the case of the Chinese, special funds sometimes were obtained for these students. The establishment of an Italian fellowship exchange, by which the Italian government offered Americans five fellowships to universities in Italy for five similar fellowships for Italian students in the United States, was another example. In order to obtain one such fellowship Yale had to reciprocate. Most, if not all, of the needed $1,500 was given by the wealthy local movie operator, Sylvestre Z. Poli. The exchange, which began in 1929-30, brought "consistently good" Italian students to Yale. [29]

By providing some scholarship aid for a few foreign students, Yale enriched itself as it helped others. Because both Hadley and Angell believed that Yale should remain a first-rank university, they encouraged such cultural contacts. Yet in certain respects, Yale still bore the stamp of a provincial college during the 1920s and 1930s. Hardly had the spirit of cosmopolitanism been fostered than it was challenged by the entrenched forces of tribalism and provincialism.

President James Rowland Angell and the Old Blues

James R. Angell was eminently qualified for the presidency of Yale, possessing the necessary scholarly attainments, administrative experience, and family background. While he lacked Yale connections, he was properly New England born. "On his father's side," wrote Professor Pierson, "[Angell] could trace back through eight generations of Scituate farmers and Providence settlers to the original founding of Rhode Island under Roger Williams." And his mother's family could trace their ancestry back to the Mayflower. His father, James Burrill Angell, had taught at Brown University before moving on to the presidency of the University of Vermont. James R. Angell was born in Burlington, Vermont, in 1869, and two years later his father began his thirty-eight-year presidency of the University of Michigan. The son graduated from the Ann Arbor public schools and received his A.B. from the University of Michigan in 1890. In his graduate study in psychology, James R. Angell worked under John Dewey at Michigan and William James at Harvard, earning two A.M. degrees. Then at the University of Halle, he all but finished a German Ph.D. thesis on Immanuel Kant, but left to accept an instructorship at the University of Minnesota. From there he went to teach at the University of Chicago, where he became dean of the faculties and finally acting president. After World War I, Angell became president of the Carnegie Corporation. While serving in this office, he received the call from Yale. [30]

According to Pierson, Angell soon won the support of both Yale students and alumni. But members of the faculty felt "neglected," and this slight added to their recent disappointments. Not only had they been "bypassed in the Reorganization" following World War I, but they also would have preferred as successor to President Hadley either his secretary, the Reverend Anson Phelps Stokes, or Charles Seymour '08, professor of history. By 1920, however, the Yale Corporation was dominated by businessmen and it, along with most of the alumni, was against reinstating an ordained minister in the president's office. To break a deadlock in the voting among Yale candidates, the corporation solicited nominations from the outside. Angell was the best candidate, and after some dickering—the salary initially offered was modestly low—he was unanimously elected president of Yale University. [31]

The faculty's doubts were not resolved by their first impression of the president-elect. Admittedly, he was eloquent, if not "a little wordy and long-winded." At times he seemed personally "ill at ease, cordial, a little jocose." Some of the faculty missed in Angell "the breeding and cultivation so conspicuous in Hadley." For his part, Angell found the college led by "men whom he would not have chosen and about whose intellectual convictions he was extremely dubious." [32]

In his inaugural address delivered at commencement in June 1921, Angell announced that he would work to enhance Yale's "character as a national University." This end could be accomplished in part by enrolling talented high school graduates and in part by strengthening the graduate and professional schools. And finally he urged that the "content of liberal culture" be redefined and broadened. While speaking of the need for "change and adjustment," Angell did not say those words of praise for languages, literature and "the classical or Christian heritage" that the college faculty wanted to hear, wrote Pierson. 33

Angell's emphasis on intellectual training seemed to encroach upon another part of a traditional Yale education—extracurricular and social activities. Many of the professors, themselves former Yale undergraduates, considered these essential. The new president had come to Yale after more than twenty years' association with the ethnically and socially more diversified and urban University of Chicago. In contrast, many of the Yale faculty wanted the college to preserve its basic homogeneity, by educating first and foremost middle-class Anglo-Saxon Protestants. True enough, the college educated boys from all parts of the country, some of them from humble backgrounds and inferior secondary schools, but the faculty held a strong stereotypical view of the ideal Yale undergraduate. 34

As an outsider to the Yale family, Angell could not count on allies within the college faculty. By custom, moreover, the Yale president was *primus inter pares*, first among equals; he could consult, but he neither presided at faculty meetings nor directly initiated legislation. At Harvard the president very largely governed; Charles W. Eliot had held the chair at the meetings of all faculties, the professional schools as well as the college. At Yale, Angell could not even choose his own dean. The permanent officers of Yale College wanted one of their own kind, a man who could "handle students, . . . lead the faculty, and . . . guard the interests of the College." After forty-four faculty members signed a petition in favor of the appointment of Clarence Whittlesey Mendell '04, Angell reluctantly yielded. On this matter, as on admissions decisions, the views of the Old Blues prevailed. 35

The "Jewish Question": How to "Protect" Yale?

President Angell certainly did not intend to make radical changes in Yale admissions policies, but he did want to broaden them. In contrast to President A. Lawrence Lowell, he never advocated adoption of a quota system at Yale, although apparently he acquiesced in such a policy when it was instituted. Indeed, Angell attacked prejudice in an address entitled "The Public Schools and the Spirit of Tolerance," delivered at the annual meeting of the Northeastern Ohio Teachers' Association, October 26, 1928 (the year in which Governor Alfred E. Smith of New York became the first Catholic to run for president of the United States). The public schools, he declared, had an important role in discouraging "local and provincial bias and prejudice" and in cultivating "an atmosphere of tolerance and fair play concerning controversial issues, whether in the field of politics, or religion, or in the larger world of ideas." To this end, schools should exemplify the principle that religious belief was a personal right whose protection was essential to the well-being of the nation. He then addressed himself to another type of prejudice:

> Perhaps the most socially and morally disintegrating of all the forms of bigotry, outside of religion, is that found in national and especially racial prejudice. The Jew against the Gentile [sic], the white against the black, the Nordic against the yellow races—the number of these instances is legion.

Angell's publicized denunciation of religious and racial prejudice was unequivocal, and his sympathy for immigrant stocks who had often been "exploited industrially" and "despised socially" was explicit. 36

But there were those in the corporation, on the faculty, and among the alumni who believed, as did their Harvard and Princeton counterparts, that the Jewish student body at their university should be limited. Unfortunately, Angell lacked the presidential power and personal influence to block them. Instead he tried to defuse the issue by urging a balanced and unemotional discussion of its ramifications. His sense of perspective and of humor were evident in the following exchange with Robert N. Corwin. The chairman of the Board of Admissions informed him that 115, or about 13 percent, of the class of 1927 were Jewish, half of these from New Haven and neighboring towns, by a count that was "approximately correct," although "not as accurate as that employed by Jephthah at the passages of the Jordan." The president wittily replied: "Perhaps what we really need is a rejuvenation of the house of the Philistines." 37

An early, if not the first, sign of the policy that was to come was the vote by the Board of Admissions, on October 18, 1921, to refer the "question of a possible limitation" of future freshman classes to the University Council, a body under the chairmanship of Provost Williston Walker. Following an affirmative vote by the council, President Angell was appointed chairman of a committee "to investigate the matter of limitation of numbers." The other members included Deans Frederick S. Jones (Yale College), Roswell P. Angier (freshman year), and Wilbur L. Cross (graduate school) and Director Russell H. Chittenden (Sheffield Scientific School). 38

While this subject was under investigation, the question of whether Jews in particular should be limited became the topic of some correspondence and several meetings. In January 1922, for example, at about the same time that President Lowell was making inquiries about the number of Jews at Harvard, President Angell began to ask his deans and administrators for similar information. In response to questions raised during a conversation over dinner, Director Chittenden sent Angell statistics showing that Jewish enrollment had increased during the Students' Army Training Corps period of the war

years and, as of December 1921, promised to maintain these gains during the
coming decade (see Table 5.2). Furthermore, "practically all members" of
Sheff's premedical course were "of Jewish or South European origin."[39]

No immediate action was taken on these statistics, but during the next five
months, especially in April and May, a great deal of data was collected on
Jewish students at Yale. This was done chiefly by Corwin and Dean Jones.
Requested by the corporation's Committee on Educational Policy to report
on Jewish students at Yale, Corwin in turn asked Deans Jones and Angier and
Registrar A. K. Merritt for information and their views. Data supplied by
Merritt, for example, showed that the tiny percentage of Jewish students in
Yale College had more than tripled in twenty years. In 1901-02, the number
of Jewish students in the three upper classes was 18, or 2 percent of the 878
total (whereas Congregationalists and Episcopalians were about 18 and 14
percent, respectively, of the university's enrollment). By 1911-12, Jewish students had increased to 40 out of 852. Ten years later, the 78 Jewish students
constituted 7.4 percent of the 1,042 total.[40]

To some Yale officials, this was a disturbing realization. And the dean of

Table 5.2
JEWISH STUDENTS IN THE SHEFFIELD SCIENTIFIC
SCHOOL, CLASSES OF 1910-24

Class	Total Men in Class	Number of Jews	Percentage of Jews
1910	405	24	6
1911	426	24	5
1912	384	14	3
1915	434	24	5
1916	399	24	6
SATC Period			
1921/1922	556	67	12
1923 (Fall 1920)	324	29	9
1923 (December 1921)	190	12	6
1924 (December 1921)	254	24	8

Source: Russell H. Chittenden to Angell, January 26, 1922, Records of the President,
James Rowland Angell, Yale University Archives, box 84, file Jewish Problem, Etc. Chittenden gave two figures for 1923, because this case "lost over a hundred men through
withdrawal and dropping, in connection with changes in courses, etc., but mainly because
of the dropping of a group of Pre-Medical men who had violated the Honor System—all
Hebrews. . . ." See also Table 5.7.

the freshman year confirmed these trends. In his letter of May 9, 1922, to Corwin, Dean Angier noted that the 96 Jews in the freshman year comprised 11 percent of the class of 1925. At midyear, their grades averaged 73.2, while the class average was 70.0. Moreover, in intelligence rating, Jewish students averaged 61.3, which was over 11 percent more than the class as a whole. While Jews constituted seven out of nineteen freshmen suspected of cheating during the past two years, Angier added that the Student Discipline Committee found only five students guilty, one of them Jewish. Jewish students were "very likely to be eager for all sorts of scholarship aid," he continued, even when their need was not great. Contributing little to college life, many of them were "personally and socially unacceptable." In short, Angier felt that Jews somehow were "more or less in the nature of a foreign body in the class organism." To "protect" Yale, he suggested four methods of selection: the requirement of passing knowledge of English A; a personal interview with the chairman of the Board of Admissions for applicants living within a fifty-mile radius of New Haven; a more careful selection of those admitted "on trial"; and "extreme care in the award of scholarships."[41]

To stem what he felt was a swelling tide of Jewish students, Jones, like Angier, justified "our rule not to award the honorary scholarships in the upper years to Jews," because they were established to aid "deserving students of the Christian religion." Jones may or may not have been correct about the donors' intentions—Dean Wright thought he was. But Jones would even place a low limit on the beneficiary aid and Connecticut scholarships awarded to Jews. Moreover, the amount of aid available to them would remain static, irrespective of their number in the student body.[42]

Dean Jones was hardly popular among most students, though he could be kindly in his relations with some of them. His prejudice against Jews and blacks was indisputable; family and social background suggested some explanations. Born in Missouri and prepared for Yale in Minnesota, Frederick Scheetz Jones was the son of a physician who had graduated from Princeton and Jefferson Medical College. At Yale, where he paid part of his expenses, he had been an excellent student and, like Corwin, a member of Psi Upsilon and Skull and Bones. After graduation in 1884 and two years of European study, he began a successful twenty-year career at the University of Minnesota, first as professor of physics and electricity and then as dean of the School of Engineering. This success was repeated at Yale, where he served as dean of the college (1909-27). His religious and political affiliations were Episcopalian and independent Republican.[43]

The following note, written to Professor Corwin during the height of the Jewish question at Yale, indicated Jones's prejudice against blacks:

> Yours rec'd. *Too many Freshmen!* How many Jews among them? and are there any *Coons*?

> Pennypacker is here & much disturbed over the Jew Problem at Harvard.
> *Dont let any colored* transfers get *rooms* in College. I am having a big
> rest.

Both Jones and Pennypacker, chairman of the Harvard Committee on Admission, were summering on Cape Cod, in or near Chatham. [44]

With the assistance of Registrar Merritt, Jones compiled the most interesting report on Jewish students at Yale. Using Senior Class Histories as well as their own recollections, they traced the careers of Jewish students from the class of 1911 to that of 1926. In a way, Jones, Merritt, and Corwin were Yale's equivalent to Harvard's Committee on Methods of Sifting Candidates for Admission. Jones's memory may have been something less than perfect for classes early in his deanship; some students classified as Jews actually were not. But on the whole, the head count for each class showed the trend of Jewish enrollment at Yale over a fifteen-year period. Until the 1920s that increase had been gradual (see Table 5.3). [45]

The tabulation of the nationality of Jewish students illuminated immigration patterns. The 135 Russian Jews, 39 of whom were born in Russia, constituted the largest group. Of those parents for whom information was known, almost half (48 percent) were born in Russia; 29 percent were born in the United States, 11 percent in Germany, and 12 percent in other European countries. Since most of the 515 students (see Table 5.4) were immigrants or sons of immigrants, Jones simply did not believe that they could mix well into the student body. [46]

Understandably, the majority of Yale's Jewish students lived in Connecticut. New York, Ohio, Illinois, Pennsylvania, and New Jersey sent the only other sizable contingents. That three-fourths of the Jewish students came from either Connecticut—particularly New Haven, Hartford, and Bridgeport—or New York convinced some faculty that the so-called Jewish problem was really a local one (see Table 5.5).

Although the Yale authorities were unhappy with the increasing local influx, the other tables revealed Jews to be good students academically, which would make it difficult to exclude them on the basis of present admissions tests (see Table 5.6). While 7.3 percent of all students made A grades, only 4.8 percent of the Jewish students attained this standing. On the other hand, only 20 percent of the Jews made D and E grades, as compared to 30 percent for all students. Moreover, 45, or 10.7 percent, of the Jewish students achieved Phi Beta Kappa. And the dean's report noted, "of 633 awards of Prizes and Premiums, the Jews took 68 or 10.7 per cent, a somewhat higher percentage than their share." [47]

Jewish students both registered at the Bureau of Appointments and applied for scholarship aid and loans. Indeed, Jones was alarmed by the fact that in 1922, of 106 Jewish freshmen 56 had sought financial assistance. In Yale Col-

Table 5.3
ENROLLMENT OF JEWISH STUDENTS IN YALE COLLEGE,
CLASSES OF 1911-26

Class	Enrollment	Jews	% of Jews	4-Year Average of % of Jews
1911	345	23	6.7	
1912	322	18	5.6	
1913	308	12	4.0	5.5
1914	339	17	5.0	
1915	348	27	8.0	
1916	390	21	5.4	
1917	394	22	5.6	6.4
1918	392	26	6.6	
1919	400	28	6.5	
1920	387	32	8.3	
1921	310	28	9.0	7.5
1922	390	25	6.5	
1923	466	38	8.2	
1924	356	32	9.0	
1925	534	71	13.4	10.2
1926	878	95	10.8	
Total	6,559	515	7.9	

Source: [Frederick S. Jones], eleven-page memorandum of report consisting of statistical tables and conclusions drawn therefrom [ca. September-October 1922], Records of the Dean of the College, Frederick Scheetz Jones, Yale University Archives, box 5, file Jews. Note: Note on table reads, "It will be observed that the Jewish element has nearly *doubled* in this period."

lege, 78 of 105 Jewish students also applied for scholarships or loans. But only about 40 percent of them in each case received grants. In contrast, the university awarded scholarships to 72 and 75 percent, respectively, of the other freshman year and college applicants. Jewish scholarship students were thus not only culturally "undesirable," but also considered economic liabilities. 48

Between 1911 and 1922, however, about the same proportion of Jews, 77 percent, graduated as non-Jews. Of the 64 Jewish nongraduates, 22 were dropped for unsatisfactory academic standing. But of the 42 leaving with satisfactory academic records, only 4 were dismissed for disciplinary reasons. Six left to "go into business," 4 transferred to Sheff, and 5 went to other colleges, including Oxford University. Of the 213 Jews listing their occupational choices in the Senior Class History, 41 percent wanted to take up law and 20

Table 5.4
NATIONALITY OF JEWS IN YALE COLLEGE, CLASSES OF 1911-26

Class	American	Austrian	French	German	Hungarian	Polish	Roumanian	Russian	Total
1926									95
1925									71
1924									32
1923									38
1922	3	3			1			18	25
1921	8	1	1	1				17	28
1920	11	1		5		1		14	32
1919	6	1						21	28
1918	3	2		5	4		1	11	26
1917	10	1		1	1			10	22
1916	6	4		1	1	1		8	21
1915	11	1		1	1	1		12	27
1914	5			5	1			6	17
1913	3			2				7	12
1912	5			4	1	1		7	18
1911	11			8				4	23
Total	82	14	1	33	9	4	1	135	515

Source: Records of the Dean at the College, file Jews.
Note: Nationality was determined by student responses in the class book, which was published senior year. Data for the classes 1923-26 was not then available, but the ethnic or national origins of these Jewish students conformed to earlier distribution patterns.

Table 5.5
GEOGRAPHICAL DISTRIBUTION OF JEWISH STUDENTS
IN YALE COLLEGE, CLASSES OF 1911-26

Connecticut	Number	% of Total Number of Jews
New Haven	178	34.5
Hartford	46	9.0
New Britain	12	2.3
Bridgeport	19	3.7
All other towns	44	8.5
	299	58.0
Outside Connecticut		
New York State	100	19.4
Ohio	19	3.7
Illinois	17	3.3
Pennsylvania	12	2.3
New Jersey	10	2.0
Massachusetts	8	1.6
All other states	50	9.7
	216	42.0
Total	515	100.0

Source: Records of the Dean of the College, file Jews.

percent medicine, as opposed to the 30 percent who planned to enter business. For them, Yale was a steppingstone into the professions, which offered greater opportunities and also freedom from corporate bureaucracies, where the higher echelons were invariably closed to Jews.[49]

As far as participation in undergraduate life was concerned, Jewish students had a limited, but not completely negligible, role. They were least represented in the snobbish social clubs. Only one was elected to a senior society —Elihu Club, the most recently established of the four. In twelve years, five were members of junior fraternities: Beta Theta Pi, Delta Kappa Epsilon, Alpha Delta Phi, Alpha Sigma Phi, and Psi Upsilon. A far larger number were members of (Jewish) university fraternities: Zeta Beta Tau, Sigma Alpha Mu, and Tau Epsilon Pi. Jews also belonged to the Menorah Society and, perhaps disproportionately, to the Society for the Study of Socialism.[50]

Jews were active in certain extracurricular activities, especially in debating and in the orchestra. Although few made the university teams, there were "many Jewish aspirants in football and basket-ball, fewer in swimming and

Table 5.6
SCHOLARSHIP RECORDS OF JEWISH STUDENTS IN YALE
COLLEGE, CLASSES OF 1911-25

Year	A	B	C	D	E	Total	Phi Beta Kappa	Sigma Xi
1911	2	4	12	5		23	3	
1912		4	9	5		18	2	
1913		4	6	1	1	12	2	1
1914	3	6	4	3	1	17	7	
1915	3	6	13	5		27	4	
1916	1	5	11	4		21	2	
1917		7	9	4	2	22	2	
1918	2	9	11	2	2	26	2	
1919	1	7	15	1	4	28	3	
1920	2	8	17	3	2	32	5	1
1921	1	8	16	2	1	28	7	1
1922		16	4	2	3	25	6	
1923	3	13	15	2	4	37[a]		
1924	2	8	13	4	5	32		
1925		19	36	11	5	71		
	20	124	191	54	30	419	45	3

Source: Records of the Dean of the College, file Jews.
[a]This number probably should have been 38, which would have increased the total to 420, the total given in table 5.3.

base-ball." On the whole, the dean's report concluded that "the Jew in Yale College is as active in extra-curricular activities as he is encouraged to be." The committee on methods at Harvard had reached a similar conclusion.[51]

Whatever may have been its original intent, the evidence compiled on the Jewish student's position at Yale was surprisingly favorable. At a 1918 meeting of the Association of New England Deans, Jones had said: "We have got to change our policies and get them into shape." But four years later, he and other Yale officials had to concede:

> The Jew, with ten and two-tenths per cent of the College enrollment, does not at present constitute an *acute evil* [italics added], but if the percentage increases during the next four College generations at the same rate as in the last four, it will become a serious problem.

To say that Jews were not "an acute evil" implied that they were still something of an evil. At the same time, they deserved praise:

> The best Jewish students have not the ability of the best students in College, but despite the handicaps of poverty and the necessity of working their way, the Jews make better average records than their Gentile fellows. They are ambitious and industrious and distinctly worth educating.

After studying their college careers, Jones acknowledged, as had his Harvard counterparts, that most Jews were educable. Indeed, some of these deans and professors even may have admitted privately to and among themselves that the hue and cry raised over the alien onslaught was not based on fact.[52]

Limitation of Numbers, 1922-23

By the time the director of admissions presented his data to the corporation's Committee on Educational Policy, Corwin knew the sentiments of leading administrators and faculty. The notes of its May 12, 1922, meeting were cryptic. In effect, the Committee on Admissions was asked to advise the Yale Corporation whether means "other than those established by scholastic examination" should be used in admitting applicants to the freshman class. If other means were "desirable," what "form" should "such limitation" take? Undoubtedly, the Committee on Educational Policy had discussed possible percentage limitations on Jewish students.[53]

Two memoranda in the Angell Papers cast some light on this meeting and proved conclusively that discussion of a Jewish quota at one college had a snowballing effect. By the very nature of their formal and informal contacts, moreover, administrators and professors at the prestigious eastern colleges and universities were in a position to formulate what amounted to a concerted policy of restriction. The May 12 memorandum noted that the Jewish question came

> before the Harvard Faculty, Wednesday, May 9, for report and discussion—514 Jews in undergraduate body—well over 20% and some increase in Freshman class—60% of Jews in Honor List—60% in discipline list. Proposed to reduce immediately and radically in spite of Judge——

Though Judge Julian W. Mack, Harvard's first Jewish overseer, was not fully identified, it was clear that Yale was closely attuned to events in Cambridge. And the statement that 60 percent of Harvard's Jewish students were on the discipline list, subsequently proven to be a gross exaggeration, gave support to similar allegations with respect to Jews at Yale and at other institutions. Publicly, Yale denied that it was even considering a quota policy; privately, it was.[54]

Whereas President Lowell at Harvard led the movement for restriction in the face of a wavering faculty, the situation at Yale was quite the opposite.

There the overwhelming majority of the faculty was sympathetic toward limiting the number of incoming freshmen, especially local Jewish youths. Such a limitation, it argued, would make possible greater selection among academically qualified applicants. Tests, other than scholastic, could be imposed; they would be subjective, in both definition and application. In addition to scholarship, other characteristics existed "essential to success in college,—manliness, uprightness, cleanliness, native refinement, etc." Such qualities, it was believed, were not usually found among recent immigrants from eastern and southern Europe.[55]

Probably the faculty would have gone beyond the policy of limitation of numbers to some specific restrictions on the total of Jews admitted. At the very least, they would have favored a policy restricting the number of scholarships awarded to Jews to their percentage within the student body. A majority of both Yale faculty and students came from the American middle class —whom the faculty, with some smugness, felt was "usually too self-respecting to ask such assistance."[56]

But some alumni associations chose "the corner newsboy or the son of the janitor of their building or a boy similarly circumstanced in the evident belief that the boy who is in the most distressing financial circumstances must be the most needy intellectually." Many of those so chosen were Jewish. The extent to which Yale alumni wanted a Jewish quota is undeterminable, because discussion of the subject was closely guarded. But in all probability few would have objected to restriction based on "the general principle that the University must provide the greatest good for the largest number." A quota of 6 percent was suggested, which some considered generous, because it was twice the percentage of Jews in the national population.[57]

Before any definite actions could be undertaken, further discussion and investigation were necessary. A second memorandum in the Angell Papers raised several questions about the corporation's intent. For example, what percentage should the quota be: 6, 8, or 10 percent? Who should discuss the matter, the three undergraduate faculties or the Board of Admissions? Did the corporation prefer to announce the policy or did it wish that the Board of Admissions "exercise such powers of restriction as expediency and experience shall dictate"? What means of restriction should Yale employ?[58]

Following the May 12 meeting of the corporation's Committee on Educational Policy, President Angell instructed Professor Corwin to obtain from the three undergraduate deans information on the number of Jews subject to disciplinary action. This data was subsequently sent by Corwin to Angell with a "Memorandum on Jewish Representation in Yale," in the event that the president desired to present it to the corporation's Prudential Committee. The latter's records did not indicate such a discussion, but one may well have taken place. The conclusions that Corwin presented in his memorandum on May 26 were critical of Jewish students. While the three undergraduate deans reported that Jewish students conformed "in general to the routine regulations of college," most were commuters and "therefore rarely involved in any campus disturbances or like breaches of discipline." Although few Jewish students participated in campus riots, many Jews did not uphold the honor system at Yale, nor were they honest in financial matters, maintained Corwin and the undergraduate deans. [59]

These allegations may have been based largely on one incident in Sheffield Scientific School. Director Chittenden said that the high number of Jews subject to discipline in 1920-21 resulted from a single case of ten Jewish sophomore premedical students, nine of whom were held to have violated the honor system. While "it was distinctly understood that not all of these nine men violated directly the Honor System," they had refused to cooperate in providing information, and so the majority were dismissed. The problem in regard to the honor system was complicated by the existence of group loyalties. As an insecure minority at Yale, some Jews may have felt it would be far worse to turn against an erring brother than to maintain a silence that implicated themselves as well. Chittenden himself admitted that if this premedical group were eliminated, "we find men dismissed for violation of the Honor System amount to seven non-Hebrews for the last three college years, and two Hebrews" (see Table 5.7). [60]

Clearly, the facts did not prove that a consistently higher proportion of Jews were subject to disciplinary action than of non-Jewish students. Data

Table 5.7
DISCIPLINARY CASES IN SHEFFIELD SCIENTIFIC
SCHOOL, 1915-22

Year	Jews	Non-Jews
1915-16	2	7
1916-17	0	11
1917-18	0	8
1918-19	3	15
1919-20	4	10
1920-21[a]	10	10
1921-22 (May)	2	5
Total	21	66

Source: Russell H. Chittenden to Robert N. Corwin, May 23, 1922, Records of the President, James Rowland Angell, Yale University Archives, box 84, file Jewish Problem, Etc.
[a]In 1920-21, nine of the ten Jewish students were in the sophomore premedical group disciplined for violation of the honor system. See also Table 5.2.

provided on the freshman year showed that Jews numbered 5.4 percent of those on cut probation, 10.2 percent on mark probation, and 5.6 percent on gymnasium probation. But Jews composed 11 percent of the freshman year in 1921-22. These figures certainly suggested that the percentage of Jews subject to discipline was in proportion to their percentage within the student body.[61]

The so-called facts, however, received a different interpretation. And Corwin again tentatively proposed the following measures: limitation on the size of the freshman class, restriction on the number of Jewish students proportionate to their number in the country, and reduction in scholarship aid to Jews. "Many feel," he wrote, "that the saturation point has already been passed" in terms of the Jews that the university could handle. Not only had Jews had a harmful effect on Yale, he alleged, but they also resisted the beneficent values of a Yale education. The real problem was

> here as at Harvard . . . the local Jew, who lives at home, knows nothing of dormitory associations, sees nothing of Chapel or Commons, and graduates into the world as naked of all the attributes of refinement and honor as when born into it. His wits have probably been sharpened but he has not gained wisdom, at least not the kind expected of college men.

The Jew was thus stereotyped as a crafty and crude interloper.[62]

In spite of Corwin's strong and persistent endorsement of a quota, President Angell and the Yale Corporation did not act on these proposals. Angell's reply to President Harry A. Garfield, who had written him concerning the Jewish situation at Williams College, stated Yale's official position as of June 1922: "Some of our people here have been getting a little nervous, but we have as yet taken no action of any kind." At the same time, the Yale president expressed interest in the handling of the Jewish question at Williams, while noting "that our Harvard friends have been passing through a rather unpleasant experience as a result of their discussion of methods of discouraging Hebrew patronage."[63]

The Jewish question had appeared at Williams as early as 1910, with "demonstrations" by Gentile students against the increased number of Jews who had entered with the class of 1914. These demonstrations were sufficiently serious to receive comment from President Garfield in a morning chapel exercise. Subsequently, one Mr. Greenbaum, an alumnus, personally offered to select only the "desirable" Jews from a list of applicants to Williams. In effect, Greenbaum had divided Jews into two categories: The desirable ones— implicitly the culturally assimilated German Jews—had decided to assume responsibility for keeping out their undesirable coreligionists—the immigrant Russian Jews. Garfield did not know whether Greenbaum actually took any action along these lines. Thereafter the number of Jewish applicants declined, but other selective factors were involved. As Garfield wrote to

Charles H. Grandgent at Harvard, "the influence of fraternities, required attendance at chapel, and the rural situation of Williams College had kept Jews out of that institution."[64]

President Angell's interest in Greenbaum's proposal suggested that he was looking for some way to handle Yale's alleged Jewish problem, while avoiding the publicized controversy currently afflicting Harvard. And he was kept informed about Harvard developments by Alfred L. Ripley, president of the Merchants National Bank of Boston and a member of the Yale Corporation. In the fall of 1922, the Committee on Limitation of Numbers reported to the University Council that it had held two meetings, appointed two subcommittees and "requested that publicity in connection with its deliberations be avoided for the present."[65]

To obtain information for the Committee on Limitation of Numbers, Corwin wrote letters to Brown, Columbia, Dartmouth, Princeton, Vassar, and Williams. Although it was "difficult to get frank statements," unofficially Yale learned of measures taken at Columbia, Harvard, and Princeton specifically to reduce Jewish enrollment. Within the decade, Yale would use most of their methods, but chiefly the following: limitation on the size of the freshman class, rejection of transfer students, a more searching application form, psychological tests, personal interviews with local candidates, the New Plan examinations, and restriction of scholarship aid. The information received from other colleges and New York City medical schools was summarized in a memorandum entitled "Limitation of Numbers."[66]

Corwin prepared still a second one, with the same title, presenting recommendations for Yale. He urged the corporation "to authorize the admission of approximately eight hundred Freshmen." According to the general criteria of admission, no candidate who presented satisfactory examinations and references "would be excluded because of parentage." But all "doubtful candidates" should present themselves to the Board of Admissions, which would admit them "upon the basis of visible evidence of educability"—no doubt linked to the faces of freshly scrubbed, if adolescently pimply-faced, "American" boys.[67]

Corwin's arguments finally prevailed. After about fifteen months of intermittent discussion, considerable letter writing, and compilation of numerous statistical tables, Yale made a significant policy change. On January 19, 1923, the University Council "voted to informally approve of the proposal to limit the numbers of the entering Freshman Class." With corporation approval, President Angell announced on Alumni Day that the freshman class would be limited to 850. In supporting this measure, he pointed up its supposed educational benefits—smaller classes and more effective instruction. Although the Committee on Admissions argued that limitation involved "no radical change either of principle or of procedure," there was conclusive evidence that one major reason for the policy was to restrict the number of Jews by increasing the weight given to character tests. [68]

First Attempts to Stabilize Jewish Enrollment, 1924

The new emphasis did not immediately result in a reduction of the number of Jews admitted to Yale. Three reasons seemed to underlie Yale's caution in altering admission procedures. First, it wished to see how successful limitation of the size of the freshman class would be in excluding "undesirables." Second, it undoubtedly wanted time to weigh the probable effects of the changes adopted elsewhere, especially at Harvard, following publication of its "Report of the Committee on Methods of Sifting Candidates for Admission." And third, certain members of the corporation, administration, and faculty may have restrained or soothed the exaggerated fears of their fellows. Although President Angell's precise role in these deliberations did not appear in any of the available correspondence, he expressed "the gravest anxiety" on hearing "the views of many presumably intelligent people about certain of these more acutely controversial questions involving prejudice of race, nationality and religion." To deny the existence of "racial and national peculiarities" would be "purely sentimental." But believing that the "cure" for bigotry was "the habit of full and dispassionate examination and evaluation" of the issues, Angell undoubtedly encouraged such an attitude among his Yale colleagues. And to some extent, he succeeded. [69]

When limitation of the size of the freshman class failed to reduce the percentage of entering Jewish students, as Corwin reported to Angell in February 1924, the Board of Admissions voted in June to refuse to admit as transfer students "those from this general district (New Haven, Hartford, Bridgeport) who have attended schools which regularly prepare for the admission examinations." (Almost three-fourths, or 307, of the 420 Jewish students in the classes of 1911 through 1925 had prepared in the local high schools.) The following February, two other votes were passed that would decrease, it was believed, the number of Jewish students. First, the board voted in favor of intelligence tests as offered by the College Entrance Examination Board. (Yale would later require psychological tests of those September candidates who had not satisfied grade requirements the previous June.) Second, the Board of Admissions voted

> that the limitation of numbers shall not operate to exclude any son of a
> Yale graduate who has satisfied all the requirements for admission.

Any change in policy would not infringe on the priority accorded to alumni sons. [70]

President Angell was keenly interested in the effects of the new procedures.

In December 1926, he expressed concern to Corwin that Yale's "selective limitation of students" would tend to discourage applicants from high schools, especially those outside New England. He urged the Board of Admissions to study the entire problem in its broadest implications and to compare Yale's student body with Dartmouth's in terms of "the representation of the different social, industrial and economic strata." Angell was himself a product of the public school system and clearly did not want Yale to be patronized almost exclusively by the privately educated sons of the well-to-do. Such a development, he added, would be "little short of calamitous in terms of the ultimate welfare of the University."71

Meanwhile, in April 1926, Clarence Whittlesey Mendell, soon to be the new dean of Yale College, reported to Angell on what he had learned during a ten-week trip to twenty universities, private schools, and public schools in the South and West. The best of the western colleges, he thought, were Pomona, Stanford (which was limiting numbers), and the University of Washington, but entrance requirements at these institutions were not difficult.72

Even more interesting were the reports of Mendell's visits to Harvard and Dartmouth in the late fall of 1926. He conferred with leading Harvard administrators and faculty about admissions policies, the college's tutorial system, and a proposed Harvard-Yale-Princeton academic competition. Relations were cordial between the two universities, judging from Mendell's reception by President Lowell, Admissions Director Henry Pennypacker, and Deans Chester N. Greenough, Clifford Moore, and Edward Allen Whitney. Cordiality bred a certain frankness in discussion, particularly about methods devised to reduce the percentage of Jewish students at Harvard from 25 percent to 15 percent. And very likely this decision by Harvard's Committee on Admission led to similar resolutions in New Haven. The Harvard deans and President Lowell also tried to persuade Yale, through Mendell, to adopt its tutorial system, which Lowell considered "his real achievement during his administration."73

Although Jews were not mentioned specifically in Mendell's report on Dartmouth, the latter's policy of selective admissions was obviously designed to bring a certain type of student to Hanover. The administration claimed that certification was "better than exams and character a better criterion than intellect" and that "Dartmouth gets the very best." But faculty members who had not attended Dartmouth conceded that their freshmen were a year or more behind those at Harvard or Yale and "a poorer group intellectually." "No one questions the fact," Mendell added with a touch of irony, "that they are a fine group of attractive gentlemen and excellent sportsmen." Most Dartmouth freshmen were chosen without examination from those standing in the highest fourth of any one of over 1,200 accredited schools. Preference was given to alumni sons, to New Hampshire applicants, and to those from the West and South. Candidates from these regions were rated by alumni groups on the basis of personality, rather than on scholarship. And Mendell concluded that Dartmouth's so-called new curriculum, involving course distribution, major and minor studies, and comprehensive examinations, was "really a terrific let down—never have I seen more of a case of the mountain and the mouse." He was fully convinced that Yale should not only maintain but, more importantly, raise its academic standards by offering greater opportunities for scholarship aid to the academically better third of undergraduates. [74]

Considerable alumni pressure, however, was exerted on the Yale Board of Admissions to admit alumni sons to the undergraduate schools. In September 1929, a memorandum entitled "The Admission Requirements as Applied to the Sons of Yale Alumni" was sent to members of the Board of Admissions. While the percentage of alumni sons admitted had indeed increased, some of those connected with the university's endowment campaign in 1927 urged that "more specific assurances" be given the alumni. Others felt that such statements "might look like a thinly disguised plan for the sale of indulgences." Nevertheless, many alumni believed that the university had committed itself during the fund drive to provide for "Yale sons of good character and reasonably good record . . . , regardless of the number of applicants and of the superiority of outside competitors." Any Yale affiliation and even friendship with those having such alumni connections was seen as according special status in the quest for admission. [75]

While recognizing "the pitfalls of a double or doubtful standard," the board reluctantly felt obliged to continue, "for the time being . . . its present procedure" of regarding sons of Yale College and Sheffield Scientific School graduates "as having satisfied the scholastic requirements for admission upon their passing examinations in fifteen units with a mark of 60 or above." Other candidates probably had to average ten points higher. Even so, the academically weakest alumni sons would be denied admission. [76]

Despite the advantages accorded alumni sons, Jewish applicants continued to threaten the position of Yale's traditional clientele. In 1929, Francis Parsons, a fellow of the Yale Corporation, complained to Corwin about a newspaper piece that published the list of Jewish names among incoming freshmen from Connecticut. Referring to the list, Corwin agreed that it "reads like some of the 'begat' portions of the Old Testament and might easily be mistaken for a recent roll call at the Wailing Wall." Yet the format of the article, he reassured Parsons, gave an exaggerated impression of the number of Jews at Yale, which had "not as yet run to embarassing proportions, though I should not put on black if it were less." While an exact count of Jewish freshmen had not been made, it would "not be far from ten per cent,—a little under," Corwin thought and hoped. "This racial problem," he added, was "never wholly absent from the minds of the Board of Admissions," for Yale would "become a different place when and if the proportion of Jews passes a certain as yet unknown limit." Effective limitation—to guard Yale from the "peaceful penetration" of New York City colleges—would be easy if the corporation agreed to stand by such a decision. Harvard had learned its lesson and was now "sawing wood and saying not a word." But those excluded by this "present silent process expect us to take up the slack which she is paying out." While "the more intelligent and influential members of the race" said they preferred to send their sons to a university that practiced some limitation, local Jews in prominent positions might raise the taxation issue if Yale was known to discriminate. If they handled the situation "without publicity and firmly," even this "agitation would probably exhaust itself largely in threats and innuendoes."[77]

Whether indeed the corporation accepted Corwin's proposal that a quota on Jewish students be formally adopted cannot be known for sure. But considerable evidence pointed to the existence of an *informal* quota. The Board of Admissions was given broad discretionary authority in selecting the Jewish students to be admitted, with the result that their number and percentage would fluctuate somewhat from class to class. The graduate school was affected as well as the freshman year, Yale College, and Sheffield Scientific School. As of 1926-27, Jewish enrollment in the graduate school was "down to nearly four per cent," although in previous years the percentage had run "up to eight or nine per cent."[78]

In contrast to Harvard, Yale's admission form did not ask for the applicant's race and religion. Not until 1934 was there a major change in the questions asked with regard to parental background. Previously, Corwin had advised against "asking questions which might seem to indicate a sudden anti-Semitic attitude." The father's full name and birthplace and mother's maiden name, "together with the comments of principals and headmasters, rarely leave us in doubt as to the ethnological classification of the applicant." That information was sufficient: The percentage of Jews in the class of 1934 was only 8.2 percent, down 5 percent from the high of 13.3 percent in the class of 1927. Between 1926 and 1930, the number of Jewish students from Connecticut declined from fifty in the class of 1930 to thirty-five in the class of 1934.[79]

The depression did not change this policy. Not until 1932 did Yale feel the impact of declining applications. In May of that year, Corwin reported to the Board of Admissions that the number of applicants was 1,330, down 140 from the previous May. The dean of Sheffield Scientific School, Charles H. Warren, opposed increasing the number of transfer students, however, because most of the recent applicants were Jews, interested in a medical career and asking for a scholarship.[80]

After a difficult three-day session in July, the board admitted 959 applicants to the class of 1936, including 10 transferees and 9 men dropped from the class of 1935. The corporation had voted to allow the admission of an additional 85 freshmen beyond the limitation of 850. More Jewish applicants were also admitted. Noting that "the racial quota among the provisionally accepted applicants" was "somewhat larger than [was] usual or desirable," Corwin trusted that it would "be reduced by the conditions imposed in the letters sent to those requesting aid." But Jews constituted 11.6 percent of the class of 1936, a 3.4-percent increase over the previous two classes. Nearly 30 percent of the 884 entering freshmen had Yale fathers, a gain of almost 3 percent over the class of 1935 and almost 6 percent over 1934. Alumni sons were becoming the backbone of Yale in times of financial adversity (see Table 5.8).[81]

During these same years, Jewish enrollment fluctuated between 8.2 and 13.3 percent. In response to Corwin's letter, enclosing statistics on Jewish enrollment from 1926 through 1936 (see Table 5.9), President Angell commented ironically:

> The oscillations from year to year are rather larger than I would have expected. In any case, the material is very informing and it seems quite clear that, if we could have an Armenian massacre confined to the New Haven district, with occasional incursions into Bridgeport and Hartford, we might protect our Nordic stock almost completely.

An "Armenian massacre" was not necessary. In 1934, another check was added to the admission form, by asking the applicant to include his mother's birthplace. Jewish enrollment would remain within certain bounds—averaging around 10 percent for at least another decade—until World War II placed new demands on the Old Campus.[82]

Whatever his personal views, President Angell seemingly acquiesced in this policy. Moreover, he expressed some concern about "a possible influx of undesirable racial groups" from urban areas. When he suggested that Yale admit the "upper fifth" of secondary schools without examination, he recognized that it might be necessary to exclude from this category schools in eastern urban areas. This was to be Yale's answer to Harvard's highest seventh plan. Like Harvard, Yale wanted to attract boys from high schools and small private schools. Benefiting from Harvard's experience, Angell would not extend this privilege to high schools that produced a large proportion of "undesirable racial groups."[83]

Angell, like most American college presidents, condemned Nazism. But he did not have thrust upon him the publicity that Dr. James Bryant Conant of Harvard received in refusing the $1,000 traveling scholarship offered by Dr. Ernst F. S. Hanfstaengl, Harvard '09 for support of a Harvard student in Germany. Although Angell wrote Rabbi Edgar E. Siskin of Congregation Mishkan Israel of New Haven that he would cooperate in efforts to halt Nazi practices, he feared that "public demonstrations" in the United States would be distorted in the "muzzled" German press. The president declined to address a mass meeting in New Haven's Shubert Theatre in protest against "the

Table 5.8
SONS OF YALE MEN IN THE CLASSES OF 1924-36

Class	Total Membership	No. of Freshmen Whose Fathers were Yale Men		Total[d]	% of Freshmen Whose Fathers were Yale Men
		Graduates	*Nongraduates*		
1924	681	86	4	90	13.2
1925	866	126	4	130	15.0
1926	886	125	12	137	15.4
1927	863	110	9	119	13.7
1928	880	187	0	187	21.2
1929	864	143	4	147	17.0
1930	881	153	11	164	18.6
1931	884	177	13	190	21.4
1932	894	182	15	197	22.0
1933	834	157[a]	18	175	20.9
1934	850	189[b]	13	202	23.7
1935	850	213[c]	14	227	26.7
1936	884	242[b]	20	262	29.6

Source: Robert N. Corwin, chairman, Board of Admissions, to James R. Angell, February 10, 1933, enclosing table, dated October 19, 1932, on "Yale Fathers," Records of the President, James Rowland Angell, Yale University Archives, box 2, file Board of Admissions.
[a]4 Yale fathers with 2 sons each in class—8 counted in total.
[b]6 Yale fathers with 2 sons each in class—12 counted in total.
[c]3 Yale fathers with 2 sons each in class—6 counted in total.
[d]Only 137 of the Yale fathers were nongraduates.

anti-Semitic excesses" in Germany. Yet in 1934, the *Jewish Advocate* published his strong denunciation of the loss of academic freedom in German universities. Yale was reluctant, however, to offer positions to refugee scholars during the 1930s and 1940s, thereby losing the opportunity to bring outstanding academicians to New Haven. [84]

In December 1933, Angell noted that Yale's Jewish enrollment "remained fairly constant" and that "we have not as yet felt any additional pressure as the result of anti-Semitic policies abroad." Indeed, during his administration, Yale had stabilized its Jewish population and accorded to it a certain percentage of the scholarship awards. Officially, the university also approved the existence of Jewish clubs and fraternities. In achieving this stabilization and quasi-acceptance, Yale avoided both the drastic quota imposed at Columbia and the heated controversy at Harvard. Though little public discussion of the issue took place in New Haven, there was virtually no doubt that Yale's policy of leveling off the percentage of Jews received tacit support from the great majority of non-Jewish undergraduates and alumni. [85]

Table 5.9

NUMBER AND PERCENTAGE OF JEWISH STUDENTS IN YALE CLASSES, 1926-36

	1926	1927	1928	1929	1930	1931	1932	1933	1934	1935	1936
Total number of students in class	886	863	880	864	881	884	894	834	850	850	884
No. of Jews in class	92	115	88	97	106	108	90	106	70	70	103
% of Jews in class	10.4	13.3	10.0	11.2	12.0	12.2	10.1	12.7	8.2	8.2	11.6
% of Jews in class residing in Connecticut	47.8	49.5	45.4	47.4	47.1	44.4	46.6	48.5	50.0	34.2	38.8
% of Connecticut residents being Jewish	17.0	24.5	20.1	20.5	23.4	20.0	19.0	25.2	17.5	11.4	18.0

Source: Robert N. Corwin, to James R. Angell, January 3, 1933, enclosing table, dated October 19, 1932, "showing our Jewish population for the last ten years," Records of the President, file Board of Admissions.

One of the better barometers of undergraduate opinion was the *Yale Daily News*, which, on March 30, 1926, declared editorially that "Yale must institute an Ellis Island with immigration laws more prohibitive than those of the United States government." A personnel bureau should be established, it said, "to study the character, personality, promise and background of men who wish to enter the University." Unless this was done, the day would be "fast dawning"

> when potential captains of industry must absent themselves from the groves of academe and take up their unpurposeful studies elsewhere, while the intelligentsia of the approaching renaissance Americanize even such an isolated province as Yale in a merciless competition for seats in the University. If this era is admitted, Yale will no longer be a heterogeneous group of average citizens, but will be essentially a brain plant.

To keep the university open, "Yale would be justified even with her ideal of 'service to the nation' in sloughing off the unkempt at the same time she drops the unlettered." The previous day's editorial had approved of Harvard's new admissions policy, which would consider character and personality in admitting freshmen to a class limited to 1,000 students. Harvard also required applicants to submit personal photographs. The *News* urged that Yale "might go them one better and require applicants to submit photographs of their fathers also." These two editorials criticized the ambitious sons of immigrants—mostly Jewish—who gained admission to Yale on the basis of their scholastic abilities. Such an attitude undoubtedly struck responsive chords in the hearts of Yale fathers, for whom admission to the alma mater was simply a matter of perpetuating the family line.[86]

· 6 ·

PRINCETON: THE TRIUMPH OF THE CLUBS, 1900S TO 1950S

> I hope the Alumni will tip us off to any Hebrew candidates. As a matter of fact, however, our strongest barrier is our club system. If the graduate members of the clubs will ram the idea home on the undergraduate bicker committees and make the admission of a Hebrew to a club the rarest sort of a thing, I do not think the Hebrew question will become serious.
>
> Varnum Lansing Collins, secretary of Princeton University and member of the Committee on Admission, to Henry M. Canby, November 23, 1922[1]

By the 1920s, the upper-class eating clubs completely dominated undergraduate life at Princeton. Not only did they provide sustenance for alumni sons, but they even became unofficial arbiters as to who should be admitted to the college. Any Jewish or other applicants who were deemed not "clubable" but defied their unwritten policy by obtaining admission to Princeton could look forward to four years of social isolation. Neither intellectual achievement nor even athletic prowess would open the door to the clubs if a man were labeled an outsider. Woodrow Wilson had fought hard against the clubs because he rightly saw them as competitors with the college. In 1910 he wrote that there should be "no elective membership" in a university, which "must be . . . a social unit and community in the fullest meaning of those words." The only inequalities, he said, should be "the natural inequalities of age and experience." Free of artificial barriers, such a community would be democratic because, by Wilson's definition, "democracy [was] made up of unchosen experiences." But his defeat over the Quadrangle Plan—a proposed social reorganization of all students into residential colleges—meant the defeat of a broader concept of democracy at Princeton for almost half a century. Not until the last decade or so have the upper-class eating clubs diminished in importance in the eyes of Princeton undergraduates. As long as the clubs embodied ultimate undergraduate ambition, Princeton would, by its social values, discourage—if not reject—students of diverse ethnic backgrounds.[2]

In spite of the volumes written on the controversies over the Quad Plan and the graduate school, a few important questions remained unanswered about Wilson's presidency of Princeton. How "radical in character," as Wilson described his proposal, was his Quad Plan in comparison with the social systems existing at Harvard and Yale? How "democratic" was Wilson compared to other college presidents—for example, to A. Lawrence Lowell? Was his democracy essentially an elitist concept according to which only the clubable would be encouraged to attend Princeton? Or was it a rather generous conception of the potential intellectual and social enrichment that would result from faculty and student commingling? And to what extent did Wilson's conception of democracy grow during the subsequent graduate school controversy? Some answers to these questions may be found by examining his intellectual development and attitudes toward minority groups as well as the two major controversies of his Princeton years.[3]

President Woodrow Wilson: An Intellectual Revitalization of Princeton

In Cambridge, on July 1, 1909, Woodrow Wilson delivered an eloquent oration before Harvard University's chapter of Phi Beta Kappa. Into his address, "The Spirit of Learning," Wilson claimed to have put "the whole of my academic creed." He extolled the intellectual values and mental discipline gained from a four-year, liberal, and "generalized" college education in which extracurricular activities were secondary. College should give students

> insight into the things of the mind and of the spirit, a sense of having lived and formed their friendships amidst the gardens of the mind where grows the tree of the knowledge of good and evil, a consciousness . . . of having undergone the discipline, never to be shaken off, of those who seek wisdom in candor, with faithful labor and travail of spirit.

As the very quintessence of his educational philosophy, the oration went beyond Wilson's current campaign to win over the Princeton alumni in his epic struggle with Dean Andrew Fleming West over the location of the graduate school. He was addressing the entire American academic community.[4]

Much to Wilson's "great astonishment" his address was "received with enthusiasm (Think of enthusiasm at Cambridge!)." But the applause that greeted it "where he had been king" ruffled Charles W. Eliot. Indeed, the Harvard president acknowledged that he and Wilson "struck fire like flint and steel in many a Teacher's Meeting." After receiving a Harvard LL.D. degree at the 1907 Commencement, Wilson had won friends when he drew distinctions between Eliot's and his own philosophies. His Quad Plan was warmly supported by those at Harvard who were dissatisfied with their president's limited concern for collegiate education. Convinced that Eliot had "done much to demoralize our youth," Charles Francis Adams, treasurer of Harvard, had spoken the year before of the need to reform both the elective and the collegiate social systems.5

In addition to his commitment to a liberal arts education, Wilson brought another quality to his university presidency. He was an opportunist whose conception of Princeton's educational role broadened as his audience and potential constituency expanded. Unlike his counterparts at Harvard and Yale, he was not content to spend his life wrestling in the academic lion's den. As political possibilities opened up for him, his speeches took on an increasingly democratic tone. Hence it is difficult to determine, when considering the last two years of his presidency, where Wilson the educator left off and where Wilson the nascent politician began.

Since his youth, Wilson had shown a considerable capacity to enlarge his vision. To begin with, he was hardly a "typical" southerner, though born in Staunton, Virginia, and raised in Augusta, Georgia, and Columbia, South Carolina. His father, the Reverend Joseph Ruggles Wilson, had preached sermons in support of slavery and had served as a chaplain in the Confederate army. But Woodrow Wilson argued that both slavery and secession were wrong, although he always loved the South for its traditionalism and defense of constitutional principles. After a year at Davidson College in North Carolina, he decided that Princeton would offer a more cosmopolitan educational and social experience. Following graduation in 1879, he went to the University of Virginia for legal training and then, after a year of study at home in Wilmington, North Carolina, he began to practice law in Atlanta, Georgia. But he soon came to dislike both the city's provincialism and the narrowness of the legal profession.6

On leaving the South—to undertake graduate work at Johns Hopkins (1883-85) and then to teach at Bryn Mawr, Wesleyan, and Princeton—Wilson consciously tried to lose his accent and free himself from other provincialisms. Yet Ellen Axson Wilson, a native of Georgia, reassured her husband that he had not become really "Northanized" [sic]. He was "not a 'Southerner' either in the old sense, [but] an American citizen—of Southern birth." During these same years, Wilson displayed a nationalist point of view in his historical works, as in *Division and Reunion 1829-1889* (1893), written for Albert Bushnell Hart's Epochs of American History series. When thanking the Harvard professor for his "confidence in my impartiality," Wilson stressed "this mixture of elements in me—full identification with the South, non-Southern blood [his father was born in Ohio, his mother in England], and Federalist principles."7

As president of Princeton, he urged that the college be a meeting ground for students from all sections of the country. In an address at the Peddie Institute in 1903 on "The Meaning of a College Course," Wilson said: "If the eastern young man has regarded the prairies as a benighted part of the world and referred to them with scorn, it will do him good to go to college and meet a man from Kansas," who would change that opinion. He elaborated on this theme in subsequent addresses and speeches. He praised the middle states as "the most typically American part of the United States," because they "were mixed of all races and kinds from the first," unlike New England and the South. As a result, they had "a greater elasticity of mental movement [and] more ability to see from more points of view, than any other region of the country." The development of a broad or "catholic"—the word he frequently used—outlook was extremely important to Wilson. It was "not necessary in a country like ours that you should blend in blood," he told the Friendly Sons of St. Patrick: "The real blending in this country is an intellectual and social blending."[8]

As a staunch but latitudinarian Presbyterian, Wilson advocated a considerable degree of religious toleration. He naturally had a very religious up bringing and was admitted to church membership at sixteen. But his family was not fundamentalist. In fact, his uncle, Dr. James Woodrow, was removed from his chair at the Columbia Theological Seminary (South Carolina) because he believed in and defended publicly the Darwinian theory of evolution.[9]

Wilson himself was criticized at Princeton for minimizing the role of the supernatural and of Divine Providence in his writings on government. President Francis Landey Patton, an ordained minister, made it plain to the newly elected professor of jurisprudence and political economy (1890) that Princeton's trustees "would not regard with favour such a conception of academic freedom or teaching as would leave in doubt the very direct bearing of historical Christianity as a revealed religion upon the great problems of civilization." The College of New Jersey clearly was still sectarian, even though it would assume the title of "University" in 1896, on changing its name to Princeton. When Wilson proposed two former students from Johns Hopkins for a position in the Department of History—first Frederick Jackson Turner and then Charles H. Haskins, both professors at the University of Wisconsin —Patton chose Haskins, because he "could not take the responsibility of nominating Turner," who was a Unitarian. Wilson had written Turner in November 1896: "I think I can say without qualification that no religious tests are applied here." Only by a five-year contract and an additional $2,500 a year were the trustees able to persuade a disappointed Wilson to remain at Princeton.[10]

When Wilson became Princeton's first lay president in 1902, he tried to liberate the university from its sectarianism. He assumed the right to make faculty appointments without consulting the trustees' Curriculum Committee beforehand. According to the editors of *The Papers of Woodrow Wilson*, his "initiative in offering the chair to [Harry A.] Garfield represented a turning point in the history of Princeton University." Whereas Patton sought prior approval of the Curriculum Committee, even to the point of allowing it to choose from among several nominees for faculty positions, Wilson offered Garfield the chair in politics and then asked the committee's approval. Of course, Wilson did seek the advice of department heads and faculty when conducting his search for new men. He chose them, moreover, on the basis of scholarship, not religious conformity. For example, in 1904, Wilson offered the professorship of philosophy to Frank Thilly, although he was not a church member. Thilly accepted and taught at Princeton for two years (1904-06). Wilson also appointed the first Roman Catholic to the faculty: David Aloysius McCabe, Harvard '04, and Johns Hopkins Ph.D. '09, became an instructor of economics in 1909, an assistant professor in 1910, and a professor in 1919. The next Catholic to join the Princeton faculty was probably English-born Hugh Stott Taylor, appointed professor of chemistry in 1922. Although Horace Meyer Kallen, Harvard '03, served as an instructor of English (1903-05), not until the mid-1920s were the first Jews appointed to tenured positions at Princeton. In 1924 Herbert Sidney Langfeld was brought from Harvard to be professor of psychology and director of the psychological laboratory. (He listed himself as a Republican and an Episcopalian in *Who's Who*.) And Russian-born Solomon Lefschetz, visiting professor from the University of Kansas in 1924-25, became associate professor of mathematics at Princeton in 1925 and professor in 1928.[11]

In a highly significant letter to Thomas Nelson Page, Wilson discussed the powers of Princeton's president. The institution's charter stated merely that the president had "'immediate care of the education and government' of the students" and was ex officio chairman of the Board of Trustees when the governor of New Jersey was absent. Consequently, presidential powers largely derived from the experience of previous administrations during the past 150 years. Wilson thought "that the office may be regarded as normal here as anywhere, standing midway between the autocratic presidency and the presidency which is a mere chairmanship of the Faculty." When Wilson entered the office, he sought to achieve a balance between those two kinds of presidencies, which were represented, respectively, by Harvard and Yale. As a member of both the Board of Trustees and the faculty, Princeton's president had a dual voice: representing in the board the faculty's views on education and representing and enforcing in the faculty the board's views on the administration of the university. As defined by Wilson under Princeton's "unwritten constitution," the president should play an affirmative and decisive role. And the university needed strong leadership after the do-nothing administration of the Reverend Patton, who had finally been "persuaded" to resign by the trustees, supported by a majority of the faculty. Of course, continued success as a university president required a sound grasp of the principles of military strategy: He should know when to advance and when to retreat.[12]

Between 1902 and 1906, the situation at Princeton was propitious for rapid advance. And Wilson was aided by the recent election of sixteen new men to the Board of Trustees, five of whom were the first alumni trustees. Of the sixteen, half were graduates of the 1870s, and most were businessmen and lawyers, who evaluated the purposes of a Princeton education in a rather different light than their ministerial predecessors. Among the most influential were Moses ("Momo") Taylor Pyne '77; Cyrus Hall McCormick, '79 and honorary A.M. '87; the Reverend Dr. Melanchton Williams Jacobus '77; David Benton Jones '76, alumni trustee; and Grover Cleveland, honorary LL.D. '97. These forceful men felt a deep affection for Princeton and zealously served its interests. [13]

Trustees and alumni responded well when Wilson asked for $12.5 million to build up Princeton's physical plant and to hire additional professors as well as some fifty tutors. In his first report as president to the Board of Trustees, on October 21, 1902, Wilson pointed out that Princeton had "not kept pace" with Harvard and Yale "in university development" and that while it had "lingered, other, newer, institutions, like Columbia, the Johns Hopkins, and the University of Chicago [had] pressed in ahead of her." Either Princeton had to raise the money for salaries, library endowment, laboratories, a school of science, a school of jurisprudence, and a graduate school, or it must "withdraw from the university competition" and make the best of what it had. [14]

In this same report, Wilson called for a thorough reform of the curriculum, which he subsequently outlined in his inaugural address of October 25: "Princeton for the Nation's Service." The university's purpose was to train "men of vision" and general knowledge through a humanistically oriented and balanced four-year curriculum. [15]

In April 1904, the faculty adopted the report of the Faculty Committee on the Course of Study. Under Wilson's chairmanship, it proposed unification of academic and scientific students in one undergraduate school and the development of a highly structured and prescribed curriculum. (The Bachelor of Science degree would continue to be offered to those students entering with Latin, but without Greek, and concentrating in mathematics or the sciences.) The most publicized innovation was the preceptorial system. Beginning in September 1905, small groups of students met weekly with a tutor in each department, except in laboratory sciences. These reforms succeeded in elevating Princeton's academic standards and offered a constructive alternative to the free elective system. [16]

The Quadrangle Plan Versus the Upper-Class Clubs

Having successfully carried through his academic reforms, Wilson launched his attack on the undergraduate club system at the December 13, 1906, meeting of the Princeton Board of Trustees. He remembered nostalgically his own undergraduate days before the rise of the clubs, when students chose their dining companions on the basis of compatibility, instead of preparatory school affiliation. For some years he had been mulling over a solution. In a very brief memorandum on the clubs, drawn up in February 1906, Wilson saw a "danger" that Princeton would "develop *socially* as Harvard did and as Yale is tending to do." Expanding on this theme in his supplementary report of December, Wilson pointed out that students who failed to make a club seemed "more and more thrust out of the best and most enjoyable things which university life naturally offers—the best comradeships, the freest play of personal influence, the best chance of such social consideration as ought always to be won by natural gifts and force of character." The remedy for these ills was to divide the university into a number of colleges and "to oblige the undergraduates to live together." The strongest upper-class clubs would be induced to become colleges under university supervision. They could retain their privilege of selecting new members if they agreed to build a dormitory adjoining their houses, permitted one or two unmarried faculty members to reside therein, and accepted the guidance of these faculty residents in some of their daily affairs. The new colleges would be more than dormitories; they would be self-contained social units in which undergraduates would eat and live together under "a large measure of self-government." Through them, Wilson "would substitute the college for the club." At this time, Wilson seemed to be arguing for the Quad Plan as much on social as on academic grounds. [17]

The club problem, emphasized David B. Jones, one of Wilson's strongest supporters, really centered on the four oldest: Ivy, Tiger Inn, Cottage, and Cap and Gown. These fostered the spirit of social competition and "the adoration of the athlete as the supreme emotion of the undergraduate world." In contrast, the more recent, smaller clubs were "the external manifestation of successive disappointments in failure to make the older and larger clubs." And the way they felt about the older clubs was similar to the feelings of nonclubmen toward the club system. [18]

But most Princetonians believed that their clubs were better than those collegiate systems existing at other universities. In June 1903, the Committee on Conference with Upper Class Clubs, chaired by Moses Taylor Pyne, had reported that students were pledged at Columbia, Cornell, and Pennsylvania, as well as many smaller colleges, even before they entered. And at Yale and Harvard only a few survived the rigorous process of social selection to make a senior society or final club. In contrast, Princeton clubs were neither secret societies nor chapters of national fraternities. Rather, they were eating clubs, and the fact that eleven were located on Prospect Street facilitated friendly social intercourse among them. Preferably, the number of clubs should be increased to accommodate those not receiving a bid. Between 1900 and 1904, six new clubs were organized: Campus, Quadrangle, Charter, Tower, Terrace, and Key and Seal. [19]

After discussing Wilson's supplementary report, the trustees resolved that the president appoint a committee of seven, of which he would be the chairman, to study his proposal and report on it. During the coming months, Wilson reconsidered the principles on which he should base his argument for residential quadrangles. Because his initial presentation to the Board of Trustees had not aimed at the real target, Wilson shifted his argument from that of social democracy to "academic revitalization." As long as the club system prevailed, most undergraduates would subordinate intellectual interests to social and extracurricular activities. Wilson was now against any social organizations based on student selection, because statistics showed that club membership was unquestionably a deterrent to scholastic achievement. (His secretary, Gilbert F. Close, found that in the preceding four years only 9.3 percent of the clubmen, but 41.7 percent of the nonclubmen, had achieved honors.)[20]

At the June 10, 1907, meeting of the Board of Trustees, Wilson's committee presented its "Report on the Social Co-ordination of the University." Wilson, who wrote the document, spoke about the isolation of that one-third of each class who were not elected to one of the clubs. Attempts at reforming the system had proven unsatisfactory: The inter-club treaty, forbidding the recruitment of sophomores before the spring-term "bicker" or selection week, had been broken and renewed on stricter terms several times. Beginning with the initial freshman and sophomore clubs, "the social ambitions created by the existing system of club life [were] too strong for individual honour." Moreover, Ivy and Cottage had "houses of extraordinary elegance and luxury of appointment," while five other clubs planned to replace "their present comfortable structures with buildings which will rival the others in beauty, spaciousness, and comfort." A residential quadrangle plan for all four classes was "the only adequate means" of effecting "an immediate reintegration of our academic life."[21]

Twenty-four of the twenty five trustees present on June 10 adopted the committee's recommendation that the president be authorized to develop his plan. A pleased Wilson interpreted their resolutions as a firm acceptance of his principles. During the first few weeks after publication of the report, Wilson's address to the trustees, and his memorandum to the clubs, alumni response was generally favorable. And five trustees, in particular, strongly supported him: Cleveland H. Dodge '79, Melancthon W. Jacobus, David B. Jones, Cyrus H. McCormick, and George B. Stewart '76. Wilson also heard reassuring words while attending Harvard's commencement: "The men up there bade us God-speed with the greatest earnestness, confessing that they had not had the courage to tackle the problem, and saying, of course if you do it, we shall have to do it."[22]

Convinced that his Quad Plan should be effected without delay, Wilson asked Cleveland Dodge for a letter of introduction to Mrs. Russell Sage. While believing in gradual change, Wilson fully appreciated that "money will lubricate the evolution as nothing else will." In early July, Wilson went on vacation in the Adirondacks, confident that he could win the battle for the Quad Plan. "The fight is on," he wrote, "and I regard it, not as a fight for the development, but as a fight for the restoration of Princeton." His "heart" was dedicated to it, because it was "a scheme of salvation." If victory meant "salvation," how could he fail? 23

But Wilson had consulted neither the faculty as a group nor the alumni as a body. He had his loyal faculty supporters, among them George McLean Harper (belles lettres and language and literature); Dean Henry B. Fine (mathematics); Wilson's brother-in-law, Stockton Axson (English); Winthrop M. Daniels (political economy); and Harry A. Garfield. Others, however, began to express dissatisfaction, first in personal letters to Wilson and then in the pages of the *Princeton Alumni Weekly*. Prominent among Wilson's faculty opponents were Henry van Dyke, an ordained Presbyterian minister and professor of English; Graduate Dean Andrew F. West; and John Grier Hibben, professor of logic and Wilson's intimate friend. At the very least, all three wanted the faculty to have an opportunity to discuss the merits of the proposal. 24

Alumni quickly made their opposition heard. Even graduates of the days before the ascendancy of the clubs defended their continuation. Adrian H. Joline '70 denounced the "revolutionary" nature of the Quad Plan. Some alumni argued against the Quad Plan on the quite explicit grounds that Princeton should cater to the sons of well-to-do and cultured families. Henry Fairfield Osborn '77, a former Princeton faculty member and then head of the biology department at Columbia, felt that on the basis of their father's records the scions of the privileged would have greater success in life than "the sons of obscure men." Osborn, a noted racist, would make Princeton into the very thing that Wilson deplored, "a rich man's college." 25

The clubmen felt a strong proprietary interest in their clubs, especially when graduates' dues were needed to pay off heavy mortgages. Franklin Murphy, Jr., '95, president of Tiger Inn's board of governors, was one of the first to register his protest. More recent graduates also viewed the existing club system as an integral part of their continuing relationship with Princeton. A man's club was his "second home," through which he reentered the undergraduate world, wrote Arthur H. Osborn '07. A graduate would be annoyed, if not outraged, on returning to campus to find his club abolished and others living in the house, while he had to find accommodations elsewhere. This was no less than the confiscation of private property and "contrary to the Constitution of our Country." 26

Undergraduates largely echoed the opinions expressed by the conservative, proclub alumni. While appreciating the "great benefits [to] be derived from a closer affiliation of the educational and social sides of Princeton life," the *Daily Princetonian* doubted the justification for "a change so radical that

Princeton as it is to-day would cease to exist and another, a strange and unknown Princeton rise in its place." The social system could take care of itself by the slow process of evolution. "*Class* distinctions exist to-day," it said, "and experience has long ago taught us the worth of a democracy reconciled with that wholesome aristocracy based on class seniority."[27]

Even though Wilson considered resigning, should the Quad Plan be defeated, he was convinced that the principle that he and David B. Jones had agreed on in June was "absolutely impeachable" and its purpose "entirely educational." Except for a few loyal supporters, another among them being Dr. Melancthon Jacobus, most of the trustees declined to adopt this progressive theory that Princeton guarantee "equality of intellectual and social opportunities to its students." Influenced by the cool, if not hostile, reaction from alumni in eastern cities, the trustees began to say that they had not adopted the plan, but only tentatively approved its idea. In July, Andrew C. Imbrie reported to Wilson that most Princetonians in New York were at least openminded. But about the same time, Henry B. Thompson found that in Wilmington and in Philadelphia it had "no friends." Two weeks later, Thompson wrote to fellow trustee Momo Pyne: "Wilson's eloquence has over-persuaded us." Both Thompson and Pyne wanted Wilson to withdraw his plan altogether.[28]

Trustee Bayard Henry also raised several major objections to it. Like Pyne, he had served on the committee of seven that theoretically, at least, issued the "Report on the Social Co-ordination of the University." The plan was too expensive, argued Henry: The new dormitories, dining halls, and kitchens would cost a minimum of $2 million. The method of distributing students into the different quadrangles posed additional diffficulties. If intellectual or financial means were made the basis of selection, students would become even more segregated than at present. Colleges should not, he believed, alter the socioeconomic distinctions that students brought from their home environment. Indeed, uniform room and board rates were "socialistic and not natural," because food and lodging were, like clothing and club affiliation, marks of social status.[29]

By the autumn of 1907, the Quad Plan threatened to become a fraternal battle dividing the Princeton family against itself. In an effort to persuade his faculty that the Quad Plan would continue the educational goals of the preceptorial system, Wilson made an eloquent address at their October 7 meeting. He did not talk about the evils of the clubs so much as the logic of their development. Clubs had put the faculty, "honormen," under classes, and even the university itself outside of undergraduate life. The Quad Plan was necessary to reunite them into a new collegiate body. No vote was passed at this meeting, however; further action was left up to the trustees.[30]

Fully realizing the danger of antagonizing alumni in a year of financial panic, on October 17 the Board of Trustees, led by Pyne, reversed its decision of the previous June. Then they threw a sop to Wilson's ego by saying that they understood the depth of his beliefs and that he could still try to convince the board and the alumni of the merits of his plan. In point of fact, most of them, with the exception of David B. Jones and Dr. Jacobus, wanted him to remain silent on that subject.[31]

Wilson's first major defeat profoundly influenced both his personal life and his educational philosophy. Biographers and historians agree that Wilson emerged a changed man from this bitter experience. He became aloof, somewhat cold, shying away from close personal friendships. And blaming his defeat on the men of wealth, like Pyne, who subscribed to the Committee of Fifty Fund, he began to speak for an educational democracy based on scholarship. When he encountered opposition from similar quarters during the ensuing graduate school controversy, Wilson returned to the theme of social democracy. As he saw broader horizons opening up to him in politics and sensed the growing sentiment for reform in the country, he sounded this theme even more vigorously.[32]

The Graduate School Controversy: A Fight for Social Democracy

Wilson resumed his campaign to educate the alumni in 1908 by addressing various Princeton Clubs, memorably in Chicago. These addresses fanned the smoldering controversy over the location of the graduate college to the boiling point. When Wilson carried his message, "The Spirit of Learning," to Harvard on July 1, 1909, the problems of his own university bore heavily upon him. On the one hand, the Board of Trustees had agreed in April 1908 that the new graduate college be built on the grounds of Prospect, the presidential home located in the center of campus, and then a year later had given a large measure of its control to a faculty committee friendly to Wilson. But then in May 1909, William Cooper Procter, a friend of Dean Andrew F. West's, offered Princeton $500,000 to build a graduate college if this sum could be matched by other gifts. Procter and West preferred a site removed from the campus, either at Merwick or on the golf links.[33]

On October 21, 1909, the Board of Trustees accepted Procter's conditions and agreed to the golf links location, provided that they could legally use the Swann bequest (for building on campus Thompson College, a graduate student residence) at the same site. Wilson threatened to resign unless the offer was declined, because he could not work with Dean West. Nevertheless, Wilson still hoped to win a majority of the trustees to his side by the January 13, 1910, meeting. But Momo Pyne took the president by surprise by producing a letter from Procter agreeing to Wilson's suggestion that there be two graduate colleges, one built on the golf links with his money and the other on campus with the Swann bequest. Wilson then undermined his own position by making several contradictory statements. If the graduate college were "based on proper ideals," he said, the faculty could "make a success of it anywhere in Mercer County." Finally, Wilson came out flatly against the proposal for two graduate colleges. The upshot of this meeting, wrote Professor Arthur S. Link, was that Pyne "lost all faith in Wilson's integrity and ability to govern the University." He was determined to drive him out of office. 34

By early 1910, Wilson's past resentments over the Quad Plan's defeat and his present frustrations fused into "a great crusade for social democracy," according to Professor Link. Although Wilson denied that he was attempting to bring the Quad Plan back to life, nevertheless, in his mind the two controversies shared a similar principle. If Princeton accepted Procter's offer of $500,000 for the graduate college with both explicit and implicit conditions attached, it would have meant extending to the graduate life of the university "the same artificial and unsound social standards that already dominate the life of the undergraduates." Wilson opposed "the physical isolation" and luxurious Gothic-style appointments for the graduate college, because they would foster "the spirit of social exclusiveness." Here again was the issue of social democracy: An independent graduate school under the control of the snobbish Dean West would become a super club. 35

When Procter decided to withdraw his offer on February 6, the Wilson faction thought they had won the battle. Shortly thereafter, Wilson sailed for Bermuda for a vacation. While there he began to work on an article for *Scribner's*, entitled "The Country and the Colleges." Since the world was constantly changing, the educator's "plans must be as consciously provident of the future, as those of the statesman himself." For reintegration of the college and the university, all four undergraduate classes as well as graduate students and unmarried faculty must be organized into residential units. Such a "truly American" university would "recognize uncompromisingly the radical democracy of the mind and of truth itself." It would "rank its men according to their native kinds, not their social accomplishments, and bestow its favours upon immaterial achievement." There would be no second-class collegians (neither the commuter nor the unclubbed). In the end, he decided not to publish the article, apparently for two reasons. First, he thought he might be attacked for trying to resuscitate the Quadrangle Plan. And second, believing that he had won the fight over the graduate school, he felt he had nothing to gain from further agitation. 36

But when Wilson realized that his enemies had by no means surrendered, he became determined to carry his message again to the alumni. Though he seemed to conciliate Princetonians in Baltimore, Brooklyn, Jersey City, and St. Louis, he received a cold, if not hostile, reception on April 7 in New York. Then stung by an adverse decision by the Board of Trustees, Wilson spoke intemperately a few days afterward to the Pittsburgh alumni. Because colleges, he declared, did not produce men "serviceable" to the entire country—indeed, Lincoln would not have served the American people as well "had he been a college man"—Wilson dedicated himself "to a democratic regeneration." The nation would "tolerate nothing that savours of exclusiveness." "Will America tolerate the seclusion of graduate students?" he asked and then answered in the negative. But it was doubtful that Wilson had girded himself to lead a crusade to regenerate democracy in the United States. On the other hand, with the possibilities of a political career developing into realities, Wilson may have taken such positions in response to public pressures.[37]

Meanwhile, Pyne and others on the Board of Trustees worked to settle differences between the two factions by compromise, but neither Wilson nor West was willing to accept what seemed to each a surrender to the other. In May 1910, fate intervened with the death of Isaac C. Wyman '48, who left his estate to build a graduate college for Princeton. Dean West, who had been named one of the estate's two trustees, had won. Realizing that he could not fight an estimated several million dollars—ironically, as Henry W. Bragdon has pointed out, the Wyman bequest was worth only about $660,000 to Princeton—Wilson yielded in a generous spirit. West and Pyne were less charitable, when on June 9 the Board of Trustees accepted Procter's reoffered gift. The president's lone triumph was the defeat of Pyne's candidate for alumni trustee, Adrian H. Joline. In the summer of 1910, Woodrow Wilson agreed to run as the Democratic candidate for governor of New Jersey: The educator had found a wider and more receptive audience.[38]

Minorities at Princeton: Catholics, Jews, and Orientals

Wilson came to believe that the nature of the college, the kinds of men it trained for leadership, and Princeton's mission, in the broadest sense, were at stake in his fight for social democracy. Ultimately, his Quad Plan and stand on the graduate college evolved into a struggle to determine which would prevail: the college ideal or the club system. Wilson hardly foresaw the ultimate consequences of these defeats because he viewed them primarily as personal frustrations. But the failure to establish a new social system, based on residential quadrangles, made it even more difficult for students from minority backgrounds to be accepted at Princeton.

Wilson's concept of a university community was "democratic" in spirit and organization in the sense that "the only lines of demarcation among the students" would be "intellectual, athletic, or social" attainments. On the other hand, his envisioned Princeton, "a compact and homogeneous community" in isolation from the larger world, would by its very definition have excluded commuters from urban areas. To be sure, he had spoken sympathetically of boys from the slums and praised direct experience with life, even speculating that "a whole college of youngsters who had spent their boyhood in the slums, where they had to have wits in order to live, . . . would make extraordinary progress in scholarship." But students who attended Columbia and other city universities, which lacked "the community atmosphere," were "simply going to a day school." The important effects of a university community, he believed, were felt "between the hours of 6 P.M. and 9 A.M."[39]

During the summer of 1907, Wilson began to define in greater detail the kinds of social contacts that he hoped his Quad Plan would encourage. A quadrangle, he wrote to William Belden Reed, Jr., '96, chairman of the Board of Governors of Elm Club, "should be a small cross-section of the University." Wilson recognized the need, of course, to counteract the inclination of particular cliques to congregate in one quad. In reply to H. Howard Armstrong '05, who asked about the probable effects of mixing classes and questioned whether more financially poor students could attend Princeton, Wilson defended official discretion in apportioning students so that no one quad would gain a "socially uncongenial" reputation. All members of the four undergraduate classes would be assigned by a faculty committee to a quad of 100 to 150 students; there would be no segregation of freshmen in separate halls as later developed at Harvard. To forestall the growth of commuters, a contrary development at a residential campus, Wilson proposed to Andrew C. Imbrie that the number of students admitted be limited to the available housing. Quad assignments would be made by lot, with some weight given to parental preference, family ties, and club affiliation (in the event that a club became a quad). Students would be allowed some right of transfer and their own choice of roommates.[40]

Wilson believed that economic and social circumstances should not bar a man from coming to Princeton nor exclude him on arrival from the full benefits of intellectual contacts and other university associations. It would cost less, moreover, to live in a quad than to pay the current combined charges of dormitory room and upper-class eating club membership. Poor men, who could not afford club membership (if invited), would have more opportunities to work for part of the cost of quadrangle residency. But they would not be offered opportunities to wait on table, since Wilson looked askance on those who engaged in menial labor. Although New England college students often did so, he said it was "entirely different" where such labor was "ordinarily rendered by negroes." A student waiter inevitably would lose "self-respect and social standing." Wilson even felt compelled to deny a story that he had ever been obliged to engage in menial work. In fact, his father had supported him fully until he began law practice.[41]

Despite Wilson's assertion that there should be "nothing restrictive, nothing exclusive" about a university because its members, though small in number, were "self-chosen" by their individual ambitions, Princeton had the distinct reputation of discouraging the attendance of minority groups. In an article entitled "Princeton University," published in the *Independent* of March 4, 1909, Edwin E. Slosson pointed out that Princeton's admission requirements, expense, restricted number of electives, lack of professional training, and, indeed, "traditions and atmosphere" excluded or failed to attract most students. Alone among the fourteen universities he visited, Princeton made no provision for the education of women. Blacks were excluded on racial grounds, an observation confirmed fifteen years later by W. E. Burghardt Du Bois's article, "Negroes in College," in the *Nation*. Nor, continued Slosson, did Princeton "share in the international movement . . . sweeping over the country," although its students supported missionary work by graduates in China. While Harvard, Yale, and Cornell each had at least twenty-five Chinese students, Princeton undergraduates did "not like to have them around."[42]

Anti-Semitism was "more dominant at Princeton than at any of the other" of Slosson's selected universities. "The Christian tradition of Princeton, the exclusiveness of the upper-class clubs and the prejudices of the students" discouraged Jews, although there were eleven Jewish freshmen. Typically it was said that "if the Jews once got in, . . ., they would ruin Princeton as they have Columbia and Pennsylvania."[43]

Although available evidence on Wilson's attitude toward minority groups is slight, it strongly suggests that he was more liberal than many Princetonians. He was prejudiced against blacks, but hardly more so than A. Lawrence Lowell. Like Lowell, Wilson welcomed the presence of the Irish on campus; he also regretted the persistence of anti-Semitism. Finally, in keeping with his sense of America's international mission, Wilson would have liked to increase the number of Princeton's Oriental students.

The fight over the Quad Plan and the graduate school controversy deepened Wilson's concept of social democracy, but they did not change his firm belief that Princeton's tradition of discouraging black applicants should be continued. While there was no university law preventing a black from matriculating, Wilson drafted the outline of a negative answer to "a poor Southern colored man from South Carolina," who had said that he could make his way if admitted:

> Regret to say that it is altogether inadvisable for a colored man to enter Princeton. Appreciate his desire to do so, but strongly recommend his securing education in a Southern institution perhaps completing it with a course at the Princeton Theol. Sem., which is under entirely separate control from the Univ.

Consequently, Secretary Charles W. McAlpin advised G. McArthur Sullivan to apply either to a southern college or to such northern institutions as Harvard, Dartmouth, or Brown.[44]

Princeton had not always been so uncordial, if not downright hostile, to black applicants, although not until 1947 would a black (Arthur Jewell Wilson) receive an undergraduate degree (significantly, a wartime A.B.). John

Chavis, a black Presbyterian minister and educator from North Carolina, had entered the college in 1792, but did not graduate. In 1774, free blacks Bristol Yamma and John Quamine were sent by the Missionary Society of Newport, Rhode Island, to study privately under President John Witherspoon in preparation for missionary work in Africa. And since the nineteenth century, black students at Princeton Theological Seminary had attended graduate courses at the college and then at the university. In fact, white students who protested the enrollment of a black seminary student in President James McCosh's psychology course in 1876 were themselves given the option of withdrawing. The first blacks to receive graduate degrees from Princeton were the Reverends Irwin William Langston Roundtree, A.M. '95, and George Shippen Stark, A.M. '06. [45]

Wilson's main reason for advising blacks to apply elsewhere was the college's strong antebellum connection with the South and its continuing attraction for southern students. But Princeton's student body was predominantly Middle Atlantic in origin during his presidency. In 1909, for example, 66 percent of its students came from New York, Pennsylvania, and New Jersey. And Yale outdrew Princeton in the South in 1915-16, although Princeton was to make substantial gains in that region during the 1920s. Yet in deference to a rather small constituency and a ghostly memory—in 1848 a majority of its students had come from Dixie—Princeton maintained its "southern" prejudices. [46]

Its students even resented playing against blacks in intercollegiate athletic competition. The following incident, fondly recounted by an Harvard alumnus, allegedly illustrated "the fundamentally democratic life at Harvard, where the only aristocracy of any real consequence was an intellectual one." He had been told about an incident that had occurred in the 1890s following a Harvard-Princeton football game. When the Princetonians "saw the Harvard team enter the dining room with [its one] colored member included, they (the Princeton team) arose and left in a body, the Harvard team dining without their hosts." But after the controversy developed over Harvard's exclusion of blacks from the freshman halls, the alumnus wrote President Lowell that he had "spoiled a perfectly good story" about Harvard democracy. Nevertheless, blacks played on Harvard teams fifty years before they were even admitted as undergraduates to Princeton. [47]

Woodrow Wilson, like most white Americans of his generation, was a racist. Yet in spite of a certain condescension toward blacks and a fondness for "darkey stories"—used to leaven his speeches at alumni dinners and even at formal academic occasions—Wilson occasionally expressed some concern for the situation of Negroes in America. According to his notes for an address for the Hampton Institute, he recognized that Negroes faced greater difficulties than other groups in adjusting to American society. Education and private aid would be needed to undo the damage done by Reconstruction, "a colossal example of *mal*-adjustment." Continuing this theme in an address to the Men's Association of the Witherspoon Street Presbyterian Church in Princeton, Wilson declared that "the so-called 'negro problem' [was] not of color but capacity; not a racial, but an economic problem." While he had never reached a solution in regard to the Negro's future, he felt that southern white men were the only ones who could find the answer. [48]

Princeton's racial bar against blacks was apparently never applied to American Indians, perhaps because of missionary work by graduates among the "heathen." But during the institution's first two hundred years, only ten Indians have been identified as either graduates or nongraduates. Although the College of New Jersey was not founded to further the education of Indians, as was Dartmouth, Delaware Indians had studied on government expense at President Witherspoon's Nassau Grammar School during the late eighteenth century. More than fifty years later, Princeton graduated its first Indian students: John McDonald Ross, A.B. '41; William Potter Ross, A.B. '42 and A.M. '91, chief of the Cherokee Nation; and Robert Daniel Ross, A.B. '43, A.M. '46, and University of Pennsylvania M.D. '47. Perhaps the best known Indian graduate of recent times was Joseph Paul Baldeagle, A.B. '23. A South Dakota-born Sioux—whose ancestor Chief No-Flesh had defeated General George Custer—Baldeagle was educated on scholarships at Carlisle Indian School, Mt. Hermon School, Mercersburg Academy, and Princeton. After retiring from teaching English at Bordentown, New Jersey, High School, he returned to Princeton to work at the information desk in Firestone Library. [49]

Except for his attitudes toward blacks, Wilson had few, if any, racial or ethnic prejudices. He had no religious prejudices that clouded his judgment when dealing with others of different faiths. His greatest dislikes were always directed against those men who opposed his views, as both his educational and political careers amply demonstrated. In an amusing after-dinner speech to the Friendly Sons of St. Patrick, Wilson revealed an important side to his character. "I have never objected to the race, to the blood, of other men," he said; "I have objected to their opinions." [50]

Wilson came increasingly to believe that for their own benefit the young scions of the WASP upper class should mingle with students of different socioeconomic and even ethnic backgrounds. During his years at Princeton, however, the major shift in undergraduate student body composition was a decrease in the number of those professing Presbyterian affiliation and a corresponding rise in Episcopalian representation. Presbyterians declined from two-thirds of the student body in 1890 to about one-half by 1900. Nine years later, they composed only 38 percent of the freshman class, while Episcopalians had rapidly increased from less than 20 percent to 30 percent of the total. From 1922 to 1929, when freshman classes ranged from 605 to 633, Episcopalians averaged well over 200 (from 195 to 252) students. According to historian Henry W. Bragdon, this shift in religious affiliations at Princeton began with the arrival of the sons of wealthy New York businessmen and lawyers, who built imposing mansions within a mile or two of campus. In the same classes, Presbyterians still mustered a strong second, contributing 178 to 209 members. Methodists and Congregationalists trailed with around 25 to 35 adherents. Baptists averaged between one and two dozen students, while such other denominations as Christian Scientists, Dutch Reformed, Lutherans, and Unitarians numbered from half a dozen to under twenty members. And those stating no religious preference fluctuated between a minimum of five and a maximum of thirty-odd.[51]

Wilson welcomed non-Protestant students and seems to have received without hostility a few representatives of the recent eastern European immigrants. To be sure, in volume 5 of *A History of the American People* (1901), he had drawn a very unfavorable comparison between "the sturdy stocks of the north of Europe" and the "multitudes of men of the lowest class from the south of Italy and men of the meaner sort out of Hungary and Poland, men out of the ranks where there was neither skill nor energy nor any initiative of quick intelligence." But on the other hand, in 1905 he also said, at the opening of the Institute of Musical Art in New York, that "composite America" was "being merged together." Acknowledging that his blood, the Scotch-Irish, was "good to fight with but not to play the violin with," he saw the creation of American music by peoples of many different nationalities—German, Scandinavian, Polish, and Hungarian. (Interestingly enough, he did not mention Negro jazz.) What had frightened him about the masses of immigrants pouring into eastern urban centers was the thought that they might not be assimilated. While Wilson emphasized "America's cosmopolitan nationality," according to historian John Higham, he attacked immigrants when they failed to understand the "mission" of the United States. On balance, however, Wilson's attitude toward immigrants was decidedly more positive than hostile.[52]

Despite the fact that Princeton required compulsory chapel for almost eighty years after Harvard had dropped it, the enrollment of Catholic students grew slowly, but steadily, from the early 1900s onward. By the mid-1920s, Catholics constituted about 7 percent of the entering freshman class (see Table 6.1). Both Samuel Ross Winans and his successor as dean of the faculty, Henry Burchard Fine, took special note of the number of entering Catholic students in their reports to the Board of Trustees' Committee on Morals and Discipline. In 1902, Dean Winans pointed out that ten of the fourteen Roman Catholic students were enrolled in the scientific department. This concentration might possibly be explained by the fact that a year's less preparation was required for entrance into the scientific program. Of the seventeen Catholics who signed the matriculation book in October 1902, only six declared themselves to be communicants.[53]

Among Catholic students attending Princeton during these years were the sons of James Smith, Jr., a former grocery clerk who rose to be United States Senator from New Jersey (1893-99). Smith admired Wilson until the latter, as governor, undercut him by joining the state's progressives. The future secretary of defense, James Vincent Forrestal, a contractor's son, joined Princeton's class of 1915 as a sophomore, having transferred from Dartmouth. While at Princeton, he was chairman of both the *Daily Princetonian* and the *Nassau Herald* committee and a member of the Senior Council, the Class Day Committee, and the University Cottage Club. Forrestal's religious affiliation obviously was no bar to his social success at Princeton. Nor did it hinder the efforts of Francis Scott Key Fitzgerald to become a "big man" on campus, although he lacked the self-assurance of Adlai E. Stevenson '22, a wealthy, old-stock Protestant (Stevenson listed himself as a Unitarian and a Democrat in *The Nassau Herald*). Unable to find his social niche, Fitzgerald tried almost too hard to succeed. But he did win considerable recognition: The libretto he wrote freshman year for the Triangle Club was produced the following semester. He also became an editor of the *Tiger* and the *Nassau Literary Magazine*. And having turned down invitations to Cannon, Quadrangle, and Cap and Gown, he joined Cottage Club. The next step would have been the presidency of Triangle and election to the Senior Council. But Fitzgerald's cavalier indifference, if not studied neglect, of academic work resulted in an unsatisfactory record. No longer eligible to compete for further extracurricular honors and ill with malaria, Fitzgerald left Princeton in December of his junior year.[54]

In addition to the aforementioned Catholics who became famous in later life were dozens who pursued successful careers both at Princeton and in the business world after graduation. In the undergraduate society of Princeton, success was measured principally by athletic accomplishment. (This avenue had been closed to Fitzgerald, who, at five feet seven inches and 138 pounds, was too light for football.) In practically every class during this period, there were at least one or two Catholics, if not more, who became proud wearers of the P. Such an athletic honor carried with it, unless one were Jewish, an invitation to one of the upper-class eating clubs. Many Catholic athletes received bids from Tiger Inn, which prided itself on the athletic prowess of its members.[55]

Of all the groups associated with late nineteenth-century immigration, only one—the Jews—was large enough at Princeton even to be counted (see Table 6.2). Although Wilson made no statements about Jewish students—or none that have survived—he seemed to have a much more favorable attitude toward them than most academicians of this period. Indeed, given his southern Presbyterian background, Wilson was philo-Semitic, rather than anti-Semitic. (Only once in his lifetime, as a second-year law student at the University of Virginia, did Wilson make a recorded statement disparaging a

Table 6.1
CATHOLIC STUDENTS MATRICULATING AT
PRINCETON, 1876-1925

Year	Matriculating of Catholic Students
1871-75	0
1876	0
1877	2
1878	0
1879	2
1880	3
1881	2
1882	0
1883	0
1884	1
1885	0
1886	0
1887	1
1888	1
1889	5
1890	4
1891	1
1892	1
1893	4
1894	3
1895	0
1896	6
1897	3
1898	4
1899	9
1900	11
1901	9
1902	17
1903	14
1904	12
1905	16
1906	14
1907	15
1908	25
1909	15
1910	16

Table 6.1 (Continued)

Year	Matriculating of Catholic Students
1911	23
1912	21[a]
1913	36
1914	18
1915	22
1916	28
1917	13
1918	18
1919	28[b]
1920	21
1921	38
1922	32
1923	29[c]
1924	40
1925	42

Source: Compiled from *College of New Jersey, President's Entrance-Book,* vol. 1 (1871-93), and *Matriculation Book,* vol. 2 (1893-1903); *Reports of the Dean of the Faculty to the Committee on Morals and Discipline of the Board of Trustees, Minutes of the Trustees,* vols. 9 (December 1893-March 1901) and 10 (June 1901-January 1908); *Princeton Presi-dent't Reports,* 1908-23; *The Nassau Herald, Class of Nineteen Hundred and Twenty-Three* (Princeton University Press, 1923); and Radcliffe Heermance, Office of the Super-visor [in 1925, Dean] of Freshmen, "Preliminary Analysis of Freshman Class," in Septem-ber 1921-29, Trustees' Papers, Princeton University Archives.

[a]Plus 1 qualifying student. Qualifying students were provisional students who did not have sufficient academic credits to be enrolled in one of the three upper classes. The statis-tics on religious affiliation in the *Princeton President's Reports* included qualifying fresh-men with regular freshmen.

[b]Figures for 1919 were based on biographical sketches in *The Nassau Herald, Class of Nineteen Hundred and Twenty-Three,* the senior class album. Most likely, a number of Catholic students, along with non-Catholic students, had left Princeton since matriculat-ing for academic or personal reasons.

[c]*Princeton President's Report, December 31, 1923,* gave a higher number (33) of Catholic students than the "Preliminary Analysis" of September (29).

particular Jew, the winner of an oratorical contest in Washington.) His later political career demonstrated strong support for Jews. For example, as gover-nor of New Jersey, Wilson nominated Samuel Kalisch, his political leader in Newark, as associate justice of the State Supreme Court. Kalisch thus became the first Jew to serve on this New Jersey court. Five years later, Wilson ap-pointed the first Jew to the United States Supreme Court, Louis D. Brandeis. And in an address at Carnegie Hall on December 6, 1911, Wilson spoke elo-

Table 6.2
JEWISH STUDENTS MATRICULATING AT
PRINCETON, 1876-1925

Year	Matriculating of Jewish Students
1871-75	0
1876	1
1877	1
1878	0
1879	0
1880	0
1881	0
1882	0
1883	1
1884	1
1885	0
1886	0
1887	0
1888	0
1889	1
1890	0
1891	2
1892	0
1893	2
1894	3
1895	0
1896	3
1897	2
1898	1
1899	4
1900	6
1901[a]	3
1902	2
1903	.. [b]
1904	.. [b]
1905	3
1906	8
1907	7
1908	11
1909	13
1910	6

Table 6.2 (Continued)

Year	Matriculating of Jewish Students
1911	10
1912	13[c]
1913	12[c]
1914	6
1915	19
1916	8
1917	4
1918	13
1919	16[d]
1920	20
1921	23
1922	25
1923	21[e]
1924	13
1925	11

Source: Compiled from *College of New Jersey, President's Entrance-Book*, vol. 1 (1871-93), and *Matriculation Book*, vol. 2 (1893-1903); *Reports of the Dean of the Faculty to the Committee on Morals and Discipline of the Board of Trustees, Minutes of the Trustees*, vols. 9 (December 1898-March 1901) and 10 (June 1901-January 1908); *Princeton President's Reports*, 1908-23; *The Nassau Herald, Class of Nineteen Hundred and Twenty-Three* (Princeton University Press, 1923); and Radcliffe Heermance, Office of the Supervisor [in 1925, Dean] of Freshmen, "Preliminary Analysis of Freshman Class," in September 1921-29, Trustees' Papers, Princeton University Archives.

[a]Between December 1901 and March 1902, 3 Jewish students enrolled; 2 others, who professed no affiliation, may have also been Jewish.

[b]In 1903 and 1904, the number of entering Jewish students was too small to be mentioned specifically. Undoubtedly, one or two did matriculate, but were lumped with the remainder of the class (after counting the 40 percent Presbyterians, 25 percent Episcopalians, 30 Methodists, 13 Congregationalists, 12 Catholics, and 11 Baptists) as scattered among a dozen denominations.

[c]Plus one qualifying student. Qualifying students were provisional students who did not have sufficient academic credits to be enrolled in one of the three upper classes. The statistics on religious affiliation in the *Princeton President's Reports* included qualifying freshmen with regular freshmen.

[d]Plus one who stated no affiliation. Figures for 1919 were based on biographical sketches in *The Nassau Herald, Class of Nineteen Hundred and Twenty-Three*, the senior class album. Most likely, a number of Jewish students, along with Gentile students, had left Princeton since matriculating for academic or personal reasons.

[e]*Princeton President's Report, December 31, 1923*, gave a higher number (23) of Jewish students than the "Preliminary Analysis" of September (21).

quently on "The Rights of the Jews." He argued that unless Russia lived up to the terms of an eighty-year-old treaty under which citizens—including American Jews—of both nations were to be free to travel in each other's territory on legitimate business, the United States should either sever trade relations or, at the very least, negotiate another treaty on different terms.56

It was likely that Wilson felt the same kind of concern for the rights of Jewish students at Princeton. It was brought to his attention on at least two occasions, moreover, that Jewish students were usually treated as social outcasts. In September 1904, Jacob Ridgway Wright, a Princeton classmate, wrote Wilson about John Coons of Wilkes-Barre, Pennsylvania, who was entering that fall as a freshman. The boy's father was a distinguished representative of the Luzerne County bar, a man of "sterling character and strong professional qualities," and Wright's "warmest, closest friend."57

The boy, according to Wright, was "very like his father in temperament and mentality." Not only was he intelligent, but he also loved music and might go out for one of the college musical groups. Wright then asked Wilson "to see to it" that the boy was "not 'held up' or discriminated against" because of his ethnic and religious background:

> If he should merit a place, and chance favors his winning on his merits, I do not want him to be 'thrown over' in this or any other direction because of his religious belief. Both you and I know that it is the fashion to look at the Jew unsympathetically, simply because he is a Jew. But I cannot be wrong in my belief that you would not allow this boy, or any other boy, in fact, to be discriminated against because of his race, color, belief or otherwise. . . . and I know you will keep your eye on him and see that he is protected without permitting him to know it.

Since Wilson's reply is missing, one can only guess whether or not he kept a fatherly eye on John Coons. Undoubtedly, the two met, because Wright had given Coons a note of introduction to Wilson. Although Coons did not make any of the eating clubs, he was a member of Triangle Club and got the chance to play his violin. In *The Nassau Herald* of 1908, Coons listed history as his favorite study and his political preference as Democratic. After graduating from Princeton with high honors, he attended Harvard Law School but did not finish because of ill health. Subsequently, he did practice law.58

Under the existing club system, Jewish students and any others not offered membership were effectively denied equal access to that community life (as well as to "digestible food") which was part of a Princeton education. One of the first alumni to praise the proposed "radical changes" was Leon Michael Levy, who had been a member of the class of 1905 for two years, first as a freshman and then as a special student. Although achieving some distinction by winning Whig Hall's sophomore essay contest (Cliosophic was the other campus debating and oratory society), he left Princeton and enrolled at the University of Pennsylvania. After receiving a LL.B. in 1906, he began to practice law in Scranton, Pennsylvania.59

Levy blamed the "abominable system of club life" for the "social humilia-tion" and "class prejudice" he suffered at Princeton because he was Jewish. In-itially he accepted the hazing without thinking that it was partly motivated by "racial contempt." When at the end of freshman year, he was not taken into one of the sophomore "hat lines," he felt "branded" as "an Ishmaelite and outcast" by the very "absence of a cap or insignia." Most undergraduates were "snobbish, addleheaded young cads," whose "idol [was] not a Calf of Gold, but a calf of sinew with an arm to match." In such a situation, his only friends were two other Jewish students and two Gentiles, one of whom was "an eccentric literary genius" and the other the college's "finest debater" (probably Norman Thomas).[60]

Like Levy, Harold Zeiss '07, a self-proclaimed Unitarian and a mugwump, described the clubs as "the acme of snobbish[ness]." The selection process really began during the freshman year, when undergraduate social status was "prematurely fixed, regardless of ability." If a student "'queers' himself by some little thing Freshman year," Zeiss wrote Wilson, he was "likely to be'down' for the rest of his college course."[61]

Another nonclub member, a graduate of the class of 1894, not only ex-pressed approval of the Quad Plan, but also suggested several ways for putting it into operation. Louis I. Reichner, a Presbyterian and a Republican, proposed, first, that Princeton buy all the club houses at cost and then rent certain ones, in rotation, to the upper-class clubs. Second, the university should prohibit the wearing of distinctive hatbands, neckties, and other in-signia by both undergraduates and graduates. Third, freshman and sopho-more commons should be established in which every member of these two classes must eat. Finally, all freshman and sophomore social clubs should be abolished.[62]

The club system also acted as a bar to Oriental students, although a small number did attend Princeton, Three Japanese had enrolled there as early as 1871, significantly, eight years before Ivy was founded. Two of them had presented themselves with a letter of introduction to the Presbyterian Board of Foreign Missions and had been escorted to Princeton by the board's trea-surer. They were enrolled as special students in the sophomore class. The first Japanese to graduate from Princeton was Hikoichi Orita, A.B. '76 and A.M. '79. When he matriculated in 1872, the following comment was entered beside his name in the *President's Entrance-Book:* "A Japanese not of any Christian denomination." During his years in college, he converted to Chris-tianity and joined the Presbyterian church. He was also a member of Whig Hall and a commencement orator. After graduation he had a long and dis-tinguished career in the Japanese Department of Education and was appoint-ed a life member of the House of Peers by the emperor.[63]

An occasional Japanese, like an Orita or a Motokichi Takahashi, A.M. '06, found Princeton a pleasant experience. But Wilson soon realized that the clubs did not share his sense of educational mission in regard to Orientals in general. Although refusing to lend his name to the movement for Philippine independence, Wilson authorized a favorable reply to the United States Philippine Commission in regard to "the admission of such Filipinos as may be sent us." While Princeton would extend to them "the same concessions in the matter of tuition" as to other needy students, few Filipinos ever came to Princeton.64

Wilson's sense of duty toward Orientals was most clearly expressed in regard to the Chinese. In 1909, for example, he accepted an invitation to become one of the twelve lay members—President Arthur T. Hadley of Yale was another—of the Committee of Christian Education in China, which represented Protestant foreign missions. In January of the same year, Wilson expressed great eagerness to get "the ear of the Chinese Legation in Washington" and to place Princeton "upon some preferred list" for Chinese students coming to the United States. Princeton itself would benefit only through getting "a grip upon the minds of men who may be influential in guiding the future of the Chinese empire." However, on further reflection and after several conferences with Lucius H. Miller, assistant professor of biblical instruction, and with others, Wilson soon realized that Chinese students would be better served at other universities. Princeton's less varied and less flexible program could not provide the training in engineering and the professions that most of them sought. Equally important, Wilson believed his "fear" to be "well grounded" that Princeton's social system would make any Chinese "feel like outsiders, . . . set apart for some reason of race or caste which would render them most uncomfortable." He concluded "very reluctantly" that there was "nothing" that Princeton could "wisely do to press our claims for recognition in the distribution of the numerous Chinese students" sent over by the Chinese government on the remitted indemnity funds.65

Although Wilson dropped the idea of bringing Chinese students to the college, he pursued it in regard to the graduate school, which attracted the majority of Princeton's foreign students. In April 1928, for example, the *Princeton Alumni Weekly* listed five graduate school Chinese alumni who "have given a good account of themselves in their native land." And in October 1948, Frederick Liu, secretary of Princeton's Chinese Club, claimed that "Old Nassau" was "responsible for a lion's share of the leaders in Nationalist China today," although his club was the smallest of those in leading American colleges. Most of them either entered government service or became university professors of science, in particular, physics.66

Woodrow Wilson and A. Lawrence Lowell: Comparison and Contrast

Had Wilson's social reorganization succeeded at Princeton, it was likely that the university would have taken a different path than it did. In his most progressive statements, he had said that Princeton should be a place where there was "no caste or privilege . . . but where America herself is reproduced in small." Of course, this was not meant literally because he himself agreed to the exclusion of black students from the college. On the other hand, he undoubtedly believed that Princeton should be accessible to all white students. Speaking in 1909 to the Philadelphian Society, a campus religious organization, Wilson had said that as long as the undergraduate social system standardized students, Princeton was "neither university nor Christian." But his references to Princeton as a Christian university were relatively few; above all he wanted it to be a university. [67]

It is intriguing to consider how Wilson might have reacted, had he been president of a university as ethnically diverse as Harvard. For in 1910 Harvard was surely far closer to being America "reproduced in small" than Princeton would be until the 1960s. Both Wilson and Lowell agreed that colleges should foster "social co-ordination," or cohesion, and that they needed a certain amount of homogeneity. And both believed that collegiate democracy could be achieved through some form of compulsory residence, be it Harvard's freshman halls or Wilson's quadrangles. Finally, they were critical of the impact of wealth on their respective universities. Wilson regretted the dependency of Princeton on the subscribers to the Committee of Fifty Fund and felt dejected when the wealthy—among them Andrew Carnegie—would not agree to finance his cherished Quad Plan. For his part, Lowell broke up the preparatory school cliques through the freshman halls and then undermined Harvard's Gold Coast by the House Plan. [68]

But in three important respects, Wilson differed from Lowell. First, as an educator, Wilson evaluated students according to their individual attainments, whereas Lowell considered them as members of a group, stamped with a particular identity. For Wilson, the important distinctions among students were their personal attributes of integrity and intellectual capacity. And he also contended that membership in a college community, just as citizenship in the United States, carried with it the rights of equal treatment and full participation. On the other hand, Lowell placed a greater emphasis on a student's social compatibility as a prerequisite to college membership. He seemed to believe that some students—those of Anglo-Saxon background— were more equal than others.

Second, Wilson's fascination with the art of political statesmanship led him to articulate fully his educational philosophy. He was far more insistent than the Harvardian that the purpose of an American university be to teach "democratic thinking." In presenting this theme to the Princeton Club of Chicago in March 1908, he defined such thinking as

not stopping to ask a man's origin, not stopping to ask a man's influence, but regarding a man, every man, as different from his fellows only in capacity, only in trustworthiness, only in character. . . . Whenever you have shut classes up tight, nations have begun to rot, because the individual worth has been checked and individual opportunities denied.[69]

The next year, he expounded the same theme in addresses on Abraham Lincoln, his ideal "generalized American." Unlike the clubmen who paid Princeton's bills, Lincoln "did not allow himself to be encumbered by riches"; he "was absolutely direct and fearless" in confronting the issues. But Lincoln would not have belonged at Princeton as it was then academically and socially structured. Under the current social system, "the born leaders and managers and originators" were "drafted off to 'run the college.'" Education had become "swallowed up" by the many distracting "side shows." A university, said Wilson, should train the mind to be "a radical democrat" and in the process make students "as much unlike their fathers as possible." Wilson's comments connecting Lincoln to contemporary American colleges and universities had broader implications, as suggested by his address in Philadelphia in March 1909, on the "University's Part in Political Life." He was presenting another version, though one substantially transformed, of his inaugural, "Princeton for the Nation's Service."[70]

In a third respect Wilson also differed from Lowell. His vision of American society was more generous and open than was the Harvard president's. Although Lowell and like-minded adherents to the Immigration Restriction League were ostensibly realistic in pointing out that different races and ethnic groups did not easily commingle, their advocacy of quotas on immigrants and on Jewish students was shortsighted as a long-term solution. Quotas may have temporarily eased the burdens of racial and ethnic adjustment and averted clashes between groups, but they did not educate people on the need for mutual respect and toleration. In contrast, Wilson did not favor quotas—they were socially exclusive—any more than he did tariffs—they created special privileges. In a "true democracy," he said, a community or nation must be "organized on the principle of involuntary and unselected contact." Like Charles W. Eliot, Wilson was a member of the National Liberal Immigration League. His role in this organization may have been just a perfunctory one, however, since, unlike Eliot, he apparently wrote no letters on its behalf. Nevertheless, as president of the United States, Wilson vetoed two literacy bills, in 1915 and 1917, and pocket-vetoed the Emergency Quota Act of 1921.[71]

Although A. Lawrence Lowell's commitment to curriculum reform and defense of academic freedom at Harvard during World War I should not be forgotten, Wilson became the true democratic idealist, whose interest in a political career led him to assume both radical and popular positions. Indeed, he believed so intensely that his educational and social ideals would prepare the best citizens and leaders that he began to see his presidency of Princeton as "a sort of minor statesmanship." And the theme—of keeping the channels open from the bottom to the top of society—would gain increasing usage as Wilson moved toward the governorship of New Jersey and then toward the New Freedom. 72

Circumstantial evidence thus suggests that Wilson would not have proposed a quota on Jewish students had he been in A. Lawrence Lowell's position in 1922-23. But in the assignments to the proposed residential units of his Quad Plan, Wilson might have felt it necessary to cross-section students by religious affiliation to prevent any one unit from being stigmatized as socially undesirable or from becoming a Little Jerusalem. Like Lowell, Wilson understood the social realities of his time.

On the whole, Lowell was the more successful of the two college presidents in effecting his academic reforms and residential plans at Harvard. Wilson had the broader vision, but was unable to implement his goals fully. Even Lowell, who had "a blind confidence" that Wilson was "right," wrote that he could not fully understand the issues over the location of the graduate college. Wilson's early years of great achievement at Princeton (and later at Washington as president of the United States) were followed by almost self-inflicted defeats. In large measure, his personality, perhaps already affected by two bouts with the cerebral arterial sclerosis that later paralyzed him, was to blame. In 1924, Charles W. Eliot, his educational opponent but political supporter (A. Lawrence Lowell also voted for him in 1912), astutely observed: "Woodrow Wilson, like most reformers and pioneering folk, had a fierce and unlovely side." 73

Special Committee on Limitation of Enrollment, 1921-22

John Grier Hibben, Wilson's successor at Princeton, was the kind of president "needed to hold the institution steady" in a period of transition, according to Ray Stannard Baker. Although regarded as the candidate of the anti-Wilson trustees, Hibben began the work of conciliation by appointing two Wilson men to deanships: Luther Pfahler Eisenhart (mathematics) served as dean of the faculty (1925-33) and Christian Frederick Gauss (modern languages) as dean of the college (1925-45). The graduate college, cause of so much controversy, was built on the golf links, about one mile from the center of campus; it was ceremoniously opened in October 1913. A statue of Andrew F. West sits in brooding judgment in its courtyard, but the dean lost his bid to make the school largely self-governing within the university. On the Quad Plan and Wilson's ideals of social democracy, Princeton was officially silent for at least a generation. And the Wilson and West factions remained bitter and socially divided for decades. 74

Very little evidence exists about Hibben's attitudes toward minority students, because he justified R. S. Baker's description of himself as a "self-effacing administrator." A story is told in Princeton that toward the end of his presidency, he and Mrs. Hibben spent their evenings burning his official papers. But having found administrative duties too demanding, Hibben appointed Howard Alexander Smith '01 as executive secretary of the university in the autumn of 1920. Smith served as an ex officio member of every trustees' committee and attended faculty meetings. He might have succeeded Hibben in the presidency if he had not become involved in the controversy over the influence of the evangelical Buchman movement on the activities of the campus Philadelphian Society. As a result, he resigned his office and underwent a conversion experience. Some years later, Smith found a new calling when he entered New Jersey politics. 75

One of the special committees on which he served during his years as executive secretary was asked to report on the desirability of limiting Princeton's undergraduate enrollment and to propose a new admission procedure. Although Princeton was influenced by steps taken elsewhere—notably, at Columbia, Dartmouth, Harvard, Stanford, and Yale--as early as 1904, Woodrow Wilson had privately anticipated that Princeton might have to limit its enrollment someday to 2,000 undergraduates. He wanted to preserve its homogeneous and, by his definition at that time, its "democratic character." 76

Like most American colleges, Princeton's enrollment had increased since 1900, although with some fluctuations. Exclusive of graduate students, there were 1,161 undergraduates in 1900-01, 1,814 in 1920-21, and 2,227 in 1929-30. But as of December 1920, Princeton could accommodate only between 1,275 and 1,350 students in its present dormitories and another 400 when the new dormitories were built. Its dining halls could feed about 1,200 students. For reasons of space rather than race, Princeton decided to limit its enrollment, although the latter subject was discussed in order to prevent a future problem. Following a year's deliberation by the "Special Committee to consider and report a method to be pursued in limitation of the number of undergraduates," the trustees had voted, on January 12, 1922, that "the number of undergraduates that can be adequately accommodated and properly taught is approximately 2000." 77

The Special Committee inquired into and then considered such methods as Dartmouth's "Selective Process for Admission" and the Rhodes's Scholarship requirements of "character," "scholarship," "athletics," and "leadership." H. Alexander Smith was eager to review any plan that embodied methods of selection "outside of the orthodox examination," such as psychological testing, personal interview, alumni preference, geographical distribution, school activities, and "character." Among some faculty and trustees there was considerable interest in the psychological tests used by the army during World War I, but they wished to experiment with them before making them part of admission process. Of course, the term *mental* or *psychological* test was applied during the 1920s to several different kinds of examinations: the Army

Alpha Test; the Scholastic Aptitude Test of the College Entrance Examination Board—verbal (1926) and mathematical (1930) sections; and various predictive tests used to place freshmen in appropriate course levels as well as estimating their college achievement. In June 1922, the Princeton Board of Trustees authorized the administration of psychological tests to all students who entered that autumn. Four years later Princeton required SATs and also developed an index (based on psychological test score, College Board and school averages, and age) to predict a student's probable academic success ("bogie" group) in college. 78

By early March, the Special Committee had drafted a report, which would undergo two revisions because of faculty and trustee opposition. The first and second versions, presented to the university faculty on March 14 and 21, 1921, proposed that the number of future freshmen not exceed 600 and recommended adoption of additional admission qualifications. The first version specified not only the attainment of certain examination averages, but also a satisfactory rating by the school principal on "mental," "manhood," "leadership," and "physical qualifications." Such "other qualifications" as "home environment and companions" and "religious belief and attitude toward religious activities" would also be evaluated. Moreover, alumni association districts would each be given "a quota of vacancies," with "special consideration" being accorded to New Jersey applicants. A majority of a class conceivably could be admitted on the basis of either Princeton connections or certain manly qualities attributed by Anglo-Saxons to those of the same stock. In order to carry out this rather complicated selective process, the Special Committee recommended the appointment of a new Committee on Admissions—three faculty, one trustee, and the registrar—to replace the existing Entrance Committee, which was a faculty standing committee. (In time, special personnel, either nonteaching or only part-time faculty, would assume virtually the entire work of admissions. 79

These proposed basic changes in procedure aroused faculty opposition, because it would no longer be the almost exclusive arbiter as to who would be admitted. Several faculty, among them George McLean Harper and Gordon H. Gerould (English), urged that the part on qualifications be either stricken or restated. Faculty sentiment was clearly expressed by its affirmative vote on the motion of William Starr Myers, professor of political science and a former Wilson preceptor: "That it be the sense of the Faculty that primary consideration be placed upon scholarship and that other considerations be regarded as secondary." 80

A week later, on March 21, the Special Committee presented an amended report, which placed greater emphasis on entrance examination grades. All applicants would be asked to submit blanks, now only signed by principal, president, or dean, with data on their various qualifications. These were listed briefly in the report, with the more explicit "race and nationality" substituted for "religious belief." Concerned about the proposed method of appointing the Committee on Admissions as well as its composition, the faculty voted in favor of Dean Henry B. Fine's motion that it "be a Committee of the Faculty to include the Registrar and to be appointed in the usual way."[81]

Having received two setbacks, the Special Committee decided to spend the summer and autumn reconsidering its basic objectives. H. Alexander Smith consulted extensively with Walter E. Hope '01, a New York lawyer, who had been elected alumni trustee in 1919. Undoubtedly expressing the views of the vast majority of Princetonians, Hope did "not agree that anyone should be admitted *solely* on the basis of his passing mark on examinations, irrespective of other qualifications." He also advised Smith that certain statements should be left rather "in the nature of informal regulations for the guidance of the Committee on Admissions." The provision referring to alumni sons, for example, "might not make a favorable impression on outsiders," and alumni could be adequately informed through their weekly magazine. And "requirements" in regard to "'race and nationality,' if published, might stir something up, whereas the blanks, when obtained, [would] speak for themselves."[82]

Smith sent Hope's letter to Dean Howard ("Irish") McClenahan, with the observation that the trustees would "all see the importance of some evidence besides the mere passing of examinations" and would "also favor a large discretion in the Committee." To "prevent the outbreak of any hostilities" between faculty and trustees, especially over the appointment of the admissions committee and its discretionary authority, Smith sought to work out an acceptable "practical diplomatic formula." Meanwhile, he succeeded in developing a consensus among the five members of the Special Committee. They agreed to "the principle of a short report, emphasizing a broad authority" in the Committee on Admissions. Its director should be a presidential appointee and ex officio a faculty member, because he would represent the faculty, trustees, and alumni. And he should be a full-time administrative officer.[83]

The "Report of the Special Committee on Limitation of Undergraduate Enrollment" was adopted by the university faculty at a special meeting on January 9, 1922, and by the Board of Trustees three days later. The Committee on Admissions, which would report annually to the trustees' Curriculum Committee and to the faculty, would be given virtually a free hand for two years to admit applicants under the existing entrance requirements. But instead of the extensive qualifications proposed in its first report, the Special Committee listed just two requirements: taking the College Board Entrance Examinations and submitting certificates attesting to character and school records. And only two categories of applicants—qualified scholarship candidates and those with records showing "unusual promise, seriousness of purpose, or achievement under difficulty"—were given explicit preference.[84]

Judging from editorials in the *Daily Princetonian*, undergraduates generally favored the trustees' resolution to limit enrollment to 2,000. The January 27, 1922, editorial warmly approved the decision to entrust the Committee on Admissions and its director with implementation of the new policy. Under a broad principle of limitation, nonacademic factors would be considered in order to "develop, not mere scholars, but *leaders*." The campus newspaper pointed out, moreover, that it was not "the *son* of a Princeton man who has a claim on Princeton, it is his *father*."[85]

The subject of selective admissions was even debated formally in March 1924 among Princeton, Harvard, and Yale undergraduates in their annual triangular debate. On the resolution "That Limitation of enrollment in American colleges and universities by means other than raising the competitive scholastic standards for entrance is justifiable," Princeton's negative team lost to Yale at Princeton, but its affirmative team defeated Harvard at Cambridge. Princeton won by arguing that "scholastic limitation alone discriminates against the West and South, and against those unable to afford expensive secondary school training." They also maintained that "a limitation which retained men with personality, leadership, character, and intellect [was] the only fair basis." In contrast, Harvard argued against the resolution on the grounds that high scholastic achievement was itself a test of character and should be stressed to counteract excessive emphasis on extracurricular activities. Since all three teams lost to their visitors, the year's triangular debate ended in a three-way tie.[86]

The Beginning of "Selective Admission," 1922

In October 1922, President Hibben appointed Professor Radcliffe Heermance as director of admissions; he was assisted by four faculty members. Although Princeton followed Harvard and Yale in appointing a full-time director of admissions, it predated them in limiting its total undergraduate enrollment and the size of the freshman class. A limitation of numbers, of course, was the essential first step in developing Princeton's "Selective Admission."[87]

After conferring extensively with admissions officers elsewhere, the Committee on Admissions developed its own basic procedures in 1922-23, which would last virtually unchanged for a decade, when economic conditions would compel Princeton to admit 85 percent of the applicants. Henceforth, freshmen were to be admitted only on the basis of examinations and not by transfer or "back door" admission. To aid in the selection of a class of about six hundred from about twelve hundred applicants, three forms were developed: the "Applicant's Information Blank," the "Principal's Report on Applicant Blank," and the "Report on Applicant" for letters of recommendation.[88]

On the basis of data transcribed from these three forms to a card for each individual, all applicants were sorted into four classes, even before the results of the College Board examinations were known. Classes 1 and 2 were rated "desirable," while Class 3 was "doubtful." Applicants in this latter class still had some chance of being admitted, pending examination results, but those in Class 4 had none, because they were already judged "undesirable from the point of view of character."[89]

Those whose characters were "desirable" were then subdivided into five new categories, A through E. The first three classes would provide 400 acceptable candidates, based on their weighted averages on the June entrance examinations. (A weighted average was obtained by multiplying the applicant's grade on each examination by the units per subject and then dividing this number by the total required units.) Then the 200 most promising applicants in Class D were put on a preferred list. Though they had failures on the June examinations, they would be admitted if they performed satisfactorily on the September examinations. Even a few Class E's, "exceptional cases," would be conditionally admitted. Some of these men had served in World War I and were much older than their classmates. Though lacking in credit units because of poor preparation, they had the motivation, the committee felt, to benefit from a Princeton education.[90]

This classification procedure brought to Princeton more students from cities, towns, and suburbs than it did from small towns and rural areas. Indeed, Princeton officials expressed concern that most of their students lived in the East, chiefly in New Jersey and New York (with more than 60 percent usually residing within 125 miles of the campus) and the remainder in Ohio, Illinois, and Missouri. Some felt that its undergraduate admission terms were "practically a bar to students in many Western High Schools." Yet not until 1936, in President Harold Willis Dodds's administration, did Princeton commit itself to attracting more applicants from high schools. At that time, it essentially adopted "the Harvard idea" by admitting "without examination men of exceptional achievement and promise from certain schools in the West and the South," and it would consider as well those from eastern rural high schools.[91]

Director Heermance had written the Committee on Admission at Harvard to inquire about the operation of their highest seventh plan. In reply, their committee made a veiled reference to a Jewish problem. Harvard specifically excluded from the plan applicants from New Jersey, Long Island, and eastern New York and stated that

> if we seem to be getting a preponderance of an undesirable type from any particular locality, we cut out the whole locality. There are times, consequently, when we are not very popular in certain quarters, and there is much wailing and gnashing of teeth, but we stand to our guns.

Princeton was also advised that most students applying under the highest seventh plan would seek scholarship aid. But Harvard was distinctly pleased with this experiment, because those admitted under it had done "consistently better work" than candidates entering under the other plans.[92]

In September 1937, twenty-nine of the thirty-seven applicants granted "admission without examination" entered the freshman class at Princeton. All ranked at least in the top seventh of their high school class. By residence, nine came from Illinois, five from California, and one or two each from Colorado, Iowa, Kansas, Michigan, western Pennsylvania, Ohio, Oregon, and Washington. Only three came from the South, one each from Alabama, Florida, and Kentucky. Within a decade or so, this experiment would begin to bear fruit. During the depression classes of 1932-39, the proportion of private school students had reached a high range of 82 to 86 percent. (To put it another way, only 800 students out of 5,000 were prepared in public high schools.) In 1946, however, around 28 percent of the 606 entering freshmen had graduated from high schools. At the same time, the proportion of alumni sons had risen from about 17 percent in the class of 1931 to 26 percent in the class of 1950.[93]

In addition to alumni sons, another constant in undergraduate composition was the presence of a large number of sons of businessmen. The pool from which Princeton drew most of its applicants was already preselected in terms of educational background and economic status. For example, of the 629 members of the class of 1927, about 75 percent attended private schools; 248 of their fathers were themselves college men, of whom 70 had attended Princeton and 55 had graduated. Ten of the eleven occupations represented by 20 or more fathers were concentrated in either business or the more lucrative professions: businessman (70); lawyer (63); executive (59); none (56); manufacturer (54); physician (33); merchant (31); real estate broker (28); banker (27); and securities broker (22). Twenty fathers were ministers. At the other end of the scale, the following occupations had token representation: farmer (5); clerk (3); grocer (3); and 1 each for florist, foreman, laborer, letter carrier, machinist, milliner, miner, and tanner. Sons of these men rarely could attend a university like Princeton without scholarship aid. The university had no commuter population comparable to that at Harvard or Yale, not to mention Columbia and the University of Pennsylvania. In short, Princeton was a residential college for the sons of men who could afford to pay around $1,000 per annum.[94]

Given all these circumstances, students of poor, immigrant backgrounds were rare at Princeton. In the class of 1927, for example, there were between twenty-nine and thirty-three Catholics, all of whom were of native-born Irish stock, except for one, an American-born Italian from Philadelphia. There was also an American-born Greek from the same city, who belonged to the Greek Orthodox Church. All of the Jewish students, numbering between twenty-one and twenty-three, were born in the United States. Of the non-Protestant groups, only the Catholics were club members in large numbers: twenty-one of the twenty-seven for whom data was available belonged to one of the fourteen clubs. In contrast, only one Jewish student was a member —in Court Club.95

Yet it was quite possible that the Committee on Admissions kept a count of Catholic applicants. Although the number of Catholics increased during the 1920s, especially beginning with the class of 1928—the same year that the number of Jewish students declined sharply—it grew slowly for the next six or seven years. The combined totals of Catholics and Jews fluctuated around 10 percent from the class of 1925 until the class of 1936 (see Table 6.3). Of course, Princeton admitted several times as many Catholics as Jews.

Table 6.3
CATHOLIC AND JEWISH STUDENTS AT PRINCETON,
CLASSES OF 1925-40

Class	Catholic	Jews	Total Catholics and Jews	Total Enrollment
1925	38	23	61	585
1926	32	25	57	635
1927[a]	29	21	50	629
1928	40	13	53	629
1929	42	11	53	633
1930	43	17	60	605
1931	45	18	63	606
1932	40	17	57	611
1933	46	17	63	615
1934	50	11	61	632
1935	60	5	65	635
1936	71	11	82	673
1937	81	11	92	618
1938	60	20	80	643
1939	41	12	53	625
1940	63	17	80	635

Source: Statistics on the classes of 1925-33 from Princeton University, "Preliminary Analysis of Freshman Class," entering in September 1921-29, Trustees' Papers, Princeton University Archives. Statistics on the classes of 1934-40 from *The Freshman Herald* (Student Employment Section, Department of Personnel, 1930-33; Bureau of Appointments and Student Employment, 1934-36). These two sources did not always give the same number of Catholics and Jews for the same classes. The "Preliminary Analysis" was used instead of *The Freshman Herald* for the years that they were readily available, because they were compiled by the office of the dean of freshmen and were more detailed.
a*Princeton President's Report, December 31, 1923* gave higher numbers (33 and 23) of Catholic and Jewish students than did the "Preliminary Analysis" of September (29 and 21). Former also reported total enrollment as 636.

When V. L. Collins wrote in November 1922 that "no specific action [had] been taken to date regarding the Hebrew question," he also observed: "The number of Hebrews (confessed) in the Freshman Class [was] between 4 and 5 percent which [was] about the national quota." The Committee on Admissions may have considered even this percentage too large. For example, of the twenty-seven Jewish applicants ("probable Hebrew 28") the number noted at the June 11, 1924, meeting, only thirteen enrolled that September in the class of 1928. A Jewish quota was introduced, probably in that year. Although not necessarily the instigator, President Hibben seemed to participate willingly enough in its application. While lunching with the Hibbenses "sometime between 1930 and 1932," Robert M. Hutchins, then president of the University of Chicago, inquired about the enrollment of both black and Jewish students at Princeton. Hibben said that there were no black students, because "they just don't seem to want to come." But when he declared that about two hundred Jewish students were enrolled, Hutchins asked in obvious doubt about their number the previous year. Hibben replied:

> "About two hundred." I asked how many there were the year before that. He said, "About two hundred." I said that was very odd and asked how it happened. He said he didn't know; it just happened. Mrs. Hibben was outraged and said, "Jack Hibben, I don't see how you can sit there and lie to this young man. You know very well that you and Dean Eisenhart get together every year and fix the quota."

Although Hutchins did not comment further on this conversation, his recollection was substantial evidence that Princeton did indeed limit drastically the number of Jews admitted.[96]

The profile of the class of 1935 showed that 106 sons of Princeton men, 77 Catholics, and 28 Jews had completed applications as of May 21, 1931. Among the 635 students enrolling in September were 89 alumni sons, 60 Catholics, and 5 Jews. The number of Jewish freshmen was the lowest since 1917 (even though Princeton admitted 79 percent of all applicants in 1931). Four years later, 12 Jews matriculated out of the 58 completing applications (69 percent of the applicants were admitted to the class of 1939).[97]

On several occasions, Director Heermance expressed a certain dislike or distrust of Jewish students. He questioned their loyalty as a whole because some were brought before the Discipline Committee. Heermance was reluctant to accept, if not opposed to, the adoption of the highest seventh plan at Princeton, because he feared it would bring in more Jews, especially those who would apply for financial aid. The following incident summed up the situation of the Jewish applicant at Princeton. In the summer of 1927, H. Alexander Smith was asked by a Gentile Princeton classmate to intercede with the Committee on Admissions on behalf of a friend who was Jewish. Smith had frequently been prevailed upon to put in a good word for sons or friends of the men of the class of 1901. In regard to Jewish students, he showed no evidence of anti-Semitism. Indeed, in 1922, he had inquired into a complaint of discrimination against Jews among one or more boardinghouse keepers in the town. He then reported to trustee Henry B. Thompson that while some individuals might refuse lodgings to Jews, he doubted that there was "any organized campaign against them." At any rate, Smith did write Director Heermance about the Jewish applicant, no doubt suggesting his own sense of obligation to a classmate. In late August, Heermance replied briefly: "Your little friend———has been admitted." Several weeks later, Smith received a letter of thanks from his classmate: "You have made the seemingly impossible actually possible and I feel quite sure that the boy will be a credit to the Institution." He was: Not only did he make the honor roll, but he also won numerals on the freshman basketball team and then played on the varsity basketball squad during his senior year.[98]

Princeton's methods of exclusion were well known at other colleges. Its first lines of defense against any ethnic invasion were, observed Admissions Director Robert N. Corwin of Yale, "undergraduate sentiment" and the upper-class clubs, which refused "social honors" to Jewish students. The second lines—used against those bold enough to apply—were "Selective Admission" and "a personal inspection of all doubtful candidates," aided and abetted by vigilant alumni. The possibility of Woodrow Wilson's "unchosen experiences" was thus reduced to a minimum.[99]

The problem of the upper-class clubs continued to plague succeeding administrations. President Hibben felt compelled to attack "the flagrant abuses of the club system" and to appoint yet another investigating committee. Its report, which appeared in the *Princeton Alumni Weekly* of May 21, 1924, echoed Woodrow Wilson:

> Our life here should and must be one complete whole, incapable of segregation into separate compartments. At the present time it is evident that the social life suffers from separation from the intellectual life, and clearly the intellectual life suffers from a lack of spontaneous and wholehearted recognition of its worth in our clubs.

But no effective reform resulted because neither the administration nor the students and alumni were really committed to finding alternatives to the clubs until the late 1950s. In 1955, President Harold W. Dodds and the trustees agreed to build a house for the nonclubmen. In addition to providing meals and other services at reasonable cost, Wilcox Hall had its own library. Approximately six hundred upperclassmen resided in adjacent dormitories. This quadrangle was managed by an undergraduate organization, appropriately named the Woodrow Wilson Society. Of course, Wilson had felt that a quadrangle for the unclubbed alone would not solve the evils of the social system. In 1967, a faculty subcommittee proposed that residential quadrangles or colleges be established to unify undergraduate intellectual and social life. Princeton has not as yet followed Harvard and Yale in developing either a House Plan or a College Plan.[100]

·7·

CONCLUSION: A NEW ELITE,
1940S TO 1970S

> The new upper class that is forming is one of socially valuable talent and learning, not unlike Thomas Jefferson's concept of a "natural aristocracy of talents and virtues." . . . The colleges with upper-class affiliations . . . are compounding it of the best of the old upper class and the most talented of the lower and middle classes.
>
> Gene R. Hawes, "The Colleges of America's Upper Class" (1963)[1]

As of 1963, the new elite was still overwhelmingly white (about 98 percent), though by then diversified in terms of ethnic group and religious preference. Universities had to respond to the civil rights movement of the 1960s, however, which demanded that they recruit a larger percentage of blacks and, somewhat later, that they also seek out Hispanic (or Spanish-surnamed) Americans, American Indians, and Asian Americans. In recruiting members of the newer minority groups, the Big Three and other private and state universities have developed special admissions criteria or programs. These, in turn, have resurrected the spectre of discrimination—now labeled "reverse" —and quotas—now called "benign." It even threatened to disrupt or to polarize the civil rights coalition, which united blacks, Jews, liberals, and progressive labor unions. Given the passions aroused by the controversy over preferential admissions, both proponents and opponents have and would continue to appeal to the courts either to uphold such programs or strike them down. The recently decided United States Supreme Court case, *Regents of the University of California* v. *Bakke* (1978), generated much publicity and attracted such legal talent as former Watergate Special Prosecutor Archibald Cox, Harvard A.B. '34 and LL.B. '37, who argued on behalf of the University of California. What is at stake transcended the legal battle of one particular while male applicant to gain admission to medical school; the decision may ultimately have sweeping educational and social effects. McGeorge

Bundy, former dean of the Faculty of Arts and Sciences at Harvard and now president of the Ford Foundation, summarized "the Issue before the Court" and the bar of American higher education with this question: "Who Gets Ahead in America?"[2]

Admissions decisions, contended Bundy, must take into account the society in which minority applicants lived. Since "it is not yet 'racially neutral' to be black in America," a color-blind standard would not *"produce more than a handful of minority students in our competitive colleges and professional schools."* While he would not defend obvious quotas or even the special track for disadvantaged minorities at the Medical School of the University of California at Davis, he disagreed with the California Supreme Court's judgment that Allan Bakke, a white man and unsuccessful applicant, had been denied his constitutional rights. A United States Supreme Court decision in favor of the California ruling, Bundy feared, could call into question, even nullify, affirmative action programs elsewhere.[3]

Reverse discrimination may raise the percentage of minority enrollments, but it posed uncomfortable questions, among them, What were the perimeters of legitimate discretion in admissions? Characteristics other than strictly academic criteria have always been used in selecting a student body: motivation, career interests, probable service to the community, musical and artistic skills, extracurricular activities, geographic residence, and alumni connections. But benign quotas have made "race" a key factor in selection in a way not unlike the earlier discriminatory quotas against Jewish applicants. Race, once the undesirable factor, has become a most desirable consideration —one that interferes with a selection process based on academic merit. Disadvantaged minority students may be admitted with academic records that would result in the rejection of white applicants. On the other hand, there was a crucial difference in purpose between discriminatory and benign quotas: The function of the former was to exclude; of the present, to include. Whereas Jewish quotas, for example, attempted to preserve social homogeneity (and thus, it was argued, reduced "racial" tensions), today's benign quotas helped universities to fulfill their service to the nation, their advocates maintain. By educating more minority students, they performed the broad social role of "diversifying the leadership of our pluralistic society."[4]

A "compelling" state or national interest may indeed be served by special admissions programs for minorities, but it is also in the interest of the nation to protect all citizens equally under the law. It has become a matter of weighing, if not adjudicating, rival claims that involve two conceptions of the general social good as well as the rights of individual white and nonwhite students. While the courts may properly rule against acts or measures that exclude applicants solely on the basis of race, they should give educational institutions the leeway to exercise legitimate discretion. Ideally, admissions committees would evaluate all students according to certain academic standards and then select from among the qualified applicants on the basis of a wide range of other factors.

The central issue has been and would continue to be hotly debated: Who gets into college and professional school and who, as a result, gets ahead in the United States? Before World War II, children of middle- and upper-class families, predominantly Anglo-Saxon Protestant, had found it relatively easy, if they possessed minimum academic qualifications, to be admitted to the elite colleges and professional schools. But since the war, the proportion of undergraduates and graduate students from Catholic and Jewish middle- and lower-middle-class families has dramatically increased. In large measure, the elite institutions themselves effected this shift in student composition, within a few college generations, by requiring higher academic standards for admission and graduation. They also substantially expanded scholarship aid programs. By the early 1960s, most students at the Big Three ranked in intellectual abilities among the highest 5 to 10 percent of all American college students.[5]

Even more striking than the rise in Catholic and Jewish enrollment at each of the Big Three was the breakthrough in the appointment and promotion of non-Protestant, especially Jewish, professors. Seymour Martin Lipset has written of Harvard that with the end of World War II "the dike broke," and the university "hired Jews in significant numbers." Although World War II was itself a catalyst, because it led to a reaffirmation of democratic values and a decline in anti-Semitic feeling, the way had been paved by the higher standards of scholarship established for faculty recruitment during the depression years.[6]

The war, together with the G.I. bill of rights, encouraged Jews and other minority groups to seek a college education. The United States could no longer tolerate discrimination at home while playing the leader of democracy and the "free world" abroad. American society needed all talented individuals, irrespective of family background, to staff its professions, run its bureaucracy, and manage its scientific-technological machinery. Four important reports on discrimination in higher education recognized that both institutional and personal attitudes had to change. These were published, from December 1947 to July 1949, by President Truman's Commission on Higher Education, the New York State Commission on the Need for a State University, Connecticut State Inter-Racial Commission, and the American Council on Education. According to the latter's study of some fifteen thousand high school seniors, Protestants had the highest percentage (82) of acceptance by their first-choice colleges, while Catholics were second (71) and Jews trailed (63). A higher proportion of Jews were accepted by some school, because they applied to several colleges, but they found admission to small New England liberal arts colleges to be difficult. Under the combined pressures of state fair educational practices laws (for example, in New York, Massachusetts, and

New Jersey) and of new policies by several leading institutions, most northern colleges and universities dropped from application blanks questions relating to nationality, race, and religion.[7]

These antidiscrimination measures combined with the postwar flood of applications from veterans and secondary school seniors to undermine college
quota systems. Younger faculty and administrators, themselves veterans,
sympathized with claims based on talent rather than heredity. When forced
to choose between "the extremely gifted son of a mechanic in Missouri with
his G. I. Bill benefits" and "the gentlemanly 'C' student from a prominent family and a noted prep school," wrote Gene Hawes, "intellect won, though not
easily or decisively," at the elite colleges. Many a Social Register son had to
enter less prestigious private colleges or state universities. By 1963, the proportion of upper-class sons attending the Big Three had declined from about
two-thirds to less than one-half. While this class could still maintain its social
relationships through clubs, fraternities, and societies, these lost much of
their luster during the turbulent 1960s. Children of the WASP upper class
found more satisfaction and prestige in academic achievement than in en-
hancement of their social status; and not a few of them became political activists on behalf of civil rights or against the Vietnam War.[8]

Harvard

During his twenty-year tenure as president of Harvard University, James
Bryant Conant's educational views broadened significantly, as he became a
spokesman for a "flexible classless society." Insofar as admission policies
were concerned, his administration continued to apply the highest seventh
plan in such a way as to benefit young men from small cities and towns, while
"the all-important limitations excluded would-be candidates who went to
school in New York and Boston and nearby communities." Conant also
maintained the principle of "cross-sectioning" upperclassmen in the houses
by school groups, rank list, and "race." At the same time, he committed himself to raising intellectual standards at Harvard, among both faculty and students. To commemorate Harvard's founding, the governing boards proposed that contributions be made to a Three Hundredth Anniversary Fund to
establish both university professorships and Harvard national scholarships.
Financier Thomas Lamont responded with a gift of $500,000 for one of the
university professorships "with roving commissions." Supported by attractive salaries and research funds, such professors could bring their expertise to
bear in two or more related fields, unhampered by the rigidity of specializa-
tion and departmentalization. Among the first were Roscoe Pound (law),
Werner Jaeger (philosophy), and I. A. Richards (English).[9]

The national scholarships aimed at broadening Harvard's national representation, initially in the "Old Northwest Territory." In 1934, the first group

of ten Harvard prize fellows, as they were then called, were chosen from over two hundred applicants from Ohio, Michigan, Indiana, Illinois, Wisconsin, and Minnesota; in 1935 two donors provided fellowships for Iowa and Kentucky. By 1936, there were thirty-one such scholarships offered in sixteen states. In that year, ten of the fellows prepared in private schools and twenty-one in public high schools. The amounts of scholarship aid ranged from $200 to $1,200, with financial need being determined by "the sliding scale" principle. For the neediest, a scholarship would pay "nearly all of the student's essential college and living expenses" through Harvard College and graduate school as long as he achieved honors rank. To facilitate the selection of scholarship candidates, Harvard began in 1936 to cooperate with Yale and Princeton in holding "special" April examinations in both scholastic aptitude and achievement. (Beginning in 1941, all Harvard candidates would take this same-day combination of one aptitude and three achievement tests.)[10]

During a twenty-year period, 1930-31 to 1950-51, significant shifts occurred in Harvard's geographical representation due, in part, to the national scholarships. Many of the fellows came, for example, from the smaller high schools in the South and West that were favored under the highest seventh plan. While enrollment of undergraduates from the six New England states declined by 11 percent—to 45.8 of the 4,695 in the college—that from the Northwest rose from 303 to 568 students; from the South from 77 to 221; and from the West and the Pacific states from 77 to 223.[11]

World War II and the postwar years also initiated an educational revolution at Harvard. While preserving the major reforms of the Lowell years—course distribution and concentration, tutorial system, and general examination—the Conant administration required that all students take general education courses in the humanities, natural sciences, and social sciences, a concept supported in 1939 by a committee of the Harvard Student Council. In 1943, a twelve-member committee under the chairmanship of Dean Paul H. Buck began to study and report on "The Objectives of a General Education in a Free Society." The committee concerned itself with "the whole matter of the general education of the 'great majority of each generation—not the comparatively small minority who attend our four-year colleges.'" Though once an admirer of the best German universities, Conant was appalled by their loss of academic freedom and of leading scholars under the Third Reich. For this reason, he argued persuasively that American education had an obligation to develop an appreciation in future citizens of "both the responsibilities and the benefits which come to them because they are Americans and are free."[12]

In October 1945, the Harvard faculty adopted the recommendations of the Buck committee report. Following five years of experimentation, the class of 1955 was required to pass during its freshman and sophomore years three general education courses, one each in the humanities, natural sciences, and social sciences, as well as freshman English. This reform completed, said the

Harvard Alumni Bulletin, "the cycle begun with President Eliot's revolutionary free elective system."[13]

Another "revolutionary" result of World War II was the entrance of Radcliffe women into Harvard classrooms, following a faculty vote in March 1943. Opposed to coeducation early in his administration, Conant acquiesced in the new agreement between the Harvard Corporation and the trustees of Radcliffe College. Wartime demands had so strained the Harvard faculty that they could no longer be spared to teach the same course at both colleges. In return for providing academic instruction for the women students as a regular part of the professorial teaching load, Harvard would receive almost all of Radcliffe's tuition payments. Not until the late 1960s would Yale and Princeton decide to admit women undergraduates, although the former had opened its Ph.D. program to qualified women as early as 1892. (By the 1970s, several women would achieve important administrative positions at each of the three universities.) Yet Harvard had dragged its heels in regard to the medical education of women. In 1943, the corporation turned down a vote of the Faculty of Medicine to admit women to the medical school. Following a more limited faculty recommendation the next spring, the governing boards agreed to admit each year a few superior women medical students on an equal basis with their male classmates, beginning in September 1945.[14]

During the war and immediate postwar years, the effort to recruit veterans had absorbed much of the Conant administration's energy. The university processed more than seventy thousand G.I. admission applications, all of which were answered by a personal letter. Conant, a strong advocate of the principle behind the G.I. bill, wrote in his *President's Report* of 1942-43 that such national financing would "wipe out the educational deficit created by the war and give renewed vitality to our fundamental doctrine of equality of opportunity for all." In 1946-47, for example, almost 75 percent (9,138) of the 12,225 students enrolled in the university (and 3,941 of the 5,408 in the college) were veterans, almost all of whom were subsidized under the G.I. bill. It should be pointed out, however, that three-fourths of the veterans enrolled in the college had either attended Harvard or been admitted before entering the service. But for the diversity of talents, specifically non-Anglo-Saxon, that it brought to higher educational institutions, Wilbur J. Bender, Harvard's counsellor for veterans, praised the G.I. bill as "one of the most statesmanlike pieces of social legislation I have ever seen."[15]

Conant, who taught Natural Science 4 for three years, found "the mature student body which filled our colleges in 1946 and 1947 . . . a delight to all who were then teaching undergraduates." Indicative of this new generation were responses to a questionnaire answered by 400 Harvard students, 60 percent of them veterans, and 100 Radcliffe students enrolled in Professor Gordon W. Allport's course, Social Relations 1a. The questionnaire, given in January 1947, showed that "two-thirds were basically religious in their inclinations and one-third definitely irreligious."[16]

Indeed, a majority of the students felt that distinctions among religious denominations, especially Protestant, were "outworn and unnecessary." Although "44 per cent of the Harvard students were brought up in Protestant Christian influence, only 18 per cent" declared that it brought religious fulfillment, the questionnaire revealed. Equally striking was "the drift away" from Judaism; 11 percent of the Jews felt they needed a "substantially new type of religion," many even favoring a kind of "ethical but not theological Christianity." While 82 percent of the women and 68 percent of the men declared that they still required "some form of religious orientation or belief in order to achieve a fully mature philosophy of life," regular church attendance and daily prayer had declined, especially among veterans. Of the respondents, the veterans were "more critical of existing institutions" and "less orthodox, less conventional at every point." In addition to the impact of their numbers, they influenced campus life by their healthy skepticism and seriousness of purpose.17

After veteran enrollment peaked, observed John U. Monro, Bender's successor as veterans' counsellor, Harvard "woke up in the late 1940's to the fact that we were in a relatively weak position, as compared to some of our natural rivals in recruiting students." It was "no accident" that Bender, then dean of Harvard College (1947-52), was appointed the new dean of admissions and financial aids. His task was to double, if not quadruple, the number of applicants for the 1,100 places in Harvard's freshman class.18

Bender united a personal understanding of the educational aspirations of working-class families with a deep appreciation of the Harvard experience. One of eight children of a Mennonite family, he had begun to support himself at sixteen when his father died. Bender then attended Goshen College in Indiana before transferring to the Harvard class of 1927; he graduated magna cum laude and Phi Beta Kappa. Subsequently, as an assistant dean, he helped develop the method of selecting national scholars. He left Harvard in 1936 to teach at Phillips Academy, Andover, until World War II. As a lieutenant in the naval reserve, Bender headed a V-12 unit training officers at Tufts University. After returning to Harvard in 1946 as veterans' counsellor, he was soon appointed to his successive deanships.19

With his appointment as dean of admissions, the era of essentially a one-man operation, which began with Henry Pennypacker's chairmanship in 1920, had ended; it would be replaced by a group operation. The primary function of the Committee on Admission was now seen as "a public relations job"—of making it clear to applicants, many of whom were already self-selected by academic qualifications and prior interest—exactly what kind of an education Harvard offered. To this end, Bender drafted "a comprehensive formal statement of Harvard College admission policy" in September 1952.20

Although Harvard had already become a "University College," as Provost Paul H. Buck wrote in 1946, maintaining its "balance [between] democratic selection [and] aristocratic achievement," traditional families and social groups still predominated in the college. In his study of undergraduate admissions, Bender identified seven major groups, three comprising the socially elite: first were the alumni sons, who were, on the whole, economically and socially upper-middle-class and "scholastically average." They made up about 20 percent of the class of 1951. Overlapping with them were those of "Greater Boston social and financial upper-bracket families." While this group still chose Harvard for its social contacts, some were turning to Princeton, Yale, and Dartmouth. Third was the equally small group who attended the "selected private schools." These represented the "upper-upper" social classes across the nation, although for the most part they lived in the Northeast. The three aforementioned groups provided most of the final club members and collectively embodied an "importance beyond their intrinsic worth as individuals."21

Harvard's "solid middle class" consisted of sons of successful business and professional men who usually had attended other colleges or perhaps one of Harvard's graduate or professional schools. The younger generation had probably graduated from a reputable suburban high school, a good country day school, or one of the less social boarding schools. At the other end of the socioeconomic scale were two sizable groups. One consisted of "able, ambitious boys," who had come on scholarship from other parts of the country; they were often the only representative of their school. The other group comprised the sons of middle- and lower-income families from eastern Massachusetts—some of Harvard's "finest if least polished students," together with some of its "least desirable ones." Commuters, about 15 percent of the undergraduates, were heavily represented among them. Moreover, they helped to pay Harvard's tuition bill without burdening its residential housing. Finally, there were the "intellectual, musical or esthetic individuals," a high proportion of whom were Jewish. These invariably came from culturally sophisticated and politically liberal families living in metropolitan centers. While this group produced many of Harvard's "most interesting and potentially significant students"—intellectuals, artists, poets, and writers—it also included some "effeminates."22

The success of the whole undergraduate body depended on a balance among these seven groups. The selection of freshmen should not be made, Bender argued, on only one or two criteria, such as grades and test scores. Factors of alumni loyalty and financial support, relations with feeder schools, geographical representation, and local goodwill had also to be considered. For example, three-fourths of the students must be "paying customers"; at the same time, a number of Cambridge and Boston-area applicants had to be admitted for "political considerations." And not only should a certain percentage of alumni sons be accepted—it had fallen from 25.0 in the class of 1935 to 17.7 in the class of 1960—but alumni efforts at recruitment should be rewarded by taking their most promising candidates, especially when they resided in the South and the West. (Harvard's New England location and residential student cost—together with its reputation, deserved and exaggerated, for excessive intellectualism, radicalism, social snobberry, indifference toward moral values, and lack of interest in undergraduate teaching—made it difficult to attract solid-citizen types from other parts of the country.) Bender also justified the recruitment of academically qualified athletes to the extent that competitive, if not winning, teams improved Harvard's image nationally and maintained alumni enthusiasm. In regard to these groups of applicants, Harvard did "discriminate" in admissions: "The practical question really is not whether we should give any preference, but what are the limits of preference?"[23]

In his final report as dean of admissions in 1959-60, Bender defended the selection of a diverse student body rather than just the top academic 1 percent. Harvard should always be, he argued, "a college with some snobs and some Scandinavian farm boys who skate beautifully and some bright Bronx pre-meds, with some students who care passionately if unwisely (but who knows) about editing the Crimson or beating Yale." Such diversity of undergraduate talent refuted the charges that his alma mater admitted only "super brains," fielded "terrrible football teams," and constituted "a hotbed of Communism." By 1960, moreover, Harvard was providing about $2 million in financial aid to undergraduates and had extended the national scholarships to excellent students from urban high schools. When Harvard awarded Bender an honorary LL.D. in 1961, President Nathan Marsh Pusey described him as "an architect of the post-war Harvard, sturdy exponent of excellence and opportunity in the colleges of a democracy."[24]

These same years marked the beginning of Harvard's active recruitment of black students. Since the controversy over their admission to the freshman halls, only a few blacks had enrolled in each entering class and fewer still lived in campus housing. In 1935, for example, no black undergraduates then resided on campus, although one black had been elected to Phi Beta Kappa in November 1934. As of June 1936, eight blacks, by a rough estimate, were enrolled in the college and two others were in the Graduate School of Arts and Sciences. Meager finances rather than academic deficiencies were cited as the main reason why blacks numbered only 9 of 3,574 Harvard undergraduates in May 1940. As late as October 1951, Dean Bender guessed that blacks averaged five or six a class for a total of around twenty in the whole college. Yet even these few provided, over the half a dozen years after World War II, a class marshal, a president of the *Harvard Crimson*, and a manager of the football team.[25]

In 1949, however, John U. Monro, then counsellor for veterans, who was to be dean of Harvard College (1958-67), expressed concern that Harvard had not actively recruited Negroes, "considering the unusual opportunity" that the college could offer them. He urged that Harvard "go out and get five to ten really excellent Negro students for each new freshman class." Such efforts would help "materially on one of the country's sorest social problems." He thought that Harvard could make overtures to Negro leaders in such major cities as New York, Chicago, and Detroit who could work with the college in recruiting talented Negroes and in raising the necessary scholarship money. His suggestions probably antedated those of any other administrator then at the Big Three. By working together with the National Scholarship Service and Fund for Negro Students (NSSFNS) of New York, Harvard at least doubled the number of black undergraduates. During the 1960s its percentage of blacks would rise dramatically: from 2 percent early in the decade to 4 in 1968 and 7 in 1969. To the class of 1975 were admitted 109 of the 407 black applicants, and 90 decided to attend. Black students were now "visible" on campus, and Harvard appointed two blacks as deans.[26]

Recent statistics indicated, however, that while the admission rate for blacks was higher, by perhaps 5 percent or more, than for the applicant group as a whole, it was about 15 percent below the rate for alumni children. For example, of the 882 alumni sons and daughters applying to the class of 1981, 41.7 percent (368) were admitted, under the combined Harvard-Radcliffe Office of Admissions and Financial Aids, and 85.3 percent (314) of that group entered. The corresponding percentages for blacks were 26.6 percent (174) accepted from the 655 making application, and about 71.3 percent (124) of those accepted actually registered. Several circumstances were probably responsible for the differences in percentages: first, in terms of grade point averages and aptitude test scores, the pool of qualified black applicants remained smaller than the pool of qualified whites. The effects of poorer educational preparation would take time to remedy—and require the financial commitment to provide better secondary schools. Second, able blacks might still be deterred from applying to Harvard by their belief that they did not belong there. They might think Harvard's educational advantages offset by a threatening social aura, in contrast to their own, more secure cultural milieu. Even though Harvard succeeded in projecting a more expansive image of itself—as a place where diversity was welcomed, whether of talents, religious affiliation, ethnic and social background, or geographic residence—alumni children, graduates of New England schools, and East Coast applicants felt closer to the institution. They were less likely to turn down admission if offered. To attract more candidates from outside these circles, especially blacks, Harvard would have to intensify its publicity and recruitment programs.[27]

In spite of such administrative efforts, successful black and other minority applicants might prefer, nevertheless, to shop around. Equally prestigious colleges might bid against Harvard for their share of the available qualified black, native American, and Spanish-surnamed students. For example, Harvard admitted to the class of 1981 these other minority applicants: 47 of the 149 Mexican Americans, 18 of the 61 Puerto Ricans, and 11 of the 43 native Americans. Of the Mexican Americans, 35 registered, as did 10 Puerto Ricans and 9 native Americans. The high number of Asian American applicants (567) to the class of 1981 suggested that this minority would probably seek higher education without extensive special recruiting programs. Harvard admitted 94 of them, and 71 came.[28]

Nevertheless, such older minority applicants as Irish Catholics and Jews still had substantial advantages over blacks and other newcomers to elite colleges. Their family and educational levels were higher, which in turn facilitated a greater degree of social assimilation. According to Andrew M. Greeley's study, *Ethnicity, Denomination, and Inequality* (1976), Jews were "the best educated Americans," averaging 14.0 years of education. Episcopalians and Presbyterians were second and third with, respectively, 13.5 and 12.7 years. But Catholic groups as a whole, with 11.5 years of education, were just below Methodists and somewhat above Lutherans and Baptists. Irish Catholics, moreover, were "the best educated Gentile group in American society" (12.5 years), leading even the British Protestants (12.4 years). Education attainment correlated with income level: Jewish families were the most affluent in the United States with an average income of $13,340; Irish Catholics placed second with $12,426, while Episcopalians ($11,032) and Presbyterians ($10,976) lagged behind even the Italian, Polish, and German Catholics ($11,748-$11,298). Although Catholics and Jews might still view themselves as outsiders, feeling that Protestant Americans deny them full recognition, they have achieved a degree of social recognition, reflected by their cultural and community leadership and suburban residence.[29]

By the 1970s, if not before, Harvard's Catholic and Jewish students were indistinguishable from their Protestant classmates. The university's Jewish question had largely become a thing of the past; four of its deans and probably about 25 to 30 percent of its undergraduates were Jewish. But quotas, even the so-called benign ones for disadvantaged minority groups, remained suspect, as were any new departures in admissions policy. Jewish faculty, alumni, and students were understandably worried when former Admissions Dean Chase N. Peterson (1967-72) informed a group of Jewish faculty members that "the doughnuts around the big cities" were "not as successful with the Harvard Admissions Committee as they used to be." Since these "doughnuts" were suburban areas in New York (Westchester County and Long Island), New Jersey, and Ohio, one of the Jewish faculty members wryly pointed out: "Dr. Peterson, those aren't doughnuts, they're bagels."[30]

Whatever the percentages of Jewish students, and they may indeed fluctuate from year to year, Harvard had opened wide its doors to both Jews and to the so-called newer minority groups. Although the university undoubtedly lost the support of some of its alumni and "selected private school" families both through personal choice and tougher academic selection, there was no hard evidence that Gentiles would flee Harvard, as President A. Lawrence Lowell had feared, as if it were an exclusive summer resort suddenly invaded by undesirable guests. Professor William Ernest Hocking, among others, had seen this over fifty years ago when Harvard reacted to the first waves of Jewish immigrant sons. *"There is no other Harvard,"* he acknowledged with pride:

> There can never be another oldest university in North America; there will never be another university here first in scholarship; there can never be another university which is the alma mater of the fathers of a large body of present students. Any Gentile who now or for years to come is tempted to turn away from these non-transportable advantages to some other school, merely because he finds here at present more Jewish companions than he likes, admits himself to be a man without root in what is vital to this place, and we need feel no regret at losing him.[31]

Yale

World War II forced Yale to reject in principle at least one kind of discrimination. In the spring of 1941, the Yale School of Nursing had declined to accept a Negro applicant because of "an unwritten policy." Dean Effie J. Taylor maintained that "it would be exceedingly difficult for us to arrange for the experience of a negro student here or to make for her a happy and satisfactory adjustment." In seeking to change this policy, the National Association of Colored Graduate Nurses turned to the Reverend Anson Phelps Stokes, former secretary of Yale University and then president of the Phelps-Stokes Fund. Thereupon Stokes wrote President Charles Seymour that he believed "a New England university with Yale's tradition cannot afford to decline a competent colored student who wishes professional training exclusively because of her race." Stokes considered the issue of discrimination particularly important at a time "when we are opposing Nazi ideas of race."[32]

In reply, Seymour reassured Stokes of his "detestation of distinction based upon race or color" and his "strength of sympathy" with those "who have taken such interest in the education of the Negro." The previous year, he noted, a Negro had won one of the outstanding divinity school prizes, while this year one of the best freshman scholars was a black student. But he pointed out that "special difficulties [involving] contacts with patients in the hospital and in the general life of the School," over which Yale had no control, had forced a former black nursing student "to resign." Some doubt existed about the recently rejected black applicant's "physical fitness," although she was accepted at another school. In the future, however, the Yale School of Nursing would judge applicants on the basis of student qualifications. Yale was by no means unique in its reluctance to accept black applicants. Harvard had also met opposition in providing clinical training for black medical students. 33

Not until almost twenty years later, when thirty-seven blacks applied to the college class of 1964, did Yale begin to encourage their admission. Of these applicants, eleven were admitted and ten matriculated. By the time that Yale went coeducational in 1969 there were a total of 525 black applicants for the class of 1973, of whom 138 were women. Thirty percent were admitted, and of these 62 percent matriculated (71 men and 25 women). Probably about half of the black students were the sons and daughters of the business and professional black bourgeoisie. Yale had definite attractions as a ladder to economic, and perhaps social, success for them and even for ghetto youth. Lower-middle-income black students had the most difficult adjustment problems, since they often lacked the preparatory training of the upper-middle class or the desperation of the very poor. By the early 1970s, Yale's director of minority recruitment was spending about $17,000 a year to contact blacks and such other ethnic and racial groups as Chicanos, Puerto Ricans, Asian Americans, and American Indians. 34

That blacks were the main target of a national recruitment effort was reflected by the establishment in 1969 of an Afro-American studies program, with the blessing of Yale College and grant support from the Ford and Rockefeller foundations. During its third year, 1971-72, 537 students, many of them white, enrolled in the twenty courses on Afro-American art, culture, history, and literature. The high tide of black applications, at least for a few years, came in 1970 with 755 (270 of them women), but only 146 were admitted (37 women), and of these 83 (26 women) entered. As recruitment of blacks moved into its second decade, information about educational opportunities at other colleges and universities, public as well as private, had become widely circulated. While many qualified blacks would continue to apply to at least one Ivy League school, they invariably also submitted applications to institutions with less prestige—and fewer academic and social pressures. 35

The increased black representation in higher education was largely the result of postwar economic gains and the civil rights movement. On the other hand, a significant democratization in the social and ethnic composition of white college students began with the Selective Service Act of World War II. Because public high school students graduated at a younger age (around seventeen) than those attending private schools (the average Exeter senior was over eighteen), they could go to college for a year before being subject to the draft. Whereas in July 1942 only 28.4 percent of Yale freshmen entered from public schools, a year later the percentage rose to 43.6. Among the group matriculating in March 1945, 53.6 percent were public school graduates. While they may have been less well prepared academically than those from private schools, they were usually intellectually able and well motivated. The Yale

Alumni Board encouraged their applications through its Committee on Enrollment and Scholarships, which interviewed many prospective candidates. During these same years, the percentage of alumni sons decreased from a peak of 31.4 percent in the class of 1943 to 25.8 percent in the July 1946 class (which had entered in 1943).36

According to Edward Simpson Noyes, chairman of the Board of Admissions, "Selective Service has increased the problem of Jewish applications for Yale, as for many other colleges." For several reasons, he noted, Jews finished their secondary education at a younger age than Gentiles: "It may be that they mature earlier; it may be that they permit themselves—or are permitted—fewer distractions; it may be that they are pushed as fast as possible by their families." While Jews constituted less than 10 percent of the class entering in July 1943, the figure rose to 23 percent by sophomore year, as a large number of their older Gentile classmates joined the service. For the first time in almost twenty years, Yale's stabilization policy was threatened. "Realization of this situation," wrote Noyes, "has made it necessary for the Board of Admissions to adopt standards of selection from this group more severe than in the past, in order to prevent it from reaching an undue proportion in the residential colleges." With Lowellesque candor, President Seymour explained to a Jewish alumnus in July 1944 why Yale "decided to stand by its policy of selective admission." Because the number of Jewish applicants had increased during the war years, its Board of Admissions had rejected "a number of Jewish boys who in normal circumstances might well have received favorable consideration." Seymour rationalized the quota with this observation: "It would work out unhappily for the Jewish boys at Yale if the University did not preserve their numbers in some reasonable balance with those of other elements in the student body."37

Yale's tougher standards for admitting Jewish applicants had some effect, because in October 1945, Noyes offically reported that there was "very little," if any, increase in the proportion of Jews to the total applicant pool. "But the proportion of Jews among the candidates who are both scholastically qualified for admission and young enough to matriculate" had "somewhat increased," remained "too large for comfort" at Yale and at most other higher educational institutions in the Northeast, and was beginning to affect those in the West and South.38

"Bulldog" values died hard. For example, the results of a conference between the Yale Football Committee and the Board of Admissions in December 1948 suggested continuation of a long-established policy of preferential admissions to outstanding athletes. An excellent athlete with a "superior personality" and a "mediocre" academic record provided "about as reliable an index of leadership potentiality as can be found," Yale believed. In addition to alumni information, the application blank continued to serve as a means of selection. Although the question on religious affiliation was deleted as a result of discussions by the Board of Admissions in 1948-49, the blank still asked for the applicant's photograph as well as his mother's maiden name and birthplace. 39

Undergraduate priorities naturally mirrored admissions policy. William Clyde De Vane '20, a soft-spoken southerner and dean of Yale College, was critical of the collegiate system, which provided an excellent education for "the man of action." Yale was thus "a perfect reflection of the country: the honors which the undergraduates bestow—and those are the ones which the undergraduates value—all seem to go to the athletes and managers of affairs." In 1947-48, the dean, who often spiced his official reports with his own poetry, versified on the mentally deleterious effects of valuing character above intellect. The brains of the typical Yale undergraduate "atrophied" during his arduous pursuit of athletic, managerial, and social honors. Consequently, in the area of intellectual attainment, Yale was "surpassed by Harvard, Columbia, and Chicago, in that order." To improve the academic caliber of undergraduates, De Vane urged the Board of Admissions to scrutinize with greater care "the intellectual and imaginative qualifications of candidates" and to award scholarships accordingly. In freshman and sophomore years, "the incompetent" should be dropped and replaced by qualified transfer students. 40

The Yale graduate and professional schools, De Vane wrote approvingly, admitted on the basis of college record and did not yet ask for "physical prowess, or too much for that indefinable thing called personality." Given the greater emphasis on scholarship, it was not surprising that the barriers against Jewish students were first lowered there. In his report for 1948-49, Dean Edgar S. Furniss commented on "the predicament" in which laws against discrimination would place the graduate school. While it did not discriminate nor even ask an applicant's race or religion, it could not prove that the better students scholastically were always admitted under its limited enrollment and drawn-out admissions procedure. 41

Although no "official" statistics existed on the racial backgrounds and religious affiliations of Yale students, those compiled by the university chaplain at least indicated trends in enrollment. Apparently, students were asked at registration to complete, on a voluntary basis, forms designating religious preference or affiliation. According to Table 7.1, of the twelve largest denominations, Jews became the most numerous religious group in the graduate schools—429, or just over 17 percent—in 1950-51. 42

To be sure, the total number of Protestants, all denominations lumped together—including Episcopalians, Fundamentalists, and Unitarians—still exceeded the combined totals of Catholic and Jewish students in both the college and the graduate schools. Episcopalians, as in the 1920s, were the most numerous Protestant denomination, more than twice as large as the Congregationalists, who had founded Yale. While Jewish students numbered 740,

Table 7.1

RELIGIOUS PREFERENCES OF YALE UNDERGRADUATES AND GRADUATE STUDENTS, 1947-54

Religious Preference	1947-48				1948-49				1949-50			
	Freshmen	Upper Classes	Graduate Schools	Total	Freshmen	Upper Classes	Graduate Schools	Total	Freshmen	Upper Classes	Graduate Schools	Total[a]
Episcopalian	324	1,317	298	1,939	338	1,269	307	1,914	281	1,117	338	1,790
Presbyterian	138	559	327	1,024	126	514	254	894	151	440	260	851
Congregational	105	513	263	881	97	522	250	869	89	411	244	744
Methodist	64	234	300	598	62	246	255	563	67	210	257	534
Baptist	22	113	131	266	32	102	103	237	31	100	102	233
Lutheran	22	99	117	238	27	98	91	216	16	41	38	189
Unitarian	19	54	38	111	9	52	37	98	16	40	36	92
Christian Scientist	14	68	21	103	16	56	21	93	20	53	19	92
Church of Christ									3	4	8	15
Disciples of Christ		24	54	78								
Christian or Christian church[b]	9				5	16	54	75	9	12	57	78
Interdenominational Protestant		8	12	20								
Nondenominational Protestant	27				51	142	86	279	42	112	97	251

214

Table 7.1 (Continued)

No affiliation (Protestant)												
Roman Catholic	167	747	198	1,112	212	703	280	1,195	196	611	295	1,102
Jewish	102	446	192	740	139	405	279	823	140	368	320	827
No affiliation	42	235	287	564	26	196	167	389	22	208	189	419
Total	1,055	4,381	2,238	7,674	1,140	4,321	2,184	7,645	1,083	3,781	2,260	7,217
Total number of students reporting a religious preference[c]	1,082	4,482	2,385	7,949	1,163	4,417	2,330	7,910	1,108	3,937	2,484	7,529

Religious Preference	1950-51			1951-52			
	Undergraduates	Graduates	Total	Freshmen	Upper Classes	Graduates	Total
Episcopalian	1,252	334	1,586	294	798	316	1,408
Presbyterian	512	263	775	138	386	247	771
Congregational	377	247	624	109	257	242	608
Methodist	259	114	373	73	181	280	534
Baptist	104	125	229	35	66	121	222
Lutheran	80	126	206	37	16	30	83
Unitarian	63	37	100	14	34	37	85
Christian Scientist	57	18	75	11	41	13	65
Church of Christ				10	23	53	86

Table 7.1 (Continued)

	1952-53				1953-54		
	Freshmen	Upper Classes	Graduates	Total	Undergraduates	Graduates	Total
Disciples of Christ					4	48	52
Christian or Christian Church					20	10	30
Interdenominational Protestant							
Nondenominational Protestant	36	81	106	223	251	58	309
No affiliation (Protestant)							
Roman Catholic	166	511	304	981	686	296	982
Jewish	161	365	476	1,002	462	429	891
No affiliation	16	162	242	420	78	219	297
Total	1,100	2,921	2,467	6,488	4,205	2,324	6,529
Total number of students reporting a religious preference	1,139	2,991	2,633	6,763	4,322	2,474	6,796

Religious Preference	1952-53				1953-54		
	Freshmen	Upper Classes	Graduates	Total	Undergraduates	Graduates	Total
Episcopalian	268	755	288	1,311	1,049	339	1,388
Presbyterian	125	363	223	711	504	266	770
Congregational	72	262	207	541	321	237	558
Methodist	60	174	232	466	299	278	577
Baptist	28	70	103	201	94	124	218
Lutheran	35	68	98	201	112	225	337
Unitarian	11	42	38	91	48	33	81
Christian Scientist	13	26	16	55	47	19	66
Church of Christ							

Table 7.1 (Continued)

Disciples of Christ	5	12	32	49	22	56	78
Christian or Christian Church	3	10	12	25			
Interdenominational Protestant							
Nondenominational Protestant	57	189	214	460	200	210	410
No affiliation (Protestant)							
Roman Catholic	153	481	357	991	579	447	1,026
Jewish	133	402	543	1,078	508	553	1,061
No affiliation	30	156	278	464	150	353	503
Total	993	3,010	2,641	6,644	3,933	3,140	7,073
Total number of students reporting a religious preference	1,015	3,103	2,797	6,915	4,030	3,293	7,323

Source: Based on "Religious Statistics" or "Religious Affiliations" compiled by the chaplain's office, Sidney Lovett, Church of Christ in Yale University. "Report as Chaplain of Yale University to the President and Fellows of Yale University," in *Reports to the President by the Deans and Directors of the Several Schools and Departments for the Academic Year, 1947-48 to 1953-54,* Yale University Archives.

a The total of 189 Lutherans far exceeds the number of students indicating that preference. Either there were more Lutheran students that year or the total should be reduced to 95. Another discrepancy or mistake in addition occurred in the number of Jewish students listed; the total was probably 828.

b The statistics from the chaplain's office did not indicate what "Christian" meant—whether it was a general term or the designation used by the Disciples of Christ.

c Religious groups with smaller representation were not included, for example: Atheists, Agnostics, Buddhists, Greek and Russian Orthodox, Hindus, Mormons, Muslims, Quakers, and evangelicals.

or just over 9 percent of the enrollment in 1947-48, they rose to 1,002, or between 14 and 15 percent of the enrollment in 1951-52. They also displaced Catholics as the largest non-Protestant group at Yale. In 1953-54, Catholic and Jewish students together constituted over 28 percent of the student body. Unquestionably, many students of Jewish and even Catholic backgrounds were among the 503 students stating no religious affiliation.

Jewish students seemingly were overcoming Yale's quota barrier of the 1920s and 1930s. But the data of the 1950s did not provide sufficient information to decide whether or not a quota, albeit more generous than previously, was still being imposed on them. As in the past, Protestants dominated campus organizations. Specifically Catholic or Jewish associations, like the Saint Thomas More Club and Hillel Foundation, had no "social prestige of any sort," in contrast to the Protestant Dwight Hall, wrote William F. Buckley, Jr. 43

Jews, moreover, continued to experience conflicts with the larger university community. In 1953-54, Chaplain Sidney Lovett reported that Jewish students found themselves "somewhat isolated" because of a "conflict" between their religious calendar and the Gregorian, on which Yale planned its academic schedule. This situation was "undoubtedly exacerbated by the fact that the Jew is very apt to construe a purely temporal conflict as evidence of racial discrimination, to which, alas, he and his forebears have been and still are subjected by the Gentile majority." Although this "temporal" difference was in no way deliberate, the chaplain recognized the existence of continuing social discrimination against Jews. Several steps should be taken by university officials to minimize these conflicts, specifically a consultation with the local rabbi. Through mutual adjustment of the two calendars, friction may be reduced, even avoided, "where the undoubted rights of the University are in conflict with the religious sensibilities of one of its minority groups." Lovett's attitude was far different from that held by President Lowell and others of similar persuasion during the 1920s and 1930s. The chaplain recognized not only that minorities had rights, but also that they had "sensibilities." As the Yale population had diversified, the university itself had to make certain compromises with its new clientele. The test for membership in an academic community was primarily scholastic achievement, not personality, social acceptability, or ethnic homogeneity. Jewish students had proven beyond all question that they added to the intellectual strength of Yale. 44

Princeton

Although Princeton remained "very low on the applicants' list of the Bronx High School of Science," it was not able to postpone for long an acceptance of the changes brought about by World War II and the G.I. bill. By 1940 some alumni, among them Norman Thomas and George McLean Harper, were already criticizing the university for excluding blacks. In the *Princeton Alumni Weekly*, Thomas accused Princeton of maintaining "a racial intolerance almost worthy of Hitler, and wholly alien to any ideal of a university or even a college in a democracy." And he continued, "if generation after generation of Princetonians is to support a custom which would make Princeton hell for the best qualified Negro, let us speak more respectfully of Hitler's barbarous pseudo science of race." Pressure for change intensified after the United States entered World War II. In September and October 1942, the *Princetonian* published three editorials on "White Supremacy at Princeton." The first, "A Thousand Million Colored Allies," showed that discriminatory attitudes hurt American leadership during "a global war for democratic principles." In the second, "A Time to Decide," Princeton was urged to make its professions of democracy real by "revising its admissions policy so that qualified men may be admitted to the University regardless of the accident of race or color."45

The next night, October 1, the chairman and the cochairman of the *Princetonian* participated in a forum held by the American Whig-Cliosophic Society: "Should Negroes Be Admitted to Princeton?" The negative argued that the Negro student would be shut out of extracurricular activities, "and thus denied 50 per cent of the education he had been promised." No formal vote was taken. Two days later, in the third of its series of editorials, entitled "We Make Answer," the *Princetonian* strongly countered the arguments against admission of blacks. Such a lengthy discussion and debate naturally elicited letters, both pro and con, from undergraduates and alumni. One argued that Princeton could admit whom it pleased since it was "a private institution, built and endowed with private capital, and not subject to control by any government." The writer, a southerner, advanced the corollary that just as students had the right to choose their social companions, "we don't think we should deny ourselves the right also to choose our classmates." On the other hand, the *Princetonian* received support from the Harvard Liberal Union and from Princeton Local 552 of the American Federation of Teachers. And a local-born Negro, then student chairman of the Group Prejudice Commission, National Assembly of Student Christian Movement, added his voice for the admission of qualified black applicants. But a survey undertaken by the *Nassau Sovereign* showed that 62.4 percent of the undergraduates polled (62.9 percent of those from the North and 60.0 percent of those from the South) were against admission of Negroes to Princeton. Even some of those in favor would impose such "limitations" as banning black students from Prospect Street, "dormitory segregation, much higher standards than for white people, and definite quotas."46

The United States Navy partially settled the issue in 1945 by sending four blacks to Princeton under the V-12 program. Arthur Jewell Wilson, Jr., basketball team captain in 1945-46, became the first black to earn a Princeton

A.B. in June 1947. But after the war ended, few blacks applied—only two for the fall of 1947. One of them enrolled as an undergraduate; another black was registered in the graduate school. Two years later, four blacks enrolled, three as freshmen and one as a sophomore transfer; a fifth black student attended the graduate school. Although the Princeton Liberal Union actively encouraged blacks to apply, less than a dozen matriculated between 1950 and 1961. Five black freshmen enrolled the following year. In 1963, the university decided to begin active recruitment of black students. [47]

Recruitment would not be easy, given the limited pool of qualified applicants, and Princeton's reputation was a handicap in competition with Harvard, Brown, Dartmouth, and even Yale. As many as one-fourth of those blacks matriculating at Princeton departed within the year. Some failed academically, but others probably left because they felt isolated in an alien environment. The position of blacks began to improve with the appointment in 1964 of Carl A. Fields, Princeton's first black administrator, as assistant director of the Bureau of Student Aid. According to Dr. Fields, a black student at Princeton (and this was undoubtedly true at other universities as well) had one of three choices: "Forget that he was a Negro. . . . Be quietly but militantly Negro. . . . Keep to himself." Fields helped blacks to cope with their feelings of "anonymity or invisibility" in a college in which most students were white, and he strengthened their relationship to the area's larger Negro community through the family sponsor program. [48]

In 1964, 72 blacks applied to the freshman class, 19 were admitted, and 12 came. When Princeton began coeducation in 1969-70, 150 black undergraduates were enrolled; and during the next two years, their number almost doubled to 283, or about 7 percent of the student body. Among incoming freshmen, the percentage was just over 9 percent. More than 50 black graduate students were on campus, and blacks were visible as deans, professors, and coaches. And like Harvard and Yale, Princeton has an Afro-American studies program. These developments were the result of a strong commitment on the part of the administration. [49]

But to increase the number of Mexican Americans and native Americans, the minority students themselves persuaded the admissions office to fund travel expenses (up to $600) for eight undergraduate recruiters to visit high schools in their home communities. As of the autumn of 1972, there were only 20 Mexican Americans and 18 American Indians at Princeton. Four years later, however, Princeton had a larger percentage of American Indians (0.3) and Hispanics (2.9) as well as blacks (7.4) among its undergraduates than either Harvard (respectively, 0.2, 2.3, and 6.9) or Yale (respectively, 0.1, 2.4, and 4.7). Yale had the largest percentage of Asian Americans (3.1), followed by Princeton (2.7) and then by Harvard (2.6). In diversifying its student body, Princeton had come a long way: 13.3 percent of its 4,362 undergraduates represented the newer minority groups. [50]

The "typical" Princeton student of the 1960s, however, was an athlete and leader of his classmates. In addition to the 107 valedictorians among the 767 members of the class of 1961, there were 130 class or student body presidents, 93 school editors, and over 450 athletes—200 in football, 124 in track, and 129 in basketball. When President Robert F. Goheen was asked in 1967 to describe the "kind of boy" he wanted to see at Princeton, he replied:

> We don't want any single "kind" here. There is no stereotyped Princeton boy. Oh, they've got to have a few things in common: a fairly high level of intelligence in order to stand the gaff; not to be too bothered by competition—or rather to be able to compete even though bothered; a good measure of curiosity and personal integrity—whether they're football players or classicists. But within these limits great variety is possible—and we want it.

Princeton should have "potential leaders in all walks of life." And while its undergraduates had later become prominent in business and industry, the professions, and government, Princeton had not "produced a single Nobel Laureate."[51]

Princeton sons still continued to enjoy considerable priority in admissions until the late 1960s. To preserve its traditions and to placate graduates, the university admitted a certain percentage—around 20—of sons to each class. In 1958, about 70 percent of alumni son applications were accepted for the class of 1962, as against only 35 percent of those without Princeton connections. An alumni son was not required "to compete against non-Princeton sons," but was admitted if his "character record [was] satisfactory" and if the committee could answer just one major question in the affirmative: "*Can he be expected to graduate?*" The fruits of such preference were seen in the freshman class admitted in 1957: "50% of the bottom quarter, academically speaking, was made up of Princeton sons." But by 1965, the applicants as a whole had higher average test scores than those of any freshman class enrolling before 1958. Given such competition, alumni sons could henceforth expect "preference" only if their qualifications were "roughly equal" to those of other candidates.[52]

The sheer volume of qualified applicants in the postwar era would ultimately force Princeton to relax and then remove its quota on Jewish students. Their enrollment grew slowly, even though, in March 1948, Dean Radcliffe Heermance, director of admissions, had "categorically denied a charge," cited in Carey McWilliams's book *A Mask for Privilege*, that "Princeton maintains a tight Jewish quota of less than 4 per cent of its enrollment." Table 7.2 casts doubt upon Heermance's insistent denial: "We've never had a quota system, we don't have a quota system, we never will have a quota system." More Jews did begin to enroll in 1948. By 1963, there were "nearly 400 Jewish

Table 7.2
JEWISH FRESHMEN ENTERING PRINCETON,
1930-49

Year	Number	Year	Number	Year	Number
1930	11	1937	12	1944	32
1931	5	1938	20	1945	23
1932	11	1939	12	1946	29
1933	11	1940	7	1947	24
1934	20	1941	16	1948	54
1935	12	1942	19	1949	41
1936	17	1943	16		

Source: The Freshman Herald, 1930-1949; Princeton University, Office of the Registrar, "Statistics of the Freshman Class."

students—a commonly accepted figure—on the campus," or about 100 per class. In spite of this increase, Princeton, if no longer considered overtly anti-Semitic, was still held in suspicion by some Jewish students. To overcome its past reputation, Princeton opened a kosher kitchen in 1971 and began its first classes in modern Hebrew, with outside funding provided for five years by the Memorial Foundation for Jewish Culture.[53]

Although "the first 100 per cent Bicker" took place in 1941 and elections in subsequent years were usually uneventful, "the infamous Bicker of '58" gained national notice. About half of the "23 'men in trouble'—those without bids" were Jews. During open house night some club members apparently said to Jewish sophomores, "We'd love to have you but our quota is filled." While the Interclub Committee did "not approve of religious and racial discrimination, [it had] no power to control the Bicker policy of individual clubs." Nor would the committee guarantee these sophomores bids because Prospect Club had gone "nonselective," thus opening up the possibility of a "universal 'bid'" After they declined membership in Prospect Club, President Goheen argued that they could still join the small nonselective Wilson Lodge, which had been founded in 1955. To protest the situation, some students picketed Nassau Hall, and B'nai B'rith began an inquiry. Although the prevalence of religious discrimination was not ascertained, the bicker system "never fully recovered from its scars of 1958."[54]

According to Paul Sigmund, professor of politics at Princeton, 1967-68 was "the crucial year" of change at the university. By then, a black student had been elected freshman class president. Proctors no longer enforced parietal rules on entertaining women in student rooms by using their passkeys; and a committee was appointed to examine the educational and financial aspects of coeducation. (In 1971-72, Princeton enrolled 750 women undergraduates, whose numbers were to be increased to 1,200, or 30 percent of the total, by 1974.) But the two most significant events of 1967-68, observed Sigmund, were a sit-in by the Students for a Democratic Society at the Institute for Defense Analyses and the opening of Stevenson Hall, a dining facility owned by the university. The first incident had two results: first, Princeton terminated its sponsorship of IDA; and, second, following a demonstration by 600 students that was organized by SDS in front of Nassau Hall, a faculty-student Special Committee on the Structure of the University was elected to review the decision-making process within the university.[55]

Students also initiated the other major change of 1967-68. In the autumn, eighty-four upperclassmen, among them the sophomore and junior class presidents, the president of the chapel deacons, and the *Princetonian* chairman, resigned their club memberships. Instead, they urged that a new facility, run by faculty and students, be formed from two neighboring clubs, one of which had already failed, while the other was on the verge of bankruptcy. After some hesitation, Princeton acquired the buildings and then opened Stevenson Hall in January 1968 to any member of the university community who wanted to join. In addition to its two popular eating societies—Stevenson Hall and the Madison Society—Princeton had two well-established residential colleges by the mid-1970s, the recently acquired Princeton Inn and the older, most appropriately named Woodrow Wilson College. These social alternatives, together with opposition to bicker, would cause ten of the seventeen selective clubs to close their doors.[56]

Of the five oldest clubs, Ivy, Cottage, Cap and Gown, and Tiger remained healthy and selective. But Colonial went nonselective in 1969-70. When a nonselective club could no longer keep going, it might turn the ownership over to Princeton. By 1973 and 1974, only 32 and 38 percent, respectively, of the sophomores joined the remaining seven selective clubs—in contrast to two-thirds of the class in 1968. Whatever the future of selective clubs, an era had ended at Princeton, a college once described as "the pleasantest country club in America."[57]

Since 1950, when the question was dropped from the application blank, Princeton had not, apparently, kept an official annual record of student religious preference. The cards that students filled out at registration indicated the preference of only those interested in being contacted by campus and local religious groups. Required twice-a-month chapel attendance for freshmen was abolished without protest in 1963-64. During the past fifteen years, according to the incomplete evidence of registration cards, Roman Catholic students "almost doubled" in number, while Episcopalians, Presbyterians, and Methodists each "declined by approximately 50 per cent." And while more Roman Catholic and Jewish students stated a religious preference, a growing number of freshmen indicated none at all.[58]

The most complete recent study of the backgrounds of Princeton freshmen was done in the autumn of 1970 as part of a national survey by the American Council on Education on 180,684 freshmen matriculating at 33 private and 241 public colleges and universities. "Religious Preferences of Princeton Freshmen, 1970, and Their Comparison with Maternal Preferences," Table 7.3, showed that less than 10.0 percent of the freshmen were Presbyterian at a college once heavily dominated by this persuasion. Episcopalians had declined from being the largest denomination of the 1920s through the 1940s—a third or more of the students—to 10.0 percent. In contrast, Roman Catholics had become the leaders with 18.0 percent, followed by Jews at 13.5 percent. At the same time 28.0 percent of the freshmen expressed no religious prefer-

Table 7.3
RELIGIOUS PREFERENCES OF PRINCETON FRESHMEN, 1970,
AND THEIR COMPARISON WITH MATERNAL PREFERENCES

Religious Preference	Student Percentages		Total Student Percentages	Total Maternal[a] Percentages
	Male	*Female*		
Baptist	3.6	2.4	3.4	5.3
Congregational	2.2	4.2	2.6	3.6
Eastern Orthodox	1.1	0.6	1.0	1.8
Episcopal	9.5	12.0	10.0	14.3
Jewish	12.6	17.5	13.5	15.5
Latter Day Saints	0.0	0.6	0.1	0.1
Lutheran	2.1	0.6	1.8	3.2
Methodist	3.6	4.8	3.9	6.1
Muslim	0.1	0.0	0.1	0.1
Presbyterian	9.5	10.2	9.6	13.3
Quaker	1.0	2.4	1.2	0.5
Roman Catholic	19.9	9.6	18.0	21.6
Seventh Day Adventist	0.0	0.0	0.0	0.1
Unitarian	1.1	1.2	1.1	1.7
Other Protestant	2.5	1.8	2.4	2.7
Other Religions	2.9	4.8	3.3	2.2
None	28.2	27.1	28.0	7.9

Source: "A Survey of Princeton Freshmen," *Princeton Alumni Weekly*, February 23, 1971, p. 7.
Note: Religious preferences of fathers were either not asked for by the American Council on Education or not included in the results.

ence. While Princeton remained predominantly a white institution, which attracted students from wealthy families (19.6 percent of the men and women came from families earning $40,000 or more a year), its days of exclusion based on ethnic group, race, or religion had passed. [59]

Discretion or Discrimination: Ethnic Quotas in College Admissions

Gains in Jewish representation at Princeton, as at Harvard and Yale, were due to the crumbling of quota barriers during the same period that college attendance became "practically universal among Jews of college age." As a result, Stephen Steinberg projected that "Jewish representation will either stabilize or drop off." Any future increases in enrollment, he expected, would most likely be made by Catholics (probably by those who were neither Irish nor German, since the latter had already "produced more scholars than have Italians or Poles") and by such "underrepresented" Protestant denominations as the Baptists. But Steinberg and others have contended that new restrictions threatened white ethnic groups, particularly Jews: percentage limitations imposed by state universities on out-of-state students and preferential admission programs for racial minorities. For example, the Board of Regents of the University of Wisconsin introduced in 1967 a system by which out-of-state admissions would be reduced to 15 percent of the enrollment within four years. By September 1970, the number of Jewish students had dropped by two-thirds. New York Jews were a particular target of some Wisconsin legislators because of their alleged involvement in campus activism and New Left political demonstrations. Some Jewish students were indeed conspicuous among the activists of the 1960s, but this generation of college students was a mixed bag. [60]

More serious threats to the educational aspirations of upwardly mobile white ethnic groups were the so-called benign quotas adopted to recruit underrepresented or disadvantaged students. The 1976 case of *Bakke* v. *Regents of University of California* assumed great contemporary importance because the issues it raised had been awaiting judicial resolution since the similar, but inconclusive *De Funis* v. *Odegaard* (1973). By the time his case came before the United States Supreme Court, Marco De Funis, Jr., was about to graduate from the University of Washington Law School, whose preferential program for minorities, he claimed, had resulted in his initial rejection. [61]

In the autumn of 1977, however, the United States Supreme Court began hearing arguments presented by counsel for the Regents of the University of California, petitioner, and for Allan Bakke, respondent. The previous year, the Supreme Court of California had ruled unconstitutional a "task force program" at the University of California Medical School at Davis, under which 16 of the 100 slots available each year were open only to "disadvantaged" applicants, specifically blacks, Mexican Americans, Puerto Ricans, Cubans, American Indians, and Orientals. (These groups constituted more than 25 percent of California's population.) After Bakke, a white veteran in his mid-thirties, was twice denied admission to the regular track, he brought suit against the university, beginning in 1974, in the Yolo County Superior Court. He claimed that he had been discriminated against on account of his race. The age factor aside, his test scores were high enough to have gained him admission had he been a member of a minority group. The trial court ruled the Davis program invalid but did not order Bakke admitted to medical school. Both the university and Bakke then appealed to the California Supreme Court. This court also agreed that the Davis medical school's two-track system denied Bakke equal protection under the Fourteenth Amendment. Although both white and minority students had applied to the special track, all those admitted since its inception in 1969 had been minorities. The university had not demonstrated, moreover, that its goal of increasing the number of minority doctors could not have been effected by means "less detrimental" to the excluded whites. Instead, the court suggested that colleges and universities extend preference to all "disadvantaged" applicants without regard to race, strengthen recruitment and remedial assistance, consider personal qualities and goals as well as academic criteria in admission, and expand educational facilities. Finally, the California Supreme Court ordered Bakke admitted to the Davis medical school for the fall of 1977. However, the University of California was permitted to keep its existing admission program pending appeal to the United States Supreme Court.[62]

Already primed by the *De Funis* case, the proponents and opponents of preferential admissions for minority students submitted 61 "friend of the court" briefs to the United States Supreme Court. Of the more than 120 organizations, institutions, or persons filing individual or joint briefs, over 30 were in favor of Bakke and over 80 in support of the University of California. It was no coincidence that Jews, Italians, Greeks, Poles, and Ukrainians were against an admissions track reserved for racial minorities. Among the ethnic organizations supporting Bakke were the following: American Jewish Congress, Anti-Defamation League of B'nai B'rith, Hellenic Bar Association of Illinois, Order of the Sons of Italy in America, Polish American Congress, and Ukrainian Congress Committee of America (Chicago Division). For example, the Anti-Defamation League of B'nai B'rith, together with four other "friends," among them UNICO National (the largest of the Italian-American community service organizations) denounced the two-track system as a new "numerus clausus." And the brief filed by the American Jewish Committee and the American Jewish Congress with six other non-Jewish ethnic organizations argued that equal protection under the Fourteenth Amendment was an individual right, not a right conferred on groups. The favoritism now extended to racial minorities had not been bestowed on members of other ethnic groups which credibly can claim to have been subject to generalized societal discrimination—Italians, Poles, Jews, Greeks, Slavs—as a result of which at least some such persons bear the economic and cultural scars of prejudice and thus could be deemed entitled to preference as a form of restitution.[63]

Since these ethnic groups had to overcome either discrimination or discouragement in their own quest for higher education, they did not see the necessity of protecting others through benign quotas, especially when such a device might well deny them admission to a college or to a professional school. It was not that Jews, Italians, and Poles were ungenerous toward the educational aspirations of these newer minorities, but that having once surmounted restrictive quotas, they did not again want to be barred from higher education by a process described as reverse discrimination. Indeed, the Anti-Defamation League-UNICO National brief spoke on behalf, not "of any single minority," but "of the free and open society mandated by the Constitution."[64]

Nothing more clearly illustrated the nature of the division among the older and newer minorities than the opposing briefs submitted by groups often allied in the cause of civil rights: The Anti-Defamation League of B'nai B'rith, on the one hand; the American Civil Liberties Union, the National Association for the Advancement of Colored People, and the National Urban League, on the other. Joining the latter on this side of the argument were the Black Congressional Caucus, a host of professional associations, liberal organizations, labor unions, and four of the country's most prestigious private universities. Among the many defending the University of California were the American Association of University Professors, Association of American Law Schools, Association of American Medical Colleges, American Bar Association, Americans for Democratic Action, National Education Association, National Organization for Women, National Council of Churches of Christ in the USA, the United Farm Workers of America (AFL-CIO), and the United Mine Workers of America. Fearing that minority groups would lose their recently attained foothold in the professions, such organizations as the American Indian Bar Association, Asian-American Bar Association of the Greater Bay Area, Aspira of America (national organization of Puerto Rican educators and students), and La Raza National Lawyers Association also defended special admissions programs.[65]

Consistent with their past admissions policies, elite private universities, conspicuously Harvard and Columbia, justified "race"—but now publicly—as a selective factor. They filed a brief with Stanford and the University of Pennsylvania calling for "judicial restraint" in educational matters and a reversal of the decision of the California Supreme Court. Reminiscent of Woodrow Wilson's plea for "unchosen experiences" as a vital part of a liberal education, the collective brief spoke of the way in which racial minorities enriched the learning experience of classmates while expanding the scholarly concerns of faculty. Indeed, many faculty found that "an ethnically diverse student body help[ed] them to fulfill their teaching roles" and protected them from "insensitivity to minority perspectives."[66]

Columbia, Harvard, Stanford, and the University of Pennsylvania, supported by seven other universities, were concerned that their own affirmative action programs, more "flexible" and subtle than the one at the Davis medical school, might be jeopardized if the courts extended to private institutions the Fourteenth Amendment's equal protection clause. Even if private universities were not legally affected by a ruling that dismantled preferential admissions at state universities, they might feel morally bound to bring their own programs into line. They would be subjected, moreover, to intense pressures to admit far greater numbers of minority students to counterbalance the shutting of the doors at state universities. Their argument that private universities might have to take up the slack for state universities echoed one used in the 1920s as a rationale for Jewish quotas. Once universities in New York City restricted Jews, others had to follow suit to protect themselves from being inundated. So that all universities might share the responsibility of educating disadvantaged minorities, the brief had to defend the principle behind affirmative action programs, even if benign quotas received only its token support.[67]

To achieve educational and social objectives, educators must be allowed to exercise discretion based on professional competence. Preferential admissions, the collective brief anticipated, would be needed for only a limited period of time. There were already indications that Japanese Americans and, to some extent, Chinese Americans were increasingly successful in gaining admission to colleges and professional schools. (Asian Americans, who made up about 6 percent of California's college graduates, filled thirteen of the eighty-four regular places at the Davis medical school.) In recent years, blacks, Spanish-surnamed Americans, and native Americans have made progress. As of 1976, they constituted approximately 17 percent of the national population, 12 percent of beginning undergraduates, 8.3 percent of the graduate students, 8.0 of the law students, and 9.1 percent of the medical students.[68]

For the most part, the Justice Department agreed with arguments presented by Columbia, Harvard, Stanford, and the University of Pennsylvania. Although its own brief, filed in September 1977, denounced quotas, the Justice Department made room for institutional discretion, including "reasonably selected numerical targets for minority admissions." The Fourteenth Amendment, it maintained, "protects all persons without regard to race," but it "does not call for rejection of minority-sensitive programs when employed in a remedial manner." While not upholding the procedure followed at the

Davis medical school, the Justice Department contended that the ruling of the California Supreme Court should be reversed and remanded. [69]

In a close, equivocal, 5 to 4 decision on June 28, 1978, the United States Supreme Court affirmed the judgment of the California Supreme Court on two counts: that the special admissions program at Davis was unlawful under the Fourteenth Amendment, and that, as a consequence, Bakke should be admitted to the medical school. On these issues, the pivotal justice, Lewis F. Powell, Jr., was supported by Chief Justice Warren E. Burger and by Justices Potter Stewart, William H. Rehnquist, and John Paul Stevens. But a different majority reversed that portion of the California court's ruling that had denied that race could in any way be considered a factor in the admissions process. Again, Justice Powell spoke for the majority, which now consisted of Justices William J. Brennan, Jr., Byron R. White, Thurgood Marshall, and Harry A. Blackmun. Simply stated, had Powell voted with the "Stevens Four" and declined to decide whether race may ever be taken into account in admissions, the Supreme Court might well have undermined affirmative action programs. On the other hand, had Powell voted with the "Brennan Four" in upholding the two-track system at Davis, the Supreme Court would virtually have legalized benign quotas. Since neither alternative is politically and socially acceptable to a majority of the American people, the Supreme Court judiciously avoided, at least for the present, the problems that might have resulted from a more unified and sweeping decision. But the narrowness of the majority as well as the ambiguities in Powell's opinion have opened the courtroom door to future litigation over admissions programs that favor minority applicants. [70]

In ruling against the Davis program, Justice Powell drew interesting distinctions between the medical school's "use of an explicit racial classification" and the more sophisticated, flexible undergraduate admissions program developed at Harvard. The medical school had erred by conspicuously excluding disadvantaged whites from its special program, while permitting racial minority students to compete only against each other, rather than against all applicants, in seeking admission. Quoting liberally from the statement on Harvard College admissions that was appended to the four-university brief, Powell maintained that Harvard's program treated "each applicant as an individual in the admissions process," without insulating "the person from comparison with all other candidates for the available seats." Although both the statement and the brief were purposely couched in language to protect admissions officers in their exercise of discretion, Powell recognized that the public will presume that university officials are acting in good faith where there is no evidence of specific discrimination or quotas. By praising Harvard, he reassured universities that were concerned about the future of their affirmative action programs. Yet Harvard has limited usefulness as a model, because it attracts the cream of applicants, whether white or of a racial minority. And if it so chooses, Harvard can decide to satisfy its need for diversity by admitting racial minorities from middle- and upper middle-class backgrounds. By contrast, the Davis medical school had reserved special consideration for those racial minority applicants who were also economically or educationally disadvantaged.71

Although the Fourteenth Amendment prohibits universities from using quotas to achieve diversity, Powell interpreted the First Amendment's protection of academic freedom to allow them some discretion in selecting a diverse student body. Thus race may legitimately be considered one factor in admissions. But if challenged, universities will have to show that, in weighing race, they had first evaluated all applicants individually on their qualifications. At this point, it is hard to say who has won: white males or the racial minorities. The latter may indeed have lost if universities do not voluntarily continue affirmative action programs. Blacks and other racial minorities are no longer guaranteed any quotas in admissions. Within the broad guidelines of the Fourteenth Amendment, Justice Powell left it up to the universities to decide how much weight would be accorded to the racial factor in admissions. On the other hand, although Bakke has won his long battle, most white males may not be helped by striking down benign quotas. First, universities and professional schools have allotted a relatively small number of slots to minorities, while a large number of white men continue to apply to the most competitive schools. In 1975-76, almost thirty-five thousand whites applied to medical school; twenty-two thousand were not admitted. Minority students accounted for less than 7 percent of the entering classes. Second, the biggest beneficiaries from affirmative action in the past decade have been women—of all ethnic and racial groups. Their numbers among those entering medical school climbed from 8 to 25 percent, totaling four thousand students; and women have made similar gains in the law schools. Although the national trend of declining enrollments might open up seats in some classrooms, at least for those who can afford to pay, this situation would not seriously affect the top universities and professional schools, for which demand exceeds supply.72

Higher education remains the most prestigious (even if only modestly profitable) ladder of upward mobility. In the competition for the higher rungs in American society, college and graduate or professional training makes the difference. The collegiate dandies, who once so ardently pursued the "sideshows" of undergraduate life, have yielded their seats to more serious students. Many who never would have dreamed of attending college fifty years ago now expect this educational opportunity as a matter of right. Commenting on the post-World War II era, William C. De Vane of Yale pointed to the very substantial role played by the federal and state governments in the democratization of higher education:

> One of the effects of the G.I. Bill was to show young people that college was possible for anyone with the requisite ability, and the strong trend towards the democratization of the colleges has now reached the point where many states, and soon perhaps the federal government, will regard free higher education as the right of every young person, and consequently think it the duty of government to provide it.

Today's students, De Vane predicted, would "do well in the world," though they might be "somewhat insensitive and at times ruthless" in achieving their goals. Beyond a doubt, a new generation of college students is making its mark. 73

NOTES

HGM	*Harvard Graduates' Magazine.*
HPR, year	*Reports of the President of Harvard College (Harvard President's Report)*, 1890-1955, HUA, NMPL.
HPW	Henry Parks Wright Papers, YUL.
HTR, year	*Reports of the Treasurer of Harvard College (Harvard Treasurer's Report)*, 1890-1955, HUA, NMPL.
HUA	Harvard University Archives, Nathan Marsh Pusey Library, Harvard University, Cambridge, Mass.
HUL	Harvard University Library, Cambridge, Mass.
JDG	Jerome Davis Greene Papers, HUA, NMPL. Eight boxes (including correspondence with Charles W. Eliot).
JRA	Records of the President, James Rowland Angell, YUA, YUL. Correspondence arranged alphabetically by letter, name, and topic.
NMPL	Nathan Marsh Pusey Library, Harvard University, Cambridge, Mass.
PAW	*Princeton Alumni Weekly.*
PPR, year	*Annual Report of the President of Princeton University for the Year Ending . . . (Princeton President's Report)*, 1900-50, Princeton University Archives (PUA), Princeton University, Princeton, N.J.
PUA	Princeton University Archives, Seeley G. Mudd Manuscript Library, Princeton University, Princeton, N.J.
PUL	Princeton University Library, Princeton, N.J.
PWW	Arthur S. Link, et al., eds., *The Papers of Woodrow Wilson*, 29 vols. to date (Princeton: Princeton University Press, 1966-).
RB & SC, PUL	Rare Books and Special Collections, Princeton University Library, Princeton, N.J.
WC	Woodrow Wilson Collection, RB & SC, PUL.
WP, LC	Woodrow Wilson Papers, Library of Congress.
WWP	Woodrow Wilson Papers, PUA. One box.
YAM	*Yale Alumni Monthly.*
YAW	*Yale Alumni Weekly.*
YPR, year	*Reports of the President, Provost, and Secretary of Yale University and of the Deans and Directors of Its Several Schools and Departments for the Academic Year . . . (Yale President's Reports)*, 1900-36, YUA.
YRP, year	*Reports to the President by the Deans and Directors of the Several Schools and Departments for the Academic Year . . . (Yale Reports to the President)*, 1937-54, YUA.
YUA	Yale University Archives, Yale University Library, New Haven, Conn.
YUL	Yale University Library, New Haven, Conn.

Unless otherwise noted, all official letters in university files are copies of outgoing originals; for example, those from Charles W. Eliot are in CWE or CWEB and those from A. Lawrence Lowell are in ALL.

The bibliography gives full citation for works listed in abbreviated form in the notes.

Introduction

1. B. S. Hurlbut to Joseph Warren, October 16, 1907, CWE, box 221, folder Hurlbut, Byron Satterlee.
2. Bayard Henry to Henry Burling Thompson, July 13, 1907, enclosed with letter from Henry to Woodrow Wilson, July 29, 1907, in PWW, 17: 305.
3. "Report of the Special Committee Appointed to Consider the Limitation of Numbers" [dated by hand, December 1925], pp. 18-19, in ALL, #184 Limitation of Numbers; J. E. Kirkpatrick, *Academic Organization and Control*, p. 79.
4. John Kenneth Galbraith, Text of remarks delivered . . . on Harvard Class Day, June 11, 1975.
5. Seymour Martin Lipset and David Riesman, *Education and Politics at Harvard*, pp. 179, 307-09.
6. Ibid.
7. "A Survey of Princeton Freshmen," *PAW* 71, no. 17 (February 23, 1971), pp. 6-9; Rabbi Norbert Samuelson, "Rabbi Responds," *Daily Princetonian*, September 25, 1972, p. 3; Rabbi Arnold Jacob Wolf, "Jewish Experience Is Vividly Present at Yale," *YAM*, 36, no. 4 (January 1973), pp. [14]-15; and Mark Singer, "God and Mentsch at Yale," *Moment* 1, no. 2 (July/August 1975), pp. 27-31.
8. *Brief of Columbia University, Harvard University, Stanford University and the University of Pennsylvania as Amici Curiae*, June 7, 1977, *Regents of the University of California* v. *Allan Bakke*; see its appendix on "Harvard College Admissions Program."
9. David B. Tyack, *The One Best System*, p. 228; pt. 5, chap. 3, "Victims Without 'Crimes': Black Americans," pp. 217-29; chap. 4, "Americanization: Match and Mismatch," pp. 229-55, 276-83. See also Diane Ravitch, *The Great School Wars*, chap. 15, "New Education for the New Immigration," pp. 161-80; chap. 22, "From Americanization to Integration," pp. 241-47; and part 7, "Fourth School War: Racism and Reaction," pp. 251-378.

Chapter 1. The Big Three

1. Lawrence Perry, "For the Game's Sake," *New York Sun*, undated clipping [November 1926] in box 1 "Athletics, Football Break with Harvard, 1926-1934," PUA.
2. George W. Pierson, *The Education of American Leaders*, pp. xix-xxi, 240-51; Pierson, *Yale: College and University, 1871-1937*, vol. 1, *Yale College: An Educational History, 1871-1921*, chap. 18, "The Literary Renaissance," pp. 346-68; Henry F. May, *The End of American Innocence*, pp. 298-301.
3. Gene R. Hawes, "The Colleges of America's Upper Class," *Saturday Review Magazine*, November 16, 1963, pp. 68-71.
4. Kenneth S. Davis, *A Prophet in His Own Country*, pp. 108-09.
5. Rudolf Tombo, Jr., "College Student Geography," Boston *Evening Transcript*, October 5, 1912, p. 3; "Only Ten Colleges Listed As 'National,'" *New York Times*,

May 31, 1931, clipping in subject file Administration—Statistics, Geographical Distribution, PUA. May, *The End of American Innocence*, pp. 56-62.

6. Arthur T. Hadley to Andrew F. West, March 6, 1900, ATH, September 21, 1899, to March 15, 1901, book no. 1, p. 284. See map entitled "Princeton Harvard Yale Undergraduate Geographical Distribution 1915-16," subject file Administration—Statistics, Geographical Distribution, PUA; and table and map entitled "Geographical Distribution According To Residence Harvard, Princeton, And Yale Undergraduates Classes of 1926-29, Inclusive" (figures compiled in May 1926), JRA, box 2, file Board of Admissions. See also Harvard, Yale, and Princeton alumni directories and annual catalogues.

7. Adlai Stevenson, quoted in Davis, *A Prophet in His Own Country*, p. 117.

8. Prof. George Wilson Pierson, interview, Yale University Library, May 10, 1971; James R. Angell to Robert N. Corwin, October 11, 1927, JRA, box 2, file Board of Admissions; A. Lawrence Lowell to Frederick R. Martin, May 22, 1922, ALL, #124 Admission; *HPR, 1900-30; PPR, 1900-30*; George Wilson Pierson, *Yale: College and University, 1871-1937*, vol. 2, *Yale: The University College, 1921-1937*, pp. 669-71.

9. Charles W. Eliot, quoted from *Third Proceedings of the North Central Association of Colleges and Secondary Schools*, in Harry Charles McKown, *The Trend of College Entrance Requirements, 1913-1922*, p. 86; Hugh Hawkins, *Between Harvard and America*, pp. 171-80.

10. Calvin Thomas, "A New Plan of Admission to College," *Columbia University Quarterly* 2 (1899-1900): 357-61; *HPR, 1903-04*, p. 12; Pierson, *Yale*, 1: 393-401; J. G. Hart, "New Methods of Admission to Harvard," reprinted from *HGM* June 1906, and various letters relating to admission, CWE, box 217, folder Hart, John Goddard.

11. Pierson, *Yale*, 1: 401-04, 660; John Preston Hoskins '91, chairman of the Committee on Entrance, Princeton, "Co-operation in Entrance Examinations, College Entrance Examination Board to Conduct the Princeton, Harvard and Yale June Entrance Examinations After June, 1915," *PAW* 15, no. 30 (May 5, 1915): 724-26.

12. McKown, *The Trend of College Entrance Requirements*, pp. 6-12; Harvard College bulletin on the New Plan of Admission, 1912, ALL, #15 New Plan.

13. Harvey N. Davis, "The New Harvard Plan for College Admission," reprinted from *Proceedings of the National Education Association*, San Francisco, Calif., July 1911, pp. 567-71; A. Lawrence Lowell to Alfred E. Stearns, April 24, 1911, Andrew Carnegie to Lowell, January 19, 1911, and Lowell to Carnegie, January 20, 1911, ALL, #15 New Plan.

14. McKown, *The Trend of College Entrance Requirements*, pp. 13-21; Pierson, *Yale*, 1: 404-11; Gilbert F. Close '03, "The New Entrance Requirements," *PAW* 13, no. 14 (January 8, 1913): 271-73; various reports in subject files Admission and Administration—Entrance Requirements, PUA. See also Harold Potter Rodes, "Educational Factors Affecting the Entrance Requirements of Yale College" (Ph.D. diss., Yale University, 1948), pp. 103-40; and Robert N. Corwin to James R. Angell, June 25, 1928, JRA, box 2, file Board of Admissions.

15. See autobiographical sketches of Robert Nelson Corwin in *Yale College*, the *Twenty-Fifth, Thirty-Fifth*, and *Fiftieth Year Records of '87*, YUA; and biographical information on Radcliffe Heermance, dated July 21, 1955, PUA.

16. Biographical information on Heermance, July 21, 1955, PUA. See also the following in a folder on Radcliffe Heermance, Office of Secretary of the University,

Nassau Hall: Heermance to Wilkie (Varnum Lansing Collins), January 15, 1921, and January 19, 1927; Princeton University news release on his death, October 30, 1958; and a memorial resolution proposed by C. William Edwards, Willard Thorp, and Jeremiah S. Finch and adopted at the December 1, 1958, faculty meeting. Mr. Jeremiah S. Finch, secretary of the university, interview, Nassau Hall, Princeton University, February 24, 1971.

17. *Yale College, Records, Class of 1887*; Miss Nellie P. Elliot, former executive secretary of the Yale Board of Admissions, interview, New Haven, Conn., October 2, 1970; autobiographical sketches of [Charles] Henry Pennypacker in *Harvard College, Class of '88, Secretary's Report* 8 (January 1920) and Pennypacker's *Fortieth Anniversary Report* 9 (December 1928); obituary in *Fiftieth Anniversary Report* 10 (1938), HUA.

18. See above, n. 16.

19. Pierson, *Yale*, 2: 478-80; Rudolph, *The American College and University*, chap. 9, "Financing the Colleges," especially pp. 185-89.

20. Arthur T. Hadley to Gifford Pinchot, February 1, 1905, and Hadley to [Alfred L.] Ripley, February 9, 1905, ATH, January 1, 1905, to June 30, 1905, book no. 10, pp. 135-36, 173.

21. Henry Aaron Yeomans, *Abbott Lawrence Lowell, 1856-1943*, pp. 179, 223, 245-53, 259-71, 356-57; Hawkins, *Between Harvard and America*, pp. 69, 212-16.

22. Yeomans, *Lowell*, chap. 13, "Housing the Undergraduates, The 'Houses,'" pp. 180-98; chap. 15, "Material Development of the University, Growing by Plan," pp. 219-29; chap. 16, "Material Growth of the University, Building for Needs," pp. 230-44; and chap. 17, "Material Growth: Endowment and Its Use," pp. 245-74.

23. Pierson, *Yale*, 2: 213, 236-52, 471, 505-07, 594-601. See also chap. 10, "Mr. Harkness and the Quadrangle Plan—I," pp. 207-30, and chap. 11, "Mr. Harkness and the Quadrangle Plan—II, pp. 231-52; also *Historical Register of Yale University, 1701-1937* (New Haven: Yale University Press, 1939), pp. 27-29.

24. Thomas S. Matthews '22, "Those Inflated 'Twenties," *PAW* 31, no. 22 (March 13, 1931): 568, 559-561; *PAW* 20, no. 11 (December 10, 1919): 245-46; *PPR*, 1930-31, pp. 1, 50-51.

25. For sketches on Charles Joseph Bonaparte '71 and James Byrne '77, see their respective *Harvard College Class Reports* and their quinquennial files; also *Endowment Funds of Harvard University, June 30, 1947*, pp. 100, 229; and *HTR, 1901-02, 1916-19, 1924-27*.

26. See the accounts of William Stanislaus Murphy's life in the *Harvard College, Class of 1885, Reports*, especially *Thirtieth* 8 (1915-16): 94-97; also *Endowment Funds of Harvard University*.

27. See the obituary of George Smith in *Report of the Harvard Class of 1853 (1849-1913) Issued on the Sixtieth Anniversary For the Use of the Class and Its Friends*, Commencement 1913, pp. 240-43.

28. Yeomans, *Lowell*, pp. 170-74, 220-21; V. Mott Porter to A. Lawrence Lowell, October 20, 1914, and November 18, 1914, and Lowell to Porter, October 27, 1914, ALL, #70 Freshman Halls.

29. Samuel Eliot Morison, ed., *The Development of Harvard University Since the Inauguration of President Eliot, 1869-1929*, p. 237; *HPR, 1901-02, 1920-21; HTR, 1904-05, 1908-09, 1923-25*.

30. Stephen Birmingham, *"Our Crowd": The Great Jewish Families of New York*, pp. 19-25, and pt. 4, "The Age of Schiff"; *Endowment Funds of Harvard University*, p. 399; *HPR, 1923-25, 1928-29; HTR, 1923-28*.

31. Birmingham, *"Our Crowd,"* pp. 194, 225-37, 299-302, 338, 387, 415-52; *Endowment Funds of Harvard University*, pp. 63, 137-38, 295, 333-34, 399-401; *HPR, 1908-11, 1913-14, 1923-24, 1927-30; HTR, 1900-02, 1906-07, 1908-10, 1919-20, 1923-29*.

32. Birmingham, *"Our Crowd,"* p. 26; "Memorandum on the Problems Arising from the Increase in the Enrollment of Students of Jewish Birth in the University," May 12, 1922, JRA, box 84, file Jewish Problem, Etc. According to Laurence R. Veysey, *The Emergence of the American University*, American college and university professors and presidents of the late nineteenth and early twentieth centuries were overwhelmingly WASP and middle class (nn. 134-36, pp. 300-02).

33. "Scholarships and Beneficiary Funds," *Harvard University Catalogue, 1930-31*, pp. 377-400, 595-603; Seymour E. Harris, *The Economics of Harvard*, pp. 108-11, 86-99, 298-99, 304-05, 312-13.

34. Pierson, *Yale*, 1: 411-13; *Yale*, 2: 599-600, 489-92. Northern New England was added in 1944 as a seventh region for Yale's University Regional Scholarships.

35. *PPR, 1919*, pp. 6-15, and *PPR, 1921*, pp. 14-15.

36. Pierson, *Yale*, 2: 491-92.

37. McKown, *The Trend of College Entrance Requirements*, pp. 21-31; Joel H. Spring, "Psychologists and the War," *History of Education Quarterly* 12, no. 1 (Spring 1972): 3-15; Carol S. Gruber, *Mars and Minerva*, pp. 253-59; Richard Hofstadter and Walter P. Metzger, *The Development of Academic Freedom in the United States*, pp. 496-506; and Garland G. Parker, "50 Years of Collegiate Enrollments: 1919-20 to 1969-70," pt. 1, *School & Society* 98 (March 1970): 150.

38. John Higham, *Strangers in the Land*, chap. 10, "The Tribal Twenties," pp. 264-99; E. Digby Baltzell, *The Protestant Establishment*, pp. 129-36, 209-17. Yeomans, *Lowell*, pp. 314-27, and chap. 30, "The Commonwealth of Massachusetts vs. Nicola Sacco and Bartolomeo Vanzetti," pp. 483-96. For Lowell's defense of academic freedom, see *HPR, 1916-17*, pp. 17-18, 20-21, and *HPR, 1918-19*, pp. 6-7; "A Fight for Freedom, 1921: Lest We Forget," *History Reference Bulletin* 8, no. 23 (November 1934), pp. 37-38; Lowell to C. D. Velie, April 8, 1924, and other letters in ALL, #108 Reds; and Charles W. Eliot to Howard Elliott, September 19, 1921, CWE, box 387, A-L.

39. B. S. Hurlbut to Joseph Warren, October 16, 1907, CWE, box 221, folder Hurlbut, Byron Satterlee; Frederick S. Jones to R. N. Corwin, May 6, 1922, FSJ, box 5, file Jews.

40. Stephen Steinberg, *The Academic Melting Pot*, pp. 1-3; James R. Angell to Conrad Hoffman, Jr., December 7, 1933, JRA, box 84, file Jewish Problem, Etc.; Heywood Broun and George Britt, *Christians Only*, pp. 53-66, and chap. 4, "A Liberal Education," pp. 72-124; and Stephen Birmingham, *Real Lace*, chap. 21, "Sons of the Priory, Daughters of the Sacred Heart," pp. 235-42.

41. "Professional Tendencies Among Jewish Students in Colleges, Universities, and Professional Schools" (Memoir of the Bureau of Jewish Social Research), *American Jewish Year Book, 5681*, vol. 22 (September 13, 1920, to October 2, 1921), pp. [381]-93.

42. Minutes of Meeting of Association New England Deans Held in Princeton, 9th and 10th of May [1918], pp. 21-22, FSJ, box 6, file War; Topics Proposed For Discussion, Association of Administrative Officers in New England, Middletown, Conn., May 21-22, 1920, and at the 1919 and 1922-1925 meetings, DHCCF, #22 Deans' Association, 1920-27.

43. Frederick Paul Keppel, *Columbia*, pp. 179-81; Keppel, *The Undergraduate and His College*, pp. 83-84.

44. Harold S. Wechsler, *The Qualified Student*, pp. 91-95, 99-103, and chap. 7, "Repelling the Invasion: Columbia and the Jewish Student," pp. 131-85. His dissertation is still of interest, because it was solidly researched and clearly written: "The Selective Function of American College Admissions Policies: 1870-1970" (Ph.D. diss., Columbia University, 1974), especially, pp. 204-08, 229-56, and 260-76. See also Charles W. Eliot to [Nicholas Murray] Butler, August 26, 1924, CWE, box 390, A-C, mentioning their "disagreements . . . on tough subjects, like the exclusion of Jews and Prohibition legislation."

45. Wechsler, *The Qualified Student*, pp. 147-57.

46. Ibid., pp. 157-61; McKown, *The Trend of College Entrance Requirements*, pp. 21-31.

47. Wechsler, *The Qualified Student*, pp. 162-64; H. E. Hawkes to Robert N. Corwin, October 16 and 20, 1922, Corwin to Hawkes, October 18, 1922, and a [Corwin] memorandum on Limitation of Numbers, Freshman Office Records-Ex-1926-27, file Com. on Limitation of Numbers 1922, YUA; "Minutes of the Committee Appointed by the President of the University to Consider and Report to the Governing Boards Principles and Methods for More Effective Sifting of Candidates for Admission to the University." June 1922 to March 1923, meeting of December 21, 1922, HUA.

48. Wechsler, *The Qualified Student*, pp. 164-68.

49. Ibid., pp. 168-75; "Minutes of Committee to Consider and Report Methods", meeting of November 6, 1922.

50. Archibald L. Bouton to C. N. Greenough, June 23, 1923, and clipping, "At N.Y.U.," letter to the editor, *New York Tribune*, June 18, 1922, DHCCF, #16 Subcommittee on Sifting of Candidates for Admission 1922-23.

51. See Table 1.1; memorandum on Limitation of Numbers, and George Edwin Howes to Robert N. Corwin, October 16 and December 26, 1922, Freshman Office Records-Ex-1926-27, file Com. on Limitation of Numbers 1922.

52. Tables 4.1, 5.1, 5.3, 6.1, 6.2; *HPR, 1911-12*, "Appleton Chapel and Phillips Brooks House," p. 172.

53. See Tables 4.8, 5.9, and 6.3.

54. Samuel Eliot Morison, *Three Centuries of Harvard, 1636-1936*, p. 422.

55. "Minutes of Committee to Consider and Report Methods," November 6, 1922; Frederick S. Jones to R. N. Corwin, May 6, 1922, FSJ, box 5, file Jews.

56. A. Lawrence Lowell to William E. Hocking, May 19, 1922, ALL #1056 Jews; Charles W. Eliot to Bruce L. Kennan, August 9, 1907, CWEB #96, December 11, 1906, to October 26, 1907, p. 128.

57. Stanley E. Howard to H. Alexander Smith, April 21, 1924, memorandum on Club Statistics with tables on classes of 1920-23, HASP, box 37, folder Executive Secretary Statistics.

58. F. Scott Fitzgerald, *This Side of Paradise*, p. 48; Ernest Hemingway, *The Sun Also Rises*, p. 4; Baltzell, *The Protestant Establishment*, p. 210.

59. Matthews, "Those Inflated 'Twenties," p. 568; Michael David Robbins, "Princeton, 1920 to 1929: An Historical Study of a Problem in Reputation" (Senior thesis in history, Princeton University, 1955), pp. 66-67.

60. Birmingham, "Our Crowd," p. 15.

61. "Comments from the Class," *Harvard College, Class of 1924, Secretary's First Report* (1925), p. 29; Cleveland Amory, *The Proper Bostonians*, pp. 298, 291-97.

62. Amory, *The Proper Bostonians*, p. 299; Silas Bent, "Harvard Stirred by Attack on Cliques, Lamont and MacVeagh Try to Bridge Student Chasm," *New York Times*, December 9, 1923, sec. 10, p. 3; "Charges a Clique Runs Harvard Life, Corliss Lamont Assails Alleged Domination of Classes by Private School Men," *New York Times*, November 26, 1923, p. 3; "Butterfly and Ant," editorial, *New York Times*, December 16, 1923, sec. 2, p. 6. Charlton MacVeagh '24 (Spee) and Corliss Lamont '24 (Delphic) had written articles entitled respectively, "The College B. Damned" and "Who Runs Harvard and Why" for the *Harvard Advocate*, February and November 1923.

63. Amory, *The Proper Bostonians*, pp. 300-10; Yeomans, *Lowell*, pp. 35-38; Hawkins, *Between Harvard and America*, p. 12; Baltzell, *The Protestant Establishment*, p. 210.

64. *Harvard Class Albums*, 1912 and 1940, HUA.

65. Bernard Berenson, *The Bernard Berenson Treasury: A Selection from the Works, Unpublished Writings, Letters, Diaries, and Journals, 1887-1958*, ed. Hanna Kiel (London: Methuen, 1964), pp. 104-05, 209. The professors mentioned were William James (psychology and philosophy), Crawfold H. Toy (Hebrew and other Oriental languages), and Barrett Wendell (English). W. B. S. Clymer (English), one of Charles W. Eliot's personal secretaries in the 1880s, was not promoted to professorial rank. *Harvard College, Class of 1924*, pp. 32, 155-68.

66. Morison, *Three Centuries of Harvard*, p. 417; and Z. B. T., *1898-1923*, pp. 13-19, 25, 32, 68-70, 82-83, 110-12.

67. The two best accounts are by Loomis Havemeyer: *"Go to Your Room"* and *Sheff Days and Ways*.

68. Prof. Rollin G. Osterweis, interview, New Haven, Conn., May 20, 1971; Baltzell, *The Protestant Establishment*, p. 65; *History of the Class of 1925, Yale College*, YUA.

69. Prof. Osterweis, interview, May 20, 1971; Z.B.T., 1898-1923, pp. 124-26.

70. "Report to the University Council by Special Committee Appointed to Investigate Position of Pi Lambda Phi Fraternity for Official Recognition by the University Authorities," April 12, 1923, and other reports in FSJ, box 3, file Fraternities; Arthur T. Hadley to William Allen Wood, April 19, 1906, ATH, January 1, 1906, to May 20, 1906, book no 12, p. 620; "Foundation of Societies," *Yale Banner and Pot-Pourri* 22 (1930): 171.

71. W. D. Washburn to Fred Jones, April 7, 1914, and Jones to Washburn, April 13, 1914, FSJ, box 6 file Temperance and Prohibition.

72. Robbins, "Princeton, 1920 to 1929," p. 66; folder on Ku Klux Klan at Harvard in "Clippings on the Race Question, 1922," HUA; James Weldon Johnson, telegram

to the president and Board of Overseers of Harvard University, October 23, 1923, ALL, #507 Ku Klux Klan.

Chapter 2. Portraits and Philosophies of Two Harvard Presidents: Charles W. Eliot and A. Lawrence Lowell

1. Charles W. Eliot to Jerome D. Greene, June 7, 1922, JDG, box 6, folder 1922-23 the Jewish question—and Negro question.

2. Charles W. Eliot to Jerome D. Greene, January 25, 1923, JDG, box 6, folder the Jewish question; Henry James, *Charles W. Eliot, President of Harvard University, 1869-1909*, 2: 133-34. For Greene's career, see *Harvard College, Class of 1896, Twenty-fifth Anniversary Report, 1896-1921* (1921), pp. 225-28.

3. Henry Aaron Yeomans, *Abbott Lawrence Lowell, 1856-1943*, chap. 1, "The Family," in general, and pp. 7-8, 14, 21, in particular. See James, *Eliot*, vol. 1, chap. 1, in general, and pp. 26-28, in particular.

4. Yeomans, *Lowell*, pp. 6-9, 12, 15, 27. James, *Eliot*, 1: 29, 7.

5. James, *Eliot*, 1: 12-14, 73-75.

6. Ibid, pp. 22-23, 29-35; Charles W. Eliot to Dr. A. C. McCrea, March 7, 1921, CWE, box 387, M-Z; Eliot to Rev. Charles H. Parkhurst, December 21, 1923, CWE, box 389, folder Interesting; letters from Eliot to his mother, Mary Lyman Eliot, from Interlaken, July 1864, and from Düsseldorf, September 7, 1864, as quoted in James, *Eliot*, 1: 133-34, 126-27; Eliot to Rev. Edwin P. Parker, October 14, 1905, CWEB #95, May 5, 1903, to December 11, 1906, p. 99. Eliot's son, Rev. Samuel A. Eliot, was president of the American Unitarian Association.

7. Yeomans, *Lowell*, p. 17.

8. James, *Eliot*, 1: 34.

9. Yeomans, *Lowell*, pp. 22-23, 28; Eliot to Charles F. Thwing, January 31, 1923, CWE box 389, M-Z.

10. Eliot to Theodore Tebbets, March 13, 1856, as quoted in James, *Eliot*, 1: 72, 305; Jerome D. Greene, "Years with President Eliot" (printed pamphlet) p. 16, JDG, box 4.

11. Lowell to Sherrard Billings, November 23, 1921, ALL, #981 Freshman Dormitories; Lowell to Charles D. Johnson, October 17, 1924, ALL, #741 Religion in College.

12. Eliot to Frederick B. Adams, April 21, 1899, CWEB #92, January 17, 1898, to March 23, 1903, p. 28a; circular letter from secretary to president to Cambridge churches, December 21, 1903, CWE, box 205, folder Cambridge Churches; *HPR*, *1903-04*, pp. 47-48; Eliot to Frederick H. Rindge, June 3, 1892, CWEB #91, February 8, 1889, to November 3, 1898, p. 31a; Eliot to George Wigglesworth, January 18, 1909, CWEB #98, July 16, 1908, to June 4, 1909, p. 112.

13. Frederick S. Jones to Dr. Henry Sloane Coffin, November 20, 1922, FSJ, box 1, file Chapel (Battell); see Chapel file also for opposition to compulsory attendance; Ralph Henry Gabriel, *Religion and Learning at Yale*, pp. 225-29; George Wilson Pierson, *Yale: College and University, 1871-1937*, vol. 2, *Yale: The University College, 1921-1937*, pp. 84, 87-93; Loomis Havemeyer, *Sheff Days and Ways*, p. 2; *(PPR)*, *1915*, pp. 48-49; Michael David Robbins, "Princeton, 1920 to 1929, An Historical

Study of a Problem in Reputation" (Senior thesis in history, Princeton University, 1955), pp. 46-55; *Daily Princetonian*, March 2, 1927, p. 1 (results of questionnaire on undergraduate religious beliefs); Thomas S. Matthews '22, "Those Inflated 'Twenties," *PAW* 31 (March 13, 1931): 561; H. W. Dodds, "A Statement by the President Regarding the Place of Religion in the Curriculum and on the Campus," April 11, 1935, PUA; and Princeton University, "Report on the Special Committee of the Faculty on Religious Education," April 11, 1935, PUA.

14. Samuel Eliot Morison, *Three Centuries of Harvard, 1636-1936*, p. 417; *HPR, 1907-08*, p. 28; *HPR, 1911-12*, p. 172; *Harvard Crimson*, April 12 and 23, 1958.

15. James, *Eliot*, 2: 179-81; report on Eliot's speech, "College Spirit, Class Feeling, and the Social Aspects of the Dormitory Question," *Harvard Crimson*, January 10, 1906, p. 1; Eliot to Bruce L. Keenan, August 9, 1907, CWEB #96, December 11, 1906, to October 26, 1907, p. 128.

16. Yeomans, *Lowell*, pp. 68-69, 65-82, 123-35; Christopher S. Jencks and David Riesman, chap. 22, "Patterns of Residential Education: A Case Study of Harvard," in Nevitt Sanford, ed. *The American College*, pp. 738-39. For Lowell's preference for undergraduate teaching, see Eliot to Julian W. Mack, copy, September 29, 1922, FF, box 191, folder 17, Sifting Committee, 1922-1924.

17. Lowell to Eliot, April 2, 1902, CWE, box 114, folder Lowell, A. Lawrence; Yeomans, *Lowell*, pp. 165-69.

18. Lowell, "Inaugural Address," October 6, 1909, reprinted from *HGM*, December 1909, in his *At War with Academic Traditions in America*, pp. 35, 32-46; *HPR, 1918-19*, pp. 11-13.

19. Laurence R. Veysey, *The Emergence of the American University*, pp. 248-51; Yeomans, *Lowell*, pp. 142-46, 152-63; Greene, "Years with President Eliot," pp. 15-16. Eliot did not approve of the tutorial system (James, *Eliot*, 2: 182-85). See also "Ten Years of President Lowell," *HAB*, September 25, 1919, pp. 4-11; and the following *HPR: 1918-19*, pp. 11-13; *1919-20*, pp. 13-17; *1921-22*, pp. 8-15; *1924-25*, pp. 8-12; *1925-26*, pp. 15-18; and *1926-27*, pp. 10-15.

20. Yeomans, *Lowell*, pp. 175-79, 198; Eliot to Jerome D. Greene, January 22, 1923, JDG, box 6, folder the Jewish question.

21. Woodrow Wilson to Mary Allen Hulbert Peck, July 3, 1909, and Lowell to Wilson, July 14, 1909, in Arthur S. Link et al., eds., *The Papers of Woodrow Wilson*, 19: 290, 310.

22. Lowell to F. C. Woodman, December 4, 1914, ALL, #70 Freshman Halls; Henry W. Bragdon, "Woodrow Wilson and Lawrence Lowell: An Original Study of Two Very Different Men," *HAB* 45, no. 16 (May 22, 1943), pp. 597-98; Yeomans, *Lowell*, pp. 175-79, 196-97. On November 3, 1925, Lowell wrote Henry James that "the question of dividing Harvard College into separate groups, or colleges, . . . has been in my mind and that of others for the last twenty years, but until very recently it has not been ripe for discussion." Lowell was now "looking for resources to begin" (ALL, #184 Limitation of Numbers). Another of Lowell's steps toward his goal of a complete undergraduate education was the introduction, in September 1919, of required physical training for all freshmen (*HPR, 1918-19*, pp. 13-15).

23. Yeomans, *Lowell*, p. 68.

24. Barbara Miller Solomon, *Ancestors and Immigrants*, pp. 101-06, 118-30, 134-43, 150-51, 204-07.

25. Lowell to Sidney L. Gulick, August 28, 1918, ALL, #399 Immigration (Gulick's league emphasized regulation rather than restriction of immigration); Lowell, *Public Opinion and Popular Government*, pp. 35-36.

26. Robert De C. Ward, corresponding secretary pro tem, Immigration Restriction League, to Lowell, March 30, 1922, with reprint of his "Immigration and the Three Per Cent Restrictive Law," *Journal of Heredity*, 12 (August-September 1921): 319-25; and Lowell to Hon. Le Baron B. Colt, March 31, 1922, ALL, #1077 Immigration Restriction. See also R. M. Bradley to Lowell, March 18 and 24, 1924, Lowell to Bradley, March 19, 1924, Lowell to Colt, March 25, 1924, and Colt to Lowell, March 28, 1924, enclosing "Objections to Going Back to the Census of 1890 as a Quota Basis," 68th Cong., 1st sess., Senate Committee Print, 1924 [printed for the use of the Committee on Immigration], ALL, #592-C Immigration.

27. Eliot to F. A. Rupp, M.D., June 4, 1924, CWE, box 390, folder Interesting; Eliot to John W. Burgess, May 9, 1921, CWE, box 387, A-L.

28. Hugh Hawkins, *Between Harvard and America*, pp. 140-41, and "Removing the Welcome Mat: Changing Perceptions of the Immigrant," in Howard H. Quint and Milton Cantor, eds., *Men, Women, and Issues in American History*, 2: 91-92; and Eliot to *Home Journal*, November 21, 1892, CWEB #91, pp. 36a, 36b.

29. Eliot to B. G. Follansbee, February 6, 1906, Eliot to Richards M. Bradley, February 7, 1906, and Eliot to David A. Ellis, June 19, 1906, CWEB #95, pp. 133, 133½, 156½. Eliot wrote Ellis: "We need them whether they are Jews or Gentiles, Greeks or barbarians, literate or illiterate, skilled or unskilled, children or adults; and all restrictive or forbidding legislation is, in my opinion, foolish and ungenerous." In 1906, Eliot was a member of the Immigration Department of the National Civic Federation (Solomon, *Ancestors and Immigrants*, p. 188).

30. Eliot to Edward Lauterbach, January 10, 1911, CWE, special box #413, National Liberal Immigration League 1910-1913; Eliot to E. S. Richards, December 29, 1905, CWEB #95, p. 125½, on the patriotism of the immigrant. Eliot to William T. Forbes, April 10, 1900, CWEB #92, p. 57a, for his earlier view of assimilation. On Italians, see Ernesto G. Fabbri, president of the Society for Italian Immigrants, to Eliot, January 11, 1907, and Eliot's January 15 reply, CWE, box 247, Society for Italian Immigrants; Eliot to Vittorio Orlandini, May 17, 1922, box 388, M-Z; Mrs. Jessie L. Gardner to Eliot, December 18, 1924, and Eliot's December 23, reply, CWE, box 390, D-J. For Eliot's later view, denying the existence of the melting pot, see letter to F. H. Newell, November 3, 1924, CWE, box 391, A-O. Eliot felt that the main reason that different immigrant groups remained separate was "racial," not religious: The Irish did not mingle with the Italians, even though they shared the same religion.

31. Eliot to Henry R. Gall, February 14, 1921, outlined his views on necessary regulations on immigration and called for the abolition of the literacy test (CWE, box 387, A-L); Madison Grant to Eliot, December 29, 1924, and Eliot's reply, January 2, 1925, CWE, box 390, D-J.

32. R. M. Bradley to Lowell, March 18, 1924, ALL, #592-C Immigration. For a reprint of Lowell's leter to Hon. Bird J. Vincent, May 1, 1928, urging passage of Senate Bill 2450, which would allow foreign teachers employed by Harvard and other institutions to enter the United States, see "Immigration of College Professors, Hearings Before a Sub-committee on Immigration and Naturalization," U.S. Congress, House of Representatives, 70th Cong., 1st sess., on S. 2450 and H.R. 9284, May 9, 1928, Hear-

ing no. 70.1.7 (Washington, D.C.: Government Printing Office, 1928), pp. 13, 22. There were 25 alien teachers on Harvard's faculty of 751. The Senate passed S. 2450, as amended (Congressional Record, February 23, 1928, vol. 69, no. 55, p. 3540).

33. Harvard was among the eighty-five higher educational institutions that provided data to the United States Immigration Commission on 32,882 students enrolled in the fall of 1908 in these departments or schools: academic, engineering and technological, medicine, law, postgraduate, pharmacy, theology, dentistry, and veterinary. Students were asked to complete at registration the special educational inquiry blanks sent by the Immigration Commission: name, sex, age at last birthday, country of birth, years in the United States, year in course of study, and father and mother's country of birth and race. After tabulating the information gathered on public and parochial schoolchildren and public kindergarten and elementary schoolteachers as well as on students in higher education, the commission published its findings: U.S. Congress, Senate, Reports of the Immigration Commission, *Children of Immigrants in Schools.* See especially vol. 1, Introductory, and pt. 5, pp. 154-64, 168-77; vol. 5, pp. 707-13 and, for tables on Harvard, 725, 744, 762, 781, 793, 811, 817, 827, 834, 842, 850, 854, 860, 863. See also Timothy L. Smith, "Immigrant Social Aspirations and American Education, 1880-1930," *American Quarterly* 21 no. 3 (1969), pp. 523-43.

34. Solomon, *Ancestors and Immigrants*, pp. 98-99. In 1894, one Scott F. Hershey, Ph.D., alleged, in an unidentified magazine clipping entitled "Papal Harvard," that the university had become "a papal training ground" because Overseer Charles J. Bonaparte had lectured on the "Catholic Church in the United States" in Sanders's Hall (CWE, box 135, folder 1080 Roman Catholic Church).

35. *Is East Cambridge a 'Whitechapel' Town?* February 14, 1903, issued by the clergy of the Sacred Heart Church, East Cambridge, and published by the *Sacred Heart Review*, CWE, box 135, folder 1080 Roman Catholic Church. The Harvard senior was Phillip Endicott Osgood '03.

36. Solomon, *Ancestors and Immigrants*, pp. 112-18, 153-55. Eliot to Hon. James M. Curley, July 30, 1923, and Eliot to Godfrey L. Cabot, September 5, 1923, CWE, box 389, A-L; Eliot to Viscount [James] Bryce, January 7, 1922, CWE, box 388 A-L; Robert Walcott to Eliot, August 9, 1923, and Eliot to Walcott, August 14, 1923, CWE, box 389, M-Z. During Eliot's active years in Democratic politics, "he developed a hearty respect for the first two Irish mayors of Boston, Hugh O'Brien and Patrick Collins" (Hawkins, *Between Harvard and America*, pp. 139-43, 184).

37. Eliot to L. A. Stout, April 10, 1891, CWEB #91, pp. 16a, 17, 18; Eliot to Grace W. Minns, August 31, 1903, and Eliot to Miss McConkey, July 23, 1903, CWEB #95, pp. 19½, 15. See also Eliot to Mrs. William Tilton, February 7, 1921, CWE, box 387, M-Z; Eliot to Jerome D. Greene, April 14, 1925, JDG, box 6 Harvard: Material on Charles W. Eliot, folder 1925; and Hawkins, *Between Harvard and America*, pp. 184-85. Eliot favored instruction in religious and church history in public schools under the supervision of the three major faiths and the school committee (December 2, 1893, CWEB #91, pp. 48a, 49, 49a, and CWE, box 114, folder 193 Gilman, D. C.).

38. Hawkins, *Between Harvard and America*, pp. 186-89. J. Havens Richards to Eliot, July 16 and September 21, 1893, CWE, box 137, folder 1224 Georgetown College. Eliot wrote Rabbi Charles Fleischer that Harvard made a limited "but an imperfect provision" for Roman Catholic students by renting seats in the Holyoke Street

Roman Catholic Church; Catholic students did not share in university-sponsored religious services (November 14, 1901, CWEB #92, p. 134a). See sketch on James Jeffrey
Roche, editor of the *Pilot* during Eliot's controversy with the Reverend Richards, in
Arthur Mann, *Yankee Reformers in the Urban Age*, chap. 2, "Irish Catholic Liberalism: The Spirit of 1848."

39. Eliot to Rt. Rev. Monsignor Thomas J. Conaty, October 24, 1898, Eliot to Rev.
W. G. Read Mullan, S.J., December 8, 1899, and February 6, 1900, and Eliot to James
Higgins, January 13, 1900, CWEB #92, pp. 11a, 55, 53a, 49a. See also James Higgins to
Eliot, January 12 and 15, 1900, CWE, box 135, folder 1080 Roman Catholic Church.

40. Charles W. Eliot, "Recent Changes in Secondary Education," *Atlantic Monthly* 84 (October 1899): 443; Rev. Timothy Brosnahan, S.J., "President Eliot and Jesuit
Colleges: A Defence," *Sacred Heart Review* (January 13, 1900), pp. 24-25; Bliss Perry
to Eliot, January 17, 1900, CWE, box 128, folder 608 Perry, Bliss; Rev. John O'Brien
to Eliot, February 12, 1900, CWE, box 135, folder 1080 Roman Catholic Church;
Eliot to Rev. John O'Brien, February 14, 1900, CWEB #92, p. 54.

41. Eliot to Rev. W. G. Read Mullan, S.J., June 2, 1900, CWEB #92, p. 69a; Eliot
to Walter B. Cannon, February 26, 1908, CWEB #97, p. 93; and Eliot to John Duff,
February 8, 1907, CWEB #96, p. 40½. (The Catholic Club, for which the bishop had
appointed a spiritual adviser, then had over 350 members). See Veysey, *The Emergence of the American University*, p. 281, n. 55, for the 1881 poll of religious affiliations among 972 Harvard undergraduates and law school students. Episcopalians—
275 strong—were the largest Protestant denomination at a university that had been a
bulwark of Unitarianism earlier in the century. There were 214 Unitarians; 173 Congregationalists; 42 Baptists; 33 Roman Catholics (about 3.4 percent of the total); 27
Presbyterians; 20 Swedenborgians; 18 Universalists; 16 Methodists; 10 Jews; 2 each
of Christians, Quakers, and Dutch Reformed; 1 each of Lutheran and "Chinese"; 97
were "non-sectarian"; and 6 did not indicate affiliation. Only 26 declared themselves
"committed agnostics"; 7 were atheists.

42. Eliot to Jerome D. Greene, April 5, 1920, JDG, box 6, folder 1920; quinquennial file on Bonaparte, Charles Joseph, 1871, HUA; Bonaparte to Eliot, November 2
and 9, 1903, CWE, box 203, folder on Bonaparte; Hawkins, *Between Harvard and
America*, pp. 185-86.

43. A. Lawrence Lowell, "Irish Agitation in America," *Forum* 4 (December 1887):
397-407; Yeomans, *Lowell*, p. 214. Twelve years later, Lowell argued that "the theory
of universal political equality does not apply to tribal Indians, to Chinese, or to negroes under all conditions, [but] only to our own race, and to those people whom we
can assimilate rapidly" ("The Colonial Expansion of the United States," *Atlantic
Monthly* 83 [February 1899]: 152, 145-54).

44. Lowell to J. P. Morgan, March 3, 1920; Lowell to James Byrne, February 13,
1920, and Morgan to Lowell, March 2 and 4, 1920, ALL, #448 Byrne, James. "The fact
that you are Catholic by religion," Lowell wrote Byrne, was "a very distinct advantage"; and given Massachusetts's population, it was "eminently proper that we
should have a broad-minded Catholic like yourself on the Corporation." James Byrne
was confirmed and served as a fellow (1920-26), in spite of both Morgan's insistence
that the fellows consult the most important overseers before choosing a successor to
Henry Lee Higginson and his opposition to making the governing boards as cosmopolitan as the student body.

45. Yeomans, *Lowell*, p. 215.

46. As Table 2.1 indicates, most—78.9 percent—of the Jewish academic students were under twenty-one years of age, proportionately slightly younger than their Gentile classmates.

47. Eliot to Rabbi Charles Fleischer, November 14, 1901, CWEB #92, p. 134a. See also Mann, *Yankee Reformers in the Urban Age*, chap. 3, "Judaism: Premature Radicalism Aborted," for the work of Rabbi Solomon Schindler at Temple Adath Israel and a brief reference to his successor, Rabbi Charles Fleischer.

48. Morison, *Three Centuries of Harvard*, p. 203. Weiss became a Transcendentalist.

49. Eliot to George A. Bartlett, July 22, 1901, CWEB #92, p. 123. Lowell to E. D. Brandegee, October 7, 1915, with enclosures, and Brandegee to Lowell, October 14 and 25, 1915, ALL, #70a Freshman Halls. The "Jewish" student in question left college before graduating; he entered the infantry and died as a result of wounds in France in September 1918.

50. Lowell to Rabbi Harry Levi, September 9 and 14, 1915, Lowell to Russell Gray, September 17, 1915, Rabbi Levi to Lowell, September 11 and 23, 1915, Dr. K. Kohler, president of Hebrew Union College, to Lowell, September 6, 1915, and clipping of editorial, "Harvard's Attitude Toward the Jews Is Unsuspected and Surprising," *Boston American*, September 15, 1915, ALL, #780 Jewish Holidays: Protests about examinations on. See Lowell to J. T. Ellison, June 3, 1922, in which he acknowledged the Jewish origins of Christianity (ALL, #1056 Jews).

51. Lowell to William Atkinson, September 17, 1915, and Lowell to Coleman Silbert, October 3, 1916, ALL, #780 Jewish Holidays. See also these two folders: ALL, #96 Jewish Holidays, 1930-33, and DHCCF, Jewish holidays & other questions, especially McGeorge Bundy to Judge Charles E. Wyzanski, Jr., copy, September 29, 1955.

52. Lowell to Stiles P. Jones, Marcy 7, 1916, and Lowell to Austen G. Fox, March 22, 1916, ALL, #950 Louis D. Brandeis.

53. See correspondence between Eliot and Jacob Schiff in CWE, box 245, folder Schiff, Jacob H.; Eliot to Schiff, December 15, 1899, CWEB #92, p. 46a; Eliot to Schiff, December 13, 1907, CWEB #97, p. 32½; and Hawkins, *Between Harvard and America*, p. 190.

54. Eliot to Isaac N. Seligman, June 14, 1908, and Seligman to Eliot, June 16, 1908, CWE, box 246, folder Seligman, Isaac N. Eliot to Hon. Charles R. Crane, March 10, 1921, CWE, box 387, A-L; and Eliot to Dr. Percy Stickney Grant, July 15, 1922, CWE, box 388, A-L. Eliot, "Forword," in Samuel Walker McCall, *Patriotism of the American Jew* (New York: Plymouth Press, 1924), pp. 12, 9-13.

55. Eliot in McCall, *Patriotism of the American Jew*, p. 13; Eliot to Dr. E. M. East, December 17, 1924, CWE, box 390, A-C; Eliot to Hon. Nathan Matthews, September 19, 1922, CWE, box 388, M-Z; Eliot to John J. Chapman, June 23, 1923, CWE, box 389, A-L; Eliot to Jesse Isidor Straus, March 2, 1923, CWE, box 389, M-Z. Solomon, *Ancestors and Immigrants*, pp. 17-19.

56. See above, n. 33, and Table 2.1; George F. La Piana to Lowell, March 31, 1920, ALL, #298 Americanization. See also *The Columbian* (published by the senior class of Columbia College) for the 1920s; *Harvard College Class Album, 1926* and its *Twenty-fifth Anniversary Report* (1951); and John De Raismes Storey, "The Italian in

America," disquisition, *Harvard College, Class of 1905, Secretary's First Report* (1905), pp. 241-44.

57. Paul Davis '40, law school student, "Fair Harvard," *Harvard Guardian*, May 1941, pp. 29-31, in "Negro Question Clippings (P. D. Davis) 1941, "HUA. As of 1940, some 160 blacks, a majority from the South, had entered the college and about 500 attended the graduate or professional schools: around 40 in the law school, 20 in the medical school, 25 in the divinity school, and most of the others in the Graduate School of Arts and Sciences. Thirteen Ph.D.'s and almost one hundred master's degrees were conferred on Negroes. Emory J. West '72, exhibit on "Black Students of Harvard 1847-1900," Widener Library, Spring 1971; and West's "Harvard and the Black man, 1636-1850: The first stages of struggle, "*Harvard Bulletin* 74, no. 4 (November 22, 1971), pp. 21-26; and his "Harvard's first Black graduates, 1865-1890," *Harvard Bulletin* 74, no. 10 (May 1972): 24-28.

58. Davis, "Fair Harvard," p. 29.

59. Ibid., pp. 29-30. Washington was elected an honorary Harvard Phi Beta Kappa in 1904.

60. Eliot to Bruce L. Keenan, August 9, 1907, CWEB #96, p. 128; Davis, "Fair Harvard," pp. 28, 31; and Paul Daniel Davis, "Harvard Students Blast Navy Jim-Crowism," and other articles in *Afro-American*, April 19, 1941, from "Negro Question Clippings," HUA. Lucien Alexis, Jr., whose father, Harvard '18, was a high school principal in New Orleans, prepared at Phillips Exeter Academy. In the early 1920s, Harvard refused to compete with the U.S. Naval Academy and the University of Virginia, because they requested that its two black athletes be withdrawn from field and track events (Howard T. Ball to Lowell, January 13, 1923, ALL, #42 Negroes).

61. DHCCF, #29 Freshman Halls Committee 1913-16, for December 2, 1913, faculty vote, and "Harvard Men Here Fight Ban Against Negro," *New York Sun*, June 16, 1922, clipping in ALL, #981 Freshman Dormitories.

62. See n.61; also Lowell to John B. Olmstead, January 20, 1923, ALL, #42 Negroes. For Bruce's career, see *Secretary's Reports* for the *Class of 1902*, especially *Twenty-Fifth Anniversary Report*, HUA. Bruce listed his occupation as a writer; and see below, n. 72.

63. Lowell to Roscoe Conkling Bruce, December 14, 1922, and January 6, 1923, Bruce to Lowell, January 4, 1923, and clippings from the Boston *Transcript*, January 11, 1923, and New York *World*, January 12, 1923, ALL, #42 Negroes.

64. Lowell to Jerome D. Greene, January 15, 1923, JDG, box 1 Harvard: Memorial Church Controversy—Presidents Lowell, Conant, and Pusey, folder Lowell, Lawrence; and Lowell to A. B. Hart, December 2, 1921, ALL, #981 Freshman Dormitories.

65. Lowell to Charles K. Bolton, January 16, 1923, and Lowell to Witter Bynner, March 29, 1923, ALL, #42 Negroes; and Lowell, *Conflicts of Principle*, chap. 6, "Race," pp. 62-63.

66. Lowell to James Ford Rhodes, January 16, 1923, quoted in Yeomans, *Lowell*, pp. 176-77; Rhodes to Lowell, copy, February 6, 1923, ALL, #42 Negroes.

67. Lowell to Edward S. Drown, January 9, 1923, and "Extract from 'Up From Slavery' by Booker T. Washington, Page 223," ALL, #42 Negroes; Lowell to Cleveland G. Allen, January 19, 1927, ALL, #641 Washington, Booker T.

68. Albert Bushnell Hart to Lowell, January 18, 1923, ALL, #42-A Negroes; and Hart to Lowell, November 29, 1921, ALL, #981 Freshman Dormitories.

69. Hart to Lowell, November 29, 1921, and Lowell to Hart, December 2, 1921, ALL, #981 Freshman Dormitories; and W. F. Low '07 to Lowell, January 16, 1923, ALL, #42-A Negroes.

70. Low to Lowell, January 16, 1923, ALL, #42-A. See also Eliot to Robert L. O'Brien, January 16, 1923, CWE, box 389, M-Z; Eliot to R. R. Moton, March 18, 1924, CWE, box 391, A-O; and Hawkins, *Between Harvard and America*, pp. 190-92. See also Booker T. Washington to Eliot, March 7 and October 20, 1906, CWE, box 255, folder Washington, Booker T.

71. Eliot to W. Monroe Trotter, May 5, 1909, CWEB #98, p. 155; and Eliot to Trotter, April 30, 1909, CWE, box 240, folder Race.

72. Eliot to Frederick G. Bromberg, June 14 and December 6, 1901, and Eliot to Rev. S. A. Steel, October 25, 1901, CWEB #92, pp. 116, 139a, 132; and *Harvard College, Class of 1858, Report Prepared for the Fortieth Anniversary of Its Graduation*, pp. 15-18. See also CWE, box 123, folder 407 Bromberg, Frederick G.; box 234, folder Negro Problem in the Southern States; and box 240, folder Race. Eliot recommended Bromberg for the district attorneyship of southern Alabama (Eliot to Hon. Philander C. Knox, January 7, 1904, CWE, box 204, folder 407 Bromberg). For Eliot's correspondence with and about Roscoe Conkling Bruce, see CWE, box 204, folder Bruce; Eliot to P. H. Hanus, March 19, 1921, CWE, box 387, A-L; Eliot to Bruce, March 7, 1922, CWE, box 388, A-L; and Eliot to Jerome D. Greene, January 13, 1923, JDG, box 6, folder 1922-23 the Jewish question—and Negro question. Eliot was disturbed to learn that Bruce was "driven out" of his post as assistant superintendent of public schools for Negroes in Washington, D.C. (1907-21), because it did "great injustice to Bruce" and "hurt the policy of separate schools for colored children." On a personal level, Eliot advised Bruce "to get the best education chance" for his son and that was "to fit him for Harvard College at Phillips Exeter Academy" (March 7, 1922, and see above, n. 62).

73. The Eliot family, many of whom were members of the Society for Propagating the Gospel among the Indians and Others in North America, was particularly concerned with improving the condition of Indian life. Eliot's son, the Reverend Samuel A. Eliot, was appointed by President William H. Taft to the United States Board of Indian Commissioners, on which he served from 1912 to 1934, first as member and later as chairman. See Eliot to Hon. Frederick W. Dallinger, July 18, 1922, CWE, box 388, A-L, and May 10, 1924, with Dallinger's reply of June 4, 1924, CWE, box 390, A-C; see also Lowell's letter of November 22, 1922, in ALL, #141 Indians.

74. The Lowell Institute, founded in 1836, brought over distinguished foreigners and sponsored evening lectures. In 1907-08, the institute began free evening collegiate courses taught by Harvard instructors, and in January 1910 the university joined with seven other Boston-area colleges and institutions in establishing the "Commission on Extension Courses," through whose programs adults, chiefly schoolteachers, could earn an associate in arts degree at Harvard, Radcliffe, Tufts, and Wellesley (*HPR, 1909-10*). Harvard's summer school program for teachers also expanded its clientele (Pierson, *Yale*, 1:239). In 1900, some 1,450 Cuban schoolteachers came to Harvard for the six-week summer session; 353 Puerto Rican schoolteachers were brought to Cambridge in the summer of 1904 (*HPR, 1900-01, 1903-04*; A. L. Pitcher, A.M.,

'Porto Ricans At School," Boston *Evening Transcript*, August 10, 1904, p. 14; and a half a dozen letters in CWE, box 238, folder Porto Rico). Harvard's first formal exchange with foreign universities—with Germany—began in 1905-06. Professorial exchanges with France evolved more slowly, but survived the outbreak of World War I. Due to the generosity of James Hazen Hyde, Harvard or one of the other American universities began sending in 1904-05 a professor to lecture a half-year at the University of Paris and a half-year at six of the provincial universities. A Frenchman, on the Cercle Français Foundation, delivered a course of six public lectures at Harvard. But because Harvard wanted the benefit of a full semester's instruction, it proposed to the French government in 1910-11 that professors be exchanged every two years. The same year, Harvard began a half-year annual exchange with four western colleges— Knox, Beloit, Grinnell, and Colorado—to which Carleton and Pomona were subsequently added (*HPR, 1904-06, 1910-11, 1912-16;* Jerome D. Greene, "The Interchange of Professors in Universities: The Experience of Harvard University," March 8, 1906, JDG, box 3 Harvard: Miscellaneous, folder Harvard [#1 of 2]; and CWE, box 212, folder Exchange Professorship).

75. Rudolf Tombo, Jr., "The Geographical Distribution of the Student Body at a Number of Universities and Colleges," *Science,* n.s. 30 (October 1, 1909): 427-35; and Tombo, "College Student Geography," Boston *Evening Transcript,* October 5, 1912, p. 3.

76. Benjamin Rand, "Canadian Students in Harvard University, 1889-1894," with letter to Dean [L. B. R.] Briggs, January 5, 1893 [1894], and Briggs to Dr. Justin Winsor, January 5, 1893 [1894], DHCCB, book I, 417; and *Harvard College Scrap Book Registration, Geographical Distribution,* HUA. See also Wu Ting fang, Chinese Legation, Washington, D.C., to Eliot, May 12, 1902, CWE, box 118, folder 293 Wu Ting fang.

77. John K. Fairbank, "East Asia and the University," *Harvard Today,* October 1973, pp. 8-10; and Paula Cronin, "East Asian Studies at Harvard—A Scholarly Bridge Between Two Worlds," *Harvard Today,* Spring 1976, pp. 7-9, 13; also George Marvin, "The American Spirit in Chinese Education," *Outlook* 90 (November 28, 1908): 667-72. In 1872 the first group of Chinese were sent to American educational institutions, but were later recalled before receiving their university degrees. In 1907-08, 155 Chinese were supported by either the imperial or one of the provincial governments, while about another 200 were educated at their family's expense at American schools, colleges, and universities.

78. Eliot to Baron Kentaro Kaneko, October 4, 1905, Eliot to Edwin D. Mead, February 7, 1906, and Eliot to Sir Chentung Liang Cheng, March 1, 1906, CWEB #95, pp. 96, 134, 137½; also CWE, box 223, folder Japanese; CWE, box 108, folder 122 Japan Admission Requirements; CWE, box 224, folder Kaneko, Baron Kentaro; and these *HTR: 1905-06,* pp. 40-42; *1906-07,* p. 24; *1908-09,* p. 33; and *1910-11,* p. 27.

79. C. D. Tenney to Jerome D. Greene, October 12, 1906, "Facts in Regard to Chinese Educational Mission," CWE, box 252, folder Tenney. Eliot to Tenney, January 30, 1907, CWEB #96, p. 28½; CWE, box 207, folder Chinese Students; C. N. Greenough to Lowell, June 15, 1923, DHCCF, #37 President Lowell 1922-27.

80. Jerome D. Greene to Committee on Admission, J. G. Hart, chairman, July 30, 1908, CWE, box 208, folder Committee on Admission; "Proposal Concerning the Admission of Japanese and Chinese Students," October 27, 1908, CWE, box 223,

folder Japanese; "Voted to recommend to the Faculty that Japanese candidates for ad- mission to Harvard College . . . ," CWE, box 212, folder Faculty of Arts and Sciences; Greene to Eliot, June 10, 1913, JDG, box 5, unmarked folder; and above n. 2.

81. Lowell to Rev. Anson Phelps Stokes, Jr., May 2, 1910, and Lowell to Nicholas Murray Butler, January 5, 1912, ALL, #229 Chinese Students; F. W. Hunnewell to Henry Yeomans, January 2, 1918, ALL, #1986 Chinese Students; and above nn. 25 and 43.

82. Albert Bushnell Hart to Lowell, May 11, 1922, with enclosures: Government 13b, People of the United States, classroom paper no. 1, "Personal Race and De- scent"; tabulation on "Family and Race History"; and forty-two student papers, ALL, #1056 Jews.

83. Ibid.

Chapter 3. Harvard: Debate on Restriction, 1922

1. *Records, Faculty of Arts and Sciences* 11 (1918): 236 (Office of the Secretary, Faculty of Arts and Sciences, Harvard University).

2. Eliot to Jesse Isidor Straus, December 21, 1922, CWE, box 388, M-Z; Lowell to Rufus S. Tucker, May 20, 1922, and H. Henneberger, Jr., to Henry Pennypacker, December 24, 1921, ALL, #1056 Jews; *HPR, 1918-19*, pp. 21-23; and *HPR, 1923-24*, pp. 28-29. See E. Digby Baltzell, *The Protestant Establishment*, pp. 7-10, for use of term *caste* or *WASP establishment*.

3. Author of letter unidentified, but referred to in Dean C. N. Greenough's Mem- orandum for President Lowell, February 17, 1920; also memorandum for Mr. Greenough, February 16, 1920, and Greenough to Lowell, April 6 and 28, 1922, all in DHCCF, #36 President Lowell, February 1919-1922; and Greenough to Assistant Dean K. B. Murdock, January 1922, DHCCF, #42 Mr. K. B. Murdock, 1919-1927.

4. Julian W. Mack to Lowell, March 27 and 30, 1922, and Lowell to Mack, March 29, 1922, ALL, # 1056 Jews. See Judge Mack's obituary in the *New York Times*, August 6, 1943, and his quinquennial file, HUA.

5. Mack to Lowell, March 30, 1922, and Lowell to Mack, March 31 and April 4, 1922, ALL, #1056 Jews; and Julian W. Mack to Eliot, copy, June 19, 1922, FF, box 191, folder 17, Sifting Committee, 1922-1924.

6. Memorandum from President Lowell, April 6, 1922, DHCCF, #36 President Lowell, February 1919-1922.

7. C. N. Greenough to Lowell, April 6, 1922, DHCCF; and Jerome D. Greene to Lowell, April 15, 1922, ALL, #1056 Jews.

8. Henry Pennypacker to Lowell, May 3, 1922, ALL, #1056 Jews.

9. Ibid.

10. Minutes of Meetings of the Faculty of Arts and Sciences [hereinafter cited as FAS], May 9, 1922, *Records* 11 (1918): 226; R and P 309, *FAS Reports and Papers* 11 (1918); and Eliot to Felix Frankfurter, July 28, 1922, FF, box 191, folder 19.

11. Meetings of the FAS, May 16, 1922, *Records* (1918): 228.

12. Ibid., p. 229; William Ernest Hocking to Felix Frankfurter, May 24, 1922, FF, box 191, folder 18.

13. In ALL, #1056 Jews, see Prof. Edward H. Warren, law school, to Lowell, with page of statistics, May 12, 1922; Elizabeth C. Putnam, medical school, to Lowell,

May 12, 1922; Students of Hebrew Nationality, from the Business School; Percentage of Jews in Various Departments of the University, 1921-22; Enrollment of Jewish Students; Students Under Discipline; Connections Severed; Connections Severed for Improper Conduct (two tables); Distribution of Students by Rank List Groups; Degrees with Distinction; and A. B. Hart to Lowell, May 27, 1922. See also eight pages on Enrollment of Jewish Students 1921-22 and other tables on discipline, rank list, degrees with distinction, FF, box 192, folder 2. Although 43 Jewish students, or 11.2 percent of the total, were under discipline as of April 1, 1922, none of these students ranked above Group IV, and 21 of them were in the bottom group, VII. Percentages were deceptive, however: According to the table on Connections Severed 1921-22, 100 percent of all students charged with offenses at the library were Jewish. Only one student, however, was involved.

14. William Ernest Hocking to Lowell, May 18, 1922, ALL. #1056 Jews; Hocking to Felix Frankfurter, July 17, 1922, FF, box 191, folder 19.

15. Lowell to Hocking, May 19, 1922, ALL, #1056 Jews.

16. Ibid.

17. Lowell to Rufus S. Tucker, May 20, 1922, ALL, #1056 Jews.

18. [William Ernest Hocking] to Jerome D. Greene, copy, May 29, 1922, FF, box 191, folder 17, and statistics, box 192, folder 2; Meetings of the FAS, May 23, 1922, *Records* 11 (1918): 230-31. See also Lowell to Hocking, June 1, 1922, ALL, #1056 Jews; and Eliot to Straus, December 21, 1922, CWE.

19. Meeting of the FAS, May 23, 1922, pp. 231-32.

20. Ibid., p. 232; Hocking to Frankfurter, May 24 and June 8, 1922, and Edmund E. Day to Felix Frankfurter, June 13, 1922, FF, box 191, folder 18; and [Hocking] to Greene, May 29, 1922, FF.

21. Meeting of the FAS, May 23, 1922, p. 232; Hocking to Frankfurter, May 24, 1922, and [Hocking] to Greene, May 29, 1922, FF.

22. Meeting of the FAS, May 23, 1922, pp. 232-33; Hocking to Frankfurter, May 24, 1922, FF.

23. Meeting of the FAS, May 23, 1922, pp. 233-34; Hocking to Frankfurter, May 24, 1922, and [Hocking] to Greene, May 29, 1922, FF.

24. Four petitions dated May 28 and 29, 1922, signed by various members of the faculty, requesting President Lowell to call a special meeting of the faculty to reconsider the votes of May 23, ALL, #1056 Jews.

25. L. B. R. Briggs to Lowell, May 29, 1922, Briggs to F. W. C. Lieder, May 31, 1922, and Briggs to Julian W. Mack, June 2, 1922, DFASCB, letters from April 3, 1922, to July 26, 1923, pp. 146-47, 150, 153-54.

26. Harry Austryn Wolfson, "Remarks on proposed changes in admission policy in Harvard University," May or June 1922 (Estate of David Gordon Lyon, Jr.), HUA.

27. Prof. Harry A. Wolfson, interviews, Widener Library, Harvard University, July 30 and 31, 1973.

28. Lowell to Hocking, June 1, 1922, ALL; Briggs to Mack, June 2, 1922, DFASCB.

29. William Ernest Hocking to Lowell, May 30, 1922, ALL, #1056 Jews; Hocking to Frankfurter, July 17, 1922, and Ralph Barton Perry as quoted by Hocking to Frankfurter, FF.

30. Lowell to Hocking, June 1, 1922, ALL; Lowell to George F. Moore, October 3, 1922, ALL, #8 Jews; Eliot to Straus, December 21, 1922, CWE. Many overseers so dis-

agreed with Lowell's conclusions about increasing Jewish enrollment that they influenced faculty members to call for a special meeting in which to rescind their controversial votes.

31. Special Meeting of the FAS, June 2, 1922, *Records* 11 (1918): 235-36.

32. Ibid., p. 235; Paul J. Sachs to G. W. Cram, May 31, 1922, R and P 311, *FAS Reports and Papers* 11 (1918); and Lowell to Sachs, June 3, 1922, ALL, #1056 Jews. McDougall, author of *Is America Safe for Democracy?* (1921), signed the petition, but voted for the restrictive measures of May 23 and June 2, 1922.

33. Special Meeting of the FAS, June 2, 1922, pp. 235-36; Hocking to Frankfurter, July 17, 1922, FF. The following were among those voting against Henderson's motion: Professors Briggs, Wiener, G. G. Wilson, Hurlbut, McIlwain, Lyon, Greenough, Sachs, Hocking, Holmes, Day, Langfeld, Holcombe, Graustein, and Wolfson and Messrs. Cram, Merk, Phoutrides, Tucker, and Hanford. Among those voting for the motion were Professors Hart, Kittredge, Bullock, Cabot, Ropes, Ward, Carver, McDougall, J. L. Coolidge, Merriman, Henderson, Birkhoff, and Conant and Mr. Pennypacker.

34. Special Meeting of the FAS, June 2, 1922, pp. 236-37; dictated statement from Lowell to George W. Cram on June 3, 1922, to be incorporated in the minutes of the special meeting of June 2, 1922, R and P 312, *FAS Reports and Papers* 11 (1918); Day to Frankfurter, June 13, 1922, FF.

35. Lowell to George L. Kittredge, June 3, 1922, ALL, #1056 Jews.

36. Record of a Meeting of the Board of Overseers of Harvard College in Cambridge, Winthrop H. Wade, secretary, June 5, 1922, ALL, #184 Limitation of Numbers; Meeting of the FAS, June 6, 1922, *Records* 11 (1918): 238.

37. "Report of The Committee Appointed 'To Consider And Report To The Governing Boards Principles And Methods For More Effective Sifting Of Candidates For Admission To The University,'" April 11, 1923, pp. 1, 6, ALL, #387 Admission to Harvard College: Report of Committee on Methods of Sifting Candidates; and see ALL, #1056 Jews.

38. Jerome D. Greene to Eliot, June 10, 1922, CWE; Eliot to Greene, January 13, 1923, JDG, box 6, folder 1922-23 the Jewish question—and Negro question. See also Eliot to Felix Frankfurter, July 6, 1922, FF, box 191, folder 18; and Le Baron Russell Briggs to T. F. Taylor, July 17, 1922, DFASCB, p. 236. Briggs felt that the "Jew question . . . has been somewhat mismanaged, though the management is on the right track now in forming a committee with some Jews in it." He considered Paul Sachs to be an excellent choice.

39. Eliot to Jerome D. Greene, June 7, 1922, JDG, box 6, folder 1922-23 the Jewish question—and Negro question; Greene to Lowell, June 10, 1922, DHCCF, #16 Subcommittee on Sifting of Candidates for Admission, 1922-23; Julian W. Mack to Lowell, June 6 and 9, 1922, ALL, #1056 Jews.

40. Julian W. Mack to Lowell, copy, June 13, 1922, FF, box 191, folder 18; Mack to Eliot, copy, June 19, 1922, and Mack to Samuel Williston, copy, June 13, 1922, FF, box 191, folder 17.

41. Mack to Lowell, June 6, 1922, and telegram to Lowell, June 15, 1922, ALL, #1056 Jews. In FF, box 191, see Mack to Eliot, copy, June 19, 1922, Eliot to Mack, copy, June 16, 1922, and Mack to Louis E. Kirstein, copy, June 27, 1922, folder 17; Mack to H. A. Wolfson, copy, June 15, 1922, and Joseph M. Proskauer, copy, "A

Letter on the Harvard Question," folder 18; Julian [W. Mack] to Frankfurter, October 26, 1922, Richard A. Feiss to Frankfurter, December 8, 1922, and *"Extract of Letter—Sachs to Rosenwald—August 25, 1922,"* folder 19. CWE wrote Mack (June 16, 1922) that he might be "agreeably disappointed in Sachs' work on the committee," because the latter was "keenly interested in the subject, and is a hard and persistent worker on any matter which really interests him." See also Morton Rosenstock, *Louis Marshall: Defender of Jewish Rights*, pp. 251-52; and Harry Barnard, *The Forging of an American Jew: The Life and Times of Judge Julian W. Mack*, p. 299.

42. Lowell to Julian W. Mack, June 7 and 14, 1922, Mack to Lowell, June 9 and 13, 1922, and telegram from Mack to Lowell, June 15, 1922, ALL, #1056 Jews; and Ernest Hocking to Frankfurter, June 8, 1922, with draft of letter to [Lawrence J.] Henderson, June 7, 1922, FF, box 191, folder 18.

43. Felix Frankfurter to Lowell, copy, June 19, [1922], Lowell to Frankfurter, copies, June 20 and 24, 1922, and Frankfurter to Lowell, copies, June 21 and June 29, 1922, FF, box 191, folder 17.

44. Eliot to Jerome D. Greene, June 7, 1922, JDG; and Mack to Eliot, June 19, 1922, FF, box 191, folder 17.

45. Eliot to Greene, June 7, 1922, JDG.

46. Arthur S. Pier '95 to Eliot, June 5, 1922, and Eliot to Pier, July 6 and 11, 1922, CWE, box 388, M-Z; Langdon P. Marvin to Eliot, June 4, 1923, CWE, box 389, M-Z; and "Harvard to Keep Faith, Says Eliot," *Boston Post*, June 17, 1922, pp. 1-2. See also Rosenstock, *Louis Marshall*, pp. 246-50.

47. "Jewish Ban Is Opposed at Harvard," *Boston Post*, May 31, 1922, pp. 1, 11; and "Clippings on the Race Question, 1922," HUA; Prof. Harry A. Wolfson, interviews, July 30 and 31, 1973.

48. Harry Starr, "The Affair at Harvard: What the Students Did," *Menorah Journal* 8 (October 1922): 271-73. See also *New York Tribune*, June 2, 1922, and *Boston American*, June 3, 1922, in "Clippings on the Race Question, 1922." Both Dr. Richard C. Cabot and Prof. Roger B. Merriman voted affirmatively on the two restrictive measures of May 23 and June 2, 1922, but Lowell advised Cabot not to write an article for the *Alumni Bulletin* suggesting that Harvard follow national percentages in admitting those of immigrant stock. It would stir additional controversy at a time when they were already at work on a plan "for restricting the percentage of immigrant Jews in the College" (Cabot to Lowell, March 11, 1922, and Lowell to Cabot, March 14, 1922, ALL, #1056 Jews).

49. Starr, "The Affair at Harvard," pp. 273-75.

50. Ibid., pp. 263-66; *Boston Post*, May 31, 1922, p. 11.

51. Starr, "The Affair at Harvard," pp. 266-67.

52. Ibid., pp. 267-70, 276.

53. William T. Ham, "Harvard Student Opinion on the Jewish Question," *Nation* 115 (September 6, 1922): 225-26. President Lowell reinforced undergraduate anti-Semitism. According to Victor Kramer '18, Lowell told him, during a Christmas Eve train ride to New York, that the Jews must totally assimilate, that he planned to limit the proportion of Jewish students at Harvard to 15 percent, and that irrespective of their individual merits, "too many Jews at Harvard were to be feared." It was surprising that this conversation took place since Lowell did not, as a rule, give interviews. Although he said that Kramer "grossly misrepresented his views," Lowell made simi-

lar statements in his letters (*Boston Herald*, January 16, 1923, "Clippings on the Race Question, 1922"; Prof. Wolfson, interviews, July 30 and 31, 1973).

54. Ham, "Harvard Student Opinion on the Jewish Question," pp. 226-27.

55. Boston *Telegram*, June 5 and 6, 1922.

56. *New York Herald*, June 18, 1922, "Clippings on the Race Question, 1922"; "Bunker Hill K.C. Banquet," *Boston Post*, June 17, 1922, p. 11.

57. For George Pearl Webster's order, see *Journal of the House*, Tuesday, June 13, 1922, p. 1199, and for the General Court of Massachusetts's expression of disapproval of racial discrimination in admissions, see *Journal of the Senate*, Tuesday, June 13, 1922, p. 947; also Representative Coleman Silbert to Felix Frankfurter, June 13, 1922, FF, box 191, folder 18. Boston *Telegram*, June 2, 1922; Boston *Traveler*, June 2, 1922; *New York Herald*, June 3, 1922; *New York Times*, June 4, 1922, "Clippings on the Race Question, 1922." Samuel Gompers sent Lowell a copy of a resolution presented to the American Federation of Labor's convention in Cincinnati, June 12-24, 1922. Lowell promised to send him a copy of the investigating committee's report when issued (Gompers to Lowell, July 26, 1922, and January 15, 1923, and Lowell to Gompers, August 8, 1922, and January 19, 1923, ALL, #8 Jews).

58. *New York Herald*, June 18, 1922, and unidentified clipping dated June 19, 1922, from "Clippings on the Race Question, 1922"; "Harvard President Explains University's Position," *American Hebrew*, June 23, 1922, p. 162. For statements by other prominent Jews, see Joseph M. Proskauer, *A Letter on the Harvard Question*, and copies of the correspondence between Albert I. Stix '94 of St. Louis, Missouri, and President Lowell: Stix to Lowell, June 6 and 19 and July 3 and 17, 1922, and Lowell to Stix, June 9 and 23 and July 7 and 24, 1922, FF, box 191, folder 18.

59. *Extract of Letter—Sachs to Rosenwald—August 25, 1922* and *Extract of Letter—Rosenwald to Sachs—August 30, 1922*, FF, box 191, folder 19.

60. Jesse Isidor Straus to Eliot, December 18, [1922], CWE, box 388, M-Z.

61. Jesse Isidor Straus to Eliot, February 28, 1923, and Eliot to Straus, March 2, 1923, CWE, box 389, M-Z.

62. "Adler Suggests Limit on Alien Students in Colleges of U.S.," *Boston Herald*, December 4, 1922.

63. Letter to Lowell, June 5, 1922, ALL, #1056 Jews. See also letters to Lowell, January 16, 1923, and January 13, 1925, and Lowell's reply, January 14, 1925, ALL, #8 Jews.

64. Emmet Russell, Nan Kai College, Tientsin, China, to Lowell, August 15, 1922, "Harvard Faces Problem of Cutting Down Number of Students Attending by Refusing Admission to Jews," *North China Star*, August 15, 1922, p. 6, and Lowell to Russell, December 18, 1922, ALL, #8 Jews. See also Russell to law school professor [Francis B.] Sayre, November 19, 1922, FF, box 191, folder 19.

65. "Racial groups at Harvard," subject of column "From a Graduate's Window," *HGM* (September 1922), pp. 64-66; also pp. 71-72.

66. Robert C. Benchley "To the President and Fellows of Harvard College," September 25, 1922, the "memorial," and "Alumni Signing the Inclosed Memorial," ALL, #42 Negroes; Benchley to Lowell, June 15, 1922, and "Harvard Men Here Fight Ban Against Negro," *New York Sun*, June 16, 1922, clipping, ALL, #981 Freshman Dormitories.

67. See n. 66.

68. Lowell to each member of the committee of seven, October 10, 1922, the reply

of several members, and Lowell to Witter Bynner, March 29, 1923, ALL, #42 Negroes. See also Albert Bushnell Hart to Lowell, January 18, 1923, ALL, #42-A Negroes; and Nell Painter, "Jim Crow at Harvard: 1923," *New England Quarterly* 44, no. 4 (1971), p. 627-28. Judge Julian W. Mack felt that the Roscoe Conkling Bruce-President Lowell correspondence seemed "to have redounded only to Harvard's good: it has stirred up the old Harvard spirit to many sections: so far as I have seen most of the expressions have been against Mr. Lowell's position" (Mack to Eliot, January 31, 1923, box 389, folder Interesting.

69. A. B. Hart to Lowell, January 19, 1923, ALL, #42-A Negroes; Lowell to M. E. T. Brown, December 18, 1925, ALL, #184 Limitation of Numbers.

70. Letters to Lowell, December 17 and 21, 1925, ALL, #184 Limitation of Numbers.

71. Rev. George W. Lay to Lowell, January 17, 1923, ALL, #42 Negroes; W. Banks Meacham to Lowell, February 2, 1923, and Andrew R. Sherriff to Lowell, January 23, 1923, ALL, #42-A Negroes.

72. George Foster Peabody to Lowell, January 13, 1923, and James C. Manry to Lowell, March 18, 1923, ALL, #42 Negroes; and Manry to Lowell, January 25, 1923, ALL, #42-A Negroes. See also Manry's letter to the editor of *HAB* 25, no. 20 (February 15, 1923), pp. 595-96.

73. Hamilton Fish, Jr., to Lowell, January 15, 1923, and Edward S. Drown to Lowell, January 18, 1923, ALL, #42-A Negroes. For text of Representative Fish's letter, see Robert Choate, "Calls Negro Policy 'Jim Crow Method,'" *Boston Herald*, January 16, 1923, in "Clippings on the Race Question, 1922"; Drown's letter was published in *HAB* 25, no. 18 (February 1, 1923), p. 529.

74. Louis T. Wright to Lowell, January 21, 1923, ALL, #42-A Negroes.

75. George L. Paine '96 to the editor of *HAB* 25, no. 20 (February 15, 1923), pp. 590-92.

76. Ibid., pp. 590-91; "Commencement, Thursday, June 22, 1922," *HGM* (September 1922), p. 27. On the recommendation of Judge Julian W. Mack, Julius Rosenwald supported Mordecai W. Johnson in his doctoral studies (Barnard, *The Forging of an American Jew*, p. 300).

77. "The Color Line," subject of column "From a Graduate's Window," *HGM* (March 1923), p. 372; "The Colored Student and the Freshman Dormitories," *HAB* 25, no. 17 (January 25, 1923), pp. 469-70. See also alumni letters to the editor of *HAB* for January 18 and 25, February 1, 8, 15, and 22, and March 1, 8, and 15, 1923 vol. 25, nos. 16-24. See *HAB* (February 15, 1923), pp. 589-90, for Richards M. Bradley's letter generally supporting Lowell's position. Although Bradley felt Negroes could be allowed in "one of the Freshman Dormitories, while refraining in other dormitories from forcing such association upon students who do not wish it," he agreed with Lowell's position of "refusing to ignore the race question."

Chapter 4. Harvard: Methods of Sifting Candidates for Admission, 1920s to 1950s

1. Letter from the Committee on Methods of Sifting Candidates for Admission to Lowell, April 7, 1923, ALL, #387 Admission to Harvard College: Report of Committee on Methods of Sifting Candidates, HUA.

2. See chap. 3, nn. 26 and 30.

3. "Minutes of the Committee Appointed by the President of the University to Consider and Report to the Governing Boards Principles and Methods for More Effective Sifting of Candidates for Admission to the University," June 1922 through March 1923, Meeting of June 21, 1922, HUA.

4. Ibid.; Prof. Harry A. Wolfson, interviews, Widener Library, Harvard University, July 30 and 31, 1973; and [Harry Wolfson] to [Henry W.] Holmes, copy, August 13, 1922, FF, box 191, folder 19.

5. See n. 4.

6. "Minutes of Committee to Consider and Report Methods," June 21, 1922, HUA; and DHCCF, #16 Sub-committee on Sifting of Candidates for Admission 1922-23.

7. Eliot to C. H. Grandgent, copy, August 1, 1922, FF, box 191, folder 17; Eliot to Grandgent, November 10, 1922, CWE, box 388, A-L; see also Eliot to Jerome D. Greene, July 15 and 21, 1922, and Greene to Eliot, July 18, 1922, JDG, box 6, folder 1922-23 the Jewish question—and Negro question, for a discussion of sifting methods at Antioch College.

8. Eliot to C. H. Grandgent, November 10, 1922, CWE.

9. Eliot to C. H. Grandgent, February 1, 1923, CWE, box 389, A-L; Eliot to Hon. Julian W. Mack, February 3, 1923, CWE, box 389, folder Interesting.

10. Eliot to C. H. Grandgent, February 19 and March 6 and 19, 1923, and Grandgent to Eliot, March 5 and 7, 1923, CWE, box 389, A-L; "Minutes of Committee to Consider and Report Methods," March 22, 1923, HUA.

11. Julian W. Mack to Dr. Milton J. Rosenau, copy, January 18, 1923, FF, box 192, folder 1; Rosenau to Mack, January 17, 1923, FF, box 191, folder 19; Rosenau to Felix Frankfurter, January 25, 1923, with copy of "certain proposals," and Rosenau to Eliot, copy, February 6, 1923, FF, box 192, folder 2. See also Eliot to Jerome D. Greene, January 13, 1923, JDG, box 6, folder the Jewish question; Eliot to Julian W. Mack, February 3, 1923, CWE, box 389, folder Interesting; Eliot to Milton J. Rosenau, January 24, February 1, and March 15, 1923, and Rosenau to Eliot, January 25, 1923, with "memorandum of proposals," CWE, box 389, M-Z.

12. Milton J. Rosenau to C. H. Grandgent, copies, January 23, February 2, 17, and 20, and March 1, 1923, FF, box 192, folder 2; Julian W. Mack to Louis E. Kirstein, copy, June 27, 1922, FF, box 191, folder 17; J[ulian W. Mack] to Felix Frankfurter, October 26, 1922, FF, box 191, folder 19; Eliot to Jerome D. Greene, January 13, 1923, JDG; and Rosenau to Eliot, March 14, 1923, CWE, box 389, M-Z.

13. In FF, see *"Memorandum of Meeting with Professor Henderson and Professor Sachs, August 23, 1922, from three to six P.M.,"* copy initialed "JWM," C. N. Greenough to Mack, copies, October 27 and November 15, 1922, box 191, folder 19; J[ulian W. Mack] to Frankfurter, February 6, 1923, box 192, folder 2; and Mack to Eliot, copy, September 2, 1922, box 191, folder 17. In December 1922 and January 1923, Richard A. Feiss, '01 and LL.B. '03, a Cleveland clothing manufacturer, wrote several prominent Harvard men, urging open-mindedness: Professors Roger I. Lee and Wallace B. Donham on the committee on methods; Chicago attorney Mitchell D. Follansbee '92; John W. Hallowell '01, a former overseer and an officer (later president) of the Associated Harvard Clubs; and Overseer Samuel S. Drury '01, headmaster of St. Paul's School. Feiss's letters to Follansbee and Hallowell were drafted with the assistance of Felix Frankfurter (FF, box 191, folder 19, and box 192, folder 2).

14. Julian W. Mack to Felix Frankfurter, October 26, 1922, FF, box 191, folder 19; see Walter Lippmann handwritten draft of a 19-page letter to Lawrence J. Henderson, October 27 [1922], Walter Lippmann Papers, box 13, folder 531; and Felix Frankfurter's letters to Lippmann, May 25, Saturday [June 3], June 5, and June 8 [1922], box 10, folder 423, Lippmann Papers, YUL.

15. Jerome D. Greene to Eliot, with copy of January 12, 1923, letter to Lowell, January 12, 1923, Greene to Eliot, January 24, 1923, and Eliot to Greene, January 13, 19, 22, and 25 and February 8 and 17, 1923, JDG, box 6, folder the Jewish question. See also Lowell to Greene, January 15, 1923, JDG, box 1, folder Lowell, Lawrence; Eliot to Julian W. Mack, April 14, 1923, CWE, box 389, folder Interesting; and Eliot to Felix Frankfurter, February 14, 1923, FF, box 192, folder 2. Like several other Harvardians, Eliot thought that the views of the nominees for the Board of Overseers and of the candidates for alumni association director should be known on "Jewish and negro exclusion."

16. C. H. Grandgent to the secretary of the Board of Overseers, October 3, 1922, presented at the October 9 meeting, ALL, #184 Limitation of Numbers; Jerome D. Greene to Eliot, February 9, 1923, JDG, box 6, folder the Jewish question. See also Eliot to Julian W. Mack, February 3 and March 26, 1923, and Mack to Eliot, January 28 and 31, February 6, and March 17, 1923, CWE, box 389, folder Interesting; Felix Frankfurter to Eliot, April 1 and 2 [1923], and Eliot to Frankfurter, April 5, 1923, CWE, box 389, A-L.

17. Copies of the *Corporation Records* and the "Book of Understanding," March 26, 1923, ALL, #42 Negroes; "Explanatory Statement," ALL, #42-A Negroes; *HPR, 1922-23*, p. 32.

18. June 29, 1923, letter in DHCCF, #5 Mr. R. E. Bacon 1923-34; A. C. Hanford to Addison Hibbard, May 31, 1939, DHCCF, folder Negroes; and F. W. Hunnewell to Wallace W. Atwood, July 12, 1926, ALL, #185 Negroes. Nell Painter, "Jim Crow at Harvard: 1923," *New England Quarterly* 44, no. 4 (1971), p. 634, n. 26, and pp. 627-33.

19. Letter from the Committee on Methods to Lowell, April 7, 1923, ALL.

20. Learned Hand, *The Spirit of Liberty: Papers and Addresses*, Collected, and with an introduction and notes by Irving Dilliard (New York: Knopf, 1952), pp. 20-23.

21. "Minutes of Committee to Consider and Report Methods," February 20, 1923, HUA. In HUA, letter from the Committee on Methods to Lowell, April 7, 1923, "Report of the Committee Appointed 'To Consider and Report to the Governing Boards Principles and Methods for More Effective Sifting of Candidates for Admission to the University," April 11, 1923, p. 4 (hereinafter cited as "Report of the Committee on Methods of Sifting Candidates"), and memorandum on "Possible 1924 situation if new rules administered strictly" from W. B. Donham and Roger Lee to Lowell, April 9, 1923, ALL, #387 Admission to Harvard; and "Report on Apparent Effect of Recommendations of Sifting Committee," April 18, 1923, DHCCF, #16 Sub-committee on Sifting.

22. Meeting of the Board of Overseers, and "Harvard News for Release," April 9, 1923, ALL, #387 Admission to Harvard.

23. Newspaper clippings, April 11-12 and 18-21, and May 11, 1923, scrapbook: "Comment Upon the Race Question 1923," HUA.

24. Dr. Louis I. Newman, "The Harvard Report: An Analysis," *Jewish Tribune*

and the Hebrew Standard, April 27, 1923, pp. 1-2, 21. Questions on "Race and Color," "Religious Preference," "What change, if any, has been made since birth in your own name or that of your father? (Explain fully)," "Maiden Name of Mother," and "Birthplace of Father" were added in the fall of 1922 to the Harvard College admission application (ALL, #8 Jews). The "Personal Record and Certificate of Honorable Dismissal" asked the high school principal or private school head to "indicate by a check [the applicant's] religious preference so far as known. . . . Protestant. . . . Roman Catholic. . . . Hebrew. . . . Unknown," DHCCF, #16 Sub-committee on Sifting. After Harry A. Wolfson wrote a letter to Chairman C. H. Grandgent protesting the inclusion of such questions on the admission blank, the committee agreed to suggest privately to admissions that this information should not play a role in its decisions, but might be asked subsequently of successful candidates ("Minutes of Committee to Consider and Report Methods," March 12, 1923, HUA).

25. "Statistical Report of the Statisticians to the Subcommittee Appointed to Collect Statistics: Dean Chester N. Greenough, Chairman, Dean Wallace B. Donham, Dean Henry W. Holmes" (hereinafter cited as "Statistical Report"), 100 pp., and a letter from the whole committee to Lowell, April 7, 1923, ALL, #387 Admission to Harvard.

26. See n. 25; and C. H. Grandgent to Eliot, November 11, 1922, CWE, box 388, A-L. Although data was gathered on students from the Orient and from eastern and southeastern Europe, their number was too small to be significant (A. J. Hettinger, Jr., to C. N. Greenough, December 21, 1922, DHCCF, #16 Sub-committee on Sifting).

27. "Statistical Report," ALL; C. N. Greenough to A. J. Hettinger, Jr., September 28 and December 22, 1922, Hettinger to Greenough, October 1 and December 21, 1922, and Greenough to Julian W. Mack, November 15, 1922, DHCCF, #16 Subcommittee on Sifting; "Minutes of Committee to Consider and Report Methods," November 13, 1922, HUA.

28. A. J. Hettinger, Jr., to C. N. Greenough, December 21, 1922, DHCCF; "Statistical Report," pp. 1-4, ALL. For "Racial Classification" form, see "Committee to Study Racial Distribution in the University, Report and Work Papers, Ca. 1922," HUA. Eleven questions were on scholarship, activities, loans, discipline, and others.

29. A. J. Hettinger, Jr., to C. N. Greenough, October 1, 1922, DHCCF; "Statistical Report," pp. 3-6, ALL. For the cost of the statistical research—at least $2,066—see correspondence in DHCCF, #16 Sub-committee on Sifting.

30. "Statistical Report," pp. 5-6, 38, ALL.

31. Ibid., pp. 20, 26, 77-81; "Total Undergrad. enrollment from South. Southern % Southern Jews," FF, box 192, folder 1.

32. "Statistical Report," pp. 28-37, ALL; Number of Jews Elected to PBK, 1906-20, FF, box 191, folder 19.

33. "Statistical Report," pp. 38-47, ALL.

34. Ibid., pp. 48-60.

35. Ibid., pp. 61-74.

36. Ibid., four unnumbered pp. on fields of concentration.

37. Ibid., pp. 88-95; *HPR, 1921-22*, with chart of occupations of graduates, pp. 15-20.

38. "Report of the Committee on Methods of Sifting Candidates," ALL.

39. Ibid.; Jerome D. Greene to L. B. R. Briggs, April 12, 1923, DHCCF, #16 Subcommittee on Sifting; Briggs to Greene, April 13, 1923, DFASCB, pp. 745-46; *HPR,*

1922-23, pp. 32-33. Eliot to Julian W. Mack, April 14, 1923, and Mack to Eliot, April 17, 1923, CWE, box 389, folder Interesting. For copies of faculty, corporation, and overseers' votes, see ALL, #387 Admission to Harvard and #184 Limitation of Numbers.

40. See n. 39; Meetings of the FAS, April 10 and 24 and May 1 and 8, 1923, *Records* 12 (1922), pp. 32-37, 39-40; *HPR, 1922-23*, pp. 32-33.

41. Lowell to Alexander Meiklejohn, May 2, 1923, Laurence McKinney to R. B. Merriman, April 23, 1923, and Lowell to Merriman, April 25, 1923, ALL, #42-A Negroes; Lowell to Cyrus Brewer, December 1, 1925, and Lowell to M. E. T. Brown, December 18, 1925, ALL, #184 Limitation of Numbers.

42. Vote of president and fellows, June 20, 1923, and Lowell's October 11, 1923, memorandum appointing the committee (four from the former committee of inquiry—Grandgent, Greenough, Lyman, and Pennypacker—and Clifford H. Moore, chairman; Frank W. Taussig, economics; George H. Parker, zoology; William B. Monro, municipal government; and James Bryant Conant, chemistry), ALL, #76 Admission, Committee on, September 1922-December 1923; Meeting of the FAS, October 2 and 9, 1923, *Records* 12 (1922): 67, 69. See also "Report of the Committee on the Limitation of Students" (adopted by FAS, December 18, 1923), ALL, #184 Limitation of Numbers; copies of votes of corporation and overseers, ALL, #184 and #76-A Admission, Committee on, January-February 1924.

43. See autobiographical sketch on Henry James, Jr., in *Harvard College, Class of 1899, Twenty-fifth Anniversary Report, 1899-1924*, pp. 357-59.

44. "Report to the Overseers from the Committee to Visit the College on the Proposal to Limit Numbers in the Freshman Class," prepared by Henry James, chairman, and others and accepted at the February 25, 1924, meeting of the Board of Overseers, ALL, #76-A Admission and #184 Limitation of Numbers. For a concise summary of these votes as well as a copy of the "Report on the Limitation of Students," see *HPR, 1923-24*, pp. 35-38. The other members of the overseers' special committee were Overseer Dr. William S. Thayer; Professors Moore and Greenough of Arts and Sciences; and Comfort A. Adams of the School of Engineering.

45. Lowell to Henry Pennypacker, March 24, 1924, ALL, #76-A Admission, January-February 1924; Edward R. Gay to Lowell, June 12, 1923, with two tables compiled June 9, 1923, ALL, #76 Admission, September 1922-December 1923; Dean's Office to Lowell, October 25 and November 9, 1925, and six tables dated either November 23 or 24, 1925, ALL, #184 Limitation of Numbers.

46. Eliot to Jerome D. Greene, February 12, 1924, JDG, box 6 Harvard: Material on Charles W. Eliot, folder 1924; Eliot to Langdon P. Marvin, December 26, 1923, Eliot to Dr. Henry P. Walcott, December 26, 1923, and Marvin to Eliot, June 4 and December 28, 1923, CWE, box 389, M-Z; Eliot to Langdon P. Marvin, January 8, 1924, and Eliot to M. J. Rosenau, January 25, 1924, FF, box 192, folder 2; Eliot to C. H. Grandgent, February 1, 1923, CWE, box 389, A-L. See also Eliot to Marvin, January 8 and February 16 and 20, 1924, Marvin to Eliot, February 18 and 21, 1924, and Julian W. Mack to Eliot, January 10, February 11, and December 31, 1924, CWE, box 391, A-O; Eliot to Felix Frankfurter, February 15, 1924, and Frankfurter to Eliot, November 15, 1924, enclosing two-page memorandum, CWE, box 390, D-J; M. J. Rosenau to Eliot, January 21, 1924, and Eliot to Rosenau, January 23, 1924, CWE, box 391, P-Z.

47. Lowell to Henry James, November 3 and 6, 1925, ALL, #184 Limitation of

Numbers; Lowell to James, February 18, 1924, and Lowell to Dr. E. H. Bradford, February 27, 1924, ALL, #76-A Admission; Lowell to Eliot, April 3, 1925, ALL, #387 Admission to Harvard.

48. Henry James to Lowell, November 4, 10, and 30, 1925, ALL, #184 Limitation of Numbers; and James to Lowell, October 31, 1925, DHCCF, #15 Committee on Limitation of Numbers 1923-26.

49. "Report of the Special Committee Appointed to Consider the Limitation of Numbers" [December 1925], pp. 18-19, ALL, #184 Limitation of Numbers.

50. Ibid., pp. 11-12, 22; DHCCF, #15 Committee on Limitation 1923-26.

51. For copies of overseers' votes, see DHCCF, #15 Committee on Limitation 1923-26, and ALL, #184 Limitation of Numbers; appendix to *HPR, 1925-26,* pp. 297-98, 299-304.

52. See n. 51; and Anne MacDonald to Radcliffe Heermance, March 7, 1936, President's Office, Correspondence of Harold Willis Dodds, 1935-36, folder Admissions—Statistics on, PUA.

53. Meeting of the FAS, January 19, 1926, *Records* 12 (1922): 206. Robert De Courcy Ward, who had voted in favor of the two controversial motions of May 23 and June 2, 1922, served on the Committee on Admission from 1925-26 through 1931-32.

54. [Dean Clarence W. Mendell], report on "Harvard," stamped "Dec 8—Rec'd," JRA, box Mar-Clarence W. Mendell, file Clarence W. Mendell; "Applications for Admission from Secondary Schools" and "Recommendations from the Committee on Admission and the Committee on Instruction adopted by the Faculty of Arts and Sciences," October 16, 1928, ALL, #111 Admission: Committee on. Fifty-six of the 215 applicants rejected in 1928 had "admitting records" (of whom 11 were from New York; 2, Ohio; 2, New Jersey; 2, Connecticut; 1, Rhode Island; 1, Pennsylvania; and 37, Massachusetts). Well into the 1930s, if not into the 1940s, Harvard admission forms asked applicants specific questions about their race or color and religious preference. One member of the dean's office said that he was "very agreeably surprised by the truthfulness of the statements on the admission blanks this year." And he added that "you would catch over 90% of the Jews in this way, and it might be a much safer method." Additional information on successful applicants was supplied by the freshman dormitory blanks (letter to C. N. Greenough, July 15, 1923, DHCCF, #30 Mr. E. R. Gay; and Greenough to Lowell, April 17, 1923, DHCCF, #37 President Lowell 1922-27).

55. *HPR, 1936-37,* pp. 16-21; "The Houses, General Information for the Class of 1937," *Official Register of Harvard University* 31 (March 1, 1934).

56. *HPR, 1936-37,* pp. 16-18.

57. "Summary of Faculty Votes in Regard to Limitation of the Size of the Freshman Class in Harvard College," DHC Statistical and Other Reports and Papers, 1920s to 1950s, inclusive, with some earlier papers, folders Freshman Class—Limitation of Size, Enrollment, and Admissions—Estimates of Enrollment, HUA. Also A. C. Hanford to Lowell, October 15, 1932, ALL, #82 Dean of Harvard College; and Hanford to Lowell, October 27, 1932, ALL, #82-A Dean of Harvard College.

58. "Supplementary Memorandum Explaining Method of Arriving at Estimate of Size of Class of 1946," April 3, 1942, DHCCF, 1933-57 (and some earlier), box on Houses 1939-52, folder Houses 1941-42; and DHC, Statistical and Other Reports, folder Admissions—Estimates of Enrollment.

59. The best sources of information were the tables compiled for the house masters and the Office of the College Dean on "Distribution of Probable Freshman Applicants for Houses According to Rank List, Race, Type of School Represented," DHCCF, 1933-57, box on Houses (Parietal Rules—Tutorial), Houses (Adams—Winthrop), folders on Statistics, 1932-42; from box on House Plan—Houses (to 1938), folders on Houses 1933-38; and from box on Houses 1939-1952, folders on Houses 1938-42. According to Seymour Martin Lipset, "Jewish enrollment was to drop from well over 20 percent to about 10 percent of the undergraduate body" during Lowell's administration (Seymour Martin Lipset and David Riesman, *Education and Politics at Harvard*, p. 148). For the treatment of Jewish graduate students, see Bruce Kuklick, *The Rise of American Philosophy, Cambridge, Massachusetts, 1860-1930*, pp. 456-58; and Lewis S. Feuer's review, "The Professionalization of Philosophy," *Chronicle of Higher Education* 16, no. 2 (March 6, 1978), pp. 21-22. For restrictions on the admission of Jews, blacks, and women to the Harvard Medical School, see Henry K. Beecher and Mark D. Altschule, *Medicine at Harvard*, chap. 26, "Special Groups of Students," pp. 461-85. The authors, who entered the medical school in 1928, reported "a commonly heard assertion that Jews were admitted in numbers up to 10 percent of the class," but were unable to document it. Their count of "patently Jewish names" in the fourth-year class, over a sixty-year period, showed that the percentage of Jews rose from 5.5 percent in 1910, to 8.0 in 1932, and to 9.5 in 1939. By 1953, Jewish enrollment was 22.3 percent; in 1972, it was 20.0 percent (pp. 484-85).

60. Kenneth B. Murdock to A. C. Hanford, March 20, 1933, DHCCF (A. C. Hanford, 1927-33), #115 Professor K. B. Murdock (Leverett House 1930-33).

61. Tables on "Distribution of Probable Freshman Applicants for Houses," DHCCF; Cleveland Amory, *The Proper Bostonians*, pp. 297-300, 306-07; Christopher S. Jencks and David Riesman, "Patterns of Residential Education: A Case Study of Harvard," in Nevitt Sanford, ed., *The American College*, pp. 737-39, 752-59.

62. Seymour Harris, *The Economics of Harvard*, pp. 20-21.

63. "Distribution in Houses of Final Club Members, 1933—," DHCCF, folder Houses 1938-39, 1939-40; and "Eliot Drops to Fifth as Lowell Recaptures First," *Harvard Crimson*, March 27, 1953, p. 1.

64. Tables on "Distribution of Probable Freshman Applicants for Houses," DHCCF; table IV "Distribution of Final Club Members by Schools," as of 1938-39 and 1948-49, in "Speculations on the Cross-Section," DHCCF, folder Dr. Elliott Perkins (Lowell House) 1940-52; Kenneth B. Murdock to A. C. Hanford, March 20, 1933, DHCCF; "Central Committee Appointed to Divide Freshmen Among Houses," *Harvard Crimson*, March 31, 1933, p. 1.

65. See n. 64.

66. Tables on "Distribution of Probable Freshman Applicants for Houses," DHCCF; "Suggested Procedure for Assignment to Houses, March 20, 1934, and form letter to all masters, March 22, 1934, DHCCF, in box House Plan—Houses (to 1938), folder Houses, 1933-34; form letter, April.

67. See n. 66.

68. See n. 66 and "Analysis of Present Membership of Houses, Classes of 1933-35," Table 1—Geographical Distribution, DHCCF, box on Houses (Parietal Rules—Tutorial) Houses (Adams—Winthrop), folder on Statistics, 1932-34.

69. Harris, *The Economics of Harvard*, p. 17; tables on "Distribution of Probable

Freshman Applicants for Houses."

70. See above, n. 66; DHCCF, box on Houses (Parietal Rules—Tutorial) Houses (Adams—Winthrop), letter to A. C. Hanford, April 18, 1934; and letter to Hanford, April 18, 1933, and "List of starred residents," April 15, 1935, in folders on the individual houses.

71. Copy of letter to dean of Harvard College, June 3, 1933, A. C. Hanford to Lowell, June 5, 1933, and Lowell to Hanford, June 7, 1933, ALL, #82-A Dean of Harvard College. Also Hanford to James B. Conant, December 24, 1936, DHCCF, folder President Conant, 1936-40.

72. David Riesman, "Education at Harvard," *Change* 5 (September 1973): 33.

73. Thomas Stephenson, "Lowell House in the Coolidge Manner," *Boston Herald,* May 5, 1940; George W. Pierson, *Yale: College and University, 1871-1937,* vol. 2, *Yale: The University College, 1921-1937,* p. 424.

74. Stephenson, "Lowell House"; table III, "Distribution of Final Club Members by Houses," for the classes of 1939-41 and 1949-51, in "Speculations on the Cross-Section," DHCCF (see above, n. 64; also n. 63).

75. Pierson, *Yale,* 2: 413, 418, 407-13, 248.

76. Ibid., pp. 421, 416-22, 425-28; John M. Cates, Jr., "The College Plan," *History of the Class of Nineteen Thirty-Six Yale College* (published with the assistance of the Class Secretaries Bureau, 1936), pp. 601-17; "The Residential Colleges at Yale University" (New Haven: Office of the Secretary, Yale University, 1977).

77. Pierson, *Yale,* 2: 440-44; Yale chart on "Allocation of Students," Samuel H. Fisher Papers, Yale Corporation, A—Committee on Colleges, box 1, file Yale University Committee on Colleges, YUL; "Report on the Possibilities of Simplifying the Admissions Procedure for the Individual Houses," DHCCF, folder Houses 1941-42.

78. "Non-Resident Students in Harvard College 1930-1955, Miscellaneous Data and Comments," March 26, 1956, in DHC Statistical and Other Reports and Papers, folder Houses—Miscellaneous Statistics; A. C. Hanford to James B. Conant, March 13, 1935, DHCCF, folder President Conant, 1933-36; and folder Non-resident Student Center, 1935-40's.

79. "Report of the Graduate Secretary of the Harvard College Non-Resident Student Center (Dudley Hall) for the year 1936-7," ibid. for 1940-41, dated November 10, 1941, and letter from the assistant secretary to A. C. Hanford, April 21, 1940, DHCCF, folder Non-resident Student Center, 1935-1940's. See also "Distribution of College Addresses of Undergraduates in Harvard College for the Academic Year 1938-39," November 1938, in DHC Statistical and Other Reports and Papers, folder Houses—Miscellaneous Statistics.

80. "Report on Ways in Which Harvard Can Be of Greater Service in the Metropolitan Area of Greater Boston and in Massachusetts," January 11, 1941, DHCCF, folder President Conant, 1940-52.

81. A. C. Hanford to Kenneth B. Murdock, May 23, 1938, Hanford to David M. Little, June 9, 1938, and "Suggestions Contributed By Freshman Committee," May 18, 1938, DHCCF, folder Houses—Circular letters to Masters. "Figures re Waiting List," October 24, 1938, DHCCF, folder Houses 1938-39; and Murdock to Hanford, May 16, 1938, DHCCF, box Memorial Church-Music, folder Professor Murdock (Leverett House), 1933-41.

82. A. C. Hanford, "Memorandum to Freshman Committee on the Houses" and

"Memorandum to the Masters," June 9, 1938, and [Hanford] to Prof. R. M. Ferry, January 12, 1939, enclosing copy of the Minutes of the Masters' Meeting, October 27, 1938, DHCCF, folder Houses—Circular letters to Masters. See also "Hanford Rejects Freshman Plan for Associated House Members," *Harvard Crimson*, June 13, 1938, p. 1.

83. In *Harvard Crimson*, "Hanford Urges New House, Concentration Changes," January 30, 1939, p. 1; editorial, "Cooperation for Association," February 27, 1939, p. 2; and "Housemasters Vote to Adopt Associate Membership Plan for Out-of-House Men," March 30, 1939, p. 1. A. C. Hanford to James B. Conant, March 22, 1939, DHCCF, folder Houses 1938-39. See "Report of Committee to Visit Harvard College," April 22, 1940, DHCCF, folder Overseers' Committee 1933-47, for summary of recommendations of the Harvard Student Council reports.

84. "Report of the Student Council on the Petition Presented by Freshmen and Concerned with Admissions to Houses," May 29, 1939, and April 13, [1939], letter to Dean A. C. Hanford, DHCCF, folder Houses 1938-39. Also Hanford to R. M. Ferry, April 15, 1939, DHCCF, folder Houses—Circular letters to Masters. Editorial, "Deep South," *Harvard Crimson*, April 13, 1939, p. 2.

85. In *Harvard Crimson*, "654 Freshmen, Upperclassmen Get House Notification Today," May 8, 1939, p. 1; "Eleven Freshmen Protest Admission Plan for Houses," May 11, 1939, p. 1; editorial, "House Selections," May 12, 1939, p. 2; "210 Men of Class of '42 Add Names to House Protest," May 16, 1939, p. 1; "The Mail," May 18, 1939, p. 2; editorial, "Second Time 'Round," May 19, 1939, p. 2; editorial, "Houses of Mirrors," May 25, 1939, p. 2; and "Student Council Demands New House to Alleviate Admission Dissatisfaction," May 29, 1939, p. 1. See also "Freshman Class Petition on the House Problem" and Walter E. Clark to A. C. Hanford, March 6, 1939, DHCCF, folder Houses 1938-39; "Report of the Student Council on the Petition Presented by Freshmen and Concerned with Admission to Houses," May 29, 1939, DHCCF.

86. "Confidential Memorandum Regarding the Matters for Discussion with the Student Council," January 22, 1942, and Faculty Docket, February 10, 1942, DHCCF, folder Houses 1941-42; "Non-Resident Students in Harvard College, 1930-1955," DHC Statistical and Other Reports and Papers, folder Houses—Miscellaneous Statistics.

87. "Analysis of Houses By Schools, etc.," March 30, 1944. DHCCF, Houses (Parietal Rules—Tutorial), Houses (Adams—Winthrop), folder Statistics 1942-43; Minutes of Informal Masters' Meeting, November 6, 1946, DHCCF, folder Houses 1946-47; "Analysis of Houses for Fall Term 1946-47," DHCCF, folder Houses—Agenda & Notes re Masters' Meetings 1943-51.

88. Agenda for Masters' Meeting, April 17, 1947, DHCCF, folder Houses—Agenda & Notes re Masters' Meetings 1943-51; table IV, "Distribution of Final Club Members by Schools," 1938-39, 1948-49, in "Speculations on the Cross-Section," DHCCF.

89. Letters to Delmar Leighton, November 28 and December 21, 1951, copy of a September 24, 1952, letter to Dr. William Barry Wood, and copy of a March 11, 1953, letter to Eric A. McCouch, DHCCF, folder Overseers' Committee to Visit Harvard College 1952-57. By the 1950s, the houses had "done much to restore the connection between intellectual and social life at Harvard," observed Christopher S. Jencks and

David Riesman, "and this has perhaps been their most significant contribution to the College" ("Patterns of Residential Education," in *The American College*, pp. 746, 764-65).

90. Jencks and Riesman, "Patterns of Residential Education," p. 762. "Speculations on the Cross-Section," DHCCF; "Distribution of Residents by Date of Degree (Not Based on Social Standing)," October 15, 1950, DHCCF, folder Houses 1950-51 & 1951-52; "Analysis of House Applications," April 14, 1951, and April 15, 1952, DHC, Statistical and Other Reports and Papers, folder Houses—Miscellaneous Statistics.

91. Harvard College Office of Housing, University Hall.

Chapter 5. Yale: Reaction and Stabilization, 1900s to 1940s

1. Arthur T. Hadley to Frederick B. Luquiens, November 25, 1920, ATH, April 26, 1920, to February 28, 1921, book no. 36, p. 393; Robert N. Corwin to Frederick S. Jones, May 3, 1922, FSJ, box 5, file Jews.

2. Hadley to Luquiens, November 25, 1920, ATH.

3. "Memorandum on the Problems Arising from the Increase in the Enrollment of Students of Jewish Birth in the University," May 12, 1922, JRA, box 84, J.-JOH, file Jewish Problem, Etc.; Corwin to Jones, May 3, 1922, FSJ, box 5, file Jews.

4. George W. Pierson, *Yale: College and University, 1871-1937*, vol. 1, *Yale College: An Educational History, 1871-1921*, p. 109; Morris Hadley, *Arthur Twining Hadley*, pp. 1-5, 12-13, 16-17.

5. Hadley to Angell, June 29, 1921, ATH, March 1, 1921, to August 24, 1921, book no. 37, p. 235; Pierson, *Yale*, 1: 109, 113-19; and Hadley, *Hadley*, pp. 58-59.

6. Pierson, *Yale*, 1: 123, 107, 130, 147, 151-53; Hadley to Jones, March 27, 1908, ATH, June 10, 1907, to April 30, 1908, book no. 15, p. 665. In addition to choosing the dean, the faculty selected their colleagues, controlled income from tuition and room rents, and allocated expenses.

7. Reuben A. Holden, *Profiles and Portraits of Yale University Presidents*, p. 100; Hadley to H. S. Pritchett, May 5, 1906, ATH, January 1, 1906, to May 20, 1906, book no. 12, p. 700.

8. Pierson, *Yale*, 1: 491, and chap. 24, "The Great Reorganization," pp. 477-92; chap. 25, "Reconstruction," pp. 493-512; and pp. 539-45; *YPR, 1920-21*, pp. 32, 124; Hadley to Angell, February 16, 1921, ATH, book no. 36, p. 555.

9. Charles Reznikoff, "New Haven: The Jewish Community, A Portrait Sketch," *Commentary* 4, no. 5 (November 1947): 476-77; I. George Dobsevage, comp., "Jews of Prominence in the United States," *American Jewish Year Book, 5683*, vol. 24 (September 23, 1922, to September 10, 1923), pp. 109-218; Prof. Rollin G. Osterweis, interview, New Haven, Conn., May 20, 1971. See also Jones to Angell, November 14, 15, and 21, 1922, Angell to Jones, November 28, 1922, Jones to William L. Phelps, December 15, 1922, Jones to Max Mandell, December 21, 1922, and February 28, 1924, and Mandell to Jones, December 26, 1922, FSJ, box 3, file Faculty.

10. Reznikoff, "New Haven: The Jewish Community"; Dobsevage, "Jews of Prominence in the United States"; and Osterweis, interview. Meyer Wolodarsky, Ph.B. '94, taught Russian (1899-1902); Isidore Troostwyk was an instructor in violin

playing (1894-1923) and an assistant professor of applied music (1901-23); Dr. Max Mailhouse, Ph.B. '76, was a clinical professor of neurology (1907-20); and Frank Schlesinger, honorary M.A. '20, was appointed director of the observatory in 1920 and chairman of the Department of Astronomy in 1921. Paul Weiss was the first Jew to be hired by Yale as a full professor; he taught philosophy from 1946 to 1962 and was appointed Sterling Professor in 1962. Jews also became coaches or instructors in those sports which were completely open to them: "Izzy" Winters in wrestling and "Mosey" King in boxing. The little information available on the number of Catholic professors at Yale indicated that, as of 1930, Professor Albert G. Feuillerat (French) and Assistant Professor John E. McDonough (political economy) were both known to be members of the Catholic church (Elizabeth B. Sweeney, National Catholic Welfare Conference, to Angell, May 16, 1930, and secretary to the president in reply, May 21, 1930, JRA, box Cas-Chem, file Roman Catholic).

11. *The Graduates Club* (The Graduate Club Association, New Haven, Conn., 1919), p. 11; see also the membership lists for 1921, 1925, 1930, and 1938.

12. Hadley to Frederick B. Luquiens, November 25, 1920, ATH; Luquiens to Hadley, November 30, 1920, ATH, last Hadley correspondence La-Ma, divider Lu. Dean Winternitz married a Gentile and did not socialize with Jews (Dan A. Oren '79, "Jews at Yale—A Preliminary Examination," Passover, 1977, in Yale Miscellaneous Manuscripts #94, YUA).

13. Hadley to Committee on Admissions, the Graduates Club, New Haven, March 5, 1918, ATH, November 12, 1917, to April 24, 1918, book no. 32, p. 479; and Hadley's letter to Dr. Guy M. Winslow, Lasell Seminary, February 20, 1920, on behalf of the Jewish alumnus's daughter. Hadley accepted the existence of Lasell's published quota on Jews, but he asked that an exception be made in this case, because the family was "distinctly of the right sort" (ATH, September 1, 1919, to April 24, 1920, book no. 35, p. 525).

14. Hadley to Otto T. Bannard, April 19, 1918, ATH, book no. 32, p. 739; and Hadley to George Parmly Day, April 24, 1918, ATH, book no. 32, p. 748; YPR, 1923-24—1928-29.

15. Edward Sapir (1884-1939) emigrated to the United States with his parents in 1889. He earned all his degrees at Columbia University; in 1931, he came to Yale (honorary M.A. '31). He also served as chairman of the Department of Anthropology (1937-38). For an account of who may have "blackballed" Sapir—either history professor George Woodbine or philosophy professor Wilmon H. Sheldon—see Dan A. Oren, "Jews at Yale—A Preliminary Examination."

16. Jones to Lawrence Mason, December 6, 1915, Mason to Jones, December 11, [1915], and Anson Phelps Stokes to Jones, January 6, 1916, FSJ, box 3, file Faculty. Louis Sachs, New Haven, Conn. letters to Marcia Synnott, October 6, 1971, and August 8 and September 7, 1972.

17. Louis Sachs to Marcia Synnott. Dean Jones also engaged in some campus humor at the expense of Jews and Jewish students (Jones to William A. Taylor, April 11, 1924, FSJ, box 4, file Harvard Verses).

18. "Yale College 1912 Statistical Blanks," filled out by seniors for *History of the Class of 1912, Yale College*, vol. 1, YUA; Albert Beecher Crawford, ed., *Football Y Men—Men of Yale Series*, 3 vols. Another 1912 Football Y man, an Episcopalian,

converted to Catholicism sometime after graduation. At least one other Catholic student in Yale College '12 won a Y—in track; he was also a member of DKE and Skull and Bones.

19. Sidney N. Deane '02, "Wooster Square," from the *Yale Courant* [ca. 1901] in New Haven Colony Historical Society, A. G. Dana Collection, vol. 6, p. 56; John A. Thomas, "Catholicism," *Yale Literary Magazine* 85 (April 1920): 297; Terence L. Connolly, S.J., to Hadley, undated, and May 31, 1920, ATH, box 16 Coi April 1, 1917, to Daz May 31, 1904; Hadley to Rev. Connolly, May 26 and June 1, 1920, Hadley to J. W. Andrews, May 26, 1920, and Hadley to James A. Flaherty, June 18, 1920, ATH, book no. 36, pp. 72-73, 93, 137. See also Morty Miller, "New Haven: The Italian Community" (History 90 essay, Yale University, 1969), pp. 25, 56, 56-65; histories of the *Class of 1927 Yale College* and *Sheffield Scientific School* (published under the direction of the Class Secretaries Bureau); George W. Pierson, *Yale: College and University, 1871-1937*, vol. 2, *Yale: The University College, 1921-1937*, p. 152; and Rollin G. Osterweis, *Three Centuries of New Haven, 1638-1938*, pp. 367, 370-75, 388.

20. Robert Austin Warner, *New Haven Negroes: A Social History*, pp. 246-47, 254-55.

21. Ibid., pp. 175-76, 279; Hadley to Nellie L. Mebane, August 16, 1920, ATH, book no. 36, p. 238, endorsing Booker T. Washington's views on achieving "industrial independence" for Negroes.

22. Warner, *New Haven Negroes*, p. 176; *Yale College Class Book 1904*, p. 111. Rev. A. F. Beard to Henry P. Wright, July 26, 1902, HPW, Applications for Entrance and Correspondence Pertaining Thereto, box N-Z, file P; Rev. G. W. Andrews to Wright, March 1, 1904, and William Pickens to Wright, December 31, 1906, Henry P. Wright Correspondence, 1865-1908, file 737; and Wright to M. P. Shawkey, April 21, 1915, HPW, Historical Manuscripts, box no. 1. See also William Pickens to Charles W. Eliot, May 9, 1909, CWE, box 240, folder Race, expressing agreement with Eliot's views on the "race question."

23. Alfred E. Stearns to Frederick S. Jones, September 30, 1909, Dean's Office—General (FSJ), Miscellaneous Correspondence and Student Material, filed under S.

24. W. E. B. Du Bois to Angell, May 15, 1931; Robert N. Corwin to Angell, May 20, 1931; and Angell to Du Bois, May 21, 1931, JRA, file Negroes at Yale; Levi Jackson, as quoted in E. Digby Baltzell, *The Protestant Establishment*, p. 279; Tim Cohane, *The Yale Football Story*, pp. 333-36. Jackson's father was employed as a butler by former Yale fullback Frank Butterworth and later became a master steward and chef of Pierson College. After graduating from Hillhouse High School in New Haven, Levi Jackson served in the army and was discharged as a sergeant. He entered Yale on the G.I. bill of rights in September 1946. He earned a major Y in both football and basketball (*Yale 1950 Class Book*, p. 333, YUA).

25. Yung Wing, *My Life in China and America*, pp. 170-75, 207-11; *Book of the Class of 1882 Sheffield Scientific School of Yale University*, 25th Reunion (July 1910). There were three Chinese and one Japanese in Sheffield class of 1882.

26. Rev. F. L. Hawks Pott to Henry P. Wright, November 13, 1907; Thomas D. Goodell to Wright, January 9, 1908, enclosing memorandum "From the Committee, T. D. Goodell," and B. S. Hurlbut to Wright, January 13, 1908, HPW, file College Curriculum Scholastic Requirements.

27. Hadley to Sir Chentung Liang Cheng, May 22, June 1, 7, and 18, 1906; Hadley to Rev. Harlan P. Beach, June 29, 1906; and Hadley to F. W. Williams, December 10, 1906, ATH, May 21, 1906, to December 21, 1906, book no. 13, pp. 12-13, 48, 82-83, 134, 197, 682. The Chinese legation recommended only two of the applicants for the scholarships at Yale; Harvard was given the first choice of Chinese students.

28. Angell to R. N. Corwin, February 10, 1922, and Corwin to Angell, February 13, 1922, JRA, box 2, file Board of Admissions; "What Yale is Doing in China," supplement to the *YAW*, March 21, 1913, especially pp. 2-3, 5-6; and Reuben Andrus Holden, *Yale in China; The Mainland, 1901-1951* (New Haven: Yale in China Association, 1964).

29. Albert Beecher Crawford to K. P. Damlamian, February 2, 1922, JRA, file Scholarships and Fellowships; and Vote of Thanks of the President and Fellows to Sylvestre Z. Poli, January 11, 1930, and Edgar S. Furniss to Angell, May 20, 1931, JRA, file Italian Fellowship Exchange.

30. Pierson, *Yale*, 2: 16-19, and chap. 1, "Electing a New President," pp. 3-15.

31. Ibid., pp. 25, 5-7, 10-11, 15.

32. Ibid., pp., 25, 175.

33. Ibid., pp. 26-29.

34. See Floyd W. Reeves and John Dale Russell, *The Alumni of the Colleges*, University of Chicago Survey no. 6 (Chicago: University of Chicago Press, 1933), "Table 6, Percentage Distribution of Graduates of Each Period According to Religious Preference," p. 15. Jews numbered 437 of the total 3,975 who responded (560 graduates did not provide information), or 11 percent for the period 1893-1930; during the 1920s, Jews reached 15 percent. Only Presbyterians (17) and Methodists (16) had larger percentages for the entire period. The Baptists, who had comprised 27 percent of the graduates of 1893-1900, sharply declined in numbers thereafter—to 8 percent in the 1920s. The percentage of Catholics was much smaller at Chicago than at either Harvard or Yale, a modest 6 percent for the entire period. And in contrast to their large representation at the Big Three, Episcopalians totaled only 9 percent of the graduates.

35. Charles W. Eliot to Angell, August 26, 1924, CWE, box 390, A-C; Pierson, *Yale*, 2: 172-76; Holden, *Profiles and Portraits of Yale University Presidents*, p. 111.

36. The original title of "The Public Schools and the Spirit of Tolerance," which Angell delivered in Cleveland, Ohio, on October 26, 1928, was "The Duty of the Schools to Break Through Local Provincial Prejudices and Purely National Prejudices" (JRA file O; see pp. 2, 7-9).

37. Robert N. Corwin to Angell, February 29, 1924, and Angell to Corwin, March 8, 1924, JRA, box 84, file Jewish Problem, Etc.

38. Meeting of the Board of Admissions, October 18, 1921, Freshman Office Records, box 1, 1920-1922, file A 1. 10, Admissions Committee, Prof. Corwin Chairman; Minott A. Osborn to Angell, November 17, 1921, Freshman Office Records, box 2, 1921-1922, file A 3. 60 Council; Corwin's "Memorandum of Matters *to be brought before the University Council*," October 19, 1921, Freshman Office Records-Ex-1926-1927 (3), student folders Van Camp-Budd, file Admissions 1920-22 incl.

39. Russell H. Chittenden to Angell, January 26, 1922, and Angell to Chittenden, January 26, 1922, JRA, box 84, file Jewish Problem, Etc.

40. A. K. Merritt to Robert N. Corwin, April 11, 1922, copy, JRA, box 84, file

Jewish Problem, Etc. See *Two Centuries of Christian Activity at Yale* (New York: G. P. Putnam's Sons, 1901), ed. James B. Reynolds, Samuel H. Fisher, Henry B. Wright, Committee of Publication, appendixes D (1) "Church Members in Academic Classes 1873-1904" and D (2) "Religious Composition of Yale University, January 1, 1901." Statistics collected from the senior class (1873-98) and from freshman registration (1899-1904) on a total of 3,628 students indicated the number of church members for each denomination: Congregational, 1,205; Episcopal, 948; Presbyterian, 755; Baptist, 214; Methodist, 186; Roman Catholic, 130; Jewish, 44; Reformed, 35; Lutheran, 17; Disciples (Christian), 17; Unitarian, 12; and scattering, 65. As of January 1, 1901, 59 percent of all Yale University students (63 percent in the college, as compared to only 50 percent in Sheffield Scientific School) were church members.

41. [Roswell P. Angier] to R. N. Corwin, May 9, 1922, Freshman Office Records, box 1, 1920-1922, file A 1. 10, Admissions Committee. Angier was president of the Harvard Club of New Haven.

42. Jones to R. N. Corwin, May 6, 1922, FSJ, box 5, file Jews.

43. For biographical sketch on Frederick S. Jones, see *History of the Class of 1894, Yale College, Twenty-Five Year Record*, YUA, pp. 213-15; Pierson, *Yale*, vol. 1, chap. 9, "Tyrannosaurus Superbus," pp. 155-63.

44. Jones to Bob [Corwin], August 15, 1922, and [Corwin] to Jones, August 11, 1922, Freshman Office Records-Ex-1926-1927 (3), file Admissions 1920-22 incl. Corwin asked Jones to convey to Henry Pennypacker his "hope that the Hebraic question is not interfering with his summer's rest." See also "A human document. Dean Jones paid these bills & saved the receipts," a file in Dean's Office—General (FSJ), Miscellaneous Correspondence and Student Material.

45. [Frederick S. Jones], eleven-page memorandum consisting of statistical tables and conclusions drawn therefrom [ca. September-October 1922], FSJ, box 5, file Jews. Note also Jones's lists of Jewish students in Yale classes from 1911 through 1925, written on scrap paper.

46. Ibid.

47. Ibid.

48. Ibid.

49. Ibid.

50. Ibid.

51. Ibid.

52. Ibid., and Minutes of Meeting of Association New England Deans Held in Princeton, 9th and 10th of May [1918], pp. 21-22, FSJ, box 6, file War.

53. Minutes of the Meeting of the Committee on Educational Policy, May 12, 1922, *Reports of the Committee on Educational Policy to the Yale Corporation, 1919-1929* (Office of the Secretary, Yale University, Woodbridge Hall), p. 97.

54. "Memorandum on the Problems Arising from Students of Jewish Birth," May 12, 1922, JRA.

55. Ibid.

56. Ibid.

57. Ibid., and [Robert N. Corwin], "Limitation of Numbers," one of two two-page memoranda, Com. on Limitation of Numbers 1922, Freshman Office Records-Ex-1926-1927 (3).

58. "Memorandum on Jewish Problem," undated, containing "the tentative propo-

sals for restriction discussed with the Corporation's Committee on Educational Policy . . . ," JRA, box 84, file Jewish Problem, Etc.

59. Robert N. Corwin, "Memorandum on Jewish Representation in Yale," May 26, 1922; and Corwin to Deans Jones and Angier and to Director Chittenden, May 19, 1922, JRA, box 84, file Jewish Problem, Etc.

60. Russell H. Chittenden to Robert N. Corwin, May 23, 1922, JRA, box 84, file Jewish Problem, Etc.; and Table 5.2, "Jewish Students in the Sheffield Scientific School, Classes of 1910-24."

61. J. R. Ellis, Memorandum for Dean Angier, May 25, 1922; and A. K. Merritt to R. N. Corwin, May 25, 1922, JRA, box 84, file Jewish Problems, Etc., citing cases of dishonesty among Jews, four in the Class of 1920 and one in 1921. If the two classes were combined, the number would be five out of fifty-two, or about 9.6 percent.

62. "Memorandum on Jewish Representation in Yale," May 26, 1922, and "Memorandum on the Problems Arising from Students of Jewish Birth," JRA; "Limitation of Numbers," Freshman Office Records. See also Albert Beecher Crawford to Angell, June 8, 1922, JRA, box S, file Scholarships and Fellowships, suggesting "the possibility of some territorial restriction on tuition scholarships." This would, in effect, reduce the number of scholarships to Jews, since almost one-half of the Jews and over one-half of the Jewish scholarship holders came from the New Haven area.

63. Angell to H. A. Garfield, June 5, 1922, JRA, box 84, file Jewish Problem, Etc.

64. Ibid., and H. A. Garfield to Angell, June 1, 1922, enclosing copy of a May 31, 1922, letter from Garfield to William Ernest Hocking, JRA, box 84, file Jewish Problem, Etc.; and "Minutes of Committee to Consider and Report Methods," November 6, 1922, HUA.

65. Alfred L. Ripley to Angell, June 3, 1922, JRA, box 84, file Jewish Problem, Etc.; and Minott A. Osborn to Robert N. Corwin, October 14, 1922, Freshman Office Records, Com. on Limitation of Numbers 1922.

66 "Limitation of Numbers," Freshman Office Records.

67. Ibid.

68. Robert M. Hutchins to Robert N. Corwin, January 22, 1923; "Selection of Candidates for Admission to the Freshman Class under the Provision for the Limitation of Numbers," March 16, 1923; and "Admission to the Freshman Class," March 23, 1923, Freshman Office Records, Com. on Limitation of Numbers 1922. See also Minutes of the Meeting of the Committee on Educational Policy, January 12 and February 9, 1923, *Reports of the Committee on Educational Policy*, pp. 102, 105.

69. Angell, "The Public Schools and the Spirit of Tolerance," pp. 10-11, 18; also Minutes of a Meeting of the Board of Admissions, March 14, 1923, JRA, box 2, Admissions-Advisory Committee on Secondary Schools; H. E. Tuttle, file Board of Admission, Minutes.

70. Minutes of the Board of Admissions, June 10, 1924, and February 16 and October 26, 1925, JRA, box 2, file Board of Admissions, Minutes; see above, n. 45.

71. Angell to R. N. Corwin, December 2, 1926, JRA, box 2, file Board of Admissions.

72. Report of Dean Clarence W. Mendell, January-April 1926, p. 34, JRA, box Mar—Clarence W. Mendell, file Clarence W. Mendell.

73. [Clarence W. Mendell], report on "Harvard," stamped "Dec. 8—1926 Rec'd," JRA, file Mendell.

74. [Clarence W. Mendell], report on "Dartmouth," stamped "Dec. 8—1926 Rec'd," JRA, file Mendell; Pierson, *Yale*, 2: 193-206.

75. Memorandum for Members of the Board of Admissions, "The Admission Requirements as Applied to the Sons of Yale Alumni," September 28, 1929, JRA, box 2, file Board of Admissions.

76. Ibid., and Minutes of a Meeting of the Board of Admissions, October 22, 1929, JRA, box 2, file Board of Admissions, Minutes.

77. Robert N. Corwin to Francis Parsons, October 1, 1929, copy, JRA, box 2, file Board of Admissions. Parsons, B.A. '93, LL.B. '97, and honorary M.A. '25, was a fellow of the Yale Corporation (1925-37).

78. W. L. Cross, dean of the graduate school, to Provost Henry Solon Graves, January 20, 1927, in *Reports of the Committee on Educational Policy* pp. 170, f, g.

79. Robert N. Corwin to Angell, January 7, 1930, and October 17, 1930, together with statistics on Jewish students in the classes of 1926-1934, and on "Distribution of Jews in Connecticut in the Classes of 1930-34," JRA, box 2, file Board of Admissions.

80. C. H. Warren to Angell, April 29, 1932, JRA, box 2, file Increasing Number of Admissions, 1932-33.

81. Robert N. Corwin, memorandum "To Members of the Board of Admissions," May 20, 1932; Corwin to Angell, July 26, 1932 (see handwritten postscript), Corwin to Angell, January 3, 1933, enclosing table, dated October 19, 1932, on "our Jewish population for the last ten years," and Corwin to Angell, February 10, 1933, enclosing table on "Yale Fathers," dated October 19, 1932, JRA, box 2, file Board of Admissions.

82. Corwin to Angell, January 3, 1933, Angel to Corwin, January 6, 1933; and Alan Valentine to Angell, January 9, 1934, ibid. Alan Valentine succeeded Corwin as chairman of the Board of Admissions in 1933.

83. Angell to Alan Valentine, March 9, 1934, ibid.

84. Angell to Rabbi Edgar E. Siskin, March 25, 1933; Siskin to Angell, March 24, 1933; and Irving Goleman to Angell, November 21, 1934, JRA, box 84, file Jewish Problem, Etc.; *Jewish Advocate*, October 5, 1934, p. 1-2; Brooks Mather Kelley, *Yale: A History*, p. 416. See also below, chap. 7, n. 12, for James Bryant Conant's refusal of Hanfstaengl's offer.

85. Angell to Conrad Hoffman, Jr., December 7, 1933, JRA, box 84, file Jewish Problem, Etc.

86. Editorials, "Applicants Submit Photographs" and "An Ellis Island for Yale," *Yale Daily News* 49 (March 29 and 30, 1926): 2.

Chapter 6. Princeton: The Triumph of the Clubs, 1900s to 1950s

1. Varnum Lansing Collins '92 to Henry M. Canby, B.S. '95, Endowment Fund chairman for Delaware, copy, November 23, 1922, HASP, 1920-27, box 37, folder Executive Secretary Trips—to Alumni Meetings ex Number of Students Receiving Financial Aid for the Year 1922-23. Collins also served as clerk of the faculty.

2. Woodrow Wilson draft of "The Country and the Colleges" [ca. February 24, 1910], *PWW*, 20: 161, 166, 157-72.

3. "A Supplementary Report to the Board of Trustees of Princeton University" [ca. December 13, 1906], Trustees' Papers, 10 (June 1901-January 1908), PUA.

4. Wilson, "The Spirit of Learning," *HGM* 18 (September 1909): 1-14, especially pp. 9-10, 14. Wilson to Mary Allen Hulbert Peck, July 3, 1909, *PWW*, 19: 290.

5. Wilson to Peck, July 3, 1909; *PWW*; Charles W. Eliot to [John Grier] Hibben, August 26, 1924, CWE, box 390: 1924, D-J; Wilson, Address, June 26, 1907, *HGM* 16 (September 1907): 85-87; Charles Francis Adams, "Some Modern College Tendencies," June 12, 1906, *Columbia University Quarterly* 8, no. 4 (1906), pp. 347-71; and Adams to Wilson, October 2, 1907, *PWW*, 17: 409-10.

6. Arthur S. Link, "Woodrow Wilson: The American as Southerner," *Journal of Southern History* 36 no.1 (February 1970): 3-17. See also Wilson's criticism of "Convict Labor in Georgia" [ca. February 24, 1883], printed in New York *Evening Post*, March 7, 1883, *PWW*, 2: 306-11.

7. Ellen Axson Wilson to Wilson, May 22, 1886, *PWW*, 5: 251; Albert Bushnell Hart to Wilson, April 23 and June 1, 1889, *PWW*, 6: 174-75, 242-43.

8. Wilson, "News Report of an Address at the Peddie Institute" [February 13, 1903]; and "News Report of an Address to the Alumni of Western Pennsylvania" [March 8, 1903], *PWW*, 14: 356-57, 383-86. Wilson, "News Report of a Lecture in New York on Americanism" [November 20, 1904], and "Address of Welcome to the Association of Colleges and Preparatory Schools of the Middle States and Maryland" [November 25, 1904], *PWW*, 15: 536-42. See also Wilson, "After-Dinner Remarks in New York to the Friendly Sons of St. Patrick" [March 17, 1909], *PWW*, 19: 105.

9. From the Minutes of Session, First Presbyterian Church, Columbia, S.C., July 5, 1873, *PWW*, 1: 22-23. Dr. Joseph Ruggles Wilson was then pastor of the First Presbyterian Church of Columbia, S.C. Wilson to Ellen Louise Axson, June 26, [1884,] and n. 1, *PWW*, 3: 216-19.

10. Francis Landey Patton to Wilson, February 18, 1890, and Patton to Cyrus Hall McCormick, April 4, 1898, Patton Letterpress Books, PUA. Frederick Jackson Turner to Wilson, November 8, 1896, and April 3, 1897; Wilson to Turner, November 15, 1896, and March 31, 1897; Wilson to Ellen Axson Wilson, January 29, 1897, also n. 1, and February 2 and 16, 1897; Wilson to Patton, March 28, 1897; Patton to Wilson, March 29, 1897, and Wilson to Charles Ewing Green, March 28, 1897, *PWW*, 10: 42-45, 213, 50-53, 201-02, 123-24, 138-39, 163-64, 199-200, 196-97. For an interesting letter on Turner's view of Wilson, see Turner to Charles W. Eliot, April 5, 1924, CWE, box 391: 1924, P-Z. When Dean Andrew F. West learned that Turner was a Unitarian, he was against even introducing him to the Princeton faculty (Henry Wilkinson Bragdon, *Woodrow Wilson: The Academic Years*, pp. 226-27.) See also George C. Osborn, *Woodrow Wilson: The Early Years*, pp. 277-80.

11. Rev. David Ruddach Frazer, a member of the trustees' Curriculum Committee, to Wilson, October 23, 1903, referring to the dissatisfaction of Rev. Elijah R. Craven, the chairman, over Wilson's offer to Garfield, and n. 2, *PWW*, 15: 26. For letters from Thilly to Wilson, see WP, LC, and for typed copies of letters from Wilson to Thilly, see the Ray Stannard Baker Papers, LC. Of particular interest are Wilson's February 1, 1904, letter to Thilly and Thilly's reply of February 4, 1904. Both Wilson and John Grier Hibben assured Thilly that the fact that he was not a church member would not bar him from becoming professor of psychology at Princeton. Mr. M. Halsey Thomas, former archivist at Princeton University, interview, Firestone Library, Princeton University, April 15, 1971. Mr. Thomas was a source of valuable information and insights on Princeton history. According to the *General Catalogue of Prince-*

ton University, 1746-1906 (Princeton, N.J.: Princeton University, 1908), p. 58, I. Loewenthal, A.M., teacher of German (1852-55), may have been the first Jewish instructor at Princeton.

12. Wilson to Thomas Nelson Page, June 24, 1904, *PWW*, 15: 393-95.

13. Editorial note, "The Crisis in Presidential Leadership at Princeton," *PWW*, 12: 292, 289-93.

14. *PPR, 21 October, 1902*, PUA.

15. Wilson, "Princeton for the Nation's Service," *PAW* 3, no. 6 (November 1, 1902): 89-98; and editorial note, "The New Princeton Course of Study," and a draft of an article on "Princeton's New Plan of Study" [ca. August 29, 1904], *PWW*, 15: 287-92, 450-60.

16. "Report of the Committee on Course of Study to the Princeton University Faculty," April 16, 1904; and "The New Princeton Course of Study," *PWW*, 15: 252-63, 277-92. See also folders on the preceptorial system and Committee of Fifty, WWP, in particular, Andrew F. West, "The Tutorial System in College," reprinted from the *Educational Review*, December 1906, pp. 500-14, and Nathaniel E. Griffin, "The Princeton Preceptorial System," reprinted from the *Sewanee Review*, 18 (April 1910): 169-76.

17. "A Supplementary Report to the Board of Trustees of Princeton University" [ca. December 13, 1906], Trustees' Papers, 10; "A Memorandum on the Clubs at Princeton," February 17, 1906, *PWW*, 16: 314-15.

18. David B. Jones to Wilson, June 12 and September 28, 1907, *PWW*, 17: 210-11, 404-05.

19. "A Report to the Board of Trustees of Princeton University on the Club Situation" [ca. June 8, 1903], *PWW*, 14: 479-84. Bragdon, *Wilson*, p. 470, n. 26.

20. Minutes of the Meeting of the Board of Trustees of Princeton University, December 13, 1906, Trustees' Papers, 10. Wilson to Cleveland Hoadley Dodge, February 20, 1907, and n. 2, *PWW*, 17: 47; and Wilson, "Report on the Social Co-ordination of the University" [ca. June 6, 1907], Trustees' Papers, 10, reprinted from *PAW* 7, no. 36 (June 12, 1907); 606-11, and [Wilson] to David B. Jones, September 26, 1907, WWP.

21. Wilson, "Report on the Social Co-ordination of the University"; "President Wilson's Address to the Board of Trustees" and "Memorandum Concerning Residential Quads," reprinted from *PAW* 7 (June 12, 1907): 606-15, in WWP.

22. Minutes of the Board of Trustees of Princeton University, June 10, 1907, Trustees' Papers, 10. Cyrus H. McCormick to Wilson, June 10, 1907, *PWW*, 17: 206-07. Wilson to Rev. Dr. Melancthon W. Jacobus, June 27, 1907, WWP, folder Curriculum Committee of the Board. Jacobus and Stewart were ministers, while the other three trustees were businessmen: Dodge (vice president of Phelps Dodge Corporation); Jones (lawyer, successful Chicago businessman, and director of New Jersey Zinc Company); McCormick (president of International Harvester Company). Dr. Stewart later became one of Wilson's opponents.

23. Wilson to Cleveland H. Dodge, July 1 and 3, 1907; Dodge to Wilson, July 2, 1907; and Wilson to Melancthon W. Jacobus, July 1, 1907, *PWW*, 17: 240-41, 243, 245-46.

24. George McLean Harper to Wilson, July 18, 1907; Walter A. Wyckoff to Wilson, July 18, 1907; Henry van Dyke to Wilson, July 5, 1907; Wilson to van Dyke, July 8, 1907; Andrew F. West to Wilson, July 10, 1907; Wilson to West, July 11,

1907; John Grier Hibben to Wilson, July 8, 1907; and Wilson to Hibben, July 10, 1907, *PWW*, 17: 260-61, 263-64, 268-71, 276-80, 289-91. Henry van Dyke, "The 'Residential Quad' Idea at Princeton," July 10, 1907, *PAW* 8, no. 1 (September 25, 1907): 4-7. Ray Stannard Baker, *Woodrow Wilson: Life and Letters, vol. 2, Princeton, 1890-1910*, pp. 228, 232-33, 244, 249-52.

25. Adrian H. Joline to the editor of PAW 8, no. 3 (October 9, 1907): 36-38. Henry Fairfield Osborn to Wilson, September 17, 1907; and Wilson to Melancthon W. Jacobus, September 20, 1907, in which he enclosed a copy of Osborn's letter, *PWW*, 17: 389-91, 395.

26. Franklin Murphy, Jr., vice president of the Murphy Varnish Company of Newark (his father had been governor of New Jersey), to Wilson, June 7 and 18, 1907; Wilson to Murphy, June 20, 1907; Arthur H. Osborn to Wilson, July 9, 1907, with memorandum, "A Plan in Respect to the Club Situation in Princeton To-day," *PWW*, 17: 187, 216-17, 266-67. For a clubman's approval of Wilson's plan, see Linsly R. Williams to Wilson, June 27, 1907, ibid., pp. 234-36.

27. Editorial, "The 'Quad' System," *Daily Princetonian* (Hereinafter cited as *Princetonian*), October 2, 1907, p. 2.

28. [Wilson] to David B. Jones, September 26, 1907; WWP; Andrew C. Imbrie to Wilson, July 25, 1907, published along with Wilson's reply, July 29, 1907, in PAW 8, no. 1 (September 25, 1907): 7-9. See also W. M. Daniels to John Grier Hibben, August 9, 1907; M. W. Jacobus to Wilson, October 14, 1907; Bayard Henry to Wilson, July 29, 1907; Cleveland H. Dodge to Wilson, September 28, 1907; Henry Burling Thompson to Harold G. Murray, July 16, 1907; Thompson to Moses Taylor Pyne, July 30, 1907; and Thompson to Dodge, October 15, 1907, *PWW*, 17: 342-43, 432-35, 301-03, 405-06, 285, 308-09.

29. Bayard Henry to Henry Burling Thompson, July 13, 1907, enclosed with letter from Henry to Wilson, July 29, 1907, *PWW*, 17: 305, 301-06.

30. Baker, *Wilson, Princeton*, 2: 256-57; Wilson, "Notes for an Address to the Princeton University Faculty" [October 7, 1907] and "Draft of an Announcement," October 18, 1907, *PWW*, 17: 418-21.

31. Minutes of the Board of Trustees of Princeton University, October 17, 1907, Trustees' Papers, 10; and Baker, *Wilson, Princeton*, 2: 260-62.

32. Baker, *Wilson, Princeton*, 2: 262-67; Bragdon, *Wilson*, pp. 328-30; and Arthur S. Link, *Wilson: The Road to the White House*, pp. 54-57, 63, 74-75. Wilson to Melancthon W. Jacobus, November 6, 1907; David B. Jones to Wilson, November 12, 1907; and Wilson, "Notes for Remarks to the Board of Trustees of Princeton University," January 9, 1908, *PWW*, 17: 470-71, 495-97, 589-90.

33. Wilson, "Address to the Princeton Club of Chicago" [March 12, 1908]; and Henry Burling Thompson, et al. to the Board of Trustees of Princeton University [April 8, 1908], with "Report and Recommendations Respecting Undergraduate Social Conditions of Princeton University," *PWW*, 18: 17-34, 229-41. See also Baker, *Wilson, Princeton*, 2: 287-302; Bragdon, *Wilson*, p. 332; and Link, *Road to the White House*, pp. 63-65.

34. Woodrow Wilson quoted in Link, *Road to the White House*, pp. 70, 65-71; Bragdon, *Wilson*, pp. 336, 366-69; Baker, *Wilson, Princeton*, 2: 310-24. See also editorial note, "Wilson at the Meeting of the Board of Trustees of January 13, 1910," *PWW*, 20: 8.

35. Link, *Road to the White House*, pp. 74, 75-77; Arthur S. Link to Marcia G.

Synnott, October 14, 1976; Wilson to Herbert Bruce Brougham, February 1, 1910, *PWW*, 20: 69-71, also pp. 65, 74-76, 79-80; Baker, *Wilson, Princeton*, 2: 290-93, 327-28; and Bragdon, *Wilson*, pp. 371-72.

36. Link, *Road to the White House*, pp. 72-73; Wilson, draft of "The Country and the Colleges" [ca. February 24, 1910], *PWW*, 20: 159-61, 166-67, 157-72.

37. Wilson "Address to Pittsburgh Alumni," delivered at Pittsburgh banquet, April 16, 1910 (from *Pittsburgh Dispatch*, April 17, 1910, in *The Public Papers of Woodrow Wilson*, vol. 2, *College and State, Educational, Literary and Political Papers (1875-1913)*, ed. Ray Stannard Baker and William E. Dodd, pp. 202-03, and as reported in *PAW* 10, no. 28 ([April 20, 1910]: 471, 467-71); and "News Reports of an Address in Pittsburgh to Princeton Alumni," *PWW*, 20: 363-68, 373-76, 433-44. See also Link, *Road to the White House*, pp. 78-86; Bragdon, *Wilson*, pp. 375-78.

38. Link, *Road to the White House*, pp. 86-91; Bragdon, *Wilson*, p. 379, n. 68, and pp. 378-82; Baker, *Wilson, Princeton*, 2: 344-52. For an excellent, recent intellectual biography of Wilson, consult John M. Mulder, *Woodrow Wilson: The Years of Preparation*. Mulder examines in depth and with subtlety the relationship between Wilson's religious thought, educational philosophy, and developing political aspirations and vision. See especially chap. 8, "Conflict and Turmoil, 1906-1910," pp. 187-228; and pp. 252-54, 273-76.

39. Wilson, "News Report of an Address at Brooklyn Institute on 'A University's Use,'" *New York Times* [December 12, 1902], in *PWW*, 14: 283-85; "The Young People and the Church" [October 13, 1904], and notes for his address to the Schoolmasters Club, October 8, 1904, ibid., 15: 510-19, 505-06. Bragdon, *Wilson*, pp. 309-10, and nn. 57-58.

40. [Wilson] to William Belden Reed, Jr., August 31, 1907, in reply to Reed's letter of August 27, 1907, and H. Howard Armstrong to Wilson, August 29, 1907, *PWW*, 17: 367, 362-68. Wilson to H. Howard Armstrong, September 3, 1907, WC. For comments and letters on the Quadrangle Plan, see Andrew C. Imbrie to Wilson, July 25, 1907, and Wilson, to Imbrie, July 29, 1907, *PAW*.

41. [Wilson] to William Belden Reed, Jr., August 31, 1907, *PWW*. Wilson to Morgan Poitiaux Robinson, October 30, 1903, *PWW*, 15: 32. Students did work as waiters in the dining halls to pay for their board (*Catalogue of Princeton University, 1919-20*, p. 193n, PUA).

42. Wilson, "The University and the Nation," at Swathmore College [December 15, 1905], *PWW*, 16: 270, 267-71. See also Edwin E. Slosson, *Great American Universities*, chap. 3, "Princeton University," pp. 104-05; W. E. Burghardt Du Bois, "Negroes in College," *Nation* 122 (March 3, 1926): 229-30; and John Stewart Burgess '05, "Princeton's World Outlook: The Achievements and Future of the Princeton Center in China," supplement to *PAW* 16 (May 31, 1916).

43. Slosson, *Great American Universities*, pp. 105-06.

44. Wilson to G. McArthur Sullivan [ca. December 3, 1909]; Sullivan to Wilson, November 20, 1909, and the Secretary [Charles W. McAlpin] to Sullivan, December 6, 1909, subject file Students—Nationalities, Negro, PUA; and Wilson to John Rogers Williams, September 2, 1904, C. W. McAlpin Correspondence, file on Woodrow Wilson, 1901-11, PUA.

45. Editor's note, "A Negro at Princeton?" *PAW* 35. no. 23 (March 29, 1935), p. 533; Francis James Dallett, former university archivist, Princeton University, to the editor, *PAW*, June 2, 1970, on "Negroes at Princeton," PUA. Dallett's letter, with

some alterations, was published in *PAW* 71, no. 6 (November 3, 1970), p. 3, as "First Black Students."

46. Slosson, *Great American Universities*, p. 105; Varnum Lansing Collins, *Princeton*, appendix, pp. 408-09. See pp. 4-5 and p. 236 n. 6.

47. M. M. Boyd '12 to A. Lawrence Lowell, January 22, 1923, ALL, #42-A Negroes. Paul Robeson would not have been admitted to Princeton during this period, even though his father had been pastor of a local church. After winning a competitive state scholarship, Robeson became the third black student to enter Rutgers University. He played varsity football and was selected as an All-American player in 1917 and 1918. Robeson won three other varsity letters and was elected to Phi Beta Kappa his junior year (Richard Bardolph, *The Negro Vanguard* [New York: Vintage, 1972], pp. 216-17, 270).

48. Wilson, notes for an address, *"For Hampton Institute,"* February 26, 1909; and "News Report of an Address in Princeton at the Witherspoon Street Presbyterian Church" [April 3, 1909], *PWW*, 19: 69, 148-49; and Wilson to Louis Edelman, September 20, 1909, WC. To protect the public health, Wilson recognized that streets and sanitation had to be improved first in Princeton's poorer areas, which were inhabited mostly by blacks and Irish ("Newspaper Report on Two Lectures on Problems of City Government" [February 29, 1896], *PWW*, 9: 470-71).

49. Subject file Students—Nationalities, American Indians, PUA, especially Varnum Lansing Collins, "Indian Wards at Princeton," *Princeton University Bulletin* 13 (May 1902): 101-06; and a list of "American Indian Students at Princeton" compiled by F. J. Dallett, October 1970. For information on Joseph Paul Baldeagle, see *The Nassau Herald, Class of 1923*, p. 23; and *Princetonian*, March 8, 1963 ("Democrats Choose Baldeagle") and November 20, 1963 ("Baldeagle Discusses '2 Lives'").

50. Wilson, "After-Dinner Remarks in New York to the Friendly Sons of St. Patrick" [March 17, 1909], *PWW*, 19: 103, 102-08.

51. *PPR, 1908-23*; *Reports of the Dean of the Faculty to the Trustees' Committee on Morals and Discipline*, 1900-08, and Radcliffe Heermance, Office of the Supervisor [in 1925, Dean] of Freshmen, "Preliminary Analysis of Freshman Class" in September 1921-29, Trustees' Papers, PUA; and Bragdon, *Wilson*, pp. 272-74 and n. 9.

52. Woodrow Wilson, *A History of the American People*, vol. 5: *Reunion and Nationalization, 1865-1900* (New York: Harper & Brothers, 1902), pp. 212-13; Bragdon, *Wilson*, pp. 249-50, 260-61, 348-49; and Wilson, "Remarks in New York at the Opening Exercises of the Institute of Musical Art" [October 31, 1905], *PWW*, 16: 208-10; and John Higham, *Strangers in the Land*, pp. 251-52, 190-93, 198-200, 210, 243.

53. *Report of the Dean of the Faculty to the Committee on Morals and Discipline*, October 21, 1902, and October 21, 1903, Trustees' Papers, 10: 235, 227-35, 363; and *College of New Jersey, Matriculation Book*, 2 (1893-1903), PUA. A few members of the Catholic hierarchy, for example, the Most Reverend Dr. James Augustine McFaul, bishop of Trenton, denounced private eastern universities, because Roman Catholics were "beginning to send their sons to Princeton and Harvard and Yale" (Wilson to Lawrence C. Woods, June 23, 1909, WC).

54. See *The Nassau Herald, Classes of 1915, 1917*, and *1922* for information on James V. Forrestal, F. Scott Fitzgerald, and Adlai E. Stevenson, respectively. For the Princeton careers of Fitzgerald and Stevenson, see also Kenneth S. Davis, *A Prophet in His Own Country*, pp. 106-21.

55. See *The Nassau Herald* and *Bric-à-Brac*, 1910-30.

56. Wilson to R. Heath Dabney, May 31, 1881, *PWW*, 2: 71-72; Bragdon, *Wilson*, pp. 72-73 and n. 20; Link, *Road to the White House*, pp. 270-71; and Wilson, "The Rights of the Jews," address at Carnegie Hall, New York, December 6, 1911 (*Congressional Record*, 62d Cong., 2d sess., vol. 48, appendix, pp. 497-98), in *Public Papers of Woodrow Wilson*, ed. Baker and Dodd, 2: 318-22.

57. J. Ridgway Wright '79 to Tommy [Woodrow] Wilson, September 16, 1904, WP, LC.

58. Ibid.; and *The Nassau Herald, fifth* and *fiftieth* albums of the class of 1908.

59. Leon Michael Levy to Wilson [ca June 25, 1907], WP, LC.

60. Ibid., see "Ex-members of the Class of 1905," *The Nassau Herald, Class of 1905*, and also *PWW*, 17: 222-24 and nn. 1-3.

61. Harold Zeiss to Wilson, June 27, 1907, *PWW*, 17: 233-34; *The Nassau Herald, Class of 1907*.

62. Louis Irving Reichner to Wilson, July 17, 1907, *PWW*, 17: 288-89. Reichner was then an attorney in Philadelphia. See also *The Nassau Herald, Class of 1894*.

63. Walter Mead Rankin, M.S. '84, professor of biology, gave to Princeton the "brief account of the arrival of the first Japanese students in Princeton," written by his father, who was then treasurer of the Presbyterian Board of Foreign Missions (subject file Students—Nationalities, Japanese, PUA. For material on Hikoichi Orita, see his alumni biographical file, PUA; *President's Entrance-Book*, vol. 1 (1871-93), PUA; and his obituary notice in *PAW* 20, no. 32 (May 19, 1920), pp. 760-61.

64. Wilson to Charles W. McAlpin, May 27, 1903, C. W. McAlpin Correspondence, File on Woodrow Wilson, 1901-11, PUA. Motokichi Takahashi to Wilson, January 10, 1907, *PWW*, 16: 557-59; Wilson to Edward Warren Ordway, February 20, 1904, and a "News Report of an Address in Montclair, N.J." [January 28, 1904], *PWW*, 15: 175, 142-43.

65. Wilson to Lucius H. Miller, January 15, 1909, and Wilson to Andrew C. Imbrie, March 26, 1909, WWP, Miscellany. Arthur J. Brown to Wilson, March 17, 1909, and William Henry Grant to Wilson, December 2, 1909, *PWW*, 19: 109-10, 544-45. While noting their "unsavory" habits, Wilson praised, nevertheless, the industry of Chinese workmen (*A History of the American People*, 5: 213-14).

66. Andrew F. West to Wilson, July 12, 1909, WWP, Graduate School, Committee of the Board; and two subject files on Students—Nationalities, Chinese, and Nationalities (Undergraduate and Graduate), PUA, especially these clippings: "Chinese Grad Students Succeed," *PAW* 28, no. 26 (April 13, 1928), p. 778, and "Chinese Leaders Educated Here," *Princetonian*, October 6, 1948.

67. "The Daily Princetonian Entertains," *Princetonian*, May 1, 1909, p. 1; and "President Wilson Pleads for Social Independence Before Philadelphian Society," *Princetonian*, April 2, 1909, p. 1.

68. Wilson to Frank A. Vanderlip, February 1, 1909; and Henry S. Pritchett to Wilson, May 5, 1909, *PWW*, 19: 18-19, 185; and Bragdon, *Wilson*, p. 334.

69. Wilson, "Address to the Princeton Club of Chicago" [March 12, 1908], *PWW*, 18: 23, 22-28.

70. Wilson, "Abraham Lincoln: A Man of the People," address on the occasion of the celebration of the hundredth anniversary of the birth of Abraham Lincoln, Chicago, February 12, 1909 (taken from "Abraham Lincoln: The Tribute of a Century," pp. 14-30), *Public Papers of Woodrow Wilson, College and State*, ed. Baker and

Dodd, 2: 90, 83-101. In *PWW*, see "News Report of an Address in New York to Williams College Alumni" [February 6, 1909], "News Report of an Address to the Princeton Club of Chicago" [February 14, 1909], "Address to the Presbyterian Union of Baltimore" [February 19, 1909], "News Report of an Address in Philadelphia to the University Extension Society" [March 13, 1909], 19: 30-31, 47-48, 52-63, 98-100, and draft of "The Country and the Colleges," 20: 160. See also Wilson, "What Is A College For?" *Scribner's Magazine* 46 (November 1909): 570-77; Baker, *Wilson, Princeton*, 2: 304-05.

71. Wilson, News Report of Addresses to the New England Alumni in Boston and at the Harvard Church in Brookline, Massachusetts," "President Wilson Urges Democracy" [November 13, 1909], *PWW*, 19: 497; and Higham, *Strangers in the Land*, pp. 192-93, 203-04, 311.

72. Wilson, "Address at the Inauguration of Henry Harbaugh Apple as President of Franklin and Marshall College" [January 7, 1910], *PWW*, 19: 744, 740-47.

73. A. Lawrence Lowell to Wilson, February 9, 1910, *PWW*, 20: 91. See also Link, *Road to the White House*, pp. 90-91; Bragdon, *Wilson*, pp. 382-83; Charles William Eliot, "Woodrow Wilson," *Atlantic Monthly* 133 (June 1924): 823, 815-23. For Eliot's political preferences—"the archetypical Mugwump"—see Laurence R. Veysey, *The Emergence of the American University*, p. 88. Henry Cabot Lodge wrote Sturgis Bigelow, December 16, 1914, that Lowell, traditionally a Republican, had voted for Wilson in 1912, because "apparently college presidents stand by each other in politics as if they were a trade organization," quoted in John A. Garraty, *Henry Cabot Lodge: A Biography* (New York: Alfred A. Knopf, 1953), p. 296 and n.4.

74. Bragdon, *Wilson*, pp. 405-08; Baker, *Wilson, Princeton*, 2: 356.

75. William M. Leary, Jr., "Smith of New Jersey: A Biography of H. Alexander Smith, United States Senator from New Jersey, 1944-1959" (Ph.D. diss. Princeton University, 1966), pp. 17-28.

76. Wilson to Zephaniah Charles Felt, December 6, 1904, WC.

77. The Special Committee on Limitation of Enrollment, appointed by President Hibben at a university faculty meeting, January 17, 1921, included the following members: Howard McClenahan, dean of the college (1912-25), chairman; Varnum Lansing Collins, secretary of the university; Professor Christian F. Gauss; Fred Le Roy Hutson, registrar; and H. Alexander Smith. See *Catalogues of Princeton University, 1900-01, 1910-11, 1919-20, 1920-21*, and *1929-30*. George C. Wintringer, memorandum to H. Alexander Smith, December 10, 1920, and V. Lansing Collins to Smith, January 18, 1921, HASP, 1920-27, box 38, folder Limitation of Students Com. 1921-22. Minutes of a Meeting of the Board of Trustees, January 12, 1922, Trustees' Papers, 20 (October-June 1921-22): 6-8, PUA. H. Alexander Smith, "The Limitation of Enrollment at Princeton," *Princeton Pictorial* 10 (March 30, 1922): 268-69.

78. "Dartmouth College, The Selective Process for Admission, 1921-1922" (a small brochure), H. Alexander Smith to Dr. Ray Lyman Wilbur, January 28, 1921, Wilbur to Smith, with memorandum, February 9, 1921, M. W. Jacobus to Smith, January 22, 1921, Howard C. Warren to Smith, January 26, 1921, Smith to Jacobus, February 3, 1921, and Smith to Warren, February 3, 1921, HASP, 1920-27, box 38, folder Limitation of Students Com. 1921-22. See also Princeton University, October 3, 1921, *Minutes of the Faculty* (September 24, 1914, to April 8, 1929), p. 315, PUA; Meeting of the Board of Trustees, October 26, 1922, Trustees' Papers, 21 (October-June 1922-

23); and *PPR, July 31, 1925*, pp. 43-46. Carl C. Brigham, professor of psychology and later a member of the Committee on Admissions, thought that psychological tests would prove "the greatest usefulness" by guiding students through their college careers ("Psychological Tests at Princeton," *PAW* 24, no. 9 [November 28, 1923]: 185-87).

79. Meeting of March 7 and Special Meeting of March 14, 1921, *Minutes of the Faculty*, p. 293; HASP, 1920-27, box 38, folder Limitation of Students Com. 1921-22; and "Report of the Special Committee on Limitation of Enrollment, Presented to the University Faculty, Monday, March 14, 1921," subject file Admission, box 1, PUA.

80. Special Meeting, March 14, 1921, *Minutes of the Faculty*, p. 293.

81. March 21, 1921, *Minutes of the Faculty*, p. 295, and "Amended Report of the Special Committee on Limitation of Enrollment, Presented to the University Faculty, Monday, March 21, 1921," subject file, cabinet files, folder Enrollment, PUA.

82. Walter E. Hope to H. Alexander Smith, February 28 and July 5, 1921, and Smith to Hope, March 1, 1921, HASP, 1920-27, box 38, folder Limitation of Students Com. 1921-22.

83. H. Alexander Smith to Dean Howard McClenahan, July 17, 1921, dean of the college, old files, box 2, folder H. Alexander Smith, Exec. Secy., PUA. Smith letter on October 31 and memoranda on October 19 and November 23, 1921, to McClenahan, Smith memorandum on October 19 and letter on October 25, 1921, to V. L. Collins, Smith to Walter E. Hope, November 29, 1921, Smith to M. W. Jacobus, October 31 and November 8, 1921, and Jacobus to Smith, October 31, 1921, HASP, 1920-27, box 38, folder Limitation of Students Com. 1921-22.

84. Special Meeting, January 9, 1922, *Minutes of the Faculty*, p. 319; and Meeting, January 12, 1922, Trustees' Papers 20: 6-8. As of 1922-23, the graduate school decided to limit full-time students to 200—its instructional capacity—not including "incidental" graduate students from Princeton Theological Seminary (Trustees' Meeting, June 19-20, 1922).

85. Editorials, "Why More Than Two Thousand?" "How Shall We Limit Our Enrollment?" "Our Plan For Enrollment Limitation," and "The Claims of Princeton Men on Their University," *Princetonian*, January 26, 27, 28, and 30, 1922, p. 2; also campus comment, "Sons of Alumni," ibid., January 30, 1922, p. 4.

86. Ibid., February 4, 1922, p. 3, March 22, 1924, p. 1, and March 24, 1924, pp. 1, 5.

87. Professor Varnum Lansing ("Wilkie") Collins, secretary of the university; Fred LeRoy Hutson, registrar; Professor Luther P. Eisenhart; and Professor Charles W. Kennedy (English) also served on the Committee on Admissions. See Meeting, October 26, 1922, Trustees' Papers, 21; Alexander Leitch, memorandum to Radcliffe Heermance, November 27, 1951, "Extracts from minutes of the Faculty and Trustees dealing with various phases of admission," Secretary's Office, Miscellaneous Correspondence, 1940-51, box 2 (of 5), F-L, folder "Heermance, Radcliffe—Material re Coll. Bd. Exams, Elimination Latin, Greek, for admission; Limitation enroll; appt. Dir. of Admission." PUA.

88. Meetings, January 15 and 22, 1923, Minutes of the Meetings of the Committee on Admission (Office of the Committee on Admission). Radcliffe Heermance invited Adam Le Roy Jones, director of admission at Columbia and a former preceptor in

philosophy, to visit Princeton on January 22, 1923, and to explain Columbia's admission regulations. Both Jones and Princeton's committee were in favor of urging the CEEB to offer "psychological" examinations in June 1923. See also Heermance to A. Lawrence Lowell, December 12, 1923, with a six-page statement on "Limitation of Enrollment by the Selective Method (An Informal Statement of the Procedure Used by the Committee on Admission During the Year 1923)," ALL, #76 Admission, Committee on, September 1922-December 1923. Heermance, "The New Plan of Limitation of Princeton's Enrollment," *PAW* 23, no. 18 (February 14, 1923): 386-88, and address, "The Operation of the Plan of Selective Admission," *PAW*, 24, no. 26 (April 9, 1924): 549-51; *PPR, Dec. 31, 1923*, pp. 16-22.

89. Heermance to Lowell, December 12, 1923, ALL; "The Operation of Selective Admission," *PAW*, pp. 550-51.

90. See note 89 and H. Alexander Smith, "Entering College and Remaining There Under the New Programme," part 1, *PAW* 25, no. 28 (April 22, 1925): 681-83, and part 2, 25, no. 29 (April 29, 1925): 713-15.

91. Walter E. Hope to H. Alexander Smith, February 1, 1922, HASP, 1920-27, box 38, folder Limitation of Students Com. 1921-22, and Smith to Fred J. Elliott, September 17, 1927, ibid., box 36, folder Admissions, Director of, Sp. Cases; and Smith to Fred LeRoy Hutson, August 17, 1921, dean of the college, old files, box 2, folder H. Alexander Smith. At the December 13, 1923, meeting of the Committee on Admissions Director Heermance commented on the "danger that Princeton shall become a prep school university rather than a national one" (Minutes). See also Ledlie I. Laughlin '12, assistant to Director Heermance, "Admission Without Examination," *PAW* 37, no. 11 (December 4, 1936), pp. 235-36, in subject folder Administration, Entrance Requirements, PUA.

92. Anne MacDonald, assistant to the chairman, Richard M. Gummere, Committee on Admission, Harvard College, to Radcliffe Heermance, March 7, 1936, President's Office, Correspondence of Harold Willis Dodds, 1935-36, folder Admissions —Statistics on, PUA.

93. "Heermance Reports 29 Freshmen Entered Under New Program," *Princetonian*, November 6, 1937, also "29 Freshmen Admitted Without Examination," *PAW*, 38, no. 8 (November 12, 1937), pp. 172-73, and "Admission," *PAW* 37, no. 11 (December 4, 1936), p. 238 in subject folder Admin. Offices, Admissions, PUA; Carl C Brigham, secretary, Committee on Admission, report, "The Quality of the Classes Admitted to Princeton in the Years 1928 to 1935," President's Office, Correspondence of Harold Willis Dodds 1935-36, folder Admissions—Statistics on, PUA; "Admission to Princeton (being a Digest of Remarks Delivered by Dean Radcliffe Heermance at the Seventh Annual Dinner in honor of the Class Agents of the Princeton University Fund)," October 4, 1946, subject folder Administration, Entrance Requirements, PUA.

94. Radcliffe Heermance, Office of the Supervisor of Freshmen, "Preliminary Analysis of Freshman Class," September 1923, Trustees' Papers; *The Freshman Herald, Class of 1927*, pp. 32-33; *Catalogue of Princeton University, 1920-21*, pp. 199-200, PUA.

95. See n. 94, and *The Nassau Herald, 1927*.

96. Collins to Canby, November 23, 1922, HASP; Meetings, June 11, 1924, May 21, 1931, and June 14, 1935, Minutes of the Committee on Admission (only in a few

places were the exact number of Jewish and Catholic applicants given). See also George E. Tomberlin, Jr., "Trends in Princeton Admissions" (Senior thesis, Princeton University, 1971), pp. 130-35; and Robert M. Hutchins to Steven Buenning, December 17, 1970, quoted in Steven L. Buenning, "John Grier Hibben: A Biographical Study (1919-1932)" (Senior thesis, Princeton University, 1971), pp. 60-61. Permission to quote from this letter was granted to Marcia G. Synnott by Robert M. Hutchins, April 12, 1971.

97. May 21, 1931, and June 14, 1935, Minutes of the Committee on Admission; and Tomberlin, "Trends in Princeton Admissions," pp. 130-35.

98. See n. 97, above, and January 25, 1938, Minutes of the Committee on Admission; and H. Alexander Smith to Henry B. Thompson, November 28 and December 8, 1922, HASP, 1920-27, box 38, folder Undergraduate Life Com. 1922-27. See also Radcliffe Heermance to Smith, August 29, 1927, Smith to A. G. Bartholomew '01, September 8, 1927, and Bartholomew to Smith, September 16, 1927, HASP, 1920-27, box 36, folder Admissions, Director of, Sp. Cases. For a list of ten "outstanding" Jewish undergraduates at Princeton, see [Gordon Gowans Sikes, assistant to the secretary,] copy, to Ruth Rosenberger, *The American Hebrew*, December 9, 1931, subject file Students—Nationalities, Jewish, PUA.

99. "Limitation of Numbers," Freshman Office Records, Com. on Limitation of Numbers 1922, YUA, and above, n. 2.

100. Baker, *Wilson, Princeton*, 2: 273-74; and Bragdon, *Wilson*, pp. 408-09. See *PAW*, 24: "Princeton and the Upperclass Club System: The Report of President Hibben's Committee on the Revision of Club Elections" and Alexander Leitch's comment, no. 32, (May 21, 1924), pp. 693-97; Leitch, "Club Elections," no. 25 (April 2, 1924), pp. 531-32; and H. Alexander Smith, "A Year of Interesting Developments," no. 36 (June 18, 1924), pp. 791-94. See also Paul Sigmund, "Princeton in Crisis and Change," *Change* 5, no. 2 (March 1973), p. 37.

Chapter 7. Conclusion: A New Elite, 1940s to 1970s

1. Gene R. Hawes, "The Colleges of America's Upper Class," *Saturday Review Magazine*, November 16, 1963, p. 71.

2. McGeorge Bundy, "The Issue Before the Court," *Atlantic Monthly* 240, no. 5 (November 1977), pp. 41-54.

3. Ibid., pp. 44-45.

4. *Brief of Columbia University, Harvard University, Stanford University and the University of Pennsylvania as Amici Curiae*, June 7, 1977, *Regents of the University of California* v. *Allan Bakke*, p. 13.

5. Hawes, "The Colleges of America's Upper Class," pp. 68-70.

6. Seymour Martin Lipset and David Riesman, *Education and Politics at Harvard*, pp. 179, 307-10; Seymour Martin Lipset and Everett Carll Ladd, Jr., "Jewish Academics in the United States," *American Jewish Year Book, 1971*, vol. 72, pp. 89-128.

7. Francis J. Brown, Floyd W. Reeves, and Richard A. Anliot, eds., *Discriminations in Higher Education: A Report of the Midwest Educators Conference in Chicago, Illinois, November 3-4, 1950*, sponsored by the Midwest Committee on Discriminations in Higher Education and the Committee on Discriminations in Higher Education of the American Council on Education, American Council on Education

Studies, series 1—Reports of Committees and Conferences, vol. 15, no. 50, (August 1951), pp. 6-22, 35-39. See R. Freeman Butts and Lawrence A. Cremin, *A History of Education in American Culture*, pp. 522-23; also Nathan Glazer, "Social Characteristics of American Jews, 1654-1954," *American Jewish Year Book, 1955*, vol. 56, pp. 25-36; and Oscar Handlin and Mary F. Handlin, "The Acquisition of Political and Social Rights by the Jews in the United States," ibid., pp. 76-77, 86, 89-90.

8. Hawes, "The Colleges of America's Upper Class," pp. 70-71; E. Digby Baltzell, "The Protestant Establishment Revisited," *American Scholar* 45, no. 4 (Autumn 1976), pp. 499-518.

9. James Bryant Conant, as quoted by Richard M. Gummere, "Harvard and the Entering Freshman," *Harvard Educational Review* 18, no. 1 (January 1945), p. 29; James B. Conant, *My Several Lives*, pp. 107, 135-36; *HPR, 1934-35*, pp. 5-9; "In Terms of Men," unidentified clipping dated January 24, 1936, in DHCCF, folder President Conant, 1933-36.

10. *HPR, 1934-35*, pp. 10-11; Conant, *My Several Lives*, chap. 12, "The National Scholarships," pp. 128-38; Gummere, "Harvard and the Entering Freshmen," pp. 28, 30.

11. Conant, *My Several Lives*, p. 136; "Geographic Distribution," 1930-31, 1950-51, DHCCF, folder President Conant, 1940-52.

12. Conant, *My Several Lives*, pp. 84, 140-45, and chap. 27, "The Harvard Report," pp. 363-73; "General Education in a Free Society: Twelve Harvard Professors Examine Anew the American Educational System," *HAB* 48, no. 1 (September 22, 1945), pp. [23]-30; John Monro, dean of freshmen studies, Miles College, Birmingham, Alabama, to Marcia G. Synnott, October 4, 1976; and see p. 156 and p. 270, n. 84. In 1934, the Harvard Corporation received and declined an offer of a $1,000 traveling scholarship from Dr. Ernst F. Sedgwick Hanfstaengl '09, Hitler's friend and Nazi party foreign press chief (*My Several Lives*, p. 144).

13. Conant, *My Several Lives*, pp. 370-71. See also Ellen K. Coughlin, "Harvard Weighs Plan to Reform College Curriculum" and "Harvard's Report on the 'Core Curriculum,'" *Chronicle of Higher Education* 16, no. 2 (March 6, 1978), pp. 1, 15-19. Thirty years after adopting its general education program, Harvard again undertook a major reexamination of its undergraduate curriculum. Following three years of review, the curriculum task force presented its report to the Faculty of Arts and Sciences. Under its proposed guidelines, the number of required courses would remain about the same, but would be reorganized and redistributed. The new "core curriculum" would require all students to take from seven to ten courses in five areas: literature and arts; history; social and philosophical analysis; science and mathematics; and foreign languages and culture. Students who did not satisfy three other basic requirements by examination would have to pass courses in expository writing, mathematics (through algebra), and reading knowledge of a foreign language. To fulfill the core curriculum would take about a year's work. Students would then be free to devote about half their undergraduate courses to their chosen major and about one-fourth to electives. After heated debate, the Faculty of Arts and Sciences approved the new curriculum by a vote of 182 to 65. It is scheduled to be introduced over a three-year period, beginning in the autumn of 1979. See also Malcolm G. Scully, "Tightening the Curriculum: Enthusiasm, Dissent, and 'So What Else Is New?'," *Chronicle of Higher Education* 16, no. 11 (May 8, 1978), pp. 1, 12.

14. Conant, *My Several Lives*, chap. 28, "Coeducation in Fact If Not in Theory,"

pp. 374-83. See also Henry K. Beecher and Mark D. Altschule, *Medicine at Harvard*, pp. 139, 195-96, 227, and 461-74.

15. *HPR, 1942-43*, pp. 13-18; *HPR, 1945-46*, pp. 5-8; "Address of Dr. James B. Conant [to the Chamber of Commerce of the United States, May 1, 1947], Extension of Remarks of Hon. Robert Tripp Ross of New York in the House of Representatives, Tuesday, May 6, 1947," *Congressional Record*, 93, part 11, 80th Cong., 1st sess., April 2, 1947, to June 12, 1947, appendix, pp. A2122-25. Wilbur J. Bender, "Report on the Veteran: His Grades, His Difficulties, His Pressures and Enthusiasms," *HAB* 49, no. 11 (March 8, 1947), pp. 464-67. See also Bender, as quoted by Paul Giguere, "Harvard Dean Product of West, Opposes Inbreeding in Colleges," unidentified clipping dated December 1, 1946 [*Boston Herald*?], and Charles L. Whipple, "Many Are Culled, Few Are Chosen," *Boston Sunday Globe*, May 15, 1960, in Wilbur Joseph Bender, A.B. '27 and A.M. '30, quinquennial file, HUA; John Monro to Marcia G. Synnott, October 4, 1976. See also Francis Bertrand McCarthy, "A Study of the Admission of Veteran Students in Harvard College (1945-1947) and Their College Records," (Mimeographed, 1954, 131 pp.) HUL.

16. Conant, *My Several Lives*, p. 373; Gordon W. Allport, "Two-Thirds of Postwar College Students Religious," January 22, 1947, Radcliffe College Archives, quoted with the permission of Dr. Robert Allport, January 8, 1977.

17. Allport, "Two-Thirds of Postwar College Students Religious."

18. John Monro to Marcia G. Synnott, October 4, 1976.

19. Ibid., and see clippings in Bender's quinquennial file, HUA, especially Whipple, "Many Are Culled, Few Are Chosen," and "W. J. Bender, 65, Ex-Harvard Dean," *Boston Herald*, April 1, 1969.

20. W. J. Bender, "A comprehensive formal statement of Harvard College admission policy," September 18, 1952, DHCCF, folder Committee on Admission Policy 1952-57.

21. Paul H. Buck, "Balance in the College," *HAB* 48, no. 10 (February 16, 1946): [404]-06; Buck, "Who Comes to Harvard," *HAB* 50, no. 7 (January 10, 1948): 313-17; Bender, "Statement of Harvard College admission policy," DHCCF.

22. Bender, "Statement of Harvard College admission policy," DHCCF.

23. Ibid., and Bender, "To the Critics of Harvard," *HAB* 51, no. 13 (April 9, 1949): 545-48; "Sons of Harvard Men," DHC Statistical and Other Reports and Papers, 1920s to 1950s, folder Harvard Sons—Statistics.

24. "Is Too Much of 'The Best' Bad for Harvard? Broader Student Body Urged Lest College Defeat Its Own End," *Boston Sunday Globe*, October 8, 1961; Stephen F. Jencks, "Dean Bender's Report," *Harvard Crimson*, September 30, 1961; "Harvard No Slave to Change Says Retiring Dean Bender," *Boston Sunday Herald*, May 29, 1960; "Bender Named Charity Fund's New Director," *Cambridge Chronicle and the Cambridge Sun*, July 27, 1961, in Bender's quinquennial file, HUA. See also Bender, "To the Critics of Harvard," *HAB*.

25. A. C. Hanford to Harper Woodward, March 4, 1935, DHCCF, folder President Conant, 1933-36; in DHCCF, folder Negroes: "List of Students of Negro Descent Registered in Harvard College in 1935-36," June 3, 1936; David Klugh to Hanford, January 8, 1937; Hanford to Addison Hibbard, May 31, 1939; copy of information in response to questionnaire of the Carnegie study of the Negro in America, May 15, 1940; and W. J. Bender to Joseph H. Chadbourne, Jr., October 16, 1951.

26. John Monro to Marcia G. Synnott, October 4, 1976; Monro to Bill [Wilbur J. Bender], April 26, 1949, DHCCF, folder Mr. J. U. Monro 1947-49 (Counsellor for Veterans). See also Lipset and Riesman, *Education and Politics at Harvard*, pp. 180, 222; E. J. Kahn, Jr., *Harvard: Through Change and Through Storm*, pp. 109-11; and Penny Hollander Feldman, "Recruiting an Elite: Admission to Harvard College" (Ph.D. diss., Harvard University, 1975), "Table 5.5, Admissions Rates of Applicants in Preferred Categories," p. 111.

27. Harvard-Radcliffe Admission and Scholarship Newsletter, vol. 26, no. 1 (September 1977).

28. Ibid.

29. Andrew M. Greeley, *Ethnicity, Denomination, and Inequality*, pp. 18-24, 36-49, 56-59, 70-72.

30. Kahn, *Harvard*, pp. 53-54; Riesman and Lipset, *Education and Politics at Harvard*, pp. 179-80; Dorothy Rabinowitz, "Are Jewish Students Different?" *Change* 3, no. 4 (Summer 1971), pp. 48-49.

31. [William Ernest Hocking] to Jerome D. Greene, May 29, 1922, FF, box 191, folder 17.

32. Effie J. Taylor, dean, Yale University School of Nursing, to Mrs. Mabel K. Staupers, R.N., National Association of Colored Graduate Nurses, copy, April 18, 1941, Ruth Logan Roberts, chairman, Advisory Council, National Association of Colored Graduate Nurses, to Canon Anson Phelps Stokes, April 30, 1941, Stokes to Mrs. E. P. Roberts, May 3, 1941, and Stokes to Charles Seymour, May 3, 1941, CS, box 102, National Yale Alumni Placement Bureau to Negro Problem, file Negro Students (Problem regarding).

33. Charles Seymour to Rev. Anson Phelps Stokes, May 8, 1941, Ruth Logan Roberts to Stokes, July 2, 1941, and Stokes to Mrs. Roberts, copy, July 9, 1941, CS, box 102, file Negro Students (Problem regarding). For Harvard's reluctance to admit black medical students, see Beecher and Altschule, *Medicine at Harvard*, pp. 475-81. As of September 1968, there were 5 blacks among the 570 medical students at Harvard. In 1969, Harvard Medical School implemented an affirmative action policy, with the result that, among the 140 students who entered the class of 1975 and the class of 1976, there were 30 (21.5 percent) successful minority applicants: 15 blacks, 7-9 Hispanic Americans, 5 Asian Americans, and 1-3 American Indians. Such "special handling, itself a kind of racism," it was expected, would "not be necessary after 1985" (p. 479).

34. Orde Coombs, "Making It At Yale: The Necessity of Excellence," *Change* 5, no. 5 (June 1973), chart, "Black Candidates for Admission to Yale," pp. 51-52, 49-54.

35. Ibid., pp. 51-53.

36. Edward S. Noyes, "Report of the Board of Admissions to the President and Fellows of Yale University," *YRP, 1943-44* and *1944-45*, YUA.

37. *YRP, 1943-44*; and Charles Seymour to Leonard Shiman, July 7, 1944, CS, box 128 Schu-Shy, file Leonard Shiman.

38. Noyes, *YRP, 1944-45*.

39. Charles Seymour to Edward S. Noyes, December 20, 1948, "Revisions of Application Blank" and application to freshman class; Noyes to Seymour, November 2, 1948, and various application blanks and announcements, exhibits A-D, November 10, 1948, CS, box 2, Board of Admissions, file Minutes.

40. William C. De Vane, "Report of the Dean of Yale College to the President . . . ," *YRP, 1947-48.*

41. Ibid., and Edgar S. Furniss, "Report of the Dean of the Graduate School to the President . . . ," *YRP, 1948-49.*

42. See Sidney Lovett, "Report as Chaplain of Yale University to the President and Fellows of Yale University," *YRP, 1947-48-1953-54*; see p. 155 and p. 270, n. 78. In 1926-27, about 4 percent (29) of the 671 graduate students were Jewish.

43. William F. Buckley, Jr., *God and Man at Yale: The Superstitions of "Academic Freedom"* (Chicago: Henry Regnery, 1951), pp. 26-31.

44. Lovett, Church of Christ in Yale University, "Report as Chaplain . . . ," *YRP,* in Yale Miscellaneous Manuscripts #94. In 1965, by a write-in vote of the alumni, William Horowitz '29 became the first Jew elected to the Yale Corporation.

45. Clippings from PUA, subject file Students—Nationalities, Jewish: William A. McWhirter '63, subject of column "On the Campus," "At the Kosher Table," 9 *PAW* 63, no. 20 (March 8, 1963), p. 4. Clippings in PUA, subject file Students—Nationalities, Negro, from *PAW* 40; letters to the Editor, Norman Thomas, no. 25 (March 29, 1940), p. 571 and George McLean Harper, no. 26 (April 12, 1940), p. 59. From the *Princetonian*: letters to the editor, April 9 and 12, 1940; "White Supremacy at Princeton: 1. A Thousand Million Colored Allies," September 28, 1942, and "2. A Time to Decide," September 30, 1942; letters to the editor, September 30, 1942.

46. Clippings in subject file Students—Nationalities, Negro, from the *Princetonian*: "Whig-Clio Conducts Forum in Whig at 9 Tomorrow Evening," September 30, 1942; Benjamin H. Walker '44, "'Prince' Speakers Challenge Princeton on Policy of Racial Discrimination," October 2, 1942; "White Supremacy at Princeton: 3. We Make Answer," October 3, 1942; letters to the editor, October 3, 5, 7, 10, 12, 19, 1942; "'Prince' Stand Against Race Discrimination Gains Approval of Local Teachers' Union," October 12, 1942. See poll on "The Negro Question," *Nassau Sovereign,* October 1942; and letters to the editor, *PAW* 43, no. 11 (November 27, 1942), p. 3.

47. George E. Tomberlin, Jr., "Trends in Princeton Admissions" (Senior thesis, Princeton University, 1971), pp. 119, 136-42. See also subject file Students—Nationalities, Negro, from *PAW*: clipping, 47, no. 30 (May 23, 1947), p. 4; clipping, 48, no. 5 (October 24, 1947), p. 4; letters to the editor, 48, no. 29 (May 14, 1948), p. 11; letters to the editor, 49, no. 15 (January 28, 1949), p. 9; and William M. McWhirter '63, "Negro Undergraduates," subject of column "On the Campus," 62, no. 15 (January 26, 1962), p. 14. From the *Princetonian*: letters to the editor, June 3, 1946; "Yale Will Seek Negroes; Princeton Stays Neutral," March 15, 1955; and Fred Stuart, Jr., "Report Cites Evolution of Negro at Princeton," January 10, 1963. Walter White, "Princeton University Signifies Color Bar Is Crumbling There," New York *Herald Tribune,* December 26, 1948. See also in same file on Students—Nationalities, Negro, an excerpt from Minutes of Executive Committee, Board of Trustees of Princeton University, meeting of September 23, 1949, dated December 14, 1954.

48. Carl A. Fields, "One University's Response to Today's Negro Student," *University: A Princeton Quarterly,* no. 36 (Spring 1968), pp. 14, 17, 19.

49. Tomberlin, "Trends in Princeton Admissions," pp. 119, 127-28, 136-52, 159-60; Paul Sigmund, "Princeton in Crisis and Change," *Change* 5, no. 2 (March 1973), pp. 35, 38; and "A Survey of Princeton Freshmen," *PAW* 71, no. 17 (February 23, 1971), pp. 6-9.

50. Denny Chin, "Admissions Grants Recruiting Funds to Chicano, Indian Undergraduates," *Princetonian*, October 25, 1972, pp. 1, 6; and "Undergraduate Enrollment of Minorities in U.S. Higher Education," "Fact-File," *Chronicle of Higher Education*, March 20, 1978, pp. 16-21. By comparison, in the autumn of 1976, Harvard's undergraduate enrollment was 6,349 and Yale's 5,231. See also William McCleery, "The Admission Process at Hard-to-Get-into Colleges," *University: A Princeton Quarterly*, no. 45 (Summer 1970), pp. 23-30. To its long-held preferences for alumni sons (and daughters since 1969) and athletes, Princeton established a "target number" for three other groups: engineers; "blacks and other racial minorities," such as Puerto Ricans, Mexican Americans, and American Indians; and "disadvantaged white students."

51. "Answers to your questions about the admission of Princeton Sons," Alumni Council of Princeton University, June 1, 1958, subject file Admission I; President Goheen quoted in McCleery, "The Admission Process at Hard-to-Get-into Colleges," p. 26.

52. See above, n. 51; E. Alden Dunham '53, director of admission, "A Look at Princeton Admissions," *PAW* 65, no. 13 (January 19, 1965), pp. 6-9, 14-15. From 1940 to 1970, the percentage of high school graduates almost tripled—from 21.6 to 63.4 ("A Survey of Princeton Freshmen," *PAW* 71, no. 17 [February 23, 1971], p. 7); Harold Willis Dodds to Montgomery B. Angell, January 20, 1948, President's Office, Correspondence of Harold Willis Dodds, Miscellaneous Correspondence with Individuals (to 1957), A-L, folder A, and "Review of Princeton's Current Admission Policy," Graduate Council of Princeton University, May 7, 1948, subject file Admin. offices, Admissions, PUA.)

53. "Dean Heermance Denies Claim That Quota System Used Here," *Princetonian*, March 24, 1948; "Getting into Princeton," *Nassau Sovereign*, April 1949, in subject file Admin. offices, Admissions, PUA; McWhirter, "At the Kosher Table," *PAW*; David Zielenziger, "First Hebrew Classes Begin," *Princetonian*, September 20, 1972, p. 6; and Adele Simmons, dean of student affairs, Princeton University, to Marcia G. Synnott, July 28, 1976.

A university's once deserved anti-Semitic reputation may persist years after the institution has begun to change. In 1972 and 1973, Arthur B. Cooper '74 formally complained to B'nai B'rith, the New Jersey Division of Civil Rights, the United States Department of Health, Education, and Welfare, and the University Council Judicial Committee about "the massive, institutional Jew-hatred which infests" Princeton. College Dean Neil L. Rudenstine's denial of the existence of any "restrictive Jewish quota" was sustained by both the Anti-Defamation League of B'nai B'rith and the New Jersey Division of Civil Rights (Arthur Cooper to Marcia G. Synnott, June 1 and July 5, 1972; and the following articles from the *Princetonian*: Cooper, "Jew-baiting: The Princeton Pastime," September 19 and 20, 1972, p. 2, and "J'accuse . . . ," February 8, 1973, pp. 4-5; Laird Hart, "Cooper files anti-Semitism Charges Against Princeton Trustees, Officials," February 7, 1973, p. 1; and Neil L. Rudenstine, letter to the Chairman of the *Princetonian*, September 21, 1972, p. 2.

According to Rabbi Norbert Samuelson, director of Princeton Hillel Foundation, their records showed "minimal change" in the number of Jewish undergraduates until the admission of women. Even then, Princeton's Jewish enrollment was still "significantly below the percentage in attendance at comparable universities such as Harvard and Yale." More Jewish students would be attending Princeton if admission were "based totally on academic qualifications [rather] than on a system that considers additional factors." Rabbi Israel S. Dresner, national vice president of the American Jewish Congress, requested that Princeton drop from its application blanks the question on national origin of parents, which had been added two years earlier to recruit minority students with low scores on the verbal part of the Scholastic Aptitude Test. In the future, the admissions office would ask "whether English is the primary language spoken at home" (See *Princetonian*: Rabbi Norbert Samuelson, "Rabbi Responds," September 25, 1972, p. 3, and David Zielenziger, "Admissions Ends Origin Query at Jewish Congress' Request," November 28, 1972, p. 1).

54. Andy Pollack, "Color, Controversy Highlight 70 Years of Bicker," *Princetonian*, February 7, 1973, pp. 1, 3.

55. Sigmund, "Princeton in Crisis and Change," pp. 36, 34-43. In 1963, the color barrier was broken at almost all the clubs in order to accept African students who came to Princeton under the African Scholarship Program of the American Universities. President Goheen was one of the program's directors.

56. Ibid., pp. 35, 37; Adele Simmons, dean of student affairs, Princeton University, to Marcia G. Synnott, November 11, 1976.

57. Susan Stupin, "Non-Selective Clubs Show Varied Support," *Princetonian*, October 4, 1972, pp. 1, 7; F. Scott Fitzgerald, *This Side of Paradise*, p. 36.

58. Alfred W. De Jonge '50, "Godolphin Favors Non-Discrimination," *Princetonian*, May 8, 1947, in subject file Admin. offices, Admissions, PUA; Tomberlin, "Trends in Princeton Admissions," p. 135; Sigmund, "Princeton in Crisis and Change," p. 36; excerpts from a letter from Vice-President for Public Affairs William H. Weathersby to James W. Carter, Division on Civil Rights, Newark, New Jersey, [April 25, 1972], published as "University's Reply to Cooper's Charges," *Princetonian*, September 25, 1972, p. 3.

59. "A Survey of Princeton Freshmen," *PAW* 71, no. 17 (February 23, 1971), pp. 6-9; and Diana Savit, "Bring Back the Old Princeton? Survey Finds 1971 Frosh Liberal, Wealthy," *Princetonian*, March 1, 1971, p. 3.

60. Stephen Steinberg, *The Academic Melting Pot: Catholics and Jews in American Higher Education*, pp. 130, 88, xvii-xviii, 91-96, 100-15; Steinberg, "How Jewish Quotas Began," *Commentary* 52, no. 3 (September 1971): 67-76; Rabinowitz, "Are Jewish Students Different?" p. 49.

61. *DeFunis* v. *Odegaard*, 82 Wash. 2d 11, 507 P.2d 1169, 1182 (1973). DeFunis, who is Jewish, became a symbol for members of the white minority groups.

62. *Bakke* v. *Regents of the University of California*, 18 Cal. 3d 34, 553 P.2d 1152, 132 Cal. Rptr. 680 (1976).

63. "Briefs in the Bakke Case," *Chronicle of Higher Education* 15, no. 3 (September 19, 1977), p. 4. *Brief Amici Curiae of Anti-Defamation League of B'nai B'rith; Council of Supervisors and Administrators of the City of New York, Local 1, AFSA, AFL-CIO; Jewish Labor Committee; National Jewish Commission on Law and Public Affairs ("COLPA"); and UNICO National*, in the Supreme Court of the United States, October Term, 1977, no. 76-811, *Regents of the University of California, Petitioner*, v. *Allan Bakke, Respondent*, p. 5. Prepared by the attorneys for the amici curiae: Philip B. Kurland, Daniel D. Polsby, Rothschild, Barry & Myers, Two First National Plaza, Chicago, Illinois 60603, (312) 372-2345. printed pamphlet, 30 pp.

(New York: Bar Press, Inc., [1977]). *Brief of American Jewish Committee, American Jewish Congress, Hellenic Bar Association of Illinois, Italian-American Foundation, Polish American Affairs Council, Polish American Educators Association, Ukrainian Congress Committee of America (Chicago Division) and Unico National, Amici Curiae,* August, 1977, in the Supreme Court of the United States, October Term, 1977, no. 76-811, *Regents of the University of California, Petitioner,* v. *Allan Bakke, Respondent,* pp. 41-42, 15. Prepared by the attorneys for the amici curiae: Howard L. Greenberger, Samuel Rabinove (American Jewish Committee); Abraham S. Goldstein, Nathan Z. Dershowitz (American Jewish Congress); Themis N. Anastos, Philip S. Makin (Hellenic Bar Association of Illinois); Arthur J. Gajarsa (Italian-American Foundation); Anthony P. Krzywicki (Polish American Affairs Council); Thaddeus L. Kowalski (Polish American Educators Association); Julian E. Kulas (Ukrainian Congress Committee of America [Chicago Division]); and Anthony J. Fornelli (Unico National). printed pamphlet, 70 pp. (New York: Bar Press, Inc., [1977]). The American Federation of Teachers (A.F.L.-C.I.O.), which has substantial Jewish membership, also filed a brief in support of Bakke.

64. Brief of the Anti-Defamation League of B'nai B'rith et al. as *Amici Curiae,* p. 5.

65. "Briefs in the Bakke Case," see n. 63.

66. *Brief of Columbia University, Harvard University, Stanford University and the University of Pennsylvania as Amici Curiae,* pp. 2, 13-14, 16.

67. Ibid., pp. 1-7, 24-27, and n. 18. Seven other universities generally supported this brief: Brown, Duke, Georgetown, Massachusetts Institute of Technology, Notre Dame, Vanderbilt, and Villanova. Rutgers, the University of Washington, and Howard University also urged that the ruling of the California Supreme Court be reversed.

68. Ibid., pp. 32-34, and n. 29. In 1975, the University of California at Berkeley decided that Japanese-Americans had been sufficiently successful in gaining admission to its law school that they no longer needed to be included in the special admissions program; the extent of Chinese-American participation in the program was cut back. See also "Text of Justice Department's Brief in Bakke Case," *Chronicle of Higher Education,* 15, no. 4 (September 26, 1977), p. 12; Cheryl M. Fields, "Carnegie Panel Backs Racial Criteria for Admitting Qualified Applicants," *Chronicle of Higher Education,* 15, no. 6 (October 11, 1977), p. 4; and Ralph R. Smith, "Bakke's Case vs. the Case for Affirmative Action," *New York University Education Quarterly* 9, no. 2 (Winter 1978): 2-8.

69. "Text of Justice Department's Brief in Bakke Case," pp. 11, 10, 9-12.

70. Warren Weaver, Jr., "High Court Backs Some Affirmative Action By Colleges, but Orders Bakke Admitted" and "Excerpts from Opinions by Supreme Court Justices in the Allan P. Bakke Case," *New York Times,* June 29, 1978, pp. A1, A20-22. "What the Court Said in Two 5-to-4 Rulings on the Bakke Case: Text of the Opinion by Justice Powell, Text of the Opinion by Justice Brennan, Text of the Opinion by Justice Stevens," *Chronicle of Higher Education,* 16, no. 17 (July 3, 1978), pp. 3-12; and "3 separate opinions in the Bakke case: The Opinion of Justice Marshall, Text of the Opinion by Justice Blackmun, Text of the Opinion by Justice White," *Chronicle of Higher Education,* 16, no. 18 (July 10, 1978), pp. 11-13. The following were helpful for interpreting the arguments in the Bakke decision: Larry M. Lavinsky, Arnold Forster, and Harry Keaton, participants in a forum on the Bakke case, held at the Anti-Defamation League of B'nai B'rith in New York City on August 9, 1978; and Alan Der-

showitz, "Powell's Beau Idéal," *The New Republic*, July 22, 1978, pp. 14-17.

71. See all of the above, especially, "Text of the Opinion by Justice Powell," pp. 6-7.

72. See n. 70; and Bundy, "The Issue Before the Court," pp. 49-50. In the twenty-six years since the Harvard Medical School began to admit them as degree candidates, the number of women accepted has risen substantially. The 32 women admitted in the fall of 1971 represented about 20 percent of the class of 1975 (Beecher and Altschule, *Medicine at Harvard*, p. 473).

73. William Clyde DeVane, *Higher Education in Twentieth-Century America*, pp. 149-50.

BIBLIOGRAPHY

Unpublished manuscripts provided most of the essential information for this book, with the exception of published collections of Woodrow Wilson's papers, notably *The Papers of Woodrow Wilson*, edited by Arthur S. Link et al. Hence, the list of secondary sources is very selective. No attempt has been made to include a comprehensive bibliography of works relating to higher education in late nineteenth- and early twentieth-century America. As others have already noted, Frederick Rudolph, *The American College and University: A History*, has largely fulfilled this need with a twenty-page bibliography. Discussion of the various manuscript sources cited should prove of greater value to the reader.

Essential starting points for any investigation of archival material at Harvard, Yale, and Princeton are the published *Annual Reports of the President*, with their reports by or on the various departments or schools within the respective universities. Alumni publications were useful forums for both the administration and the graduates: *Harvard Alumni Bulletin, Harvard Graduates' Magazine, Yale Alumni Weekly*, and *Princeton Alumni Weekly*. College newspapers—*Harvard Crimson, Yale Daily News*, and the *Daily Princetonian*—revealed undergraduate opinion and reaction to current issues. Senior class albums and histories were the best sources of biographical information on undergraduates and alumni during this period. Each archives has one or more useful collections of newspaper clippings and scrapbooks. Harvard has three on controversies involving Jewish and Negro students: "Clippings on the Race Question, 1922"; "Comment Upon the Race Question, 1923"; and "Negro Question Clippings (P. D. Davis) 1941." For *Yale Old And New*, see the seventy-three scrapbooks compiled by Arnold Guyot Dana. Researchers should also consult Princeton's large assortment of boxes and files on subjects relating to admissions, to students of different nationalities or ethnic backgrounds, and to undergraduate life.

Manuscript and Archival Sources

Harvard has both the most voluminous and the most rewarding of all the archival collections examined. For the most part, access to them is restricted and dependent on prior permission, which is sometimes difficult to obtain, especially in the case of the

Abbott Lawrence Lowell Papers (1909-33). This extensive correspondence file contains copious documentation and statistics relating to the controversies of 1922-23. Both Harvard officials and the university archives staff have given considerable time and effort to meeting my manuscript requests, for which I am most grateful.

Corroboration and other perspectives and provided by the following manuscript collections in the Harvard University Archives: Charles W. Eliot Papers; Jerome D. Greene Papers; correspondence of Deans C. N. Greenough and A. C. Hanford of the college and L. B. R. Briggs of the Faculty of Arts and Sciences; and the minutes of the meetings of the Faculty of Arts and Sciences. The last years of Eliot's Second Chronological Correspondence File (1909-26) and the Jerome D. Greene Papers reveal the sharp differences of opinion that existed between them and President Lowell. Professor Felix Frankfurter of the Harvard Law School was the center of another faction opposing restriction on Jewish students. His letters to and from prominent Jewish alumni indicate the depth of concern within the American Jewish community.

The records of Presidents James R. Angell and Charles Seymour and of College Dean Frederick S. Jones, which are deposited in Manuscripts and Archives, Yale University Library, document Yale's reaction to internal discussions about admissions and about the policy changes elsewhere. In addition, the Freshman Office records, the correspondence between Admissions Director Robert N. Corwin and other deans and officials, and the minutes of meetings of the Board of Admissions are generally open to examination, as are other official files more than twenty years old. The archives staff was most helpful in suggesting and locating boxes and files in the voluminous Angell and Hadley correspondence.

Princeton's archival offerings are much smaller than the holdings at either Harvard or Yale. Most valuable sources are the minutes of the meetings of the faculty and of the Board of Trustees, together with reports from college, faculty, and freshmen deans. A box of Woodrow Wilson papers contains correspondence and documents relating to his presidency of Princeton. The old files of the college dean and correspondence from both the president's office and the secretary's office include several documents and letters of interest. The best single source (or rather a mine) of information on Wilson's presidency is, of course, *The Papers of Woodrow Wilson*, edited by Arthur S. Link et al., seven volumes of which (14 through 20) are devoted to the years 1902-10. By contrast, the papers of John Grier Hibben are negligible, because he and his wife destroyed most of them. Lack of information on Hibben's administration during the 1910s and 1920s is partially compensated for by the detailed *President's Reports* and by the papers of H. Alexander Smith, executive secretary of the university (1920-27), which are located in the Department of Rare Books and Special Collections. Finally, the minutes of the meetings of the Committee on Admission, although some seem to be missing, provide both revealing comments and statistics. Prior permission is required to examine the minutes of the Committee on Admission, the faculty and trustees' minutes after 1914, and the papers of H. Alexander Smith. Princeton officials and library staff members have both cooperated with and assisted my research.

Interviews

Mr. Paul Burnham, former director, Office of Educational Research, interview, Yale University, June 25, 1971.

Mr. Ralph Case Burr, director, University Financial Aids, interview, Strathcona Hall, Yale University, October 28, 1970.

Miss Nellie P. Elliott, former executive secretary of the Yale Board of Admissions, interview, New Haven, Conn., October 2, 1970.

Mr. Jeremiah S. Finch, secretary of the university, interview, Nassau Hall, Princeton University, February 24, 1971.

Dr. Reuben A. Holden, former secretary of the corporation, interview, Woodbridge Hall, Yale University, October 26, 1970.

Prof. Arthur S. Link, interview, Firestone Library, Princeton University, April 14, 1971.

Prof. Rollin G. Osterweis, interview, New Haven, Conn., May 20, 1971.

Prof. George Wilson Pierson, interview, Yale University Library, May 10, 1971.

Dr. Barbara M. Solomon, interview, Office of the Assistant Dean of Harvard College, University Hall, Harvard University, December 1, 1971.

Mr. M. Halsey Thomas, former archivist at Princeton University, interview, Firestone Library, Princeton University, April 15, 1971.

Prof. Harry A. Wolfson, interviews, Widener Library, Harvard University, July 30 and 31, 1973.

Published Sources

REPORTS AND PUBLIC DOCUMENTS

Bakke v. Regents of the University of California, 18 Cal. 3d 34, 553 P. 2d 1152, 132 Cal. Rptr. 680 (1976).

Brief of Columbia University, Harvard University, Stanford University and the University of Pennsylvania as Amici Curiae, June 7, 1977, in the Supreme Court of the United States, October Term, 1976, no. 76-811, *Regents of the University of California, Petitioner*, v. *Allan Bakke*, Respondent. On writ of certiorari to the Supreme Court of California. Prepared by counsel for amici curiae: John Mason Hammond, Albert J. Rosenthal (Columbia); Daniel Steiner (Harvard); Iris Brest, James V. Siena (Stanford); and Louis H. Pollak (University of Pennsylvania). Printed pamphlet, 40 pp. and 4 pp. appendix.

Kurland, Phillip B., and Gerhard, Casper, eds. *Landmark Briefs and Arguments of the Supreme Court of the United States: Constitutional Law. 1977 Term Supplement*, Volumes 99-100 (*Regents of the University of California v. Bakke*). 2 vols. Washington, D.C.: University Publications of America, Inc., 1978.

McKown, Harry Charles, *The Trend of College Entrance Requirements, 1913-1922.* Department of the Interior, Bureau of Education, Bulletin, 1924, no. 35. Washington, D.C.: Government Printing Office, 1925.

Regents of the University of California v. *Bakke*, 98 S.Ct. 2733 (1978).

U.S. Congress, Senate, Reports of the Immigration Commission. *Children of Immigrants in Schools.* 5 vols. 61st Cong., 3d sess., 1910-1911, S. Doc. 749.

BOOKS AND PAMPHLETS

Amory, Cleveland. *The Proper Bostonians.* New York: E. P. Dutton, 1947.

Baker, Ray Stannard. *Woodrow Wilson: Life and Letters.* 8 vols. Garden City, N.Y.: Doubleday, Page & Co., 1927-39. Vol. 2, *Princeton, 1890-1910* (1927).

Baker, Ray Stannard, and Dodd, William E., eds. *The Public Papers of Woodrow Wilson.* 6 vols. Authorized edition. New York: Harper & Brothers, 1925-27. Vol. 2, *College and State, Educational, Literary and Political Papers (1875-1913)* (1925).

Baltzell, E. Digby. *The Protestant Establishment: Aristocracy & Caste in America.* New York: Vintage Books, 1966.

Barnard, Harry. *The Forging of an American Jew: The Life and Times of Judge Julian W. Mack.* New York: Herzel Press, 1974.

Beecher, Henry K., M.D., and Altschule, Mark D., M.D. *Medicine at Harvard: The First Three Hundred Years.* Hanover, N.H.: The University Press of New England, 1977.

Birmingham, Stephen. *"Our Crowd": The Great Jewish Families of New York.* New York: Dell Publishing, 1967.

———. *Real Lace: America's Irish Rich.* New York: Harper & Row, 1973.

Bledstein, Burton J. *The Culture of Professionalism; The Middle Class and the Development of Higher Education in America.* New York: W. W. Norton, 1976.

Bragdon, Henry Wilkinson. *Woodrow Wilson: The Academic Years.* Cambridge; Belknap Press of Harvard University Press, 1967.

Broun, Heywood, and Britt, George. *Christians Only: A Study in Prejudice.* New York: Vanguard Press, 1931.

Butts, R. Freeman, and Cremin, Lawrence A. *A History of Education in American Culture.* New York: Holt, Rinehart and Winston, 1953.

Canby, Henry Seidel. *Alma Mater: The Gothic Age of the American College.* New York: Farrar & Rinehart, 1936.

Cohane, Tim. *The Yale Football Story.* New York: G. P. Putnam's Sons, 1951.

Collins, Varnum Lansing. *Princeton.* New York: Oxford University Press, 1914.

Conant, James B. *My Several Lives: Memoirs of a Social Inventor.* New York: Harper & Row, 1970.

Craig, Hardin. *Woodrow Wilson at Princeton.* Norman, Okla.: University of Oklahoma Press, 1960.

Crawford, Albert Beecher, ed. *Football Y Men—Men of Yale Series.* 3 vols. New Haven: Yale University Press, 1962-1963; Vol. 1, *1872-1919* (1962); vol. 2, *1920-1939* (1963); and vol. 3, *1940-1960* (1963).

Cross, Wilbur L. *Connecticut Yankee: An Autobiography.* New Haven: Yale University Press, 1943.

Davies, John D. *The Legend of Hobey Baker.* Boston: Little, Brown and Company, 1966.

Davis, Kenneth S. *A Prophet in His Own Country: The Triumphs and Defeats of Adlai E. Stevenson.* Garden City, N.Y.: Doubleday & Company, 1957.

De Vane, William Clyde. *Higher Education in Twentieth-Century America.* Library of Congress Series in American Civilization, edited by Ralph Henry Gabriel. Cambridge: Harvard University Press, 1965.

Doermann, Humphrey. *Cross Currents in College Admissions.* [New York]: Teachers College Press, [1968].

Endowment Funds of Harvard University, June 30, 1947. Cambridge: Harvard University Printing Office, 1948.

Fass, Paula S. *The Damned and the Beautiful: American Youth in the 1920's*. New York: Oxford University Press, 1977.

Fitzgerald, F. Scott. *This Side of Paradise*. New York: Charles Scribner's Sons, 1970.

Gabriel, Ralph Henry. *Religion and Learning at Yale: The Church of Christ in the College and University, 1757-1957*. New Haven: Yale University Press, 1958.

Greeley, Andrew M. *Ethnicity, Denomination, and Inequality*. Sage Research Papers in the Social Sciences, vol. 4, series no. 90-029 (Studies in Religion and Ethnicity Series). Beverly Hills and London: Sage Publications, 1976.

Gruber, Carol S. *Mars and Minerva: World War I and the Uses of the Higher Learning in America*. Baton Rouge: Louisiana State University Press, 1975.

Hadley, Morris. *Arthur Twining Hadley*. New Haven: Yale University Press, 1948.

Harris, Seymour E. *The Economics of Harvard*. Economics Handbook Series. New York: McGraw-Hill, 1970.

Havemeyer, Loomis. *"Go To Your Room": A Story of Undergraduate Societies and Fraternities at Yale*. New Haven: Yale University Press, 1960.

———. *Sheff Days and Ways: Undergraduate Activities in The Sheffield Scientific School, Yale University, 1847 1945*. New Haven. Preface, 1958.

Hawkins, Hugh. *Between Harvard and America: The Educational Leadership of Charles W. Eliot*. New York: Oxford University Press, 1972.

Hemingway, Ernest. *The Sun Also Rises*. New York: Charles Scribner's Sons, 1954.

Higham, John. *Social Discrimination Against Jews in America, 1830-1930*. New York, 1957. Reprinted from *Publications of the American Jewish Historical Society* 47, no. 1 (September 1957), pp. 1-33.

———. *Strangers in the Land: Patterns of American Nativism, 1860-1925*. Corrected and with a new preface. New York: Atheneum, 1968.

Hofstadter, Richard, and Metzger, Walter P. *The Development of Academic Freedom in the United States*. New York: Columbia University Press, 1955.

Holden, Reuben A. *Profiles and Portraits of Yale University Presidents*. Freeport, Maine: Bond Wheelwright, 1968.

James, Henry. *Charles W. Eliot: President of Harvard University, 1869-1909*. 2 vols. Boston: Houghton Mifflin, 1930.

Johnson, Owen. *Stover at Yale*. New York: Frederick A. Stokes, 1912.

Kahn, E. J. Jr., *Harvard Through Change and Through Storm*. New York: W. W. Norton, 1969.

Kelley, Brooks Mather. *Yale: A History*. New Haven: Yale University Press, 1974.

Keppel, Frederick P. *Columbia*. American College and University Series. New York: Oxford University Press, 1914.

———. *The Undergraduate and His College*. Boston: Houghton Mifflin, 1917.

Kirkpatrick, J. E. *Academic Organization and Control*. Yellow Springs, Ohio: Antioch Press, 1931.

———. *The Rise of Non-Resident Government in Harvard University and How Harvard Is Governed*. Ann Arbor, Mich.: George Wahr, 1925.

Kuklick, Bruce. *The Rise of American Philosophy, Cambridge, Massachusetts, 1860-1930*. New Haven: Yale University Press, 1977.

Link, Arthur S. *Wilson: The Road to the White House*. Princeton: Princeton University Press, 1947.

Link, Arthur S., et al., eds. *The Papers of Woodrow Wilson*. 29 vols. to date. Princeton: Princeton University Press, 1966.

Lipset, Seymour Martin, and Riesman, David. *Education and Politics at Harvard*. Two essays prepared for the Carnegie Commission on Higher Education. New York: McGraw-Hill, 1975.

Lowell, A. Lawrence. *At War with Academic Traditions in America*. Cambridge: Harvard University Press, 1934.

———. *Conflicts of Principle*. Reprint of 1932 ed. Cambridge: Harvard University Press, 1956.

———. *Public Opinion and Popular Government*. Edited by Albert Bushnell Hart. American Citizen Series. New York: Longmans, Green, 1913.

McCaughey, Robert A. "The Transformation of American Academic Life: Harvard University, 1821-1892." In *Perspectives in American History*, edited by Donald Fleming and Bernard Bailyn, vol. 8, pp. 239-332. Cambridge: Charles Warren Center for Studies in American History, Harvard University, 1974.

McLachlan, James. *American Boarding Schools: A Historical Study*. New York: Charles Scribner's Sons, 1970.

McWilliams, Carey. *A Mask for Privilege: Anti-Semitism in America*. Boston: Little, Brown and Company, 1948.

Mann, Arthur. *Yankee Reformers in the Urban Age*. Cambridge: Belknap Press of Harvard University Press, 1954.

Manning, Winton H.; Willingham, Warren W.; Breland, Hunter M.; and Associates. *Selective Admissions in Higher Education. Comment and Recommendations and Two Reports: Public Policy and Academic Policy, The Pursuit of Fairness in Admissions to Higher Education, The Status of Selective Admissions*. A Report of the Carnegie Council on Policy Studies in Higher Education. San Francisco: Jossey-Bass Publishers, 1977.

May, Henry F. *The End of American Innocence: A Study of the First Years of Our Own Time, 1912-1917*. New York: Alfred A. Knopf, 1959.

Morison, Samuel Eliot. *Three Centuries of Harvard, 1636-1936*. Cambridge: Harvard University Press, 1936.

———, ed. *The Development of Harvard University Since the Inauguration of President Eliot, 1869-1929*. Cambridge: Harvard University Press, 1930.

Mulder, John M. *Woodrow Wilson: The Years of Preparation*. Princeton: Princeton University Press, 1977.

Myers, William Starr, ed. *Woodrow Wilson: Some Princeton Memories*. Princeton: Princeton University Press, 1946.

Osborn, George C. *Woodrow Wilson: The Early Years*. Baton Rouge: Louisiana State University Press, 1968.

Osgood, Charles G., et al. *The Modern Princeton*. Princeton: Princeton University Press, 1947.

Osterweis, Rollin G. *Three Centuries of New Haven, 1638-1938*. The tercentenary history. New Haven: Yale University Press, 1953.

Perry, Bliss. *And Gladly Teach: Reminiscences*. Boston: Houghton Mifflin, 1935.

Pierson, George W. *The Education of American Leaders: Comparative Contributions of U.S. Colleges and Universities*. Praeger Special Studies in U.S. Economic and Social Development. New York: Frederick A. Praeger, 1969.

———. *Yale: College and University, 1871-1937.* 2 vols. New Haven, Conn.: Yale University Press, 1952, 1955. Vol. 1, *Yale College: An Educational History, 1871-1921* (1952); and vol. 2, *Yale: The University College, 1921-1937* (1955).

Pusey, Nathan M. *American Higher Education, 1945-1970: A Personal Report.* Cambridge: Harvard University Press, 1978.

Ravitch, Diane. *The Great School Wars: New York City, 1805-1973, A History of the Public Schools as Battlefield of Social Change.* New York: Basic Books, 1974.

Rosenstock, Morton. *Louis Marshall: Defender of Jewish Rights.* Detroit, Mich.: Wayne State University Press, 1965.

Rudolph, Frederick. *The American College and University: A History.* New York: Vintage Books, 1962.

———. *Curriculum: A History of the American Undergraduate Course of Study Since 1636.* San Francisco: Jossey-Bass, 1977.

Slosson, Edwin E. *Great American Universities.* New York: Macmillan Company, 1910.

Solomon, Barbara Miller. *Ancestors and Immigrants: A Changing New England Tradition.* Cambridge: Harvard University Press, 1956.

Steinberg, Stephen. *The Academic Melting Pot: Catholics and Jews in American Higher Education.* A report prepared for the Carnegie Commission on Higher Education. New York: McGraw-Hill, 1974.

Thelin, John R. *The Cultivation of Ivy: A Saga of the College in America.* Cambridge: Schenkman Publishing, 1976.

Tunis, John R. *Was College Worth While?* New York: Harcourt, Brace, 1936.

Tyack, David B. *The One Best System: A History of American Urban Education.* Cambridge: Harvard University Press, 1974.

Veysey, Laurence R. *The Emergence of the American University.* Chicago: University of Chicago Press, 1970.

Warner, Robert Austin. *New Haven Negroes: A Social History.* New Haven: Yale University Press for the Institute of Human Relations, 1940.

Wechsler, Harold S. *The Qualified Student: A History of Selective College Admission in America.* New York: John Wiley, 1977.

Wertenbaker, Thomas Jefferson. *Princeton, 1746-1896.* Princeton: Princeton University Press, 1946.

Wing, Yung. *My Life in China and America.* New York: Henry Holt, 1909.

Yeomans, Henry Aaron. *Abbott Lawrence Lowell, 1856-1943.* Cambridge: Harvard University Press, 1948.

Z.B.T., 1898-1923: The First Twenty-five Years. [New York, 1923.]

ARTICLES AND PERIODICALS

Adams, Charles Francis. "Some Modern College Tendencies." *Columbia University Quarterly* 8, no. 4 (1906), pp. 347-71.

Baltzell, E. Digby. "The Protestant Establishment Revisited." *American Scholar* 45, no. 4 (Autumn 1976), pp. 499-518.

Bender, Wilbur J. "To the Critics of Harvard." *Harvard Alumni Bulletin* 51, no. 13 (April 9, 1949), pp. [545]-48.

Berlack, Harris. "Curtain on the Harvard Question." *Zeta Beta Tau Quarterly* 7, no. 4 (1923), pp. 3-5.

Berryman, Jack W., and Loy, John W., University of Massachusetts, Amherst. "Democratization of Intercollegiate Sports in the Ivy League: A Study of Secondary School Background and Athletic Achievement at Harvard and Yale (1911-1960)." Paper prepared for the Third International Symposium on Sociology of Sport, University of Waterloo, Waterloo, Ontario, Canada, August 22-28, 1971. 32 pp.

Bragdon, Henry W. "Woodrow Wilson and Lawrence Lowell: An Original Study of Two Very Different Men." *Harvard Alumni Bulletin* 45, no. 16 (May 22, 1943), pp. [595]-98.

Brosnahan, Rev. Timothy, S.J. "President Eliot and Jesuit Colleges: A Defence." *Sacred Heart Review*, January 13, 1900, pp. 24-25.

Buck, Paul H. "Balance in the College: A Chance to Restore an Old Ideal and Point a New Way." *Harvard Alumni Bulletin* 48, no. 10 (February 16, 1946), pp. [404]-06.

————. Who Comes to Harvard?" *Harvard Alumni Bulletin* 50, no. 7 (January 10, 1948), pp. [313]-17.

Bundy, McGeorge. "The Issue Before the Court: Who Gets Ahead in America?" *Atlantic Monthly* 240, no. 5 (November 1977), pp. 41-54.

Coombs, Orde. "Making It At Yale: The Necessity of Excellence." *Change, the Magazine of Higher Learning* 5, no. 5 (June 1973), pp. 49-54.

Davis, Paul, '40. "Fair Harvard." *Harvard Guardian*, May 1941, pp. 28-31.

Du Bois, W. E. Burghardt. "Negroes in College." *Nation* 122, no. 3165 (March 3, 1926): 228-30.

Eliot, Charles W. "Recent Changes in Secondary Education." *Atlantic Monthly* 84, no. 504 (October 1899): 433-44.

————. "Woodrow Wilson." *Atlantic Monthly* 133 (June 1924): 815-23.

Galbraith, John Kenneth. Text of remarks delivered by John Kenneth Galbraith, Paul M. Warburg Professor of Economics, at Harvard University on Harvard Class Day, June 11, 1975. Released by the Harvard University News Office.

Gauss, Christian. "This New World and the Undergraduate." *Saturday Evening Post*, December 17, 1927, pp. 21, 95, 96.

Glazer, Nathan. "Social Characteristics of American Jews, 1654-1954." *American Jewish Year Book, 1955*, vol. 56, pp. 3-41.

Gordon, Milton M. "Assimilation in America: Theory and Reality." *Daedalus*, Journal of the American Academy of Arts and Sciences, 90, no. 2 (Spring 1961), pp. 263-85.

Greene, Jerome D. *Charles William Eliot, Anecdotal Reminiscences*. Paper read to the Cambridge Historical Society, May 25, 1950, and published by it, pp. 117-33.

————. "Years with President Eliot." Printed pamphlet, 46 pp. (Jerome D. Greene Papers, box 4, HUA).

Ham, William T. "Harvard Student Opinion on the Jewish Question." *Nation* 115 no. 2983 (September 6, 1922): 225-27.

Handlin, Oscar, and Handlin, Mary F. "The Acquisition of Political and Social Rights by the Jews in the United States." *American Jewish Year Book, 1955*, vol. 56, pp. 43-98.

Hawes, Gene R. "The Colleges of America's Upper Class." *Saturday Review Magazine*, November 16, 1963, pp. 68-71.

Hawkins, Hugh. "Removing the Welcome Mat: Changing Perceptions of the Immigrant." In Howard H. Quint and Milton Cantor, *Men, Women, and Issues in American History*, vol. 2, pp. 88-113. Homewood, Ill.: Dorsey Press, 1975.

Jencks, Christopher S., and Riesman, David. "Patterns of Residential Education: A Case Study of Harvard." In Nevitt Sanford, ed., *The American College: A Psychological and Social Interpretation of the Higher Learning*, pp. 731-73. Prepared for the Society for the Psychological Study of Social Issues. New York: John Wiley, 1962.

Link, Arthur S. "Woodrow Wilson: The American as Southerner." *Journal of Southern History* 36, no. 1 (February 1970): 3-17.

Lipset, Seymour Martin, and Ladd, Everett Carll Jr. "Jewish Academics in the United States: Their Achievements, Culture and Politics." *American Jewish Year Book, 1971*, vol. 72, pp. 89-128.

Lowell, A. Lawrence. "The Colonial Expansion of the United States." *Atlantic Monthly* 83 (February 1899): 145-54.

—————. "Irish Agitation in America." *Forum* 4 (December 1887): 397-407.

Marvin, George. "The American Spirit in Chinese Education." *Outlook* 90 (November 28, 1908): 667-72.

Matthews, Thomas S., '22. "Those Inflated 'Twenties (The Sixth in a Series of Articles Interpreting Princeton by Decades)." *Princeton Alumni Weekly* 31 (March 13, 1931): 559-61, 568.

Newman, Dr. Louis I. "The Harvard Report: An Analysis." *Jewish Tribune and the Hebrew Standard*, April 27, 1923, pp. 1-2, 21.

Oren, Dan A. '79. "Jews at Yale—A Preliminary Examination," Passover, 1977, in Yale Miscellaneous Manuscripts #94. Paper read to the Jewish Historical Society of New Haven. Published by the Jewish Historical Society of New Haven, 1978, in *Jews in New Haven*, edited by Jonathan D. Sarna.

Painter, Nell. "Jim Crow at Harvard: 1923." *New England Quarterly* 44, no. 4 (1971), pp. 627-34.

Parker, Garland G. "50 Years of Collegiate Enrollments: 1919-20 to 1969-70," pt. 1. *School & Society* 98 (March 1970): 148-59.

"Professional Tendencies Among Jewish Students in Colleges, Universities, and Professional Schools." Memoir of the Bureau of Jewish Social Research. *American Jewish Year Book, 5681, September 13, 1920, to October 2, 1921*, vol. 22, pp. [381]-93.

Rabinowitz, Dorothy. "Are Jewish Students Different?" *Change, the Magazine of Higher Learning* 3, no. 4 (Summer 1971), pp. 47-50.

Reznikoff, Charles. "New Haven: The Jewish Community, a Portrait Sketch." *Commentary* 4, no. 5 (November 1947): 465-77.

Riesman, David, and Denney, Reuel. "Football in America: A Study in Culture Diffusion." *American Quarterly* 3, no. 4 (Winter 1951): 309-25.

Sigmund, Paul. "Princeton in Crisis and Change." *Change, the Magazine of Higher Learning* 5, no. 2 (March 1973), pp. 34-41.

Singer, Mark. "God and Mentsch at Yale," *Moment* 1, no. 2 (July-August 1975), pp. 27-31.

Smith, Timothy L. "Immigrant Social Aspirations and American Education, 1880-1930." *American Quarterly* 21, no. 3 (Fall 1969), pp. 523-43.

Spring, Joel H. "Psychologists and the War: The Meaning of Intelligence in the Alpha and Beta Tests." *History of Education Quarterly* 12, no. 1 (Spring 1972): 3-15.

Starr, Harry. "The Affair at Harvard: What the Students Did." *Menorah Journal* 8 (October 1922): 263-76.

Steinberg, Stephen. "How Jewish Quotas Began." *Commentary* 52, no. 3 (September 1971): 67-76.

Story, Ronald, "Harvard and the Boston Brahmins: A Study in Institutional and Class Development, 1800-1865." *Journal of Social History* 8 (1974-75): 94-121.

———. "Harvard Students, the Boston Elite, and the New England Preparatory System, 1800-1876." *History of Education Quarterly* 15, no. 3 (Fall 1975), pp. 281-98.

Synnott, Marcia G. "The 'Big Three' and the Harvard-Princeton Football Break, 1926-1934." *Journal of Sport History* 3, no. 3 (Summer 1976), pp. 188-202.

Tombo, Rudolf, Jr. "The Geographical Distribution of the Student Body at a Number of Universities and Colleges." *Science*, n.s. 30 (October 1, 1909): 427-35.

Veysey, Laurence R. "The Academic Mind of Woodrow Wilson." *Mississippi Valley Historical Review* 49 (March 1963): 613-34.

Ward, Robert De Courcy. "Immigration and the Three Per Cent Restrictive Law." *Journal of Heredity* 12 (August-September 1921): 319-25.

Wolf, Rabbi Arnold Jacob. "Jewish Experience Is Vividly Present at Yale." *Yale Alumni Monthly* 36, no. 4 (January 1973), pp. [14]-15.

UNPUBLISHED DISSERTATIONS OR THESES

Buenning, Steven L. "John Grier Hibben: A Biographical Study (1919-1932)." Senior thesis in history, Princeton University, 1971.

Burr, Ralph Case. "Scholarship Students at Yale." Ph.D. diss. Yale University, 1954.

Feldman, Penny Hollander. "Recruiting an Elite: Admission to Harvard College." Ph.D. diss., Harvard University, 1975.

Leary, William M. Jr. "Smith of New Jersey: A Biography of H. Alexander Smith, United States Senator from New Jersey, 1944-1959." Ph.D. diss., Princeton University, 1966.

Miller, Morty. "New Haven: The Italian Community." History 90 essay, Yale University, 1969. (Copy at New Haven Colony Historical Society.)

Powell, Arthur G. "The Study of Education at Harvard University, 1870-1920." Ph.D. diss., Harvard University, 1969.

Robbins, Michael David. "Princeton, 1920 to 1929: An Historical Study of a Problem in Reputation." Senior thesis in history, Princeton University, 1955.

Rodes, Harold Potter. "Educational Factors Affecting the Entrance Requirements of Yale College." Ph.D. diss. Yale Univeristy, 1948.

Synnott, Marcia Graham. "A Social History of Admissions Policies at Harvard, Yale, and Princeton, 1900-1930." Ph.D. diss., University of Massachusetts, Amherst, 1974.

Tomberlin, George E., Jr. "Trends in Princeton Admissions." Senior thesis in sociology, Princeton University, 1971.

Wechsler, Harold Stuart. "The Selective Function of American College Admissions Policies: 1870-1970." Ph.D. diss. Columbia University, 1974. (See his book, *The Qualified Student: A History of Selective College Admission in America.* New York: John Wiley, 1977.)

INDEX

About the Author

Marcia G. Synnott is Assistant Professor of History at the University of South Carolina in Columbia. She specializes in the history of higher education and women's history and has published in the *Journal of Sport History* and the *History of Education Quarterly*.